THE SHIPCARVERS' ART

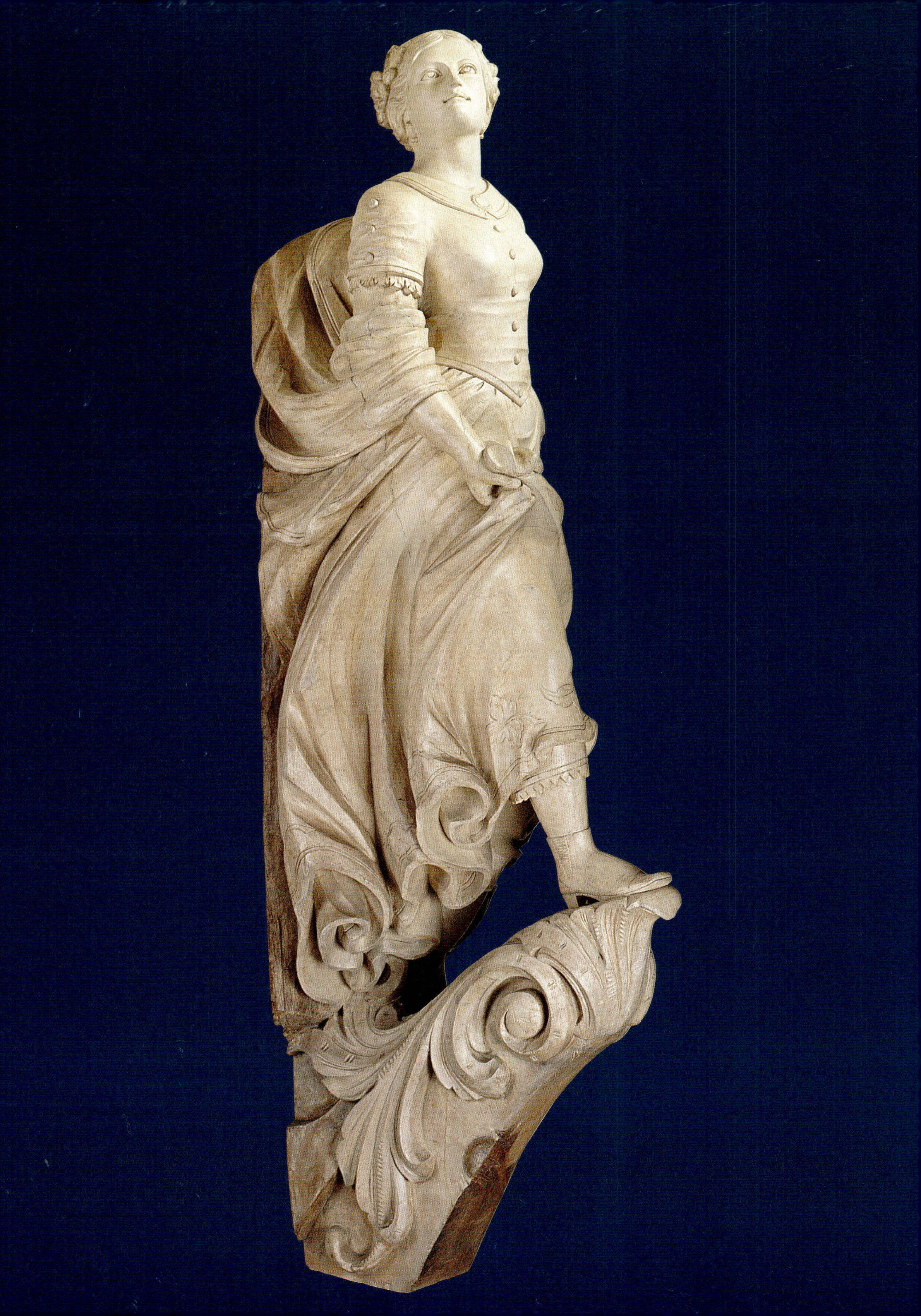

THE SHIPCARVERS' ART

FIGUREHEADS AND CIGAR-STORE INDIANS IN NINETEENTH-CENTURY AMERICA

RALPH SESSIONS

PRINCETON UNIVERSITY PRESS
PRINCETON AND OXFORD

Front cover: *Indian*, New York, 1888–1903 (detail of plate 66).
Photo: John Dean
Spine: *Volunteer Fireman*, New York, 1876–88 (plate 113).
Photo: Ali Elai, Camerarts
Back cover: Attributed to John Rogerson, *Lady Edmonton*, c. 1882 (plate 33)
Frontispiece: Isaac Howard Fowle, *Lady with a Scarf*, c. 1820 (plate 18). Courtesy of The Bostonian Society/Old State House

Published by Princeton University Press, 41 William Street, Princeton, New Jersey 08540

In the United Kingdom: Princeton University Press, 3 Market Place, Woodstock, Oxfordshire OX20 1SY
pup.princeton.edu

Publication of this book has been made possible in part by grants from Furthermore, a program of the J. M. Kaplan Fund, and from two anonymous donors.

Designed by Carolyn Eckert
Composed by Tina Thompson
Printed by Grafiche SiZ

Printed and bound in Italy
10 9 8 7 6 5 4 3 2 1

Library of Congress Cataloging-in-Publication Data

Sessions, Ralph.
The shipcarvers' art : figureheads and cigar-store Indians in nineteenth-century America/Ralph Sessions.
p. cm.
Includes bibliographical references and index.
ISBN 0-691-12081-1 (alk. paper)
1. Figureheads of ships—History—19th century. 2. Shipbuilding—United States—History—19th century. I. Title.
VM308.S38 2005
736'.4—dc22 2004049135

CONTENTS

ACKNOWLEDGMENTS

THIS BOOK IS THE RESULT of a research project that I have been pursuing for a number of years. As such, it has undergone several transformations on its long journey to publication. I have many people to thank. I only hope that I do not forget to acknowledge any of those who so generously shared their time and expertise, or who otherwise helped me along the way. I should also note that some individuals are no longer connected with the organizations mentioned below. Since they were at the time, though, I thought it best to recognize the associations.

The project began with a conversation about an exhibition of cigar-store figures with Robert Bishop, late director of the Museum of American Folk Art (now the American Folk Art Museum), New York, when I was chief curator there over a decade ago. I also had some helpful meetings with Frederick Fried in the year or so before he died. The planning continued, culminating in a traveling exhibition in 1997–98. Many people connected with the museum contributed their talents and I thank them all, including Gerard Wertkin, Stacy Hollander, Ann-Marie Reilly, and Rosemary Gabriel.

During the course of my research for the exhibition, I visited numerous public and private collections, where I received the enthusiastic support of many individuals. My conversations with curators and collectors were particularly helpful in formulating my thinking about the diversity of wooden sculpture in America. I spoke with a great many people. So many, in fact, that it would be difficult to list them all here. Among those who shared their ideas and opened their collections were David Shayt, National Museum of American History, Smithsonian Institution, Washington, D.C.; Paul D'Ambrosio, New York State Historical Association, Cooperstown; Brian Cullity and Jennifer Yunginger, Heritage Museums and Gardens, Sandwich, Massachusetts; Richard Miller, Abby Aldrich Rockefeller Folk Art Museum, Williamsburg, Virginia; Harvey Kahn; and Mark Goldman.

By the mid-1990s, the project had also become my dissertation topic at the Graduate Center of the City University of New York. I must gratefully acknowledge my advisor, William H. Gerdts, for his support and his efforts in imparting to me a portion of his knowledge of American sculpture and painting. The members of my dissertation committee, Sally Webster, Marlene Park, and David Dearinger, must also be heartily thanked for providing many insights into the breadth and depth of American art.

As I continued thinking about this book, I expanded my focus on figureheads and other types of shipcarving. In this, I was aided by a Harold S. Sniffen Fellowship at The Mariners' Museum in Newport News, Virginia, in 1998, which allowed me to study that institution's impressive collection firsthand. I would like to thank William Cogar and Claudia Pennington for that opportunity. I also had many helpful conversations with some people who are particularly knowledgeable about American shipcarving traditions, including Ryan Cooper; and Ted Miles, San Francisco Maritime National Historical Park. Others graciously shared their research and files on particular figures, including Thayer Tolles, Metropolitan Museum of Art, New York; Thomas Beckman, Delaware Historical Society, Wilmington; and Margaret Stocker, India House, New York.

This book would have never seen the light of day without the generous support of several funders. A publication grant from Furthermore was instrumental in bringing it to fruition. I must also recognize the contributions of Mark Goldman, Mom's Cigars Collection, and Ira Spanierman. And, I am eternally grateful to some anonymous donors who have been especially helpful. You know who you are.

My editors at Princeton University Press are the ones who made this book a reality. I extend my heartfelt thanks to Nancy Grubb for her support and for shepherding my manuscript down the path to publication. I would also like to thank Kate Zanzucchi and Devra Nelson for their fine work and many contributions. In addition, I would like to thank the designer, Carolyn Eckert; the copyeditor, Alison Rooney; the proofreader, June Cuffner; and the indexer, Carol Roberts.

INTRODUCTION

COUNTLESS NUMBERS OF HUMAN FIGURES were carved in wood in the United States and Canada in the eighteenth and nineteenth centuries. Most served as ship figureheads or shop signs, but they were used for a variety of other purposes as well, from architectural decoration to garden statuary to commemorative figures for civic ceremonies. The figurehead tradition had descended from antiquity and continued to be popular until the end of the era of wooden-hulled sailing ships in the late nineteenth century. As for shop figures, a journalist noted in 1886 that "few objects, policemen and lampposts excepted, are more familiar to the public than the cigar store wooden Indian."[1] Fanciful images of Native Americans were by far the most common, but especially after about 1860, any character that caught the public's imagination could and would be skillfully personified, from the more traditional Turks and Scotsmen to up-to-date baseball players and fashionable women.

The vast majority of these figures were made by shipcarvers, a tightly knit group of professional carvers bound by family ties and master-apprentice relationships who operated through a network of workshops in port cities and towns along the East Coast and, to a lesser extent, the Great Lakes. While collectively they created tens of thousands of figures, they were never very numerous, as theirs was a highly skilled art that required many years of experience. In the late nineteenth century, a newspaper reporter explained, "Twelve to fourteen years of apprenticeship is said to be necessary to make a competent workman, and that accounts for the scarcity of good hands, for the wages are low, and the demand limited."[2]

By training and tradition, American carvers were in touch with current trends in the fine arts. In this, they followed the lead of generations of European shipcarvers, beginning with Italian sculptors and carvers of the Renaissance and descending through leading French Baroque artists like Pierre Puget (1620–1694) and Charles Le Brun (1619–1690). In North America, shipcarving reflected the general stylistic developments of the time, from the Baroque-inspired designs of the eighteenth century through the Neoclassicism, Romanticism, and realism of the nineteenth.

Many talented shipcarvers worked in America in the eighteenth and nineteenth centuries, but the most influential was undoubtedly William Rush (1756–1833), who is best known today as one of the country's first sculptors and a founder of the Pennsylvania Academy of the Fine Arts in Philadelphia. Rush trained as a shipcarver, however, and operated an active workshop for over fifty years. He is generally credited with introducing into the American carver's repertoire a type of full-length, freestanding figurehead that had been developed in France.[3] His innovative designs helped determine the course that figurehead and shop-figure carving was to take throughout the nineteenth century.

Among Rush's most prominent contemporaries were John Skillin (1745–1800) and Simeon Skillin, Jr. (1756–1806), members of a family of Boston carvers who dominated the profession in that city from the mid-eighteenth century to the first decade of the nineteenth, and one of their apprentices, Isaac Howard Fowle (1783–after 1854). They are known to have created a wide range of shipcarving and architectural ornament in their time, but almost none of it exists today. In the case of John Skillin and Simeon Skillin, Jr., for example, only seven figures can be fully documented as their work.[4] This survival rate is unfortunately typical for shipcarving, rendering the researcher's task all the more difficult.

By 1820, New York City had become the leading shipbuilding center in the country, surpassing Boston and Philadelphia. Several geographical and economic factors conspired to give New York an advantage in both national and international trade, including the size and ease of access to its harbor. In addition, the opening of the Erie Canal in 1825 created a direct water link with the Great Lakes and the Midwest, consolidating New York's position as the country's commercial and cultural capital. The increased shipbuilding activity that resulted from these developments naturally enough brought more work to New York carvers, and their numbers swelled. Chief among them were Jeremiah Dodge (1781–1860), his son, Charles (1806–1886), and Jacob Anderson (1810–1857), who together continued the high level of artistry set by their predecessors.

In response to the emergence of the ocean clippers in the 1840s, American shipcarvers developed a new style of figurehead with a dynamic presence that matched the fast and sleek vessels. Due to the increased need for speed on the lucrative and highly competitive trade routes to California and the Orient, other types of ship decoration, most notably the elaborate stern carvings of the Baroque era, were greatly reduced or eliminated altogether.[5] The figurehead became the focus of the carver's creativity, resulting in some of the finest examples ever produced in this country.

At the beginning of the clipper ship era, American shipcarvers also developed new types of shop figures, often lifesize, that came to be known as show figures. By merging the tradition of full-size figureheads with that of the generally smaller shop figures, they created an imposing sculptural form that was readily adaptable to the rapidly expanding and increasingly competitive American business environment. At mid-century, nearly every tobacco store had a carved image of an Indian or some related type to advertise its wares. They were used for many other purposes as well, including, as William Demuth, a successful tobacco-products distributor, claimed around 1871, "all classes of business, such as segar stores, wine & liquors, druggists, yankee notions, umbrella, clothing, tea stores, theatres, gardens, banks, insurance companies, &c."[6] Throughout the second half of the century, the carvers created a parade of characters that reflected the latest in fashion and public opinion.

Five New York City shipcarvers—John Cromwell (1805–1873), Thomas Millard (1803–1870), Thomas Brooks (1828–1895), Thomas White (1825–1902), and Samuel Robb (1851–1928)—were largely responsible for developing the most popular types of show figures.[7] Aided by an undetermined number of journeymen and apprentices, this small group of men worked in a similar style over the course of three generations, producing thousands of figures that were marketed nationally by William Demuth and Company and a few other tobacco-products distributors. Demuth issued mail-order catalogues, sent salesmen across the country, and set up elaborate displays in major national expositions and industrial fairs, including the World's Columbian Exposition in Chicago in 1893.[8] Together, he and the carvers were instrumental in establishing New York City as the major center of production and distribution, spreading the New York show-figure style across the country.

The active carving business in America attracted other skilled artisans as well, most notably German figure carvers who came to the United States after the Revolution of 1848. Most of them had trained in a different system than their American contemporaries, in which they studied with academic sculptors and learned to carve in stone as well as wood. Several established themselves in New York City, and while they generally did not create figureheads, they did carve many other types of wooden figures, including shop figures, carousel animals, and decorative statues for architecture.

The best known European-trained sculptor and woodcarver to work in the United States was Julius Melchers (1829–1909), a native of Prussia who settled in Detroit in 1855 and operated a workshop there for nearly fifty years. He also conducted classes in drawing and modeling, providing instruction and inspiration to a number of aspiring artists, including his most famous student, his son, the painter Gari Melchers (1860–1932).[9]

In addition to these men, a third group of carvers comprised those self-taught artists who fashioned shop and cigar-store figures for local markets, often in smaller inland towns and rural areas. Throughout the eighteenth and nineteenth centuries, carpenters, cabinetmakers, and part-time woodworkers in all parts of the country produced shop figures on demand or for personal enjoyment. Little can be said about common training or techniques of these generally unidentified artists, other than what can be inferred from their work. They represent a diverse collection of individuals who usually operated independently of one another, often creating unique, one-of-a-kind pieces patterned after those made in the seaport shops. In all, they produced far fewer figures than shipcarvers, and again survival rates are low. As a result, their work is extremely rare today.

Throughout Victorian America, shop and cigar-store figures found a niche in the rapidly evolving arenas of commercial art and popular culture. The vogue did not last long. For a variety of reasons, including changing tastes, new modes of advertising, and oversupply, the production of new figures had virtually ceased by 1900. They were increasingly seen as old-fashioned, symbols of an era that was rapidly passing away. Most of the traditional shipcarvers were out of business anyway, their craft having been doomed by the advent of metal-hulled ships several decades earlier. When Samuel Robb closed his workshop on Centre Street in 1903, the end was in sight. While many figures lingered in front of shops for decades, the art of the shipcarver gradually faded from the American scene.

AS PRODUCTS OF A SHARED artistic and cultural imagination, nineteenth-century figureheads and show figures speak to several important aspects of American social history, including racial and gender stereotyping, and the emergence of a national popular culture. Based on contemporary perceptions, they reflect the opinions and prejudices of mainstream white society. Humor was injected into these stereotypical images through caricature. In this, the carvers followed English and European precedent, as seen in the work of eighteenth-century artists such as William Hogarth (1697–1764) and other social and political satirists.

Indian figures were generally rendered in the Noble Savage mode, a characterization influenced by the art and literature of late-eighteenth-century Neoclassicism and early-nineteenth-century Romanticism. As such, the imaginary American Indian assumed the dual roles of ancient stoic and doomed modern hero on an inevitable course of destruction due to forces beyond his control. Caught in the clutches of Western civilization, he was a hapless victim of progress and one of the last members of a vanishing race.

The most derogatory depictions were reserved for images of African-Americans, which were patterned after the racist characters seen in minstrel shows and the popular press. Fictitious and exaggerated physical features and dress that fit the general minstrel stereotype dominated the portrayal of most black figures. Other caricatures poked fun at contemporary urban types like vain, fashion-conscious young women and their slightly disreputable male counterparts. As for foreigners, Scotsmen, Turks, and Chinese with their respective associations with tobacco and tea, were typically rendered in exotic costumes that bespoke far-off lands.

For much of the nineteenth century, the American public found these images irresistible, and show figures occupied a prominent place in the national consciousness. They were so much a part of the scene, in fact, that no one thought to make note of them until they were threatened with extinction in the final decades of the century. Sparked by the growing antiquarian interest at the time, curious reporters visited the workshops of shipcarvers and "sign sculptors," as one journalist dubbed them,[10] to investigate the inner workings of the craft before its final demise. As a result, a handful of newspaper and magazine articles written mainly in the 1880s and 1890s, along with some photographs and magazine illustrations, are all that survive in the way of contemporary commentary.

Just as they were vanishing from city streets and bows of ships in the early twentieth century, though, the figures began to experience renewed interest as museum pieces and collectors' items. Many of the finest examples with especially long histories or links to a particular locale were donated to local historical societies. The first book on cigar-store figures, *Hunting Indians in a Taxi-Cab* by Kate Sanborn, appeared in 1911. In a breezy, anecdotal style, the author recounts her adventures and the information that she gleaned while locating figures for her country home.

By 1915 or so, figureheads and shop figures were also being collected by modernist artists searching for forms of expression that they considered to be truly American. The trend gathered momentum throughout the 1920s, culminating in the landmark exhibition *American Folk Sculpture*, organized by Holger Cahill for the Newark Museum in New Jersey in 1931.

Soon thereafter, shipcarving and shop figures finally began to receive some scholarly attention, albeit on a limited scale. A few articles on both topics appeared in *Antiques Magazine* in the 1930s, while the first major book on shipcarving, Pauline A. Pinckney's *American Figureheads and Their Carvers*, was published in 1940. Pinckney presents an interesting discussion of the subject bolstered by extensive research, but her information is not totally reliable and her text is not footnoted.[11] The best general source is still Marion V. Brewington, *Shipcarvers of North America*, which first appeared in 1962. One of the leading maritime historians of his generation, Brewington gives a well-researched and well-documented history of American shipcarving in a concise fashion.

As for shop figures, the first significant book is Anthony W. Pendergast and W. Porter Ware, *Cigar Store Figures in American Folk Art*, published in 1953. Pendergast had assembled a major collection of shop and cigar-store figures, and although his text is largely anecdotal and must be read with a critical eye, his years of collecting experience gave him an impressive knowledge of what was then an undocumented field.

The most important reference to date is Frederick Fried's *Artists in Wood*, published in 1970. Following the lead of Pendergast and others, Fried conducted extensive research and assembled a significant amount of information on the history of shop figures and related themes. His biographical research is especially important, as he was the first to establish the identities of many of the most accomplished nineteenth-century American carvers. As with Brewington and Pinckney, though, he approaches his topic as an historian and does not employ stylistic analysis or any other type of art historical methodology. As a result, the book's major problem lies in the attribution of specific figures to specific carvers, an area that merits reexamination.

Among the first writers to attempt to place figureheads, shop figures, and other types of folk sculpture in an art historical context was Jean Lipman, whose *American Folk Art in Wood, Metal, and Stone* appeared in 1948. Predating Brewington, Pendergast, and Fried, her book provides a number of important insights, but also contains information that is somewhat dated.

More recently, two art historical studies concerning the most important eighteenth- and early-nineteenth-century carvers in Philadelphia and Boston have been written. *William Rush: American Sculptor*, edited by Linda Bantel, is the catalogue of an exhibition that was held at the Pennsylvania Academy of the Fine Arts in Philadelphia in 1982. It includes scholarly essays on all aspects of Rush's career, including one on the critical reception of his work by William H. Gerdts that demonstrates that Rush's carved wooden figures, while widely admired, did not and in fact could not transcend the well-established contemporary distinctions between craft and art.

The second study is Sylvia L. Lahvis's 1990 dissertation, "The Skillin Workshop: The Emblematic Image in Federal Boston," which presents a detailed investigation of the lives and work of this important family of carvers.[12] Lahvis's principal thesis is that English figure carving evolved along with the symbolic language of civic pageantry and that eighteenth-century shipcarvers like the Skillins transformed these images into icons of American trade and commerce.

Whether rendered in detailed realism or a more stylized and individualized fashion, figureheads and shop figures represent one of the largest and most expressive of all American sculptural traditions. Along with carved wooden garden, architectural, and ceremonial figures, they can lay claim to being the first form of public sculpture in this country, particularly before about 1865, when cities and towns throughout the United States began commissioning Civil War memorials and other types of commemorative statues in large numbers.

Figure carving was generally seen as a vibrant form of contemporary expression, even if it was not considered a fine art. Its venues were the streets and wharves of America, and its intent was to speak directly to a large, popular audience. The extent of its success has been obscured by a lack of critical recognition in its own time and overshadowed by the work of native-born sculptors who began working in Europe in the 1820s and 1830s. Horatio Greenough (1805–1852) first went to Italy in 1825, followed by Thomas Crawford (1813–1857) in 1835 and Hiram Powers (1805–1873) in 1837.

Coincidentally, the decade of the 1830s was also marked by the death of William Rush, which has provided art historians with a convenient end point for the consideration of figure carving as a significant American art form. This is perhaps most clearly stated in Wayne Craven's comprehensive survey, *Sculpture in America*, which has deservedly become a standard reference. Towards the end of the first chapter, which is entitled "Artisan-Craftsmen Beginnings," Craven affirmed the major contribution that figure carvers made to the development of American sculpture up to 1830. He then wrote: "But the great era of the figurehead had passed by 1830, for such carvers failed to follow the lead of William Rush, who had elevated wood carving to a fine art. Before long, even the craft of wood carving virtually ceased to be practical as it became a victim of the woodcarving machines of the Industrial Revolution, dying out almost altogether soon after the Civil War."[13]

A central aim of the discussion that follows is to revise this widely held opinion, and to demonstrate that shipcarving retained its vibrancy until the end of the nineteenth century. The 1840s and 1850s were decades of innovation, not decline, as the carvers responded to myriad social and artistic developments, as well as the emergence of the United States as a major maritime presence.

Throughout the eighteenth and nineteenth centuries, wooden figures graced the prows of ships, gardens of well-to-do citizens, ceremonial structures built for civic celebrations, and storefronts of enterprising merchants. As sculpture, figureheads and shop figures can be appreciated more today than they could in their own time, and their place in the history of American art is more evident. As cultural images, they resonate with meaning, embodying traditional values while at the same time reflecting the attitudes, prejudices, and trends of a rapidly developing society.

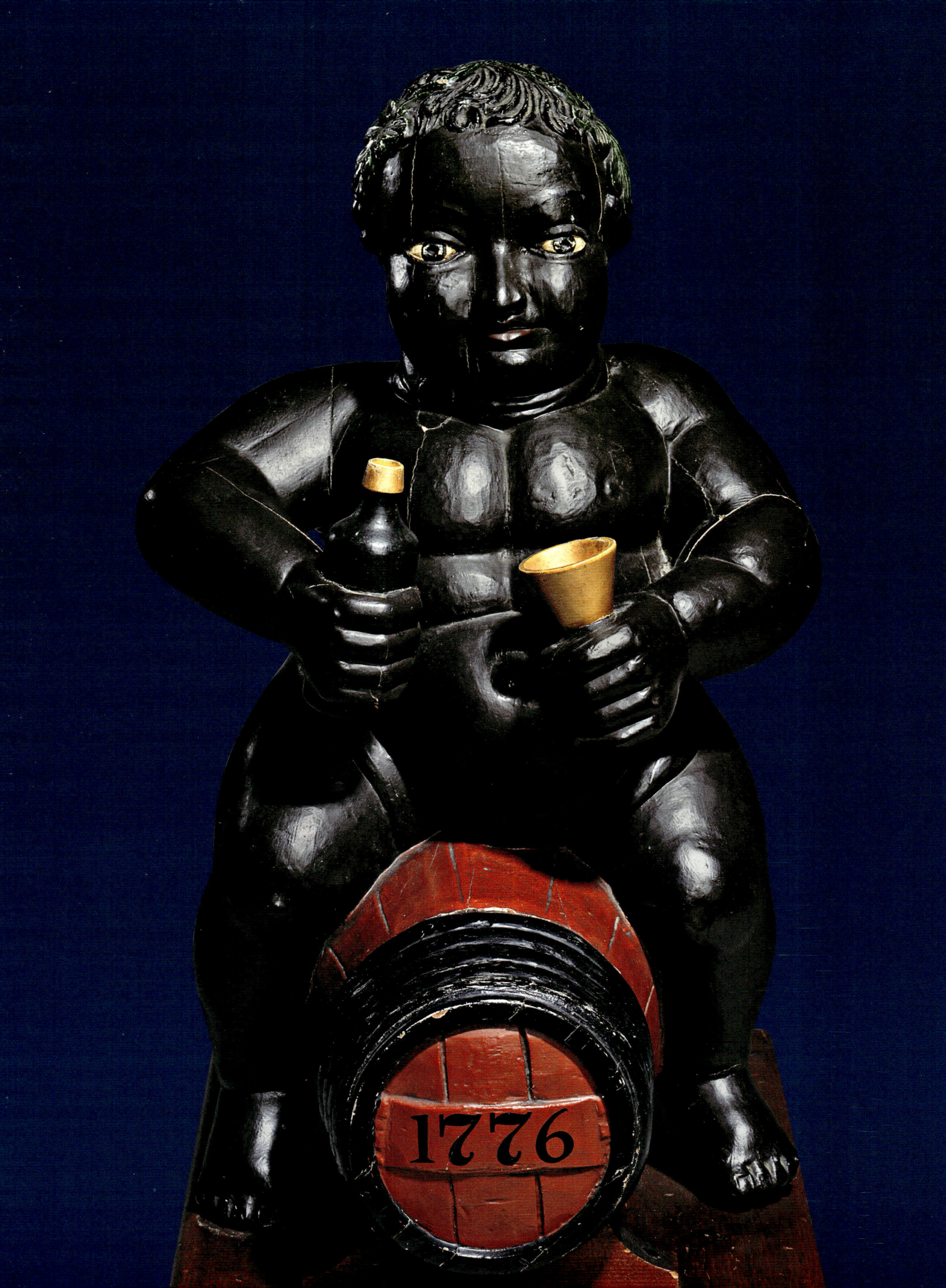
1776

CHAPTER 1 LYONS, BLACK BOYS, AND VIRGINIANS

Figure Carving in England and France

SHIPCARVING IS AN ANCIENT ART, long deemed essential for any self-respecting European maritime nation. For centuries, well-executed carvings that bespoke wealth and power were as critical to national prestige as the size of the vessels that carried them. In fact, during the period when shipcarving was at the height of ornateness, from about the mid-seventeenth century to the first decades of the eighteenth, the massive programs of Baroque-inspired ornament applied to the largest warships were so extreme that they were known to interfere with ships' operations.

Figureheads were an integral part of these design programs, which included elaborately carved, painted, and gilded decoration that covered much of the upper hull of the ship.[1] Among the most prominent features were ornamented bow timbers called cheeks and trailboards, deck rails, brackets, mullions, and most of all, complex compositions of human and animal figures and other decorative devices on the stern. Figureheads could be based on any one of a number of classical or contemporary subjects, although in the seventeenth and first half of the eighteenth centuries most European nations favored the lion for all but their largest ships. The practice appears to have derived from the traditional association of lions with royal coats of arms. In England and colonial America, lions were used almost exclusively from the mid-seventeenth century until about 1727, when the Board of Admiralty issued orders allowing other types of figureheads on its smaller vessels.[2] After that, human figures symbolizing the name of the ship became increasingly popular, and the lion soon fell out of fashion.

As for shop and cigar-store figures, their history is closely tied to that of figureheads in North America, where the vast majority of large-scale wooden sculpture was created by shipcarvers in the eighteenth and nineteenth centuries. The situation was somewhat different in Europe, however, due to the larger demand for figures and increased specialization among woodcarvers. In eighteenth-century London, for example, the carving trade was divided into five categories: framecarving, coachcarving, chaircarving, housecarving, and shipcarving.[3] Housecarving was a broad area that covered exterior and interior work for buildings of all types, including churches. Presumably, then, carvers who were experienced in either ship or architectural sculpture created figural shop signs as well. Because of this overlap, the European shop-figure tradition diverges somewhat from that of figureheads. We will avoid confusion by first considering shipcarving and then discussing shop figures.

Figureheads can be found in all parts of the world throughout history, but we need not journey to the dawn of civilization. Most important for our purposes is the intersection of shipcarving with the fine arts of western Europe that began during the Renaissance. Overall, the history of European shipcarving during the

1 Detail of plate 13

period is one of increasingly complex programs of carved and painted ornamentation. The oared galleys that had plied the Mediterranean since ancient times were the first to evidence the trend. In describing Spanish ships used in the war with the Turkish corsair and Ottoman admiral Barbarossa in the early sixteenth century, a historian wrote:

> The flagships were distinguished by their external adornment, especially those that accompanied Charles V. It was the time of the Renaissance, and ships were not exempt from its influence; which was evident from the sculpted figures on the prows, in the carving and gilding of the sterns, in the elegant form of the lanterns, in the painting of the pavesses, and the beauty of the tilts, standards and streamers. The fact that Barbarossa sent to the Sultan the scutcheon from the stern of the galley of Portuondo, as an artistic jewel, indicates the labor that was spent on it, and yet this was surpassed by the decoration of the galley in which the prince Don Felipe was at Genoa, which was the work of the best Italian artists.[4]

As the century progressed and Europe entered a period of maritime expansion fueled by the exploration and colonization of the New World, ship design and construction developed rapidly. By 1600, Spain, England, and Holland had built powerful navies of increasingly large warships and armed merchant vessels, while several other nations were committing more and more resources to shipbuilding in an effort to compete with them.

The most significant developments in ship decoration centered in France during the reign of Louis XIV. In 1665, Jean-Baptiste Colbert was appointed director of the fleet, charged with making his country into a major naval power.[5] The French had previously relied upon the Dutch for the construction of their larger ships. Colbert changed this by greatly expanding shipbuilding operations in several French ports, including Marseilles, Toulon, Brest, and Rochefort. He also turned his attention to ship decoration, initially enlisting the aid of Charles Le Brun (1619–1690), Director of the Académie Royal. In 1668, Le Brun completed ambitious designs for two major warships, *Le Royal Louis* and *Le Soleil Royal*, establishing the precedent for ornateness that characterized French work of the period. Other sculptors who made major contributions to the art include Pierre Puget (1620–1694) and later, Jean Bérain (1640–1711).[6] Colbert summarized his belief in the importance of shipcarving when he wrote that "nothing should be neglected in order to declare the magnificence of His Majesty on the seas."[7]

Strongly influenced by Italian ship work, French carvers at the Mediterranean ports of Marseilles and Toulon developed what one historian has characterized as a "flourishing French school of naval sculpture" by mid-century.[8] With Colbert's encouragement, the training of shipcarving apprentices at the major centers was formalized through the study of drawing and modeling, the use of live models, and other techniques adopted from the fine arts. As the dockyard workshops expanded and gained prominence, several of them added classrooms that came to be known locally as "academies." By 1668, more than forty master, journeymen, and apprentice carvers were employed in the carving school and workshop at Toulon.[9]

The director of ship decoration at Toulon at that time was Pierre Puget. Due to the fame that he has achieved in the annals of art history, his career has been fairly well documented. As such, it provides a rare glimpse into the development of shipcarving in seventeenth-century France and its close relationship to the fine arts. Born near Marseilles in 1620, Puget was apprenticed to a shipcarver named Roman. His talent was recognized at an early age and, according to an often-repeated story, his master recognized that he had nothing more to teach him after three months.[10] Following in the footsteps of generations of aspiring French artists, Puget left for Italy at age seventeen. He studied and worked in Florence and Rome with leading Baroque sculptors and painters including Pietro da Cortona (1596–1669).[11]

Returning to Marseilles three years later, Puget set himself up as a portrait painter while continuing to carve for ships. After a few years, he again traveled to Italy, where he continued to develop his interest in sculpture and architecture. Upon his return to France, he began receiving important painting and sculpture commissions. Working primarily in Marseilles and Genoa, Italy, he firmly established his reputation over the next decade, leading Colbert to appoint him to the post at Toulon in 1668.[12] Before long, he had also assumed the position of master sculptor at the dockyards in Marseilles, while at the same time continuing to execute major works in marble and other types of stone. Among his many accomplishments, he is credited with developing the shipcarving school at Toulon into an important center that taught generations of apprentices in southern France.[13]

As might be expected, the style that emerged was entirely Baroque. Puget was especially noted for creating complex compositions for the sterns of major vessels that included human figures in classical dress, gods and goddesses, mermaids and tritons, winged horses, portraits of contemporary subjects, caryatids, emblematic shields, and rows of huge columns. His design for the ship *Madame* featured four large figures flanking a central relief of a fashionable woman in an interior. Above and below the panel, putti and other decorative devices are combined with ornately carved balustrades and galleries (plate 2).

While Le Brun was much less directly involved in ship decoration after about 1671, he and other French artists continued to make important contributions to the development of the French style, and many influential designs have been credited to their hands.[14] It was Puget, however, who became particularly notorious among shipbuilders and seamen for creating the weighty figures, massive pillars, and other carvings that overloaded the ships to which they were applied and interfered with their handling. French ministers and naval officials quickly learned of the problems, both in terms of ship navigation and excessive expense, which resulted from a policy of unrestricted design. Puget's extravagance prompted reprimands from Colbert, including a refusal of his designs for a ship in December 1670. Three years later, a royal order was issued that limited the size and weight of stern carvings.[15] A popular story of the day recounted how one captain, having protested his ship's excessive decoration to no avail while in port, sawed off Puget's huge stern figures and set them adrift as soon as he got to sea.[16]

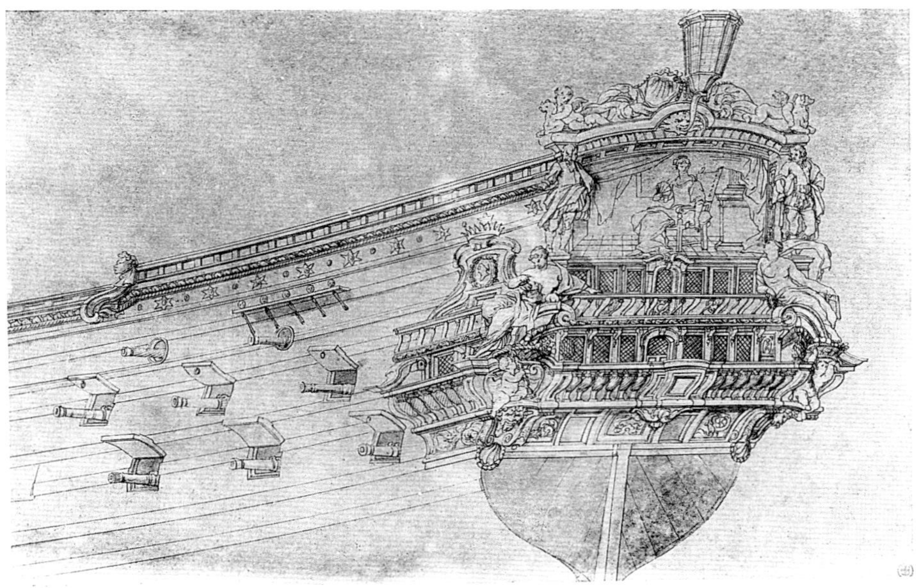

2 Artist unknown, after Pierre Puget (French, 1620–1694), drawing for the stern of the ship *La Madame*, 1669. Plate 6 in Philippe Auquier, *Pierre Puget: Décorateur naval et mariniste*. Paris: D. A. Longuet, 1909

In contrast to elaborate sterns, French figureheads of the period were generally much simpler affairs. Single figures in classical dress trailing acanthus leaves and other Baroque motifs were the general rule (plate 3). They were usually designed to emerge from the ship's head, a decorative structure built out over the water to support the figurehead and protect the bow of the vessel. Unlike most other European nations, the French never used the lion to any extent on larger vessels, except for a brief period in the late 1770s and 1780s.[17] Their emphasis on unified decorative schemes designed by leading sculptors and painters in an up-to-date aesthetic of Baroque classicism was also exceptional.

The same cannot be said of contemporary English practice. In the early part of the seventeenth century, lions, dragons, and unicorns, all survivors of late medievalism, were by far the most popular figurehead types.[18] As previously mentioned, the lion reigned supreme by the second half of the century, in compositions that were frequently embellished with cherubs or putti-type figures. The largest vessels were given equestrian portraits of the members of royalty after which they were named, or, as the tendency towards greater elaboration increased, multifigured groupings of humans and animals with complex allegorical and symbolic references.[19] In addition to classical and Baroque motifs, figureheads could also include knights in armor, double-headed horses, and other unrelated elements. The ship *Naseby* of around 1650 was described by a contemporary observer as having a figurehead of "Oliver [Cromwell] on horseback trampling six nations underfoot: a Scot, Irishman, Dutchman, Frenchman, Spaniard and English, as was easily made out by their several habits. A Fame held a laurel over his insulting head: the word 'God with us.'"[20]

Other English figureheads of the period were composed of even more complicated groups of allegorical figures. Animals, birds, armed warriors, mythological figures, coats of arms, and crowns were frequently fused in almost indecipherable masses. A carver's model for the figurehead of the *Victory* of 1765, for example, includes no less than eleven figures and busts representing the King, Britannia, Peace, Fame, Europe, America, Africa, Asia, the British lion, a five-headed Hydra, and the Genius of navigation or mathematics. The official specifications call for it to be twenty-four feet long, eighteen feet wide, and twelve feet deep.[21]

Much of the confusion in this and other English figureheads resulted from the fact that unlike the French, the British Admiralty was not particularly concerned with the quality of figurehead carving, as long as the work fit an approved subject and cost. For the most part, sculptors or shipcarvers familiar with problems of composition were not employed to design major programs of ship decoration. Instead, the ideas and allegories to be represented were conceived in the Admiralty office and passed along to the dockyards as verbal descriptions.[22] Without the aid of sketches, the carvers were then expected to translate these ideas into wood. This disjunction between conception and execution took little account of

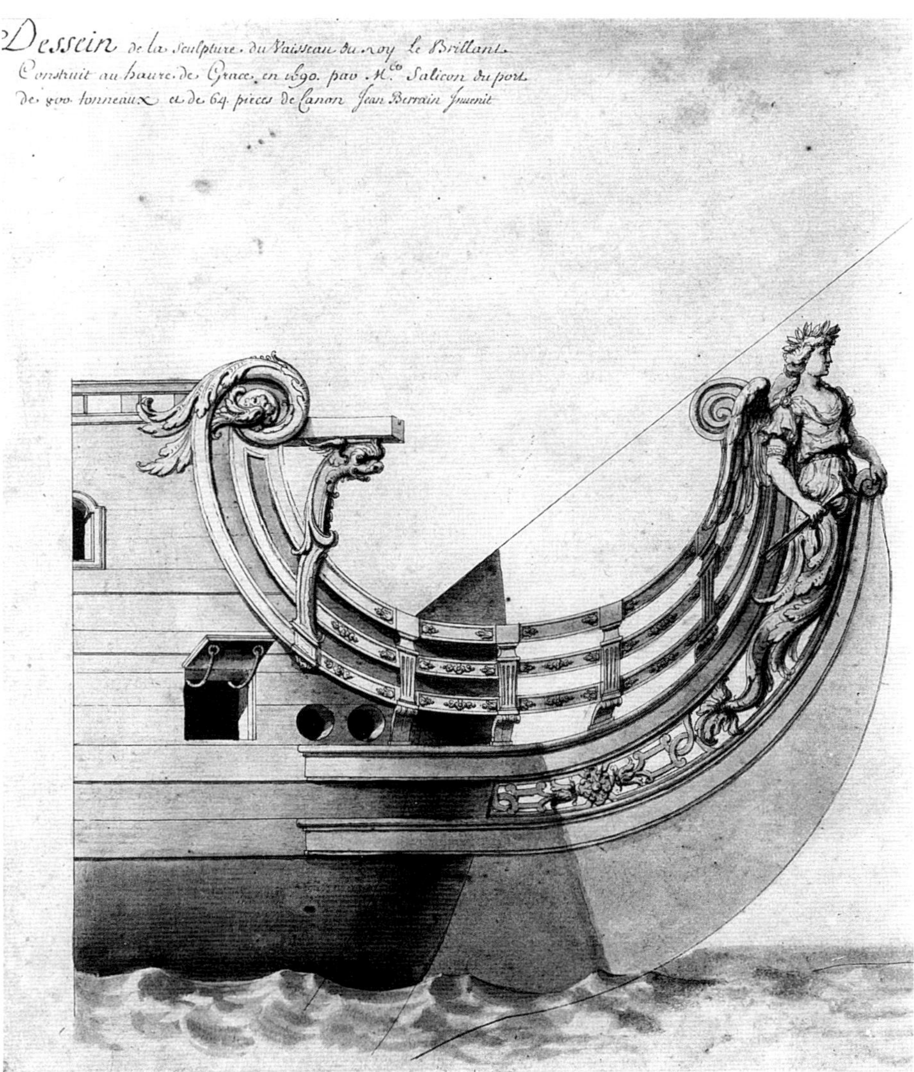

3 Jean Bérain (French, 1640–1711), after Charles Le Brun (French, 1619–1690), drawing for the prow of *Le Brillant*, Paris, 1690. Ink on paper. Musée national de la Marine, Paris

the actualities of effective design and the necessary restrictions imposed by the placement of the carvings on vessels of different sizes. Moreover, the weight of these overly complex compositions exceeded the practical limits of their purpose. They were just too heavy and too expensive.

The first serious attempt to control the size and cost of carvings on English ships came in 1703, when the Board of Admiralty issued an order that "the carved works be reduced to only a lion and trailboard for the head" and that stern and cabin decoration be greatly restricted as well.[23] The new regulations apparently had some effect, but as we have seen in the case of the *Victory* described above, the largest ships were often exempted. In both 1737 and 1773, the prices allowed for carving were restricted, while in 1742, an order to further reduce the size of stern carvings and "to make the lion or figures of the head as small and light as possible" was issued.[24] The latter order is particularly relevant to this discussion, as it was largely responsible for the replacement of hardwoods with pine as the principal wood for figureheads, a custom that was followed until the end of the era of wooden ships.[25]

The final regulation in this century-long attempt to restrict excessive decoration came in 1796, when the Board of Admiralty issued an order "to explode carve work altogether on board H.M. ships that may be built or repaired in the future, except what may be necessary for the mouldings about the scroll or billet head, and the stern and quarters."[26] The order was very unpopular, particularly in regard to billetheads, which were scrolls with a forward-curving spiral. Naval officials who sought to economize had for some time promoted them in the place of figureheads, but almost everyone else, from shipbuilders to seamen, resisted the move to discard the time-honored tradition of a representational figure on the prow. Every effort was made to evade the new regulation, and the figurehead survived a potential deathblow. The order did result in a significant reduction in the amount of carving, though, including the use of smaller and simpler figureheads. When the *Victory* received major repairs in 1802–3, for example, its complex group figurehead was replaced with a royal coat of arms, crowned and supported by a pair of cupids.[27]

Aesthetics and changing fashion also played a part in these developments, as Baroque and Rococo exuberance gave way to the more austere Neoclassical style in the latter part of the eighteenth century. The end result was a predominance of full-length, single figureheads on larger vessels, and bust portraits and billetheads on smaller ships. The figureheads were usually "straddle heads," in which the figure was placed astride the knee of the head, the principal vertical timber in the bow of the ship, often in a very awkward fashion (plate 4). The piece illustrated here is actually American, created around 1800 by the well-known Salem, Massachusetts, architect and carver Samuel McIntire (1757–1811). It is a rare example of shipcarving done by a man who is primarily known for his furniture and architectural carving. Due to its small size and fine state of preservation, it is thought to have been done either as a model or a shop sign that was never mounted on a ship.[28]

4 Attributed to Samuel McIntire (American, 1757–1811), *Model for a Figurehead*, Salem, Mass., c. 1800. Painted wood, height 26 in. (66 cm). Peabody Essex Museum, Salem, Mass.

English merchant ships generally followed the example of naval vessels throughout the period. By the closing decades of the eighteenth century, East Indiamen and other large commercial vessels that carried figureheads favored full- or three-quarter-length figures that symbolized the name of the ship, while

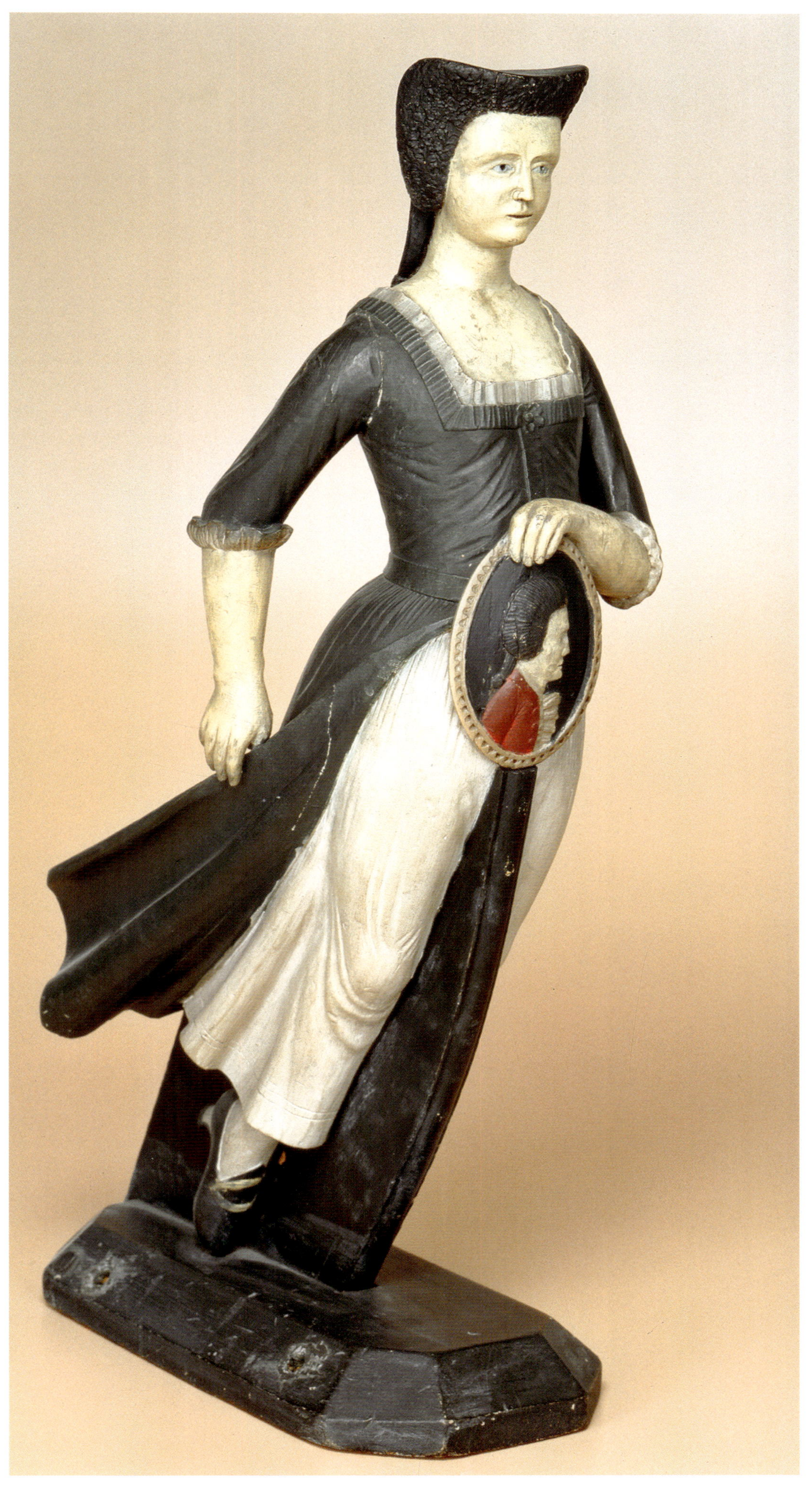

smaller craft commonly had busts of classical figures, contemporary personalities, or the shipowner himself.[29] These types remained popular throughout the nineteenth century as well, until the passing of the traditional figurehead at the end of the era of wooden sailing ships.

EUROPEAN SHOP FIGURES REPRESENT a parallel tradition in many respects, although on the whole their early history and development is more obscure than that of figureheads. In addition, little can be said about their makers, who, as mentioned earlier, were most likely a diverse group trained in several different woodcarving specialties. Still, we can assume that the use of human figures to identify a place of business dates to at least late medieval times when the resurgence of commerce and growth of trade sparked economic development throughout Europe. Given the ancient and widespread use of wooden ecclesiastical and ceremonial figures, it is not difficult to imagine that enterprising tradesmen of an even earlier date commissioned carved images as shop signs. For our purposes, though, the story begins in early-seventeenth-century England.

In 1617, Richard Brathwait wrote *The Smoaking Age, or The Life and Death of Tobacco*, a long, rambling tale of the origins of tobacco that ridiculed the extravagance of fashionable London smokers. As such, it was not a particularly remarkable piece of writing, but its frontispiece is notable as the earliest known representation of the interior of a tobacco shop (plate 5). On the counter is a sculpture of a small, vaguely African figure in a feathered skirt with a tobacco roll under his left arm, another in his mouth, and several clay pipes at his feet. Brathwait explains that this is "A Black-more upon the Stall, with rolls of tobacco, Drinking his Petoune."[30] The story that follows is presented as a quasi-mythological fable that casts Tobacco as the illegitimate son of Bacchus and Proserpine. Pluto becomes Tobacco's champion and mentor, and at one point advises him to "Plant thy selfe in the eye of the Citie; set mee the picture of some sallow-faced Blackamoore, or a Virginia-man, for that will draw custome upon the Frontispiece of thy doore."[31]

Acknowledging that Brathwait's allusions must have been familiar to his readers, his book demonstrates that counter-size figures known variously as blackamoors, black boys, or Virginians were closely associated with the tobacco trade by the early seventeenth century.[32] In fact, several other contemporary references further confirm this link between the image of black boys and tobacco. Among them is Ben Jonson's *Bartholomew Fair*, first published in 1614, which mentions "the black boy in Bucklersbury, that takes the scurvy, roguy tobacco, there."[33]

As common as the relationship was by this time, however, its origins are not entirely clear. Certainly, the association of Virginia with tobacco is understandable, as the colony was the source of much of the tobacco being imported into England. The depiction of Virginians as Africans is a more complicated issue that will be discussed later in this chapter. At this point suffice it to say that it was largely due to the unfamiliarity of most seventeenth-century Europeans with American Indians and the already-standardized conventions of artistic representation of the New World and its inhabitants.

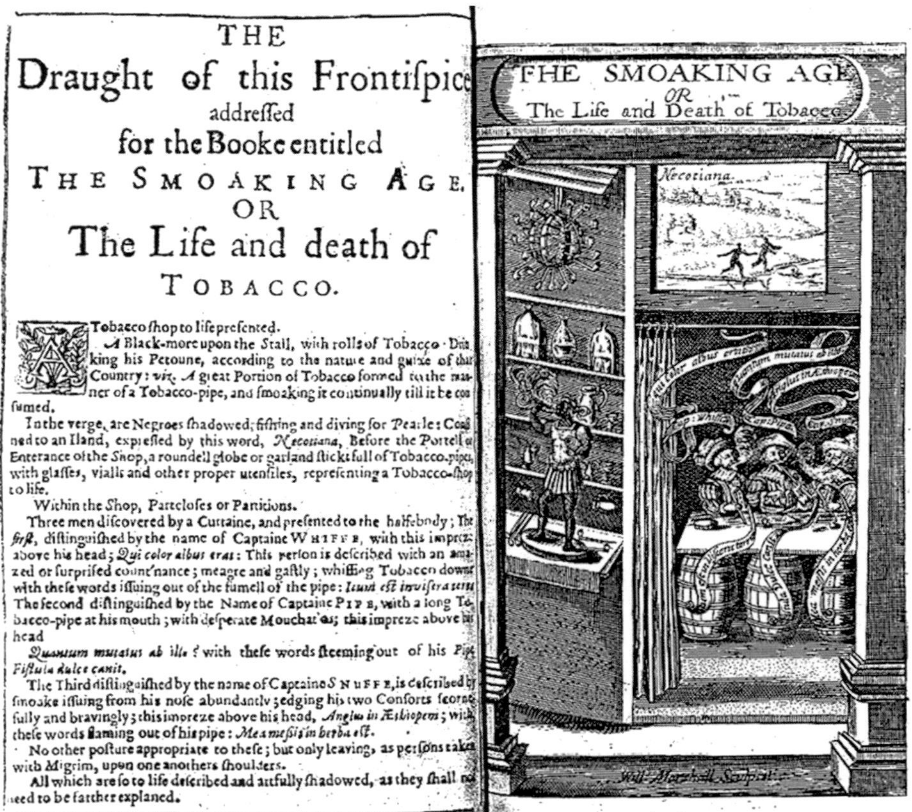

THE
Draught of this Frontiſpice
addreſſed
for the Booke entitled
THE SMOAKING AGE.
OR
The Life and death of
TOBACCO.

A Tobacco ſhop to life preſented.
A Black-more upon the Stall, with rolls of Tobacco · Drinking his Petoune, according to the nature and guize of their Country: *viz. A* great Portion of Tobacco formed to the manner of a Tobacco-pipe, and ſmoaking it continually till it be conſumed.

In the verge, are Negroes ſhadowed, fiſhing and diving for *Pearle*: Confined to an Iland, expreſſed by this word, *Necotiana*, Before the *Portell* or Enterance of the *Shop*, a roundell globe or garland ſtickt full of Tobacco-pipes, with glaſſes, vialls and other proper utenſiles, repreſenting a Tobacco-ſhop to life.

Within the *Shop*, Partcloſes or Partitions.

Three men diſcovered by a Curtaine, and preſented to the halfe body; The *firſt*, diſtinguiſhed by the name of Captaine WHIFFE, with this impreze above his head; *Qui color albus erat*: This perſon is deſcribed with an amazed or ſurpriſed count'nance; meagre and gaſtly; whiffing Tobacco downe with theſe words iſſuing out of the fumell of the pipe: *Iam est invisera sera* The ſecond diſtinguiſhed by the Name of Captaine PIPE, with a long Tobacco-pipe at his mouth; with deſperate Mouchat'os; this impreze above his head

Quantum mutatus ab illo? with theſe words ſteeming out of his *Pipe Fiſtula dulce canit.*

The Third diſtinguiſhed by the name of Captaine SNUFFE, is deſcribed by ſmoake iſſuing from his noſe abundantly; edging his two Conſorts ſcornfully and bravingly; this impreze above his head, *Anglus in Æthiopem*; with theſe words flaming out of his pipe: *Mea messis in herba est.*

No other poſture appropriate to theſe; but only leaving, as perſons taken with Migrim, upon one anothers ſhoulders.

All which are ſo to life deſcribed and artfully ſhadowed, as they ſhall not need to be farther explaned.

5 Frontispiece to Richard Brathwait, *The Smoaking Age, or The Life and Death of Tobacco.* London: E. Griffin, 1617

Images of blackamoors were often painted on two-dimensional signboards, as well as being fashioned as wooden figures. While it is not certain which came first, we do know that hanging signs themselves were universal at an early date, particularly for inns and taverns.[34] Their history can be traced through Roman and medieval times to the seventeenth century, when due to their ever expanding numbers they became subject to regulation in several European cities.

A few years after London's Great Fire of 1666, an ordinance was enacted that required signboards to be affixed to the walls of buildings instead of projecting out into the streets.[35] Apparently, the efforts of merchants and tradesmen to continually outdo one another in order to attract business had resulted in a dense, overhead canopy of large wooden signs on ornate iron fixtures that clogged narrow urban streets and threatened pedestrians. A similar ordinance was passed in Paris during the reign of Louis XIV.[36] Neither seems to have been enforced very rigorously, however, and the familiar profusion of projecting signs continued to be a part of the urban landscape in Great Britain and Europe.

In 1718, a commission of inquiry was appointed in London to investigate an incident in which the size and weight of a sign caused the wall of the building to which it was attached to collapse into the street, killing several people.[37] Then, in 1762, yet another ordinance was effected that called for "all . . . encroachments, projections, and annoyances whatsoever within the said cities . . . to be affixed or placed on the fronts of the houses, shops, warehouses, or buildings to which they belong."[38] By this time, though, the old, projecting signboards were finally beginning to disappear, in part because of these regulations, but also due to several other factors, including the increasing use of street numbers and the general rise of literacy among the population.

Throughout the seventeenth and most of the eighteenth centuries, signboards were often elaborately decorated, both by ornamental painters and well-known artists. Ornate iron fixtures were constructed at significant expense, a phenomenon that prompted the *Gentlemen's Quarterly* to comment in the mid-eighteenth century that "Long after signs became unnecessary, it was not unusual for an opulent shopkeeper to lay out as much upon a sign, and the curious ironwork with which it was fixed in the house, so as to project nearly in the middle of the street, as would furnish a less considerable dealer with stock in trade."[39]

In addition, three-dimensional hanging images of shoes, gloves, hats, and the like were common. Tobacconists frequently used a representation of a tobacco roll, a series of circular cakes of ten to twelve inches in diameter strung together for shipment. Constructed of wood, the signs were usually painted brown and gold. Several examples of this type of sign survive in the collections of English museums, while one source published in 1957 indicated that they "may be found even today hanging in the doorways of old-established Tobacconists."[40]

Small, carved human figures were sometimes attached to the more elaborate of these signboard constructions.[41] Due to the lack of documentation, it is difficult to estimate how many freestanding figures were placed outside of shops during this period. Judging by the remarkable growth in popularity of tobacco in the seventeenth century, though, images of black boys in the form of painted signboards, exterior shop signs, or carved counter figures must have been everywhere.

Tobacco began to have a significant impact on Europe around 1560, the year that Jean Nicot, the French Ambassador to Portugal, is credited with conducting the first medical experiments with it.[42] The early explorers had noted tobacco use among American Indians several decades earlier, and Columbus may have brought a few seeds to Europe on one of his return voyages, but even so it was too rare and exotic a commodity before the middle of the sixteenth century to generate much interest.[43] That was to change quickly, however, as news of Nicot's experiments caused a great stir in the French court and elsewhere. André Thevet, a Franciscan who had spent several years in Brazil, disputed Nicot's claim of being the first to recognize tobacco's potential and reported that, upon his return to Europe in 1556, he had planted tobacco seeds in his garden and had begun to investigate the plant's properties.[44] Thevet also holds the distinction of publishing the earliest-known illustration of a smoker. A plate from his *Les Singularities de la France antarctique*, first published in Paris in 1557, shows a Brazilian Indian smoking a large roll of tobacco, the direct predecessor of the cigar (plate 6).

By 1570 or so, tobacco was being cultivated in botanical gardens throughout Europe. Widely hailed by medical men as a universal panacea, it was not infrequently dubbed the "holy herb." According to the prevailing theory of bodily humors, tobacco was believed to expel phlegm and to warm and dry the body. It was therefore considered to be particularly good for older men whose brains were "cold and moist," and for all those living in damp, low-lying places.[45] Claims for its beneficial and curative properties grew more and more extravagant, and before long, "nicotian therapeutics," as its medical applications were often called, emerged as a common household remedy. Tobacco was variously prescribed for almost all known ailments, including asthma, ulcers, labor pains, rheumatism, ringworm, toothaches, constipation, deafness, and cataracts. At least one author went so far as to promote its use to counter the plague.[46]

As the list of tobacco's supposed virtues grew, some recognized the absurdity of many of the claims. By the early seventeenth century, the belief in the herb's therapeutic value was beginning to be challenged. In addition, it had become the center of an even larger controversy surrounding its social and recreational use, which many people believed to be spiraling out of control. Most medical men opposed the smoking habit on the grounds that tobacco was a medicinal agent that should not be used indiscriminately.[47] In literary circles, Brathwait's *The Smoaking Age* was just one of many satirical tracts that ridiculed the fashionableness of smoking. An earlier reference comes from a Bishop Hall, who wrote in 1597 that the young man of fashion "quaffs a whole tunnel of tobacco smoke."[48]

The most famous early opponent of tobacco use was undoubtedly James I, whose *A Counterblast to Tobacco*, published in London in 1604, characterized smoking as "A custom loathsome to the eye, hateful to the nose, harmful to the Brain, dangerous to the lungs, and in the black stinking fume thereof, nearest resembling the horrible Stigian smoke of the pit that is bottomless."[49]

The king pursued a lifelong crusade against the habit, and at one point increased the tariff on tobacco 4,000 percent in an effort to curtail consumption. He

6 Plate from André Thevet, *Les Singularities de la France antarctique*, 1557; reprint, Paris: Les Temps, 1982

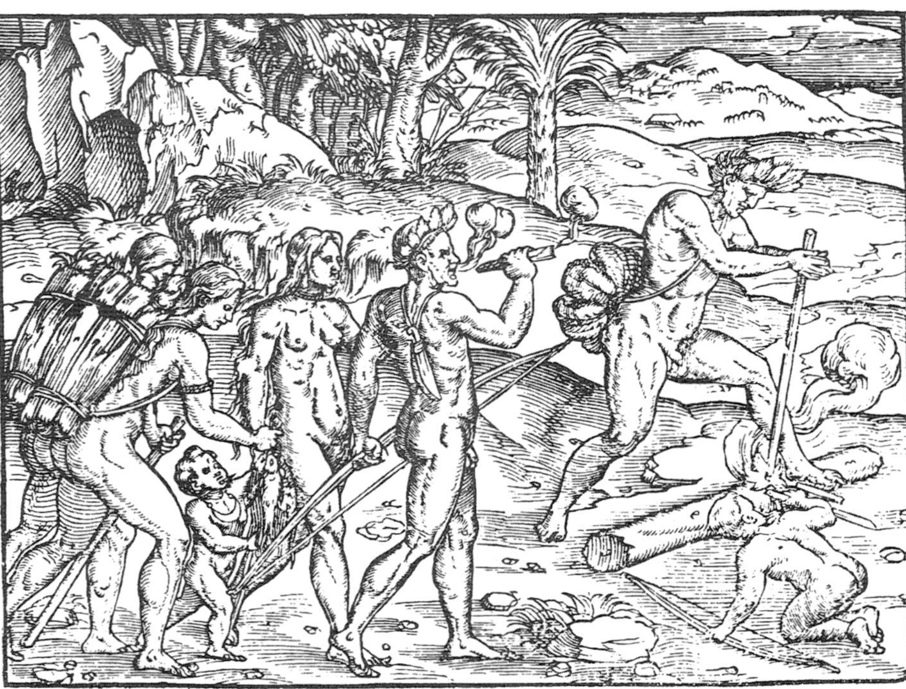

seems to have had an extreme personal aversion to tobacco, but his antipathy towards Sir Walter Raleigh, one of tobacco's great promoters, no doubt contributed to his position as well.[50] It should also be noted how useful his moral outrage was in providing a rationale for a significant new source of tax revenue.

Royal opposition to tobacco use appeared in many parts of the world in the early seventeenth century. In 1634, for example, a decree was issued in Russia that prohibited smoking or selling tobacco on pain of death or banishment for habitual offenders. Similar edicts were issued in Turkey, China, and Japan as well, not only due to tobacco's dubious health value, but also because it was considered a corrupting influence introduced by foreigners. While these laws were enforced somewhat sporadically and arbitrarily, they remained in place for several decades.[51]

Related but not quite as drastic measures have been recorded in Denmark, Sweden, Sicily, present-day Germany, and other parts of Europe.[52] The Catholic Church weighed in as well, when Urban VIII introduced a papal interdiction in 1642 that prohibited tobacco use in and around churches. The Pope noted not only the objectionable odors that filled the air, but also the frequent interruptions during religious services caused by those who left the church to have a smoke.[53]

Despite opposition in high places, tobacco consumption grew at an astounding rate. In 1603, approximately 25,000 pounds of tobacco were imported into England. By 1700, the total had reached 38,000,000 pounds.[54] As prices dropped throughout the seventeenth century, tobacco reached all corners of society and seemingly became everyone's favorite habit. As early as 1598, a German traveler named Hentzner recorded that the "English are constantly smoking tobacco," while in 1625, another observer wrote that "Tobacco shops are set up in greater number than either Alehouses or Tavernes."[55] Other European countries experienced a similar phenomenon, particularly Holland, which was consuming close to 3,000,000 pounds a year by 1670.[56]

As an exotic herb with reputed medicinal qualities, tobacco was first sold in apothecaries. Shops such as the one illustrated by Brathwait, which also sold drugs and liquors, usually offered patrons a place to indulge their habit. In this case, the three smokers are sitting in a private room that could be screened from the public by a curtain. As the popularity of smoking increased in the seventeenth century, tobacco shops quickly became more specialized concerns that were entirely devoted to the sale and consumption of tobacco products.

Although Brathwait chose to depict three gentlemen in the shop, tobacco use was not a male prerogative. On both sides of the Atlantic, it was popular among women and children of all social classes, and little evidence survives to suggest any widespread gender or age prohibition until the nineteenth century. As a visitor to backwoods America wrote in 1686: "Everyone smokes while working and idling. I sometimes went to hear the sermon; their churches are in the woods and when everyone has arrived the minister and all the others smoke before going in. The preaching over, they do the same thing before parting. They have seats for that purpose. It was here I saw that everybody smokes, men, women, girls, and boys from the age of seven."[57]

Pipe smoking was by far the most popular way to consume tobacco in seventeenth-century England, Holland, and North America. In Spain, on the other hand, cigars were preferred and the pipe was almost unknown. Evidently, Europeans adopted the prevailing custom among Native Americans in their respective colonies, as North American Indians generally used pipes, while their Central and South American neighbors rolled tobacco in a variety of vegetal wrappers.[58] The two other forms of tobacco use, snuffing and chewing, were also reported by the early explorers, although their popularity was at first somewhat limited in Europe.

Snuff came into its own in the eighteenth century. By the time of Queen Anne, it was considered much more fashionable than smoking in England and on the Continent.[59] Elaborate rituals and an extensive array of paraphernalia deemed necessary for the proper taking of snuff evolved among the aristocracy and all those with social pretensions. Snuffboxes became something of an art form, considered by many to be the equivalent of jewelry. As a Parisian observer noted in the second half of the eighteenth century: "One has boxes for each season. That for winter is heavy; that for summer light. It's by this characteristic feature that one recognizes a man of taste. One is excused for not having a library or a cabinet of natural history when one has 300 snuff boxes."[60]

Devotees of snuff disdained smoking as an uncouth habit that fouled both air and expensive wardrobes. Snuff's prominence prompted the venerable Doctor Samuel Johnson to pronounce in 1773 that "Smoaking has gone out."[61]

While this sentiment may have reflected the preference of the fashionable, however, it was far from universally true. Smoking remained popular among the middle and working classes in both city and country.[62] The image of the pipe-smoking country squire or parson became a typical artistic and literary device, while many artists, students, and other bohemian types flaunted smoking as a declaration of their independence from the dictates of fashion.

Cigars began to be seen outside of Spain only after about 1770. They had become quite popular in England by 1825, probably as a result of the influence of British soldiers returning from Napoleonic wars in Spain and Portugal.[63] By that time, cigar smoking was also common in other European countries and in North America. Unlike pipes and snuff, cigars were generally considered to be a part of the masculine domain, which would seem to be a significant comment on the emergence of new gender distinctions during the Victorian era. In the late 1850s, an English author noted that the cigar had made major inroads in the previous twenty years, and that it was a prominent feature of the gentleman's study or library.[64] Cigars continued to gain ground among smokers until the end of the century. By then, they had begun to be eclipsed by the cigarette, which is, of course, the most popular tobacco product today.

WITH THIS BACKGROUND IN MIND, we can return to the development of tobacco-shop figures in England. Due to the rapid growth in tobacco consumption in the seventeenth century, it is reasonable to assume the number of carved wooden figures advertising the sale of tobacco products must have increased dramatically. Most of them were fanciful representations of African boys, ranging from about two to three feet in height, that were intended for display on a counter of a shop that dispensed tobacco, as illustrated in Brathwait's book. They shared a number of com-

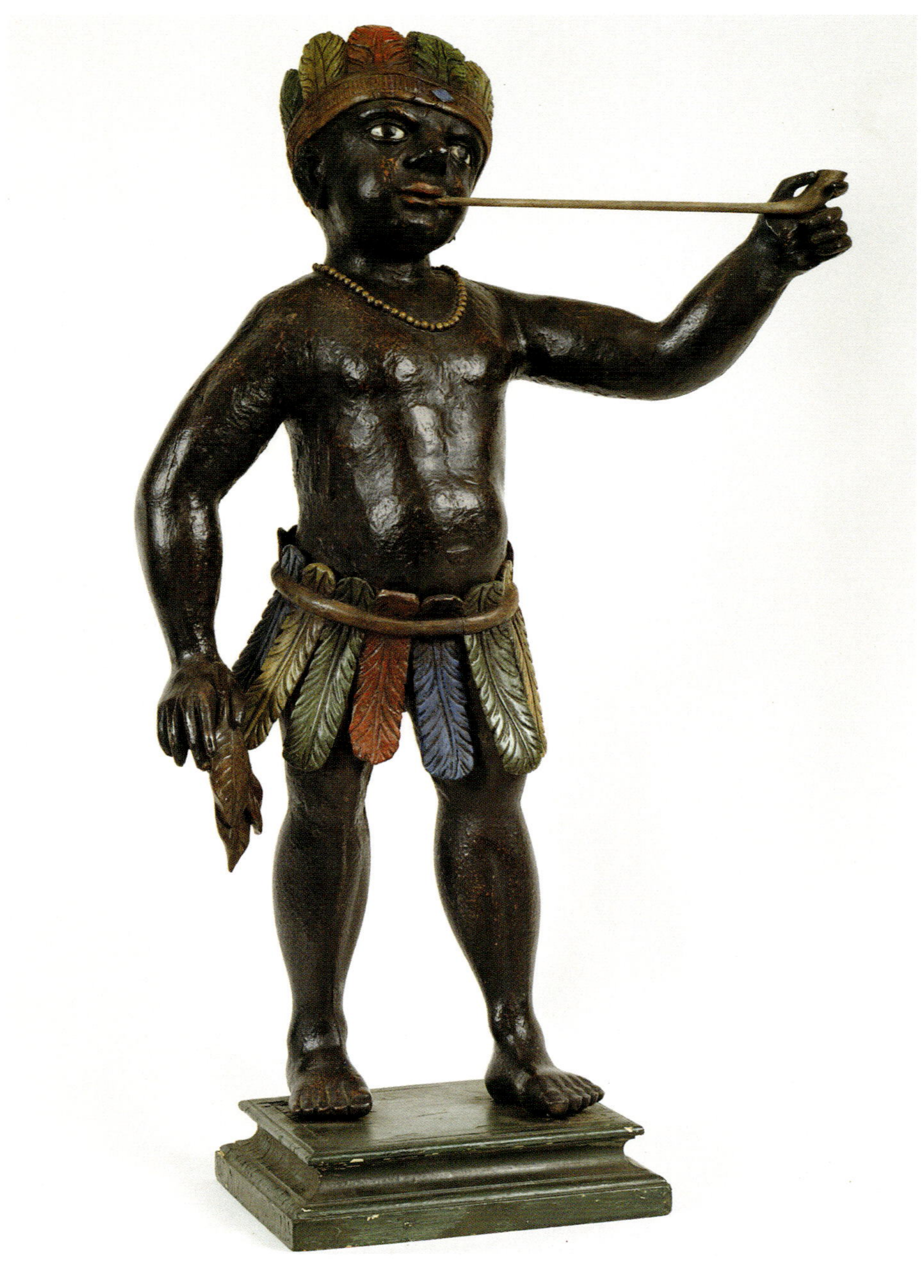

7 *Blackamoor with Pipe,* probably English, mid-eighteenth century. Painted wood, 36 x 23 x 12 in. (91.4 x 58.4 x 30.5 cm). American Folk Art Museum, New York. Gift of Mr. and Mrs. Francis S. Andrews (1982.6.3)

mon attributes and accessories that helped identify their purpose, including skirts of feathers or tobacco leaves, feathered headdresses, necklaces with gorgets, pipes, and rolls of tobacco. Their bodies were proportioned either as adults or children.

The two figures illustrated here, which are probably English dating from the mid-eighteenth century, are well carved with somewhat generalized soft and round bodies typical of representations of children during the period (plates 7 and 8). The feathers or leaves of the skirt and headdress of the figure holding the pipe are more crisply rendered and are painted in several different colors. Its lips, pupils, and necklace are also highlighted with color. Other surviving examples, such as the figure with the tobacco roll under his arm, are entirely black. Both have old surfaces. It should be noted that the issues surrounding color and surface treatment are complicated, as most shop figures were frequently repainted during their working lives. Original surfaces are rare to the point of nonexistence, and old is a relative term at best, particularly when applied to early counter figures. Nevertheless, the coloring of these two figures is both typical and traditional.

The image of the black man or African as a symbol of an exotic, far-off land certainly predates the introduction of tobacco in Europe. Commonly known as Ethiopians, North Africans had figured into the European imagination for centuries. As such, they embodied several different meanings. They could serve as fairly straightforward references to foreign places or products, as in the present instance. By the seventeenth century, black boys dressed in exotic costumes were also in much demand as pages and other types of fashionable appendages to aristocratic households.[65]

On a deeper level, images of Africans were representations of otherness from beyond the borders of Christendom that embodied a range of conflicting and generally negative characteristics more comfortably ascribed to outsiders than recognized as a part of European culture and civilization.[66] The frequent allusions to blackamoors and other African types in sixteenth- and seventeenth-century literature provide ample evidence of their many roles. In the Brathwait illustration of a tobacco shop, for example, several scrolls containing Latin phrases hover above the heads of the three smokers at right (see plate 5). The words may be translated as "How much changed from whites are these Englishmen transformed into Ethiopians." In this case, seventeenth-century racial humor is used to indict smoking through association with the negative values attached to the image of otherness.

8 *Blackamoor with Keg*, probably English, mid-eighteenth century. Painted wood, 20½ x 12 x 6 in. (52 x 30.5 x 15.2 cm). American Folk Art Museum, New York. Gift of Mr. and Mrs. Francis S. Andrews (1982.6.2)

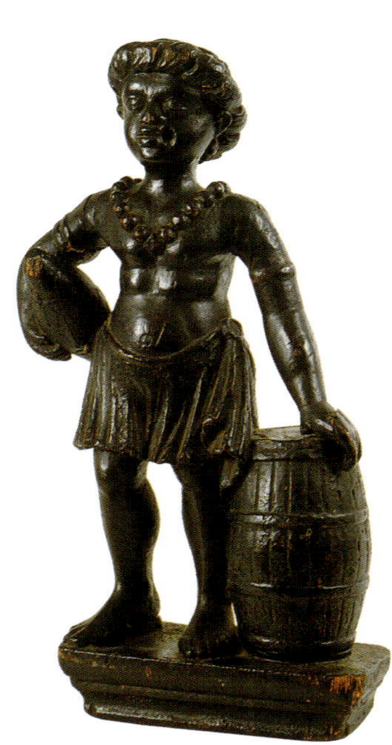

The issue is, of course, not the realistic representation of foreigners, but is rather one of European conceptions of the foreign constructed through cultural and artistic traditions. This in turn makes it easier to understand the link between the blackamoor and tobacco. The African was a much more familiar type than the Native American. Few sixteenth- and seventeenth-century Europeans had ever seen an American Indian. In the absence of existing models, artists and craftsmen relied on convention when called upon to represent the inhabitants of the New World. The Brazilian smoker and his companions illustrated in Thevet's 1557 book have idealized bodies derived from Classical and Renaissance precedents (see plate 6).

One of the earliest illustrations of the New World, a German woodcut of 1505 that relates to the letters of Amerigo Vespucci, shows Caribbean or Brazilian Indians with European beards (plate 9). It also highlights their feather ornaments, some of which are fairly accurate. The feathered skirts are not, however, and it has been speculated that they are a misinterpretation of Vespucci's verbal descriptions of people who wore no clothes but decorated themselves with feathers. European artists could not conceive of such a state of affairs, and so invented the feathered skirt.[67] Before long, this became a standard feature of representations of American Indians, surviving into the nineteenth century as the tobacco-leaf skirt of cigar-store figures.

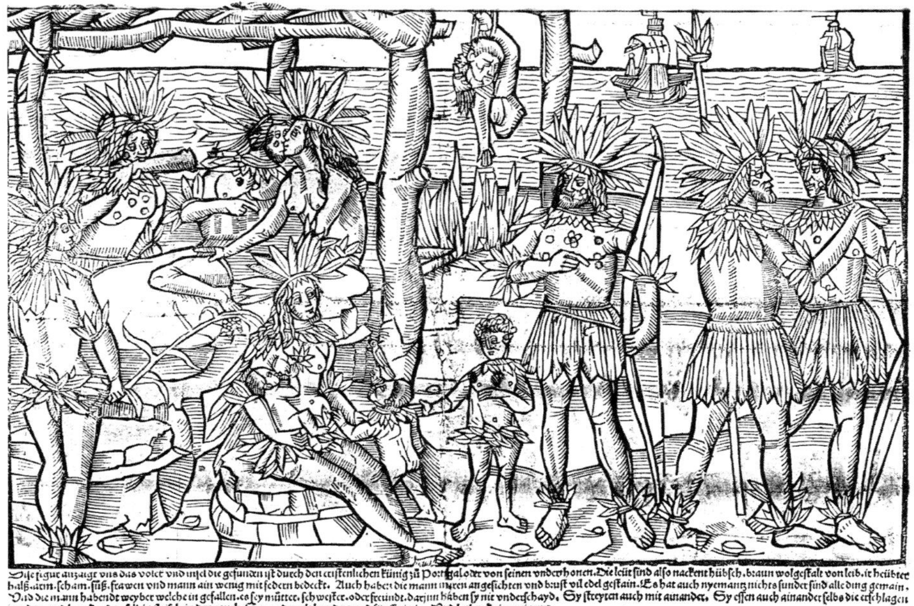

9 *America*, probably Nuremberg or Augsberg, Germany, c. 1505. Woodcut. Private collection

In Frankfurt from 1580 to 1634, Theodor de Bry and his family published a thirteen-volume series entitled *The Great Voyages*, more commonly known as the *America* series. The first attempt to create a comprehensive chronicle of the European discovery and colonization of the New World, the volumes contained over three hundred copperplate engravings, including maps, topographical views and, above all, scenes of the voyages, the conquest, and the lifestyles of American Indians. The series was widely distributed and reprinted numerous times, particularly in the seventeenth century. Its collective impact upon the popular conception of the discovery and conquest of America has been enormous. Its illustrations have served as models for many artists, while over the years, a large number of visual motifs have been extracted from the original prints and inserted into countless new contexts.

The frontispiece of volume nine, first published in 1602, features an idealized Indian man wearing a feathered skirt and headdress, and holding a bow and arrow (plate 10). His appearance demonstrates that these items had already become artistic conventions by this time. When combined with the image of the blackamoor, they result in the Virginian, an exotic figure from the distant land where tobacco is grown. Once fixed, the depiction remained remarkably consistent across a variety of formats into the nineteenth century.

AS A SHOP SIGN, the black boy reigned supreme in Great Britain until the eighteenth century. By then, he was finally being challenged by the image of the Highlander, usually a kilted Scotsman offering a pinch to passersby or holding a snuffbox or a mull, a handheld grinder used to prepare the powdered mixture. The earliest known reference appeared on the 1720 trade card of David Wishart of London, who advertised that he "Makes & sells all sorts of Snuff" at the sign of the "Highlander, Thistle and Crown."[68] Whether Wishart used a signboard or a carved wooden figure is not known, but certainly such figures existed by this time. Their numbers grew with the increasing use of snuff until, by mid-century, they were apparently encountered more frequently than the older image of the blackamoor. Their widespread popularity is confirmed by an item that appeared in 1747, two years after the English had put down the Jacobite Rebellion in Scotland and Parliament had enacted legislation to suppress Scottish dress, ballads, and other aspects of traditional culture. Veiling his criticism of English policy in satire, the author wrote:

> We hear that the dapper wooden Highlanders, who guard so heroically the doors of snuff-shops, intend to petition the Legislature, in order that they may be excused from complying with the act of Parliament with regards to their change of dress: alleging that they have ever been faithful subjects to his Majesty, having constantly supplied his Guards with a pinch out of their mulls when they marched by them, and so far from engaging in any Rebellion, that they have never entertained a rebellious thought; whence they humbly hope that they shall not be put to the Expense of buying new cloaths.[69]

Eighteenth-century Highlanders were either lifesized representations placed outside of shops or smaller figures in the tradition of their blackamoor predecessors that were displayed on counters and above doorways. Carvers generally paid great attention to details of costuming, while faces could be either generalized or quite specific in the delineation of features. All were brightly painted in the manner of one or more Highland regiments.

10 Frontispiece to Theodor de Bry, *The Great Voyages* 9. Frankfurt: Theodor de Bry, 1602

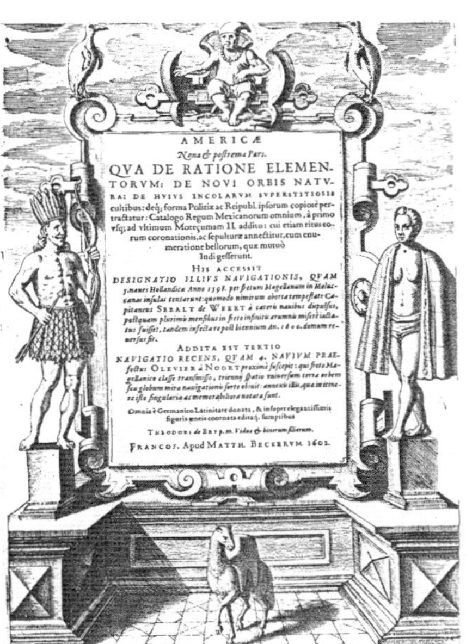
AMERICÆ
Nona & postrema Pars.
QVA DE RATIONE ELEMENTORVM: DE NOVI ORBIS NATVRA: DE HVIVS INCOLARVM SVPERSTITIOSIS cultibus: deq; forma Politiæ ac Reipubl. ipsorum copiosè pertractatur: Catalogo Regum Mexicanorum omnium, à primo vsq; ad vltimum Moteçumam II. addito: cui etiam ritus eorum coronationis, ac sepulturæ annectitur, cum enumeratione bellorum, quæ mutuò Indi gesserunt.
HIS ACCESSIT
DESIGNATIO ILLIVS NAVIGATIONIS, QVAM 5. naues Hollandicæ Anno 1598. per fretum Magellanum in Moluccanas insulas tentarunt: quomodo nimirum oborta tempestate Capitaneus SEBALT de WEERT à cæteris nauibus depulsus, postquam plurimis mensibus in freto infinitis ærumnis miserè iactatus fuisset, tandem infecta re post biennium An. 1600. domum reuersus sit.
ADDITA EST TERTIO
NAVIGATIO RECENS, QVAM 4. NAVIVM PRAEfectus OLEVIER à NOORT proximè suscepit: qui freto Magellanico classe transmisso, triennij spatio vniuersum terræ orbem seu globum mira nauigationis sorte obiuit: annexis illis, quæ in itinere isto singularia ac memorabiliora notata sunt.
Omnia è Germanico Latinitate donata, & insuper elegantissimis figuris æneis coornata editaq; sumptibus
THEODORI de BRY p.m. Viduæ & binorum filiorum.
FRANCOF. Apud MATTH. BECKERVM. 1602.

Having attained near universal popularity throughout Great Britain, the Highlander remained a common sight throughout the nineteenth century. That wry observer of English life, Charles Dickens, recognized him as such a general feature of tobacco shops around 1855 that he wrote in *Little Dorrit* that "The business was of too modest a character to support a life-sized Highlander, but it maintained a little one on a bracket on the door-post, who looked like a fallen Cherub that had found it necessary to take to a kilt."[70]

The counter-sized figure illustrated here speaks to the longevity of the tradition (plate 11). Created around 1910 for Ratray's Snuff Shop in Perth, Scotland, it is a lively characterization that features all of the Highlander's typical attributes, from snuff mull to regimental uniform. The finely detailed carving reinforces the naturalism of the little Scotsman's pose and demeanor.

While the Highlander was the most common type of English shop figure after about 1750, he was not the only character to stand alongside the older black boys. Turks and sailors were also very popular. Turbaned Turks, or Moors, as they were frequently called, were portrayed in long flowing robes and loose-fitting trousers in a generalized conception of Middle Eastern dress. They often served more than one purpose, and were just as frequently used by coffeehouses as tobacco shops.[71] It was usually just a simple matter of different accessories. With pipe in hand, a Turk identified a tobacconist; without it, he advertised a coffee shop.

It should be noted that regardless of historical and cultural realities, costuming is the most important distinguishing feature between the types of shop figures known as Moors and blackamoors. That is, while historically the European words *moor* and *blackamoor* could both refer to Islamic North Africans and, to a lesser extent, all Arabic peoples, the shop-figure tradition makes a different distinction. Generally speaking, Moors and Turks were those figures in orientalized costumes, and blackamoors, black boys, and Virginians wore feather or tobacco-leaf skirts.[72] The distinction is important because it aids in the interpretation of seventeenth- and eighteenth-century references to a variety of figures that no longer exist.

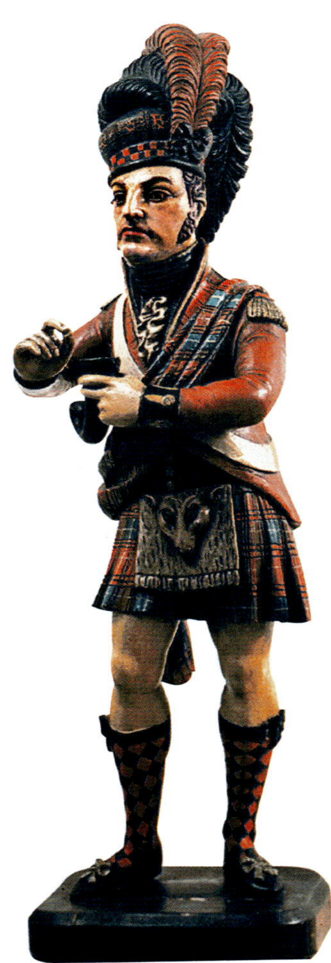

11 *Highlander*, Perth, Scotland, c. 1910. Painted wood, 41 x 12 x 12 in. (104 x 30.5 x 30.5 cm). Mark Goldman/Mom's Cigars Collection, New York

Sailors, too, played a dual role, as signs for both tobacco merchants and marine suppliers. Because smoking was usually restricted on board ships due to the fire hazard of an open flame, sailors were particularly partial to chewing tobacco.[73] Peter Kalm, a Swedish botanist, noted during a visit to Philadelphia in the mid-eighteenth century: "The English chewed tobacco a great deal, especially if they had been sailors. Not an hour passed when they did not take as much cut tobacco as they could hold in the fingers of the right hand and stuff it in the mouth. Young fellows from fifteen to eighteen years of age were often as bad as the older men."[74]

As a result of this preference, sailors were commonly identified with chewing tobacco, while sailor figures frequently presided over the sections of tobacco shops that dispensed that particular product. If, on the other hand, the sailor figure held a spyglass, sextant, or some other navigational device, he became a sign for a nautical instrument shop or a chandlery that sold all types of marine supplies. For obvious reasons, they were frequently encountered in coastal towns, and could be found in a variety of sizes, from detailed, full-sized representations standing in doorways to smaller versions in shop windows or attached to storefronts. Again Dickens provides a contemporary reference and a sly comment on their widespread use. In a description of London's maritime district in *Dealings with the Firm of Dombey and Son*, which first appeared in serialized form between 1846 and 1848, he wrote, "Anywhere in the immediate vicinity there might be seen . . . outfitting warehouses ready to pack off anybody anywhere, fully equipped in half an hour; and little timber midshipmen in obsolete naval uniforms, eternally employed outside shop doors of nautical-instrument makers in taking observations of the hackney coaches."[75]

According to a late-nineteenth-century source, the figure that inspired Dickens was a well-known sign for the shop of Norie and Wilson that was in use by 1763. Supposedly, King William IV once saluted him with a tip of the hat as he passed by on his way to Trinity House.[76]

Because these little sailors and other types of shop figures were so adaptable and provided such humorous, recognizable, and easily remembered identifications, it should come as no surprise to learn that they were also prevalent in other parts of Europe by the eighteenth century. In fact, it has been suggested that blackamoor figures were first used on the Continent and were introduced into England around 1615.[77] References to the use of carved wooden figures in Holland, Germany, France, and elsewhere are quite common, although usually they are mentioned only in passing, no doubt because it was assumed that everyone was familiar with them. In Holland, the traditional triumvirate of Highlander, Turk, and sailor was particularly popular. In addition to three-dimensional figures, the characters could also be seen together on signboards in an image inspired by a popular rhyme that translates into English as: "We three are engaged in one cause. I snuffs, I smokes and I chaws."[78]

As for shop figures in the American colonies, little evidence exists before the Revolutionary War period, but again it is certain that they were in use, at least in some of the larger coastal towns. In 1712, a "handsome wooden soldier," carved by Lemon (or Leaman) Beadle (1680–1717) was placed on top of a new watch house in Salem, Massachusetts. Beadle was one of the first native-born shipcarvers, and, although strictly not a shop sign, his soldier is among the earliest American architectural figures on record. Little more is known of his work, but he was most likely responsible for several lion figureheads carved in Salem in the 1710s and shipped to New York City, which apparently did not have a carver in residence at the time.[79]

12 *The Little Admiral*, Boston, before 1770. Painted wood, 42 x 32½ in. (106.7 x 82.5 cm). Bostonian Society, Mass.

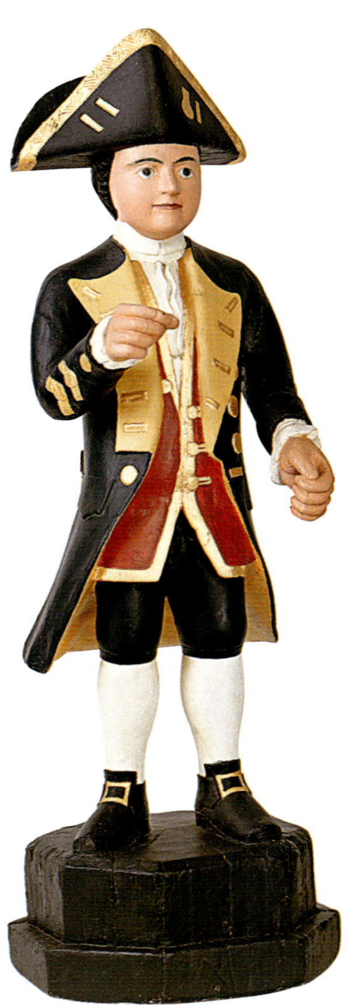

The Little Admiral, an old figure that has been in the collection of the Bostonian Society since 1916, has a more secure claim to being the oldest known American shop figure (plate 12). William Williams, a mathematical instrument maker, was using the piece as a sign for his shop at the corner of State Street and Merchants Row before 1770. The location had previously been the site of the Admiral Vernon Tavern, a popular gathering place that was in operation as early as 1743. Admiral Edward Vernon was a well-known personality who died in 1757. *The Little Admiral* has long been identified with the tavern as well as with Williams's shop, and in fact, his now empty right hand could have just as easily held a glass of grog as a quadrant.[80]

Two closely related eighteenth-century figures of Bacchus astride a keg have histories that are similarly varied. The one illustrated here is believed to have been used for many years as a sign for the Backus Hotel in Norwich, Connecticut (plate 13).[81] A nearly identical piece, painted white and holding a basket of fruit instead of a bottle and cup, has a long history in nearby Windham and is still displayed in the Windham Public Library. They are likely the work of the same carver, although tradition holds that the Windham Bacchus was made by four British seamen from the sloop *Bombrig* who were captured and imprisoned there in 1776. It was first presented to a Widow Cary as a token of appreciation for her kindness and subsequently served as a sign for several different taverns for over a hundred years.[82] One of the prisoners was a ship carpenter named John Russell, but whether or not he was the carver will never be known. Whoever was responsible for these cheerful, chubby figures can be credited with a good understanding of contemporary decorative work in a late Rococo style.

As for tobacconist figures, a colonial character in a powdered wig and knee breeches that is owned by the Demuth Foundation in Lancaster, Pennsylvania, is the earliest-known example with a documented history (plate 14). Demuth's Tobacco Shop was founded by Christopher Demuth in 1770 and remains the oldest tobacco establishment in the United States that is operated by descendants of the original owner. A counter figure approximately two feet in height, the piece

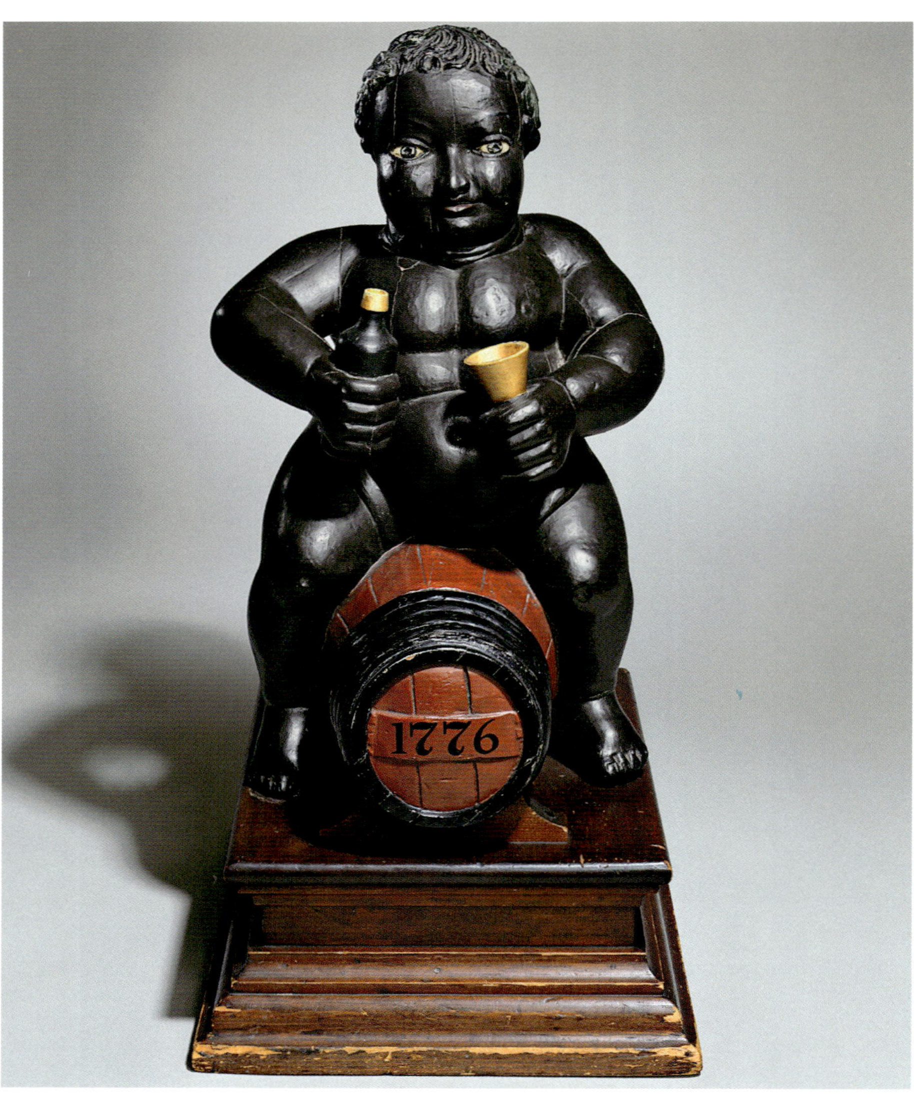

is usually dated to 1770, the year that the shop was opened. More likely it was carved a few decades later by Christopher's son, John Demuth (b. 1770), who was a woodcarver by profession.[83] While it may very well be the oldest surviving American tobacconist figure, it was certainly not the first, for, as has been shown, tobacco use was widespread in America by the late seventeenth century.

Tobacco was also a vital element of the colonial economy. One source estimates that around the time of the American Revolution, tobacco represented over 75 percent of the total value of goods exported from Virginia and Maryland. In 1770, for example, the two colonies shipped over 100,000 hogsheads of tobacco to England. The cargo was carried in from 300 to 400 vessels, employing about 4,000 seamen.[84] A case can therefore be made for the importance of tobacco not only to the growth of the shop-figure tradition, but also to the development of American shipbuilding. The link is far from being random or inconsequential.

13 (ABOVE) *Bacchus on Keg*, Norwich, Conn., c. 1776. Painted wood, 26½ x 15½ x 21 in. (67.3 x 39.4 x 53.3 cm). Connecticut Historical Society, Hartford

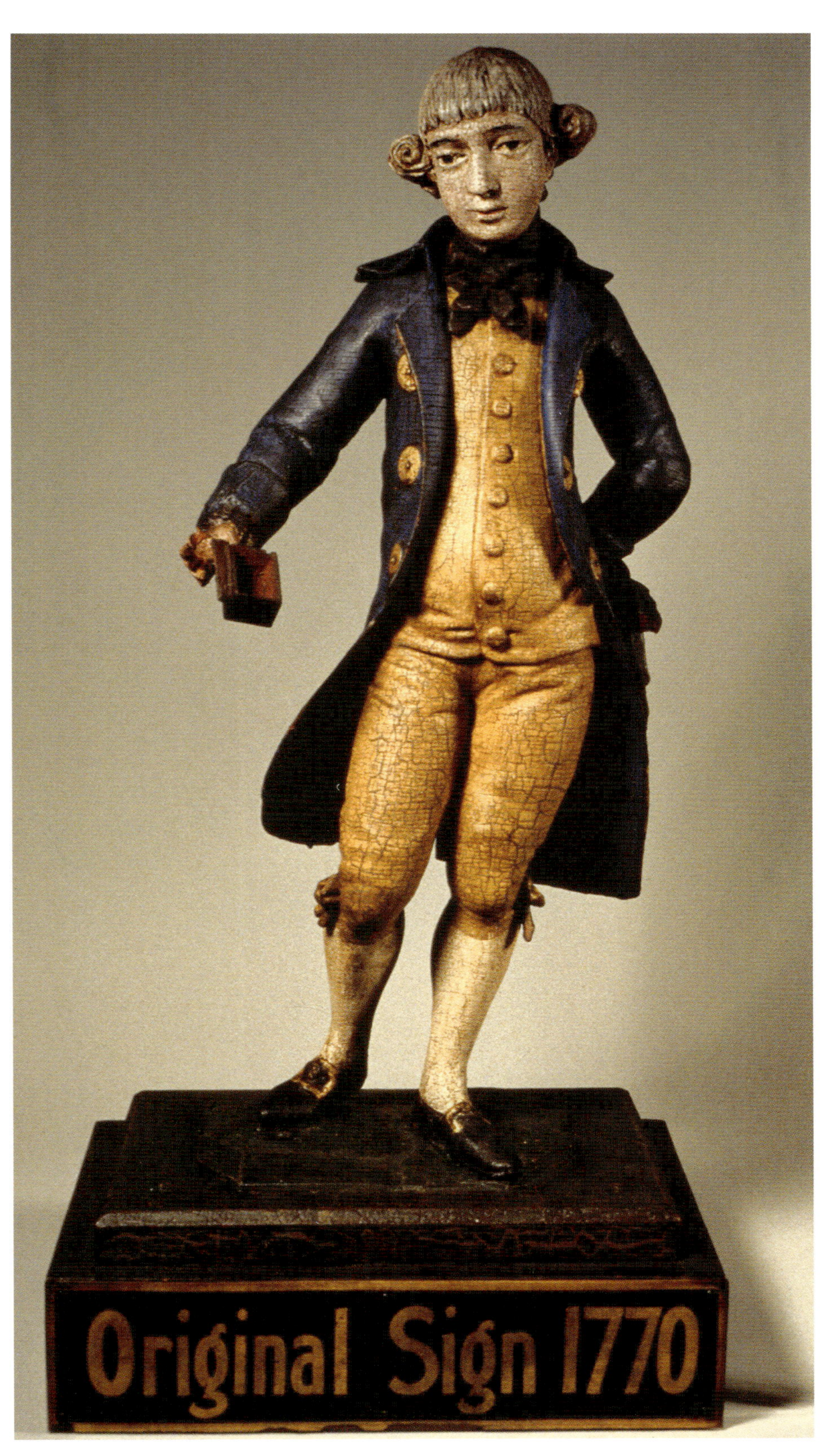

14 Probably John Demuth (American, b. 1770), *Colonial Man*, Lancaster, Pa., c. 1795. Painted wood, 25 x 10 in. (63.5 x 25.4 cm). Demuth Foundation, Lancaster, Pa.

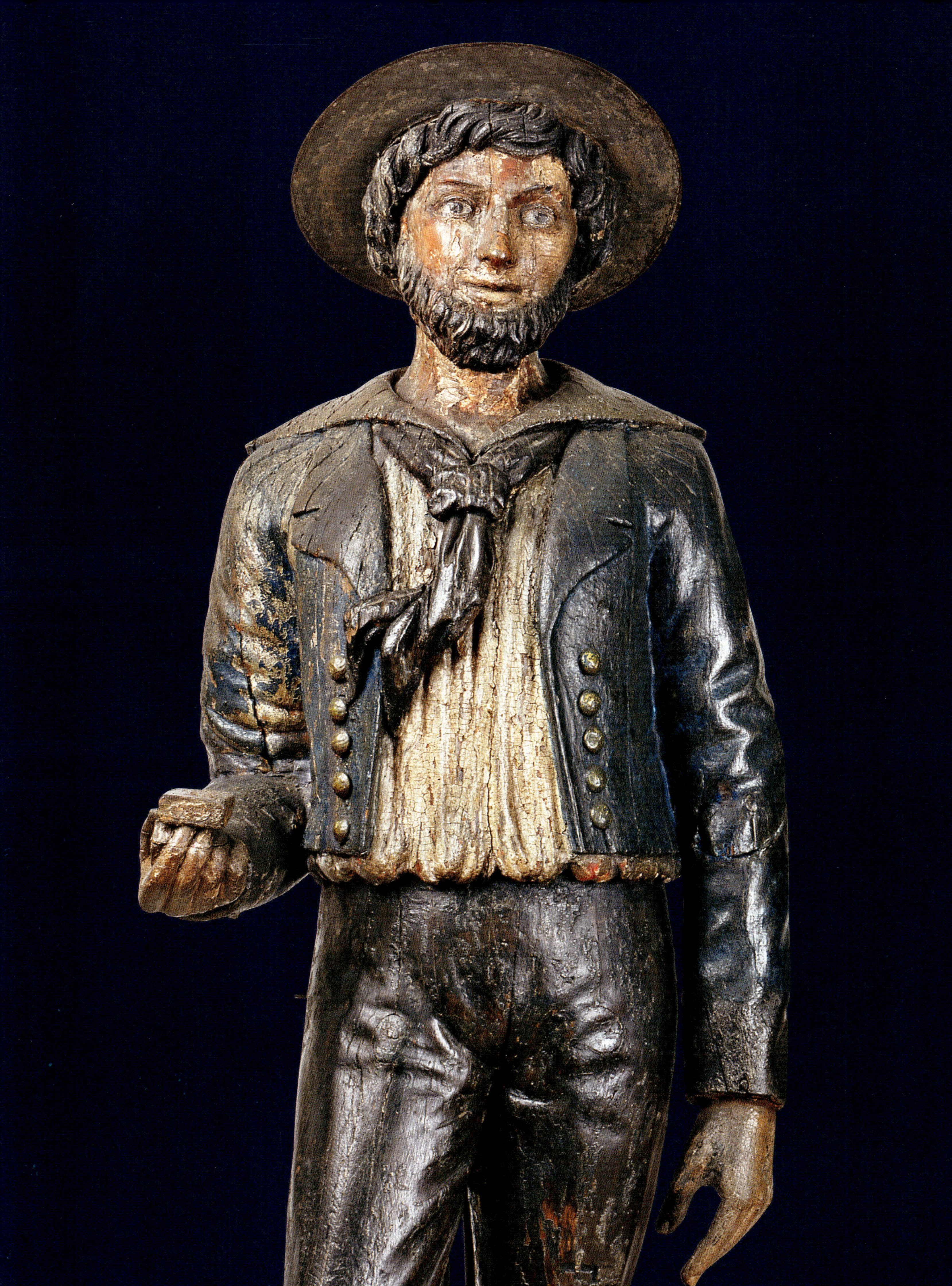

CHAPTER 2 THE ART OF THE SHIPCARVER

OF THE MANY SHIPS built along the Atlantic seaboard before the Revolution, most were small coastal vessels. American shipyards did not begin to build mid-sized, 26- and 44-gun frigates rivaling those of England and France until the 1770s, and even these were no match for the huge first- and second-rate English ships of the line that carried from 90 to 120 guns and the most ornate carvings.[1] Still, shipcarving was an important craft in colonial America, albeit on a more modest scale than in Europe.

The first vessel known to be built here was the *Virginia*, which was launched at the mouth of the Kennebec River in Virginia in 1607. Thirteen years later, the Virginia Colony established the shipbuilding industry in North America by recruiting twenty-five experienced shipwrights from England. The other colonies quickly followed suit, and the trade began to flourish, thanks in large part to the seemingly endless supply of timber. Massachusetts had the most active early shipyards, and, as one resident confidently asserted, produced "All things necessary for shipping and naval furniture." As a rough indication of numbers built, the colony owned more than 1,300 locally made vessels between 1680 and 1714.[2]

From the beginning, the larger ships carried figureheads and other kinds of carved ornament. This can be seen in some of the few surviving contracts and bills from the period. In 1671, for example, an agent for a shipbuilder in Piscataquay (now Portsmouth, New Hampshire) received an order from Barbados for a ship to be "Set forth handsomely with Carved Work."[3] In addition, shipcarvers were soon receiving other types of orders and commissions as well. By and large, they were the only artisans in a particular locale who were capable of consistently producing skilled ornamental work in wood. Because of this, they were frequently called upon to do architectural and furniture carving as well as figureheads and sternboards. Throughout the eighteenth century, their figures graced the prows of ships, gardens of well-to-do citizens, ceremonial structures built for civic celebrations, and storefronts of enterprising merchants.

Almost all of this work has long since succumbed to the ravages of time and the elements. As a result, documentary sources provide the primary evidence of the colonial carver's art. The earliest-known record of an American figurehead dates to 1689, when Edward Budd and Richard Knight of Boston presented a bill for a "Lyon" for the sloop *Speedwell*.[4] In this, they were closely following English practice, in which, as previously discussed, lion figureheads were the general rule on all but the largest naval vessels throughout the seventeenth century and the first three or four decades of the eighteenth. Numerous other references to lions carved for American vessels after 1700 attest to their widespread use during the

15 Detail of plate 35

period. The carvers themselves emphasized their familiarity with English styles, or better yet, their English training. Typical of the advertisements that appeared in American newspapers were: "Henry Crouch, Carver from London, now living in Annapolis, Makes any sort of carved work for Ships" and "Philip Witherstone, carver from Bristol, Ship Carving done as Cheap as in England."[5]

It was not until after 1727, when the British Board of Admiralty issued an order permitting the use of figures other than lions, that a wider variety of carvings began to appear, first on English ships and soon thereafter on American vessels.[6] Representations of sea horses, horses' heads, and other animals became quite popular for a time, along with human figures, both real and mythological. By mid-century, lions were decidedly out of fashion, although they continued to be seen on older ships. A decade or so later, animal figureheads of all types began disappearing in favor of human figures symbolizing the name of the vessel.[7]

In 1745, John Welch (1711–1789), a leading Boston shipcarver, submitted a bill in court for figures carved for Benjamin Bagnall during the preceding nine years. The list included nine lion's heads, two Neptunes, two sea horses, and four double-headed sea horses, one of which included a rider.[8] Twenty years later, Samuel Skillin, Sr. (1742–1793), a shipcarver who worked in both Boston and Philadelphia, presented a bill "for Carved Work Don for the Brigg *Morning Star*, To a Venus head 7 feet long."[9] Other references from the 1760s and 1770s illustrate the wide range of figures being produced, including representations of the King of Portugal, General Israel Putnam, and the Black Prince.

British Admiralty records of American ships captured by privateers during the Revolution and bought for the Royal Navy provide the first accurate sketches of the types of figureheads produced here. Several of the frigates ordered by the Continental Congress in 1775 and 1778 fell into British hands, and all of the existing drawings show single, full-length figures of the straddle-head type. The *Raleigh*, built in Portsmouth, New Hampshire, and the *Hancock*, of Newburyport, Massachusetts, bore likenesses of their namesakes, while the *Confederacy*, of Norwich, Connecticut, is shown with a representation of a Greek soldier in a breastplate and plumed helmet. Other ships captured by the British included the frigate *Boston* and the privateer *Rattlesnake*, both of which had an American Indian as a figurehead, the first-known examples of what was to become a popular motif in the next century.[10]

The number of shipcarvers working in America increased steadily throughout the eighteenth century, but, all in all, they remained a relatively small group due to the specialized nature of their craft. Testimony given in Boston in 1695 indicated that only three shipcarvers, Edward Budd (active c. 1668–d. 1710), William Shute (active c. 1693–d. 1743), and George Robinson, Sr. (active c. 1681–d. 1737), were operating there at that time.[11] Of the approximately 224 craftsmen who participated in the Boston furniture trade between 1725 and 1760, only 16 listed themselves as carvers.[12] Most of these men were primarily shipcarvers who would readily engage in other types of ornamental work when the opportunity presented itself. The previously mentioned John Welch, for example, not only carved for ships, but also worked on furniture and picture frames, and is probably best known for his *Sacred Codfish* (Old State House, Boston), commissioned for the Hall of Representatives in 1736 "as a memorial of the importance of the Cod Fishery." Later in the century, Welch also conducted a successful business importing looking glasses.[13]

The most famous Boston shipcarvers are the members of three generations of the Skillin family who dominated the trade from the mid-eighteenth century through the first decade of the nineteenth. The Skillins have received a considerable amount of attention over the years, beginning with two articles published in *Antiques Magazine* in the 1930s.[14] Interested readers are referred to these sources, as only a brief overview of biographical information will be presented here. The appendix at the end of this book should also be consulted, not only for the Skillins, but also for the other carvers discussed in this chapter and the ones that follow.

The family workshop was established by Simeon Skillin, Sr. (1716–1778), some time after he completed his apprenticeship in 1737. Three of his sons became carvers, John (1745–1800), Simeon, Jr. (1756–1806), and the previously mentioned Samuel, who moved to Philadelphia soon after he finished his training. John and Simeon, Jr., remained in Boston working with Simeon, Sr., until the latter's death in 1778, at which time they assumed control of the shop.

Two members of the next generation continued the family tradition. Simeon III (1766–1830), the son of Samuel Skillin, Sr., received his training in the family shop in Boston, but was working in New York City by 1789. Samuel II (b. 1770) was the son of Richard, a blockmaker and brother of Samuel, John, and Simeon, Jr. Samuel II was active as a carver and headbuilder—that is, a craftsman who specialized in mounting figureheads on ships—until at least 1816.

As the most prominent carvers in Boston after about 1760, the Skillins were jointly responsible for a wide range of ship and architectural work, some of which was recorded in contracts or commented upon by contemporary observers. Among the most important commissions executed by Simeon, Sr., was a bust of William Pitt for a Pillar of Liberty erected in 1767 by the Town of Dedham, Massachusetts, to celebrate the repeal of the Stamp Act. As such, it represents the earliest recorded public monument created by a native-born sculptor. The wooden bust and pillar have long since disappeared, but the stone base was still in place on the original site of Dedham's Church Green as late as 1944.[15]

The names of many of the ships for which Simeon, Sr., provided carved work in the 1740s and 1750s are known, but descriptions are lacking and no actual examples survive. Due to the sketchiness of the historical record, little else can be ascribed to him with certainty, even though he had a long and productive career.

More information is available regarding John and Simeon, Jr., the two sons who operated the Boston workshop. By the 1780s, in fact, the elder brother, John, had emerged as the most prominent carver in Boston. His standing resulted in his being chosen to lead the Boston carvers in the Federal Procession to celebrate the ratification of the Constitution in 1788 and in the entry procession of George Washington the following year.[16]

After the Revolution, the brothers continued to provide carvings for many ships, including the *America,* which was commanded by John Paul Jones and presented as a gift to the French government, and the sternboard and a figurehead

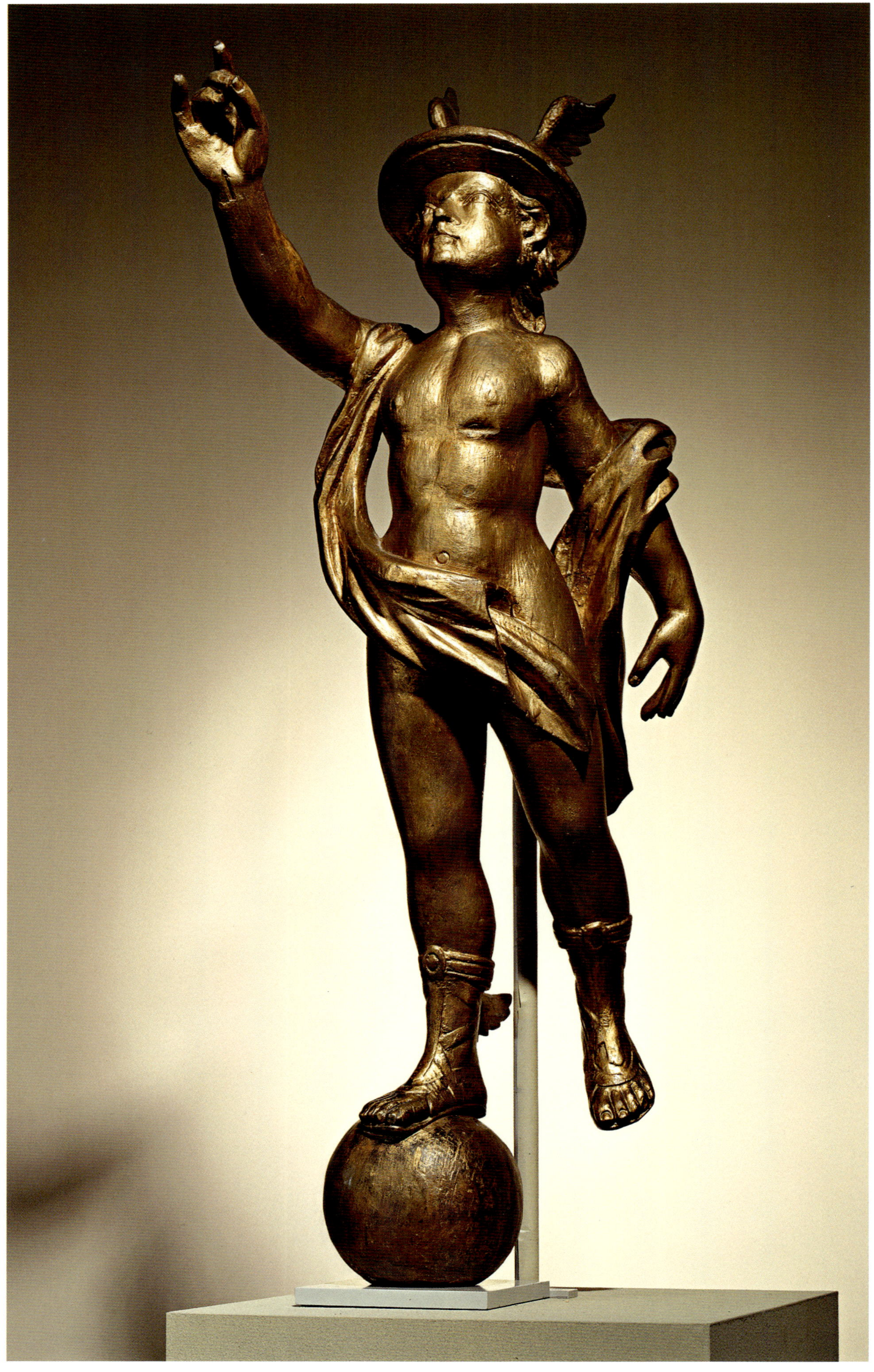

of Hercules for the famous frigate *Constitution*. By 1790, the Skillin shop was also producing most of the carved architectural ornament for Boston's major building projects, such as Charles Bulfinch's designs for the Federal Street Theatre in 1793, the Massachusetts State House in 1797, and the New North Church in 1804.[17]

The Skillins also counted several of the area's most powerful merchant families as patrons. They did much work for Elias Hasket Derby of Salem, for example, including three celebrated little figures of America, Peace, and Plenty for a chest-on-chest made in 1791 by Stephen Badlam (1751–1815). In 1793 and 1794, Derby commissioned at least six garden figures for his farm in Danvers, three of which still exist.[18]

In all, then, the Skillins were responsible for an impressive amount of figural carving in and around Boston. John and Simeon, Jr., in particular were widely recognized for their achievements, as was evident in John's obituary, which stated that "He was for many years the most eminent man in his profession." Despite their versatility and the many pieces that have been attributed to the Skillin family over the years, however, only seven figures that can be fully documented as their work have survived.[19] In addition to the three on the Badlam chest and the three Derby garden figures, they include a figure of Mercury carved for the Boston Post Office in 1793. For our purposes, the *Mercury* is the most important and merits special attention (plate 16).

The significance of this spirited, half-lifesize figure was recorded in the *Columbian Centinel* a few days after it was mounted over the door to the new post office building on State Street:

> The repairs and ornaments of the buildings add much to the beauty of the Street; and must impress foreigners, who enter the town from the water, with favorable ideas of its wealth and consequence. Among the ornaments above alluded to a very handsome one was added a few days since over the door of the Post Office. It is a winged *Mercury*, in the act of bounding from a *Globe*, supporting his *Caduceus* in his left hand—and holding in his right a letter directed to *Thomas Russell* Esq. Merchant, *Boston* per post—conveying a handsome compliment to the mercantile interest of the town, and to one of its principal supporters. The execution of the work was by Skillings—and mentioning that, precludes the necessity of saying it is elegantly done.[20]

16 John Skillin (American, 1745–1800) and Simeon Skillin, Jr. (American, 1756–1806), *Mercury*, Boston, 1793. Painted wood, 38 x 18 x 19 in. (96.5 x 45.7 x 48.2 cm). Bostonian Society, Mass.

The figure has all the characteristics of the best work of eighteenth-century American shipcarvers. Its lively forward thrust, balanced on one leg with an extended right arm that has lost the original caduceus, animates the piece and emphasizes the element of dispatch attributed to the messenger of the gods. The traditional winged helmet and sandals reinforce this quality, as does the wind-blown drapery that discreetly covers the otherwise nude figure. The emphasis on smooth planes in the handling of the face and the musculature of the torso alternates with the expressiveness of deeply cut flowing hair and drapery. At the same time, the form is strongly defined to the point of a rounded stockiness that makes it easily identifiable at a distance. Overall, the proportions are closer to that of a child than an adult, which, when combined with the figure's dynamism, further link it to the inherent conservatism of the Baroque-inspired style of shipcarvers that resisted the more fashionable aspects of Neoclassicism that were then coming into vogue in America.

According to records at The Bostonian Society, the most direct source for the piece was a contemporary logo of the Post Office Department.[21] Ultimately, though, its iconography can be traced through prints, English lead garden figures, ceramic statues, and related marbles to the famous *Mercury* created by Giovanni da Bologna (1529–1608) in 1564.[22] The Skillins' image of Mercury had many familiar connotations at the time of its installation on State Street, and its presence as a type of shop figure represented the aspirations of the "mercantile interest of the town." The traditional prestige attached to the finest shipcarvings and the vessels that bore them was transferred to the streets of Boston and transformed to symbolize the ideals of commerce and civic pride.

This was certainly not a new development, as carved wooden figures had played a prominent role in forms of English pageantry for centuries. American colonists had naturally enough continued the tradition in their own commemorative ceremonies, processions, and parades.[23] Still, the significance attached to eighteenth-century American figures like the Boston Post Office *Mercury* cannot be fully understood without recognizing the ways in which they resonated with traditional values, while at the same time operating as signs and advertisements for commercial establishments.

The sense of prestige and local pride that was invested in the shipcarvers' art extended throughout eighteenth-century America. In 1775, John Hancock instructed the superintendent of the two frigates ordered by the Continental Congress that were being built in Massachusetts to "let the heads & Galleries for the Ships be neatly carv'd and Executed, I leave the Devise to you, but by all means let ours be as good, handsome, strong & as early compleated as any building here in Philadelphia."[24]

Hancock's concern reflected the fact that Philadelphia had become Boston's chief rival in shipbuilding by the last quarter of the eighteenth century. Philadelphia was also the most populous city and the most important mercantile center south of New England. Its wharves and shipyards were busy throughout most of the Revolution, but were particularly active in the decades following the end of the war. A number of shipcarvers worked there, producing a wide range of carving that was highly regarded by local residents. As one observer noted in 1791:

> The art of carving, especially heads of ships, we may without boasting say is brought to the greatest degree of perfection in this city. A stranger walking along the wharves, must be struck with the beautiful female figures of Peace, Plenty, Love, Harmony, Ariel, Astronomy, Minerva, America, etc., etc., and also with the masculine statues of American Warriors, Alexanders, Hannibals, Caesars, etc., etc. . . . as we may allow sea Captains to be judges, they are generally of the opinion that the carving of

> heads of vessels in Philadelphia is superior to any they have seen in any part of the world.[25]

Of the many shipcarvers responsible for this diversity of figures, the most gifted and influential was William Rush (1756–1833), who is best known today as one of America's first sculptors and a founder of the Pennsylvania Academy of the Fine Arts in Philadelphia. Rush trained as a shipcarver, though, and operated an active workshop for over fifty years. His masterful and innovative work for both the federal government and Philadelphia's leading merchants and shipbuilders was widely recognized during his lifetime.

By 1788, Rush had established himself as one of the city's leading carvers, as evidenced by his participation in Philadelphia's Grand Federal Procession on July 4 of that year. Organized to celebrate the anniversary of the Declaration of Independence and the ratification of the Constitution by ten of thirteen states, the parade consisted of over five thousand people and a number of decorated pageant wagons.[26] The carvers and gilders were led by Rush's master, Edward Cutbush (c. 1735–1790), who was considered the best shipcarver in Philadelphia at the time, along with James Reynolds (c. 1736–1794) and Martin Jugiez (d. 1815), prominent furniture and architectural carvers. All three of these men had trained in London. They were followed by a group of younger craftsmen and an elaborate "federal car" designed by Rush. A detailed account of the car appeared in the *American Museum*, an extended excerpt of which is presented here, not only due to its relevance to William Rush, but also because it is a rare description of the type of work that American carvers produced for important civic ceremonies:

> The carvers and gilders exhibited an ornamental car, on a federal plan, being thirteen feet by ten on the floor, on which were erected thirteen pilasters, richly ornamented with carved work. . . . In the centre a column, with a twining laurel running in a spiral form to the capping, which was ten feet high, on the top of which was placed a bust of General Washington crowned with a wreath of laurel, and dressed in an American uniform with the thirteen stars on a collar. In the centre of the front, the head of Phidias, the most eminent of the ancient carvers, with emblematic figures supporting it; inside of the front rail a large figure for the head of a ship, richly carved and painted; the whole outside of the car decorated with figures of the seasons, the cardinal virtues, and other devices in carved work. . . . In the car was a number of artists at work, superintended by mr. Rush, ship-carver, who planned and executed the car with its principal ornaments.[27]

If this complex arrangement of historical figures, allegorical references, and symbolic columns calls to mind some of the English group figureheads discussed in the previous chapter, it is not by chance or coincidence. Whether the pageantry took place on the oceans or city streets, England was the principal source of a design vocabulary that was adapted to American circumstances.

In 1794, Philadelphia shipbuilder Joshua Humphreys was appointed the nation's first Naval Constructor, charged with establishing the beginnings of the United States Navy. He was authorized by Congress to design six new frigates, each to be built in a different city. The *United States* was launched in Philadelphia in 1797, followed by the *Constellation* in Baltimore, and the *Constitution* in Boston. The other three—the *Chesapeake* of Norfolk, Virginia; the *Congress* of Portsmouth, New Hampshire; and the *President* of New York—were completed two years later.[28]

Humphreys turned to Rush for preliminary designs for all of the figureheads and stern carvings and for a list of carvers who could accomplish the work in a timely fashion. The extent of Rush's prominence is further demonstrated in a letter from the Secretary of War, Timothy Pickering, to George Washington that stated that the decorative work for the ships being built in Philadelphia, Baltimore, and New York would take a long time because Rush was the only carver in the middle states who was competent enough to undertake their carvings.[29] Rush's shop eventually completed four of the six figureheads. The fifth was done by the Skillins for the *Constitution*, and the sixth by Daniel N. Train (active c. 1799–1812), a former apprentice of Rush, for the *President*.[30]

Rush's preliminary designs survive in a letter to Humphreys, and his descriptions of two of the figureheads that he completed are known. In each case, they were elaborate, symbolic groups that expressed American political ideals while following English design precedents. A central figure, either a mythological hero or a female allegory, was surrounded and supported by smaller figures and related motifs extending from the figurehead back into the trailboard. The best description of one of them comes from Rush himself:

> The genius of the United States: she is crest with a Constellation her hair and drapery flowing. Suspended to the ringlets of hair which fall or wave over her Breast and reclining in her bosom is the portrait of her favorite son, George Washington, President of the United States; her waist bound with a Civic Band. In her Right hand, which is advanced, she holds a spear, suspended to which is a Belt of Wampum containing the Emblems of Peace and War. On her left side is a Tablet, which supports three large columns which relate to three Branches of Government; the Scale, emblematic of Justice, blended with them. The Left Hand suspends the Constitution over the books, &c on the Tablet; the Eagle with his wings half extended, with the Escutcheon, &c of the Arms of the United States on the Right, designated the figure. The attributes, Commerce and Agriculture, and a modest position of the Arts and Sciences.[31]

As impressive as this and the other group figureheads must have been, though, they were part of a stylistic tradition that had been in decline in England for several decades. Nothing as complex would be mounted on an American ship again. In fact, William Rush's most important and far-reaching contribution to American shipcarving had its origins in France, not England.

17 William Rush (American, 1756–1833), *Peace*, Philadelphia, c. 1805–10. Painted pine, 70 x 24 1/2 x 27 1/2 in. (177.8 x 62.2 x 69.8 cm). Independence Seaport Museum, Philadelphia

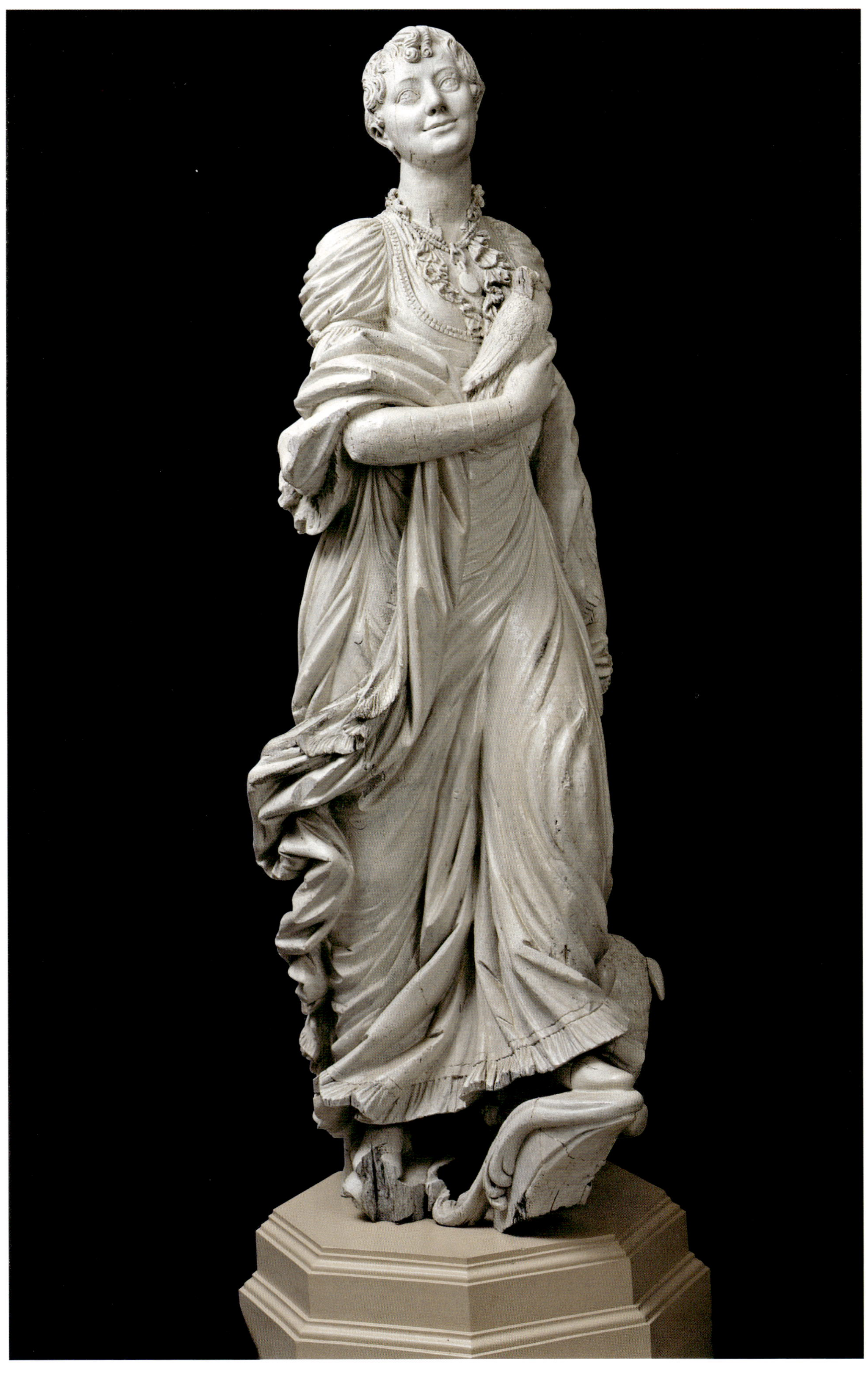

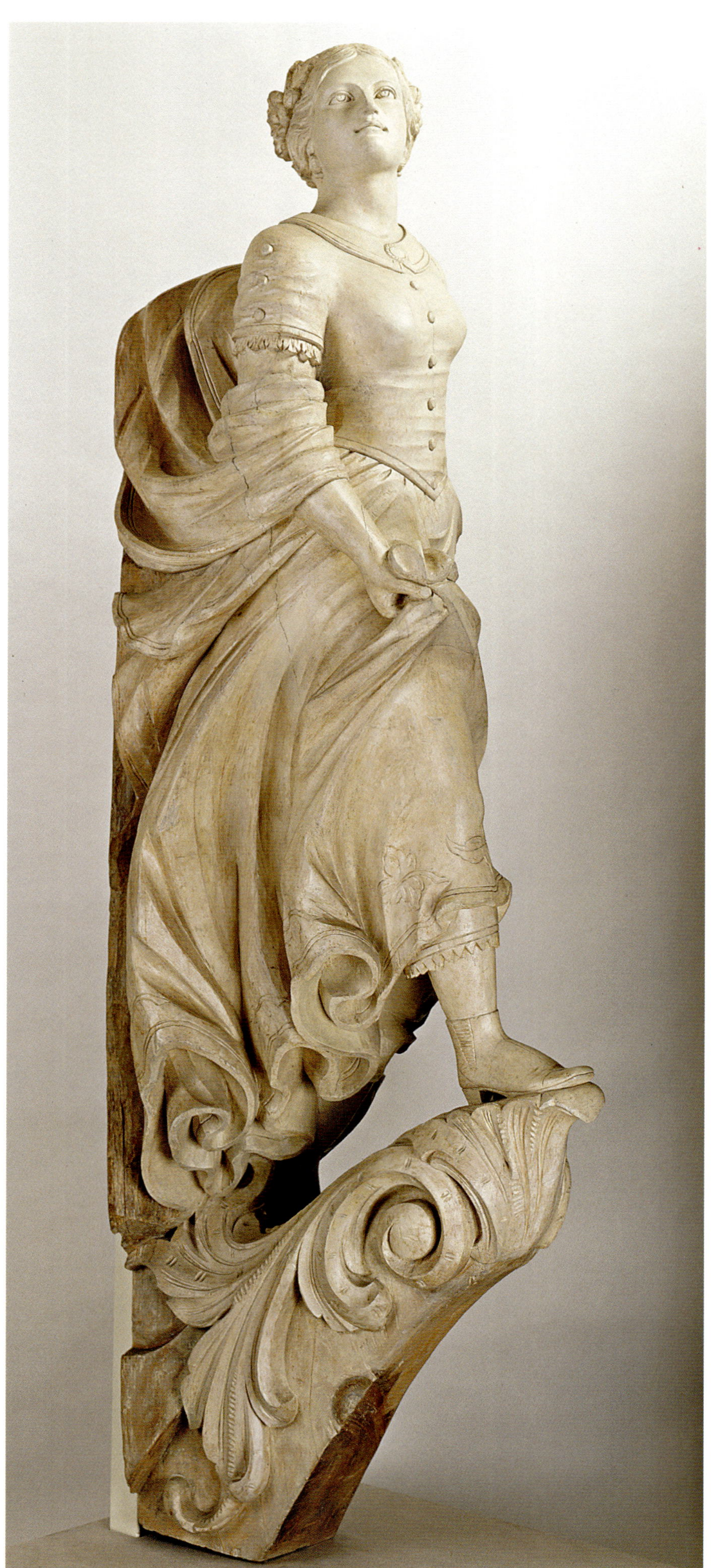

18 Isaac Howard Fowle (American, 1783–after 1854), *Lady with a Scarf*, Boston, c. 1820. Painted wood, 74 x 18 in. (187.9 x 45.7 cm). Bostonian Society, Mass.

Rush is credited with introducing the French style of full-length, freestanding figurehead into the American carvers' repertoire. He was supposedly inspired by two examples that he saw on French frigates that were being repaired in Joshua Humphreys's shipyard, probably in the late 1780s or early 1790s.[32] According to a somewhat embellished account recorded by a contemporary historian who knew him, he then "instantly conceived the design of more tasteful and graceful figures than had been before executed."[33] Unlike the somewhat stiff and unnatural straddle heads that were designed so that the knee of the head split the legs below the waist, French "walking figures," as they were often called, emphasized movement through a forward lean with one foot raised and supported on a scroll. They had been used since at least the mid-eighteenth century, but were particularly popular with French shipcarvers after 1792.[34] *Peace* of about 1805–10, the only full-length figurehead securely attributed to Rush that has survived relatively intact, is a good example of the style (plate 17).[35]

A dynamic and engaging conception, *Peace* is a masterful piece of carving that illustrates why Rush's work was so influential. The figure transmits an impression of windswept motion, seen particularly in the bold carving of the dress at the shoulders and around the feet, and in the shawl that is draped over the figure's arm. This sense of movement is entirely appropriate and traditional for a figurehead, as is the far-off look in the figure's eyes, and yet her face has a gentle expressiveness that is all too often missing in the work of lesser hands. The tendency towards mass that is especially apparent in the neck and lower body must be considered in light of the design requirements of a figurehead that was meant to withstand extreme conditions. In spite of this, Rush was able to give his figure a graceful and naturalistic presence.

Whether or not Rush was the first to carve French-style "walking figures" in the United States, he was certainly the most innovative and influential American shipcarver of his day. His approach was quickly taken up by others and was largely responsible for the course that figurehead carving was to take in the nineteenth century. Shipcarvers were a tightly knit group, bound by family and master-apprentice relationships. They were also itinerant and highly competitive, and so news of new developments traveled fast. As previously mentioned, for example, Samuel Skillin, Sr., worked in both Philadelphia and Boston, while his brothers, John and Simeon, Jr., executed Rush's designs for the *Constitution.* All of these men would have had firsthand knowledge of Rush's latest work soon after it left his shop.

Rush also designed and carved an allegorical figurehead of Wisdom for the frigate *Congress*, the sister ship of the *Constitution* that was built in Portsmouth. A local carver, William Dearing (1741–c. 1838), was commissioned to do the secondary work for the vessel. The fact that Dearing was not asked to do all the carving became something of a sore point in New England, a wound to local pride that resulted in a revealing editorial that found its way into several newspapers: "Mr. William Deering has displayed much taste and neetness in the execution of the carved work which is finished in a beautiful stil, of neet simplicity. It is only to be regretted that this gentleman's abilities were not called into more powerful action by proper encouragement, and the fanciful heads of the South would no

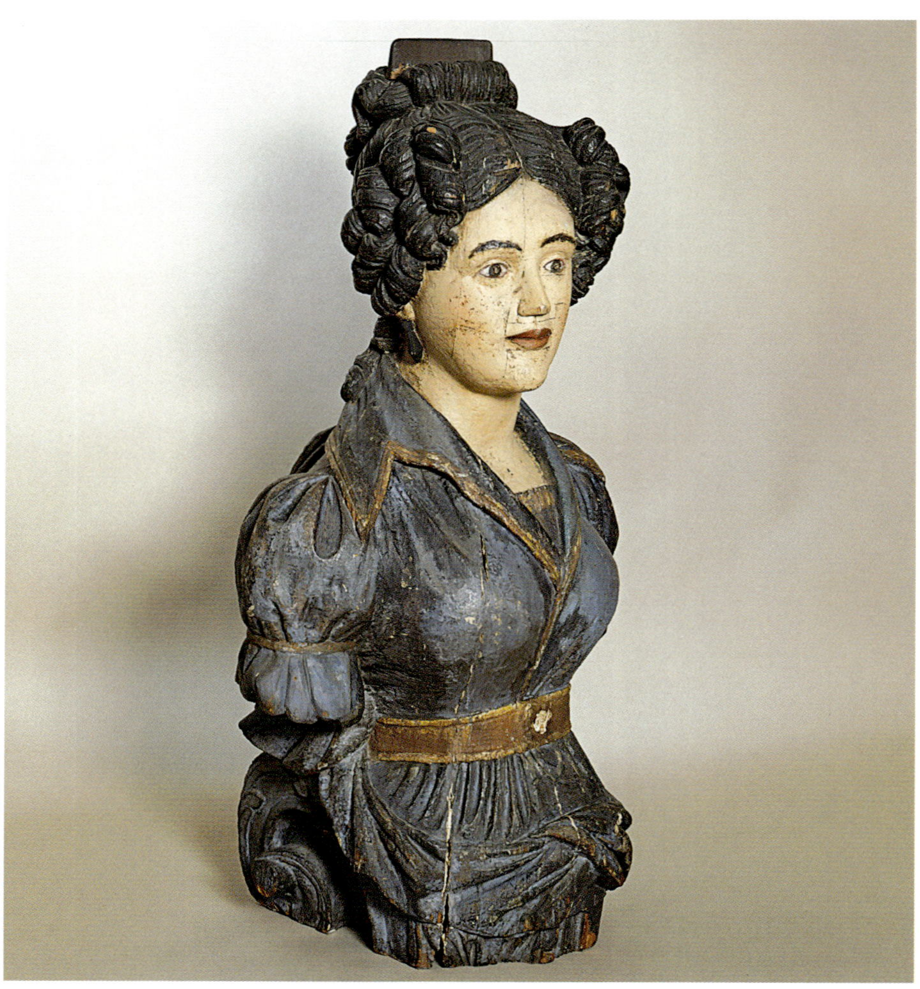

19 *Woman with a Comb*, possibly Mass., c. 1820s. Painted wood, height 44 in. (111.8 cm). Mystic Seaport, Conn.

longer take place of the more solid imagery of the North."[36] Evidently, then, some New Englanders did not approve of Rush's bold style and artistic pretensions.

The passage also provides evidence that regional stylistic preference played a role in shipcarving, just as it did in the decorative arts. Unfortunately, though, not enough ship work survives from this period to make any definitive judgments on this point. What is apparent is that, by the early years of the nineteenth century, there was a gradual shift away from the Baroque-inspired allegories that had been so popular in previous years. The next generation favored a more restrained, and in many cases, more naturalistic approach that incorporated aspects of Neoclassicism on the one hand and realistic portraiture on the other.

It should be noted that the trend was not entirely new, as the head of Rush's figure of *Peace* is relatively naturalistic, her allegorical name and flowing garments notwithstanding. Rush also carved figurehead portraits of Benjamin Franklin and George Washington in the 1780s, as well as a series of busts of French philosophers for ships owned by the wealthy Philadelphia merchant Stephen Gerard in the 1790s.[37] Still, the tendency towards realistic handling is more pronounced in

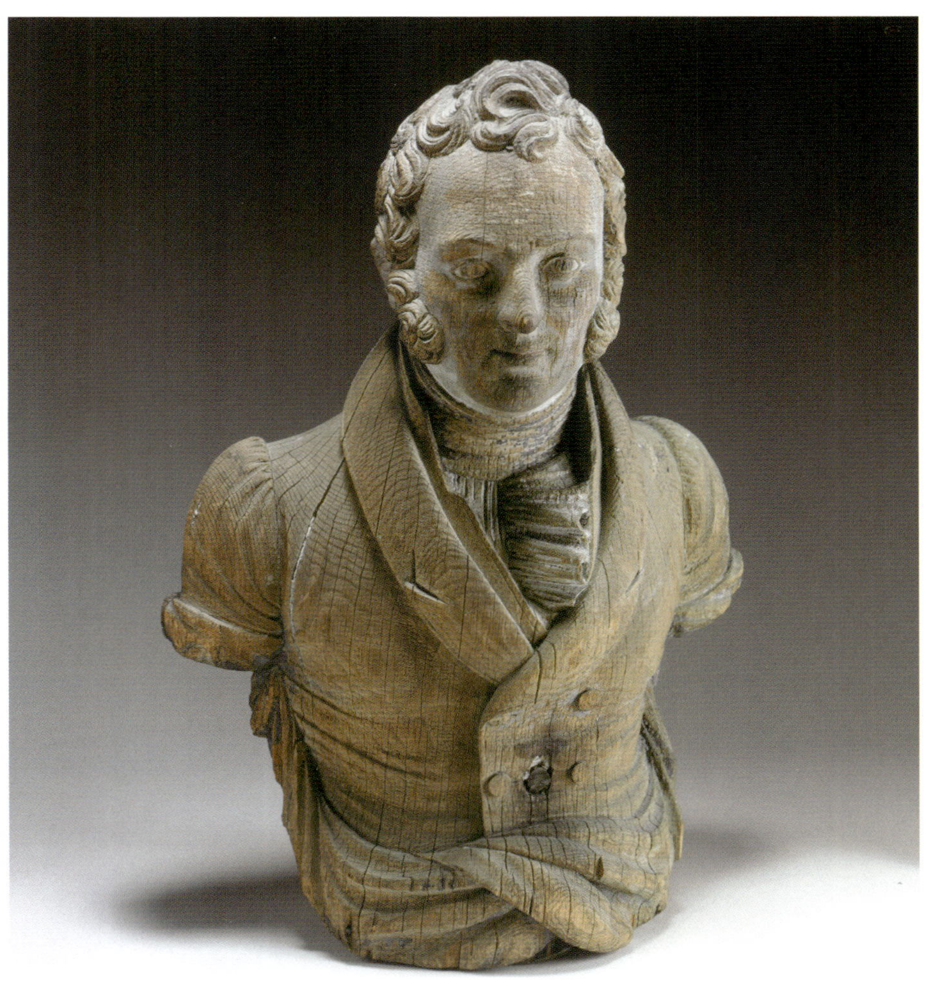

20 *Commodore Perry*, possibly New York, c. 1822. Painted wood, height 34 in. (86.3 cm). The Mariners' Museum, Newport News, Va.

the work of a number of early-nineteenth-century carvers, including Isaac Howard Fowle (1783–after 1854), a successor to the Skillin dynasty in Boston.

Fowle was one of the most prominent carvers in Massachusetts during the first few decades of the nineteenth century. He apprenticed in the Skillin shop, and was directly related to the family. In July 1806, Fowle and Edmund Raymund (active c. 1805–16), another former Skillin apprentice, advertised in the *Boston Gazette* that they "have commenced business at the shop formerly occupied by the late Mr. Simeon Skillin, carver, where they intend to carry on House and Ship ornamental Carving in its various branches."[38]

Fowle must have carved a great many figures during his lifetime, and several pieces now in museum collections are thought to be from his shop. Only one can be definitely documented to him, however, a figurehead of around 1820 known as *Lady with a Scarf* (plate 18). She is particularly important for this discussion, as she was used as a sample and a sign for the Fowle shop and was never mounted on a ship, which helps explain her excellent condition.[39] A finely executed figure, she stands dramatically poised upon a scroll wearing deeply cut and billowing skirt, petticoats, and shawl, and staring into the distance like so many of her ancestors. The individualized handling of her face, emphasized by a slight turn of the head, and the realistic treatment of her hair, earring, and costume, as well as her exposed ankle and contemporary shoe, raises the question as to whether or not she was modeled after an attractive young Bostonian. Figurehead portraits of shipowners' daughters or wives were common throughout the century.

An engaging example of this is seen in an unidentified figurehead known as *Woman with a Comb* (plate 19). The details of her dress and hairstyle date her to the 1820s, and while the scrolled base was cut down at some point, she has survived in a fine state of preservation.[40] Her graceful demeanor and alert expression suggest that she was based on a specific person and may have been intended to be a portrait. This type of half-length figure was particularly popular on smaller ships like whalers and coastal vessels.

Another fine figurehead portrait is a bust believed to represent Commodore Oliver Hazard Perry, the hero of the Battle of Lake Erie of the War of 1812, which may have been made for a ship of the same name built in New York in 1822 (plate 20). A skillfully rendered piece, it retains an old weathered surface that complements the boldly carved features of face, hair, and costuming. While its identity is not certain, the bust does bear a strong likeness to contemporary engravings of Perry. It must be noted, however, that it lacks the epaulets and other details of his naval uniform that were typically included in official portraits.[41]

Figureheads carved in a more naturalistic manner became the general rule in the early nineteenth century. The Neoclassical style that was then in vogue often called for gods, goddesses, or Greek warriors to be sure, but even so, as a less-ornate aesthetic than the preceding Baroque style, it accommodated the American shipcarver's interest in capturing a good likeness of his subject. The figure's face might be carved as either an idealized rendering of a goddess or a more recognizable portrait of a mortal, but more often than not, the costume showed great attention to detail, whether it was a toga or a contemporary outfit.

A full-length figurehead that combines classical and current references is a piece known as *Talma*, which may have been carved for a ship that was built in New York in 1825, or for one built in Medford, Massachusetts, in 1827 (plate 21). A seafaring family in Marblehead, Massachusetts, acquired the figure in 1857, and both family tradition and comparison with contemporary sources identify it as representing the French actor François Joseph Talma as Nero, one of his most famous roles. A possible model for the figure is a print published in London in 1817 entitled *M. Talma as Nero*, engraved by J. Thomson.[42] As we will see in the chapters that follow, theatrical portraits were very popular at the time, particularly as paintings and sculpture that were often copied and widely distributed as prints. In this case, the skillful rendering of form and period dress creates a convincing portrait of the celebrated actor.

Roman emperors and other tragic figures aside, it is also true that figureheads were intended to point the way, to dramatically lead a ship onward in a rush of motion, which, in the final analysis, was not compatible with the tenets of Neoclassicism. Continuing the conservatism of their predecessors, nineteenth-century carvers did not abandon one style for another. Change was more gradual, as they

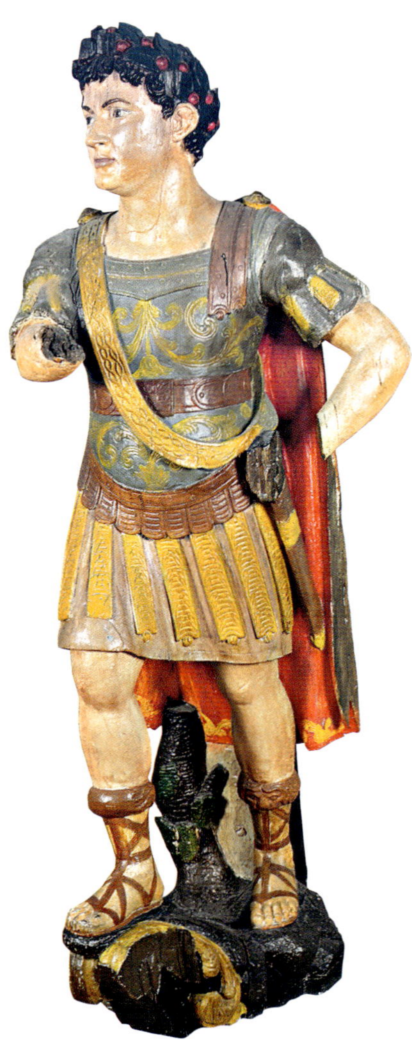

21 *Talma*, probably Boston or New York, c. 1825. Painted wood, height 84 in. (213.4 cm). Peabody Essex Museum, Salem, Mass.

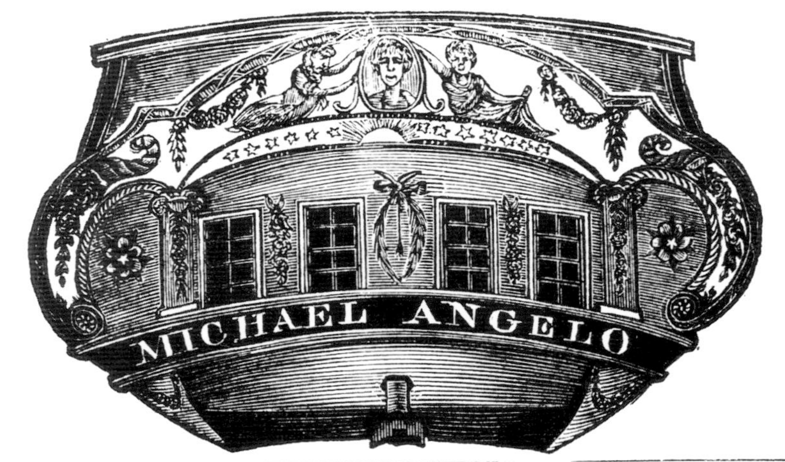

LEVI L. CUSHING,
CARVER,
No 79, Broad Street, opposite Custom House Street,
BOSTON.

Orders for carved work of any description will be attended to with fidelity and despatch.

L. L. Cushing continues the above business in Poplar Street, as usual, where orders will meet with prompt attention. ☞N. B....Models of any kind executed at the shortest notice.

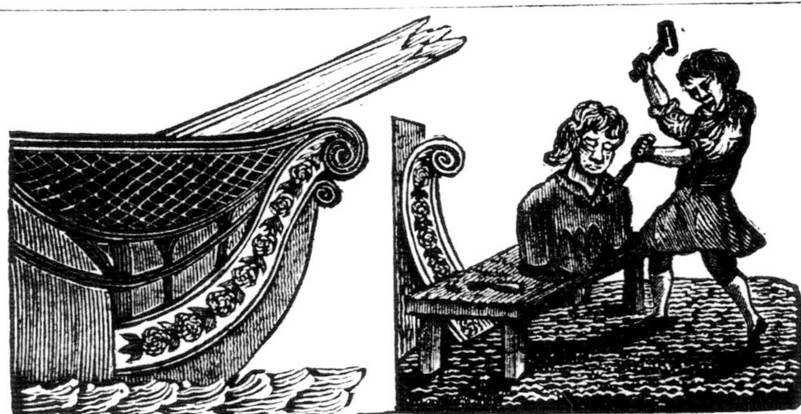

Engraved and Printed by N. Dearborn, 20, State Street.

22 Trade card of Levi L. Cushing (American, active c. 1830–75), Boston, c. 1830. American Antiquarian Society, Worcester, Mass.

modified older styles by incorporating new design elements into their traditional repertoire.

A trade card of Levi L. Cushing (active c. 1830–75) of Boston that probably dates to around 1830 illustrates this point (plate 22). At top is an elaborate design for a stern that features Neoclassical motifs, demonstrating that the carver was aware of current stylistic trends in the fine and decorative arts. By highlighting the ship's stern, which had been the focus of the most ornate programs of Baroque carving for the past two hundred years or so, he was, at the same time, adapting the new elements to an older format and placing his modern design vocabulary in a familiar context.

MOST EARLY-NINETEENTH-CENTURY SHIPCARVERS like Cushing and Fowle still worked in traditional workshop settings that bound masters, journeymen, and apprentices in close economic and personal relationships. The system was never as highly organized in America as it was in Europe, though. No craft guilds ever existed here, and while tradesmen often attempted to control local markets, the lack of skilled labor in most parts of the country and the general dislike of English institutions agitated against the development of a closed workshop system in the eighteenth century. By the second quarter of the nineteenth, growing industrialization and an increasing use of semi-skilled wage labor had rendered the old apprenticeship system obsolete in many of the larger trades like cabinetmaking, construction, and printing.[43] Due to the specialized nature and high degree of skill required for shipcarving, however, traditional apprenticeships remained the rule. Still, while most carvers served out their time with their masters before going into business for themselves, a talented individual could usually find work regardless of his particular background and training.

The varied career of Solomon Willard (1783–1861), a Boston carver, architect, and businessman, is a case in point. Although he is best known as the controversial Architect and Superintendent of the Bunker Hill Monument, Willard started in a much more humble position. Arriving in Boston in 1804 at age twenty-one, he began working as a carpenter. Five years later, he was carving capitals, panels, and other architectural elements for local builders. In 1810, he carved an eagle with a five-foot wingspan for the pediment of the Customs House, and by 1813, he was working as a shipcarver. His most important surviving work is a bust of George Washington for the ship *Washington*, built in Portsmouth, New Hampshire, in 1815–16 that is now at the United States Naval Academy in Annapolis, Maryland.

Through it all, Willard pursued a course of self-education that included lessons in drawing, perspective, anatomy, chemistry, geography, and French. Clearly an ambitious man, he seems to have given up shipcarving by the mid-1820s in favor of other pursuits that he no doubt considered more prestigious. He created architectural models for Charles Bulfinch (1763–1844), was a founder of the Boston Mechanics' Institute and Lyceum in 1826, and was an active member of the committee in charge of the Bunker Hill Monument for almost twenty years. Later in life, he was a stone contractor and architect.[44]

Willard's biographer tells us that he never served a formal apprenticeship for any of the trades in which he was involved.[45] Although he certainly learned by observing the skilled artisans with whom he was working, he was apparently largely self-taught, which makes him the earliest identifiable shipcarver who did not pass through the workshop system in the traditional manner. Surely others preceded him in this, but their names have been lost. As we will see, the issue of self-taught carvers versus those with formal training assumed greater significance later in the century. For the sake of historical perspective, then, it is important to introduce the concept at this point in the discussion.

As a self-taught carver, Willard could not depend upon the reputation of his master to help him secure his first commissions. He gained them instead through his persistence, his skill as a carver, and his growing number of personal contacts. He was also fortunate to be working at a time when the American shipbuilding industry was entering a period of major expansion and his skills were in great demand.

The trend had begun a few decades earlier at the close of the American Revolution. Peace with Britain brought an increase in international trade and renewed prosperity. The demand for new ships to meet these expanding commercial opportunities and to replace those lost during the war brought a significant increase of activity to shipyards along the East Coast. In addition, ships were much less expensive to build here than in Europe, largely because of the abundance of cheap timber.[46] As a result, American shipbuilders received many orders from English and Continental merchants, as well as from their own countrymen. In the 1790s, the European preoccupation with the escalating Napoleonic Wars created even more opportunities for American commercial interests, while the India and China trade continued to expand rapidly. American shipyards responded by producing more and more vessels of all sizes, establishing a pattern of growth that would continue until the mid-1850s. With the exception of the period around the Embargo of 1807 and the War of 1812, when shipbuilding in East Coast ports fell off significantly due to international trade restrictions and warfare on both sides of the Atlantic, the shipyards and maritime trades fueled the development of American commerce and industry.[47]

Philadelphia was generally considered to be the most important shipbuilding center around the turn of the nineteenth century. As the country's most populous city and the national capital from 1790 to 1800, it had more experienced naval architects, shipbuilders, and tradesmen than anywhere else.[48] By the close of the War of 1812, though, the tide was beginning to turn in favor of New York City. Several geographical and economic factors conspired to give New York an advantage in both national and international trade, including the size and ease of access to its harbor. In addition, the opening of the Erie Canal in 1825 created a direct water link with the Great Lakes and Midwest. Before long, the East River shipyards below 12th Street were the busiest in the country, supporting about 650 shipwrights, carpenters, and caulkers by 1830. In 1850, the number of men employed in the maritime trades in New York and the surrounding area had increased to over 2,600.[49]

The increased shipbuilding activity naturally enough brought more work to New York carvers, and their numbers swelled proportionally. The situation was quite different in the eighteenth century, when New York workshops offered little competition to those in Boston and Philadelphia. The names of only a few eighteenth-century New York carvers are known, and even less biographical information about them is available. The earliest recorded carver was George Warburton, who set up shop in 1729. At mid-century, both Henry Hardcastle (active c. 1755) and Stephen Dwight (active c. 1755–75), a former apprentice,

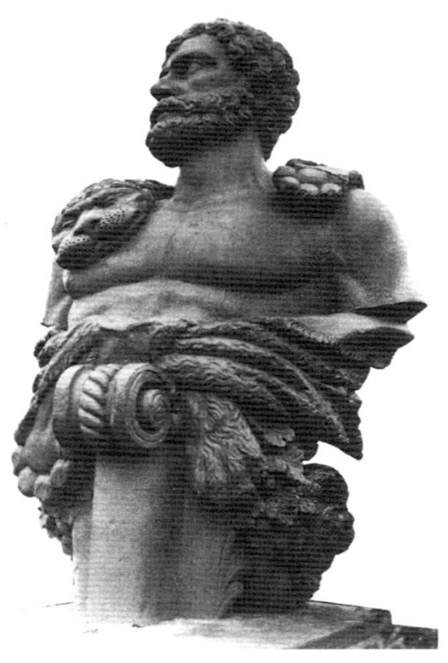

23 Jeremiah Dodge (American, 1781–1860) and Cornelius N. Sharpe (American, active c. 1810–d. 1828), *Hercules* for the USS *Ohio*, New York, 1820. Painted wood, height 42 in. (106.7 cm). Figure 42 in Marion V. Brewington, *Shipcarvers of North America*. Barre, Mass.: Barre Publishing Co., 1962

were doing "ship and house work." Dwight also advertised that he did "tables, chairs, picture and looking glass frames, and all kinds of work for cabinetmakers," as well as portraits, history painting, and instruction in drawing.[50]

As previously noted, Simeon Skillin III relocated from Boston to New York around 1789. He was active as a carver until 1822 when he entered the crockery business. In 1799, Daniel Train, the young carver mentioned earlier in the chapter as the creator of the figurehead for the frigate *President*, placed an advertisement in the *New York Gazette and Commercial Advertiser* that read: "Daniel N. Train, Carver, No. 144 Cherry-street, near the Ship Yards, offers his professional services to the citizens of New-York and others, particularly owners and builders of ships. Having studied Naval Sculpture under Wm. Rush, of Philadelphia, whose talents are extensively known, he hopes, from this advantage and his future exertion, to merit the patronage he now solicits. Heads and other ornamental parts of ships will be excepted or prepared with neatness and dispatch."[51]

WITH THEIR CONNECTIONS TO WELL-KNOWN SHOPS in Boston and Philadelphia, Simeon Skillin III and Train were the leading carvers in New York City at the turn of the nineteenth century. They are known to have produced a wide range of work, though they were probably somewhat more specialized than their predecessor Stephen Dwight.

In the mid-eighteenth century, American carvers frequently advertised that they would undertake any and all types of carving, from figureheads to furniture. Like Dwight, the Boston carver John Welch worked on furniture and picture frames in addition to being a shipcarver. He could do so due to a lack of competition and specialization. By the beginning of the nineteenth century, however, furniture and framecarving was generally done by men who had trained specifically for those tasks, often either in England or with a master who had recently emigrated from there. For the most part, nineteenth-century shipcarvers concentrated on "ship and house work," areas in which they were undeniably the most qualified.

As New York became a major shipbuilding center in its own right, other men besides Simeon Skillin III and Train assumed prominence. Chief among them are two members of the Dodge family, Jeremiah (1781–1860) and his son Charles J. (1806–1886), who together and separately operated successful workshops from about 1804 to 1870.

Three pieces known to have been executed by the Dodges illustrate the range of their work. One is a bust of Hercules carved in 1820 by Jeremiah Dodge and Cornelius N. Sharpe (active c. 1810–d. 1828) for the USS *Ohio*, the first ship to be built in the Brooklyn Navy Yard (plate 23). A fine piece of work, the figure's powerful torso rises from a well-rendered lion's pelt and scroll. After being removed from the *Ohio* when she was decommissioned in 1883, *Hercules* spent several decades in front of the Canoe Place Inn in Hampton Bays, New York. Around 1945, he was moved to the village green in Stony Brook, New York.[52]

The second carving is a head of Andrew Jackson carved by the Dodges in 1835 to replace one that was surreptitiously removed from the figurehead of the USS

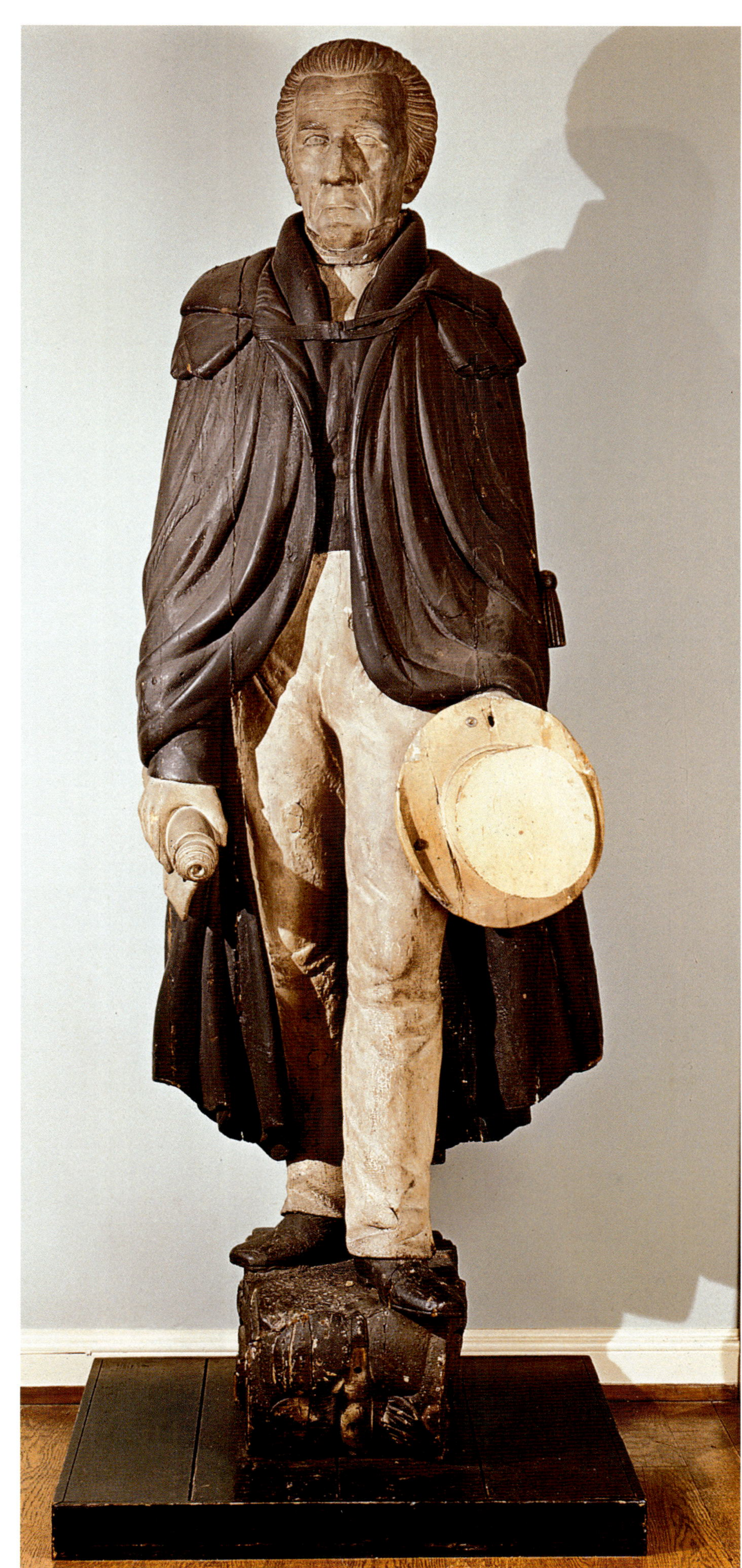

24 Laban Smith Beecher (American, 1805–1876), *Andrew Jackson* for the USS *Constitution*, Boston, 1834. Painted wood, height 118 in. (299.7 cm). Museum of the City of New York. Gift of the Seawanahaka Corinthian Yacht Club (52.11)

Constitution while she was being refitted at the Boston Navy Yard (plate 24). Therein lies a tale of political passions and the symbolic power of figureheads that bears repeating.

In the early 1830s, the Navy Department proposed scrapping the famous frigate due to the extensive damage that she had suffered during the War of 1812. Oliver Wendell Holmes led the fight to save her with his poem "Old Ironsides" and galvanized the country with his opening line, "Ay, tear her tattered ensign down!" The Navy eventually relented to public pressure and had the vessel rebuilt in Boston. During the course of the work, President Andrew Jackson visited the city and received such an enthusiastic reception that it was decided to place a figurehead of him on the *Constitution*'s prow instead of re-creating the original Hercules. Laban Smith Beecher (1805–1876) was commissioned to carve a monumental ten-foot figure of Jackson in contemporary dress, hat in hand, and draped in a cloak that was said to be his customary riding habit.

While working on the figure, Beecher received an offer of $1,500 from some ardent anti-Jacksonians to allow the piece to be stolen from his shop. This was not an insignificant sum, particularly considering the fact that his final bill to the Navy was only $300. The patriotic carver immediately informed naval officials of the plot, and the partially completed figure was moved from his shop to the Navy Yard so that the work could proceed without further interference. Nevertheless, soon after it was mounted on the *Constitution* in April 1834, the Navy received threats against it. As a precautionary measure, the ship was moved away from the docks to a mooring in the harbor.

A few months later, on a rainy night in July, a young man named Samuel Dewey rowed out to it and, escaping the notice of several armed sentries, sawed the head off the figure. The public reaction to the news of the desecration was immediate and predictable, as anti-Jacksonians responded with glee and their counterparts condemned the treachery. Political cartoons and poems from both sides appeared in newspapers throughout the country, while the Secretary of the Navy personally visited the ship and ordered the figure draped in canvas. The *Constitution* finally left Boston the following March and sailed for New York with a flag covering the still headless figure. Within a few days of its arrival, Dodge and Sons had supplied President Jackson with a new cranium, and the ship quickly departed for France.[53]

As fascinating and revealing of contemporary attitudes as this little tale of intrigue might be, the work around which the controversy swirled is not a particularly remarkable piece of carving. Beecher's figure of Jackson is somewhat stiff and lifeless, with little of the animation that might be expected in a figurehead portrait of such a dynamic national hero. The Dodges' head is an adequate representation with recognizable detailing of facial features, though again it does not transmit much of a sense of the vitality of the man it represents.

Much more accomplished is a portrait bust of Jeremiah Dodge done by his son Charles around 1835 (plate 25). The piece descended in the family until it was given to the New-York Historical Society in 1952, which makes it a rare and important example with a clearly documented history.[54] Its well-modeled face is quite distinctive and individualized in a sensitive portrait of the man, with boldly

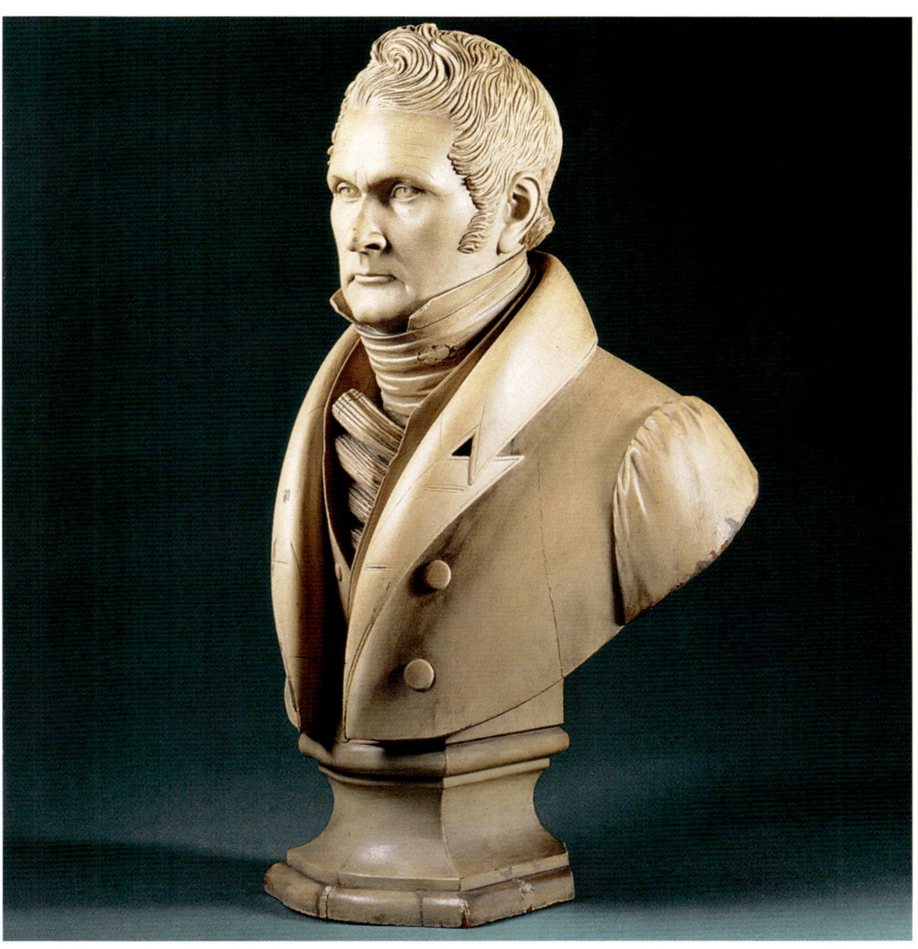

25 Charles J. Dodge (American, 1806–1886), *Jeremiah Dodge*, New York, c. 1835. Painted wood, 27½ x 17 x 11½ in. (69.8 x 43.1 x 29.2 cm). The New-York Historical Society, New York (1952.349)

swirling hair carved in the sure strokes of a master shipcarver. The costume, too, is finely detailed and crisply rendered. Overall, the carver has used his wooden medium to the best advantage, while at the same time demonstrating his familiarity with contemporary academic models more commonly rendered in marble. It is certainly a fitting tribute to a man who was one of the leading shipcarvers of his day.

Overall, Charles Dodge's career spanned the last major era of wooden shipbuilding. When he began his apprenticeship with his father around 1820, American shipyards were responding to the increased demand for merchant vessels that resulted from a period of national prosperity and the continued expansion of international trade routes that followed the wars of the previous decade. Twenty years later, when Dodge was a master carver in his own right, American shipbuilders and naval architects were perfecting the design of the clipper ship, those fast and sleek vessels that dominated international trade for a generation. The 1840s also witnessed great improvements in wooden-hulled steamships, both the paddlewheelers that plied the rivers and inland water routes and the oceangoing vessels that combined sail and steam. The California Gold Rush that began in the late

1840s brought many more orders to East Coast shipyards, and for a time, builders in major ports like New York were working at full capacity. From about 1847 to 1856, at least thirty-three shipyards were active in the New York area alone.[55]

The tide turned quickly, however, and for a variety of reasons, a significant and irreversible slowdown had begun by the mid-1850s. The economic depression of 1855 slowed ship construction considerably, and a year later the Gold Rush was essentially over, which lessened the demand even more.[56] By then, the days of wooden sailing ships were numbered anyway, as evidenced by the metal-hulled vessels built in Europe that were crossing the Atlantic in increasing numbers. American shipbuilders remained wedded to the wooden hull for some time to come, but even so, several smaller iron ships were built here before 1860.

During the Civil War, government contracts brought a short-lived period of activity to shipyards in the northern states. In 1866, though, the government sold

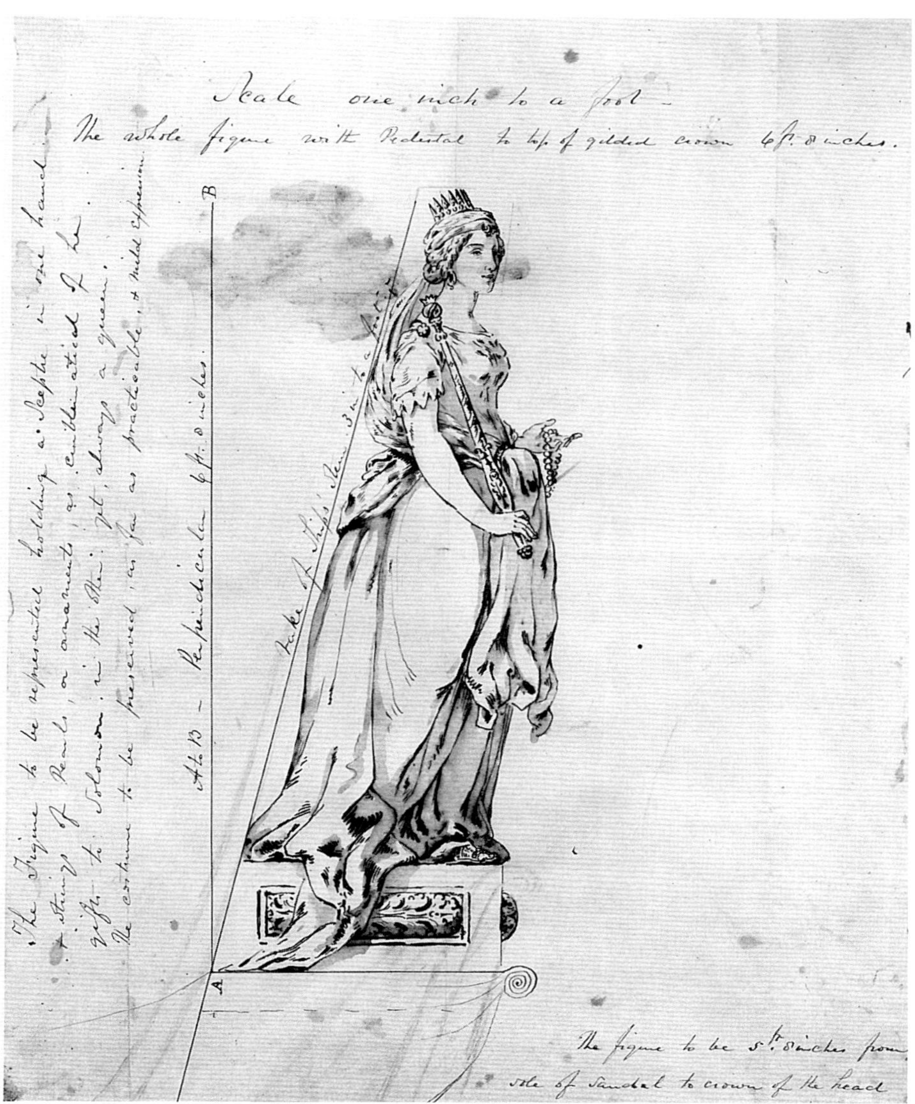

26 John W. Mason (Irish, 1814–1866), drawing for the *Queen of Sheba*, Boston, c. 1850. Ink and pencil on paper. Peabody Essex Museum, Salem, Mass.

most of its ships, causing a glut in the market that led to the final decline in major shipbuilding centers like New York and Boston.[57] When Charles Dodge retired in 1870, only one shipyard was still in operation in Manhattan, while four others in Brooklyn and across the Hudson River in New Jersey were struggling to survive. Most of the sailing ships that were still being built came from Connecticut, Massachusetts, and especially Maine, but even their numbers were steadily diminishing. From a peak of 1,781 in 1855, new construction had declined to 798 twenty years later. In 1895, only 397 larger sailing ships were built in the United States.[58]

The ocean clippers of the 1840s and 1850s represent one of the last significant developments in sailing ship design. Descendants of colonial revenue cutters and the so-called Baltimore Flyers, the most radical types, known as "sharp" or "extreme" clippers, were built with one object in mind—speed. Through the use of a modified hull design, increased length and sail area, and the elimination of unnecessary weight, the clippers were the fastest sailing vessels ever seen, developed to satisfy the increasing demand for speed in the lucrative and highly competitive routes to California and the Far East.[59]

Fast ships gained notice in the press and acclaim for the owners and builders, which in turn, attracted passengers and contracts for carrying cargo. During the boom years of the California Gold Rush, from the late 1840s until 1856 or so, extreme clippers were often very profitable, even if cargo capacity was sacrificed in the quest for speed. When the laws of economics reasserted themselves in the late 1850s, new models were developed with less streamlined hulls that carried more freight. Even so, the "medium" clippers, as they were called, were built to be as fast as possible.

Carvings were reduced to a minimum, usually only a light stern carving of some sort and a figurehead.[60] Gone were the sweeping rails, ornamental brackets, and elaborate sternboards of earlier vessels. The tendency towards the reduction in weight of shipcarving that had begun in the early eighteenth century had reached its logical conclusion.

Many builders opted to forego full-length figureheads on even their largest ships, choosing instead to use the busts and billetheads that had become standard on smaller vessels, or nothing at all. Others continued to commission standing figures, but due to the redesign of the clipper bow, the traditional position occupied by the figurehead, almost vertical on a knee of the head that was low to the water, was eliminated. The new figureheads were attached higher, at a more inclined angle at the top of a raised and elongated knee, and as a consequence appeared to extend further out, ahead of the ship. The results were even more dramatic than before, as the leaning figure, made all the more conspicuous by the lack of other carvings competing for the viewer's attention, seemed to be actively leading the ship onward in a rush of motion.

Throughout these developments, the figurehead maintained much of its traditional symbolic importance, which contributed significantly to its survival into the dawn of the era of functionalist design, despite the ambivalence of many shipbuilders and naval architects.[61] John W. Griffiths, a leading New York shipbuilder who was intimately involved with the development of the clipper ship, demonstrated his progressive views in 1850 when he wrote in his influential *Treatise on Marine and Naval Architecture* that:

> With regard to beauty in ships, we have said that it consisted in fitness for the purpose and proportion to effect the object obtained. . . . It is not the many mouldings on a ship, or the amount of carved work on the head and stern, that makes her appear to have life; so far from adding to the appearance of a handsome ship, they detract from it. . . . in very many instances, our coasting and river vessels would look much better without a head than with one; but the eye of the owner having become familiarized with its appearance, sees nothing amiss.[62]

At the same time, though, his mid-century functionalism still found a place for figureheads. Perhaps he felt that only the largest ocean clippers merited figureheads, or perhaps he, too, was just too accustomed to seeing them. Either way, the designs for bows that appeared in his book included several with full-length figureheads. Elsewhere he wrote: "There is a certain fitness about the head of a ship that at once stamps an impression on the mind in relation to the entire ship, and why? We say that the head of a ship is like a portrait, we look at the physiognomy of the man, and judge his intellectual endowments—of his internal and external qualities; so with the ship, it is the builder's mechanical portrait."[63]

In the final era of wooden-hulled sailing ships, then, the figurehead reigned supreme among shipcarvings. No longer a part of a complex program of decoration, it was the central focus. As the most important piece of carved work on the ship, the figurehead was both the survivor and inheritor of an age-old tradition.

As if in recognition of this, American carvers produced some of the finest examples of figureheads during the clipper ship period. Designs ranged from late Neoclassical conceptions like one created around 1850 for the *Queen of Sheba* by John W. Mason (1814–1866) of Boston (plate 26), to realistic portrayals of American heroes, such as a figurehead for the ship *David Crockett* carved by Jacob S. Anderson (1810–1857) of New York in 1853 (plate 27).

In Anderson's piece, the frontiersman stands poised on a scroll with rifle in hand and eyes searching the horizon, ever vigilant as the ship's protector and tutelary deity. The ship *David Crockett* was built in Mystic, Connecticut, in 1853 by George Greenman and Company. She was one of the most successful of all American clippers, plying routes between New York, San Francisco, Liverpool, and elsewhere for nearly forty years. The skillful handling of the figurehead, with its fine modeling and attention to the details of a woodsman's dress mark Anderson as one of the best carvers of his day.[64] This was recognized at the time as well. Apparently, the figurehead was so prized that it was rarely mounted on the ship, and certainly not during the rough and dangerous passage around Cape Horn on the route between New York and San Francisco. Instead, it spent most of its time in the ship's hold, which explains why it survived in such excellent condition.[65]

27 Jacob S. Anderson (American, 1810–1857), *David Crockett*, New York, 1853. Painted wood, 82 x 26 x 30 in. (208.3 x 66 x 76.2 cm). San Francisco Maritime National Historical Park

Another image believed to have been drawn from contemporary popular culture is an engaging three-quarter-length figurehead that was probably carved between about 1850–60. (plate 28) For many years, it was thought to represent the "Swedish Nightingale," Jenny Lind. This is hopeful at best. Several ships were

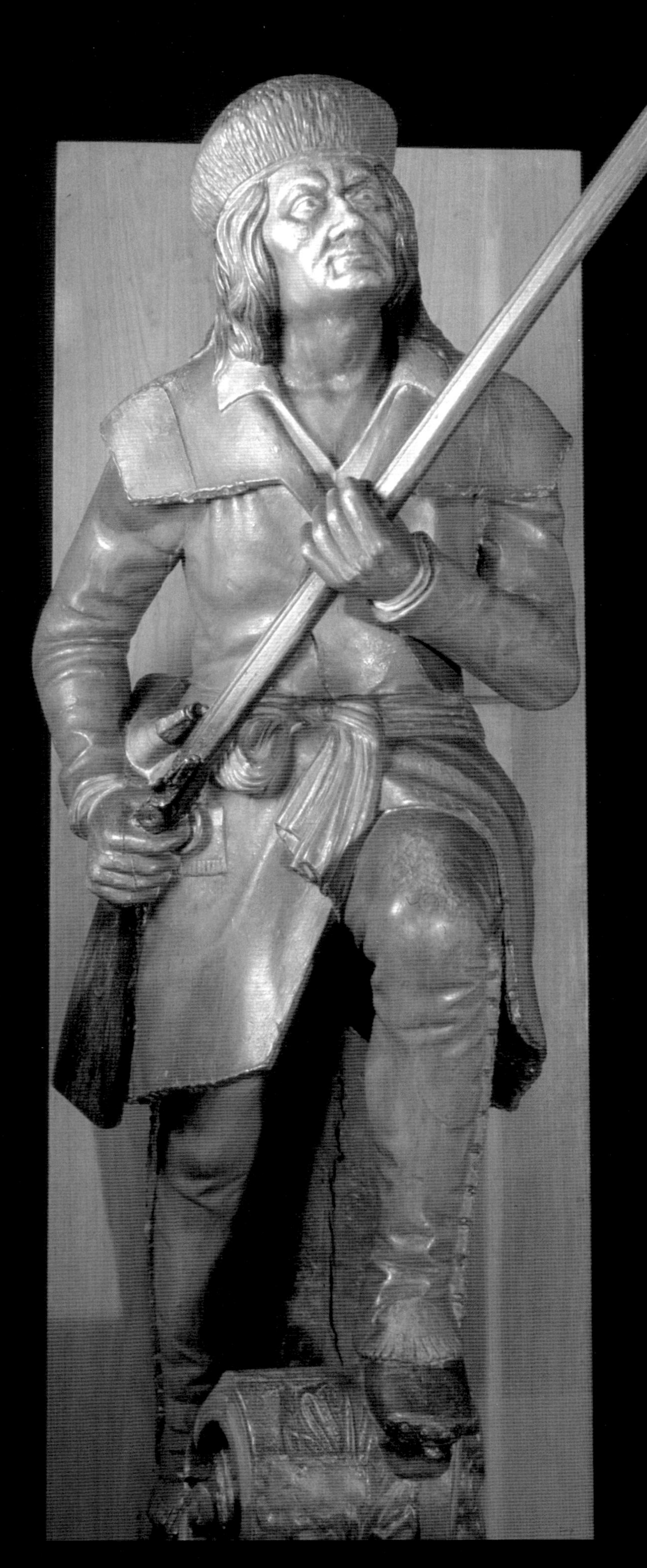

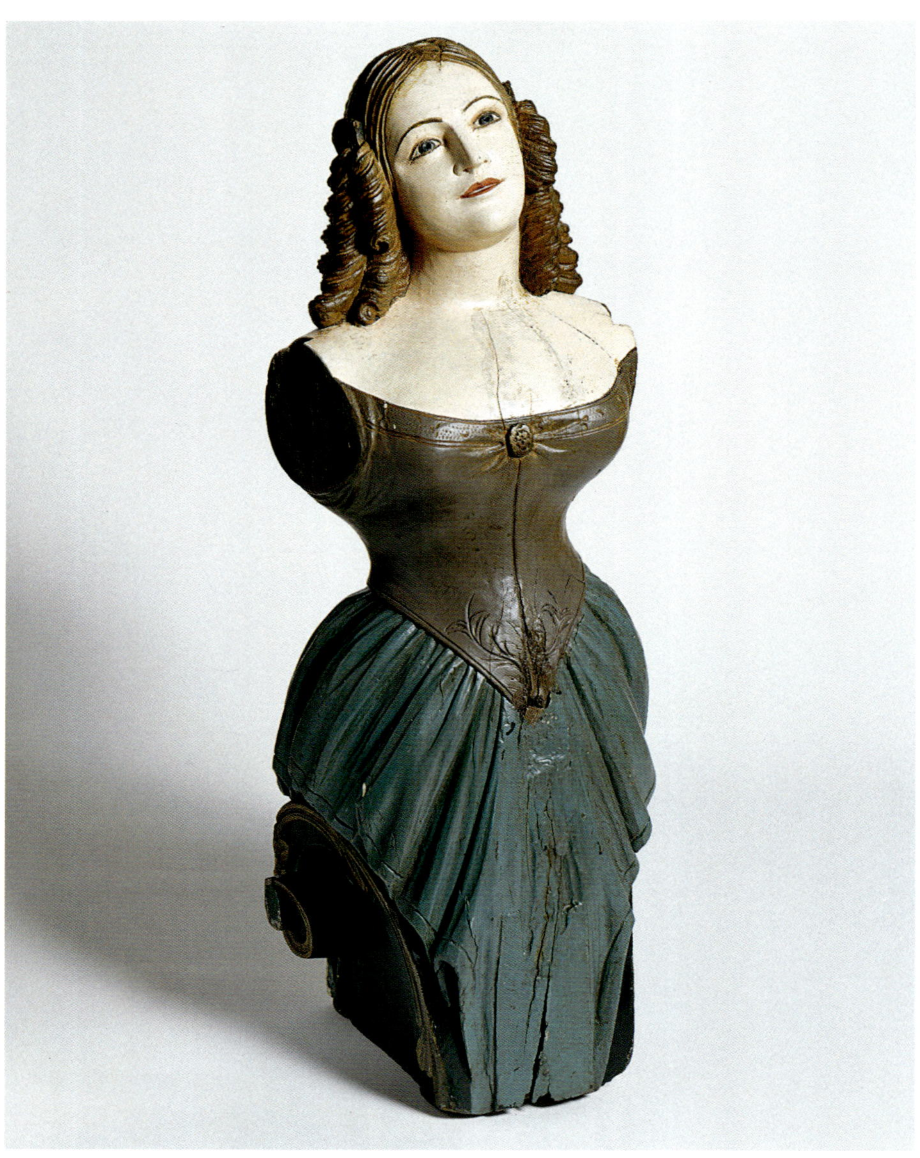

28 Possibly *Jenny Lind*, northeastern United States, 1850–60. Painted wood, $37^{1}/_{2} \times 12^{1}/_{2} \times 11^{1}/_{2}$ in. (95.2 x 31.7 x 29.2 cm). The Mariners' Museum, Newport News, Va.

named after the famous singer, and any number of comely mid-century figureheads have since been identified as her. When compared to the many representations in a variety of different media that flooded the country at the time, though, this rendering does not particularly resemble her.

Recent research suggests instead that the figurehead may portray Anna Thillon, a French actress and singer who took the country by storm in the early 1850s. During her triumphant tour of the United States in 1852, a number of engravings of her appeared in newspapers and magazines, any one of which could have served as a model for this piece.[66]

Probably the best-known ship to carry the name *Jenny Lind* was built in 1848 in Donald McKay's shipyard in East Boston, which was one of the most active operations in the country at the time. This figurehead was, in fact, once linked to that ship.[67] While it is now quite clear that no connection between the two ever existed, the attribution highlights the importance of Boston as a shipbuilding center. Throughout the period, Boston maintained its rivalry with New York, and if fewer ships were constructed there overall, the best of them were held in as high esteem as those produced anywhere. Not surprisingly, then, Boston also continued to support a number of accomplished shipcarvers.[68]

John W. Mason, the man who created the drawing for the *Queen of Sheba*, was one such carver. While no existing figureheads can be attributed to him with any certainty, he was evidently an accomplished carver who was much in demand. He worked for several leading shipbuilders, including Donald McKay, and Fernald and Pettigrew of Portsmouth, New Hampshire. He is also known to have worked in Newburyport, Massachusetts, an important, if smaller, seaport not far from Portsmouth.[69] Mason received a number of favorable notices in the press, and, in one instance in 1853, was praised as "our greatest marine artist."[70] His twenty or so surviving drawings, skillfully rendered in pencil, ink, and wash, suggest that he had some academic training, possibly through contacts with his older brother's printing business.[71] Unfortunately, though, it appears that he was a poor businessman who was plagued by financial difficulties, which led to serious family problems and a premature end to his career in the mid-1850s.

More successful workshops were conducted by members of the Gleason family. By the late 1840s, S. W. Gleason and Sons had become one of the most prominent operations in Boston. In 1850, the shop had five employees, including its founder, Samuel W. Gleason (b. 1800–active ending c. 1854), and his sons, William B. (active c. 1847–d. 1886) and Samuel W., Jr. (active c. 1847–65).[72] Among the many commissions known to have been done by the firm were several figureheads for Donald McKay, including a portrait of the English actress Julia Bennett Barrow as Minehaha and a large eagle's head for the *Great Republic* that is now in the collection of the Mystic Seaport Museum in Mystic, Connecticut.[73]

When she was built in 1853, the *Great Republic* was the largest merchant ship in the United States. As a measure of the importance of such shipbuilding ventures, the day of her launching was declared a public holiday, and the event was said to have been attended by over fifty thousand people. Her celebrity was short-lived, however, and after sailing to New York to be loaded with cargo, she caught fire and burned to the waterline before ever departing for her maiden voyage to Liverpool.[74]

As for S. W. Gleason and Sons, William seems to have been the most talented and resourceful member of the family. A review of the clipper *Shooting Star* in 1851 noted: "Her ornamental work was executed by Messrs. S. W. Gleason & Sons; but to Mr. W. B. Gleason belongs the sole credit of having made her figure head. He is a young artist devotedly attached to his profession, and exhibits a more refined taste in execution of his work than is common to carvers."[75]

In 1854, William took charge of the family shop, presumably because his father retired.[76] He diversified as well, by doing furniture carving as well as ship work. In 1868, he received a patent for a process for making molded wooden ornaments. The resulting business, William B. Gleason and Company, proved to be quite successful, eventually supporting twenty-five employees. He also developed a method for stamping ornamental designs on wood. In 1886, his obituary described him as "a leading ship carver and gilder of Boston . . . [and] inventor of the pressed ornaments commonly used on furniture."[77]

Much less is known about another shipcarver with the same family name, Herbert Gleason (active c. 1863–d. 1893). His relationship to S. W. Gleason and Sons and his better-known contemporary, William, has not been established. He was possibly his brother or perhaps a cousin, but in any event, it seems likely that he had family ties of some sort.[78]

Herbert Gleason is particularly important to this discussion because his remarkable figurehead for the famous McKay clipper *Glory of the Seas* has survived (plate 29).[79] Carved in 1869, she stands on her toes, clutching loosely flowing drapery between her breasts. Generally classical in conception, she wears a necklace and armbands that also reference American Indian adornment. The work is well done, and the figure is convincingly articulated, although her somewhat stocky body does not quite approach the Neoclassical ideal as seen in contemporary marble sculpture. What is particularly striking, though, is the extent of her nudity. Her bare feet, ankles, and arms, when combined with her exposed breasts, are extremely rare for American figureheads. At the time, public opinion was finally coming to accept nudity in the private realm of the fine art gallery or collector's home, but public display was still very controversial.[80]

The *Glory of the Seas* was the last great merchant ship built by Donald McKay. A large medium clipper, she was universally recognized as a beautiful vessel. She was built at a time when steamships were rapidly eclipsing sailing ships, though, and McKay could not sell her. He had hoped that she would reverse the tide of financial misfortune that he had been experiencing for the past decade. Instead, he was forced into bankruptcy. Still, *Glory of the Seas* was in service for more than fifty years, providing more evidence that he was one of the best naval architects and shipbuilders of his generation.[81]

E. Warren Hastings (active c. 1854–d. 1896), who was Herbert Gleason's partner from 1878 until 1893, also had a long and productive career. A number of his designs for figureheads and sterns survive, and while they are less artistically accomplished than those of John Mason, they are finely detailed pencil sketches that reveal him to be a competent draftsman.[82] As with many of his contemporaries, Hastings did other types of figure carving in addition to ship work. A rare piece of evidence appears in the journals of Leonard Cushing of Cushing and White, a firm in Waltham, Massachusetts, that specialized in copper weathervanes. In 1869, Cushing recorded that he commissioned Hastings to carve a figure of Justice for a courthouse in Delaware, Ohio, as well as a wooden model for an Angel Gabriel weathervane.[83]

Before departing this overview of Boston carvers, we must acknowledge the long shadow cast by that populist hero from earlier in the century, Andrew Jackson. Two well-carved figures of Jackson that can be documented to mid-century Boston have survived. The first is another figurehead for the *Constitution* that was done in 1846 by John and William Fowle while the frigate was in the Boston Navy Yard for repairs. While not as famous as Laban Beecher's 1834 version, it is, in fact, a better work with a more lifelike presence. Its carvers, John D. Fowle

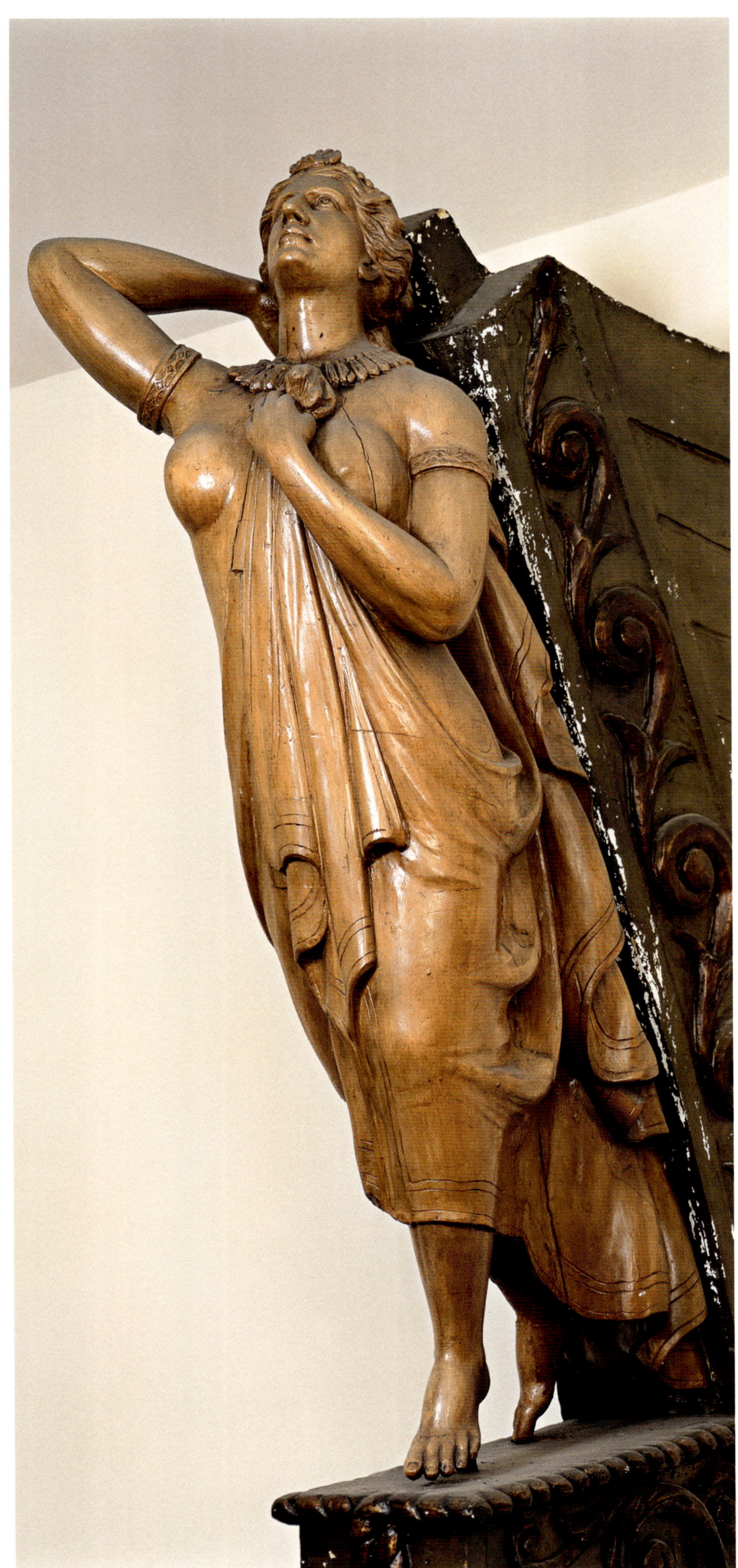

29 Herbert Gleason (American, active c. 1863–d. 1893), *Glory of the Seas*, Boston, 1869. Painted wood, height 90 in. (228.6 cm). India House, New York. Gift of James A. Farrell, co-founder of India House

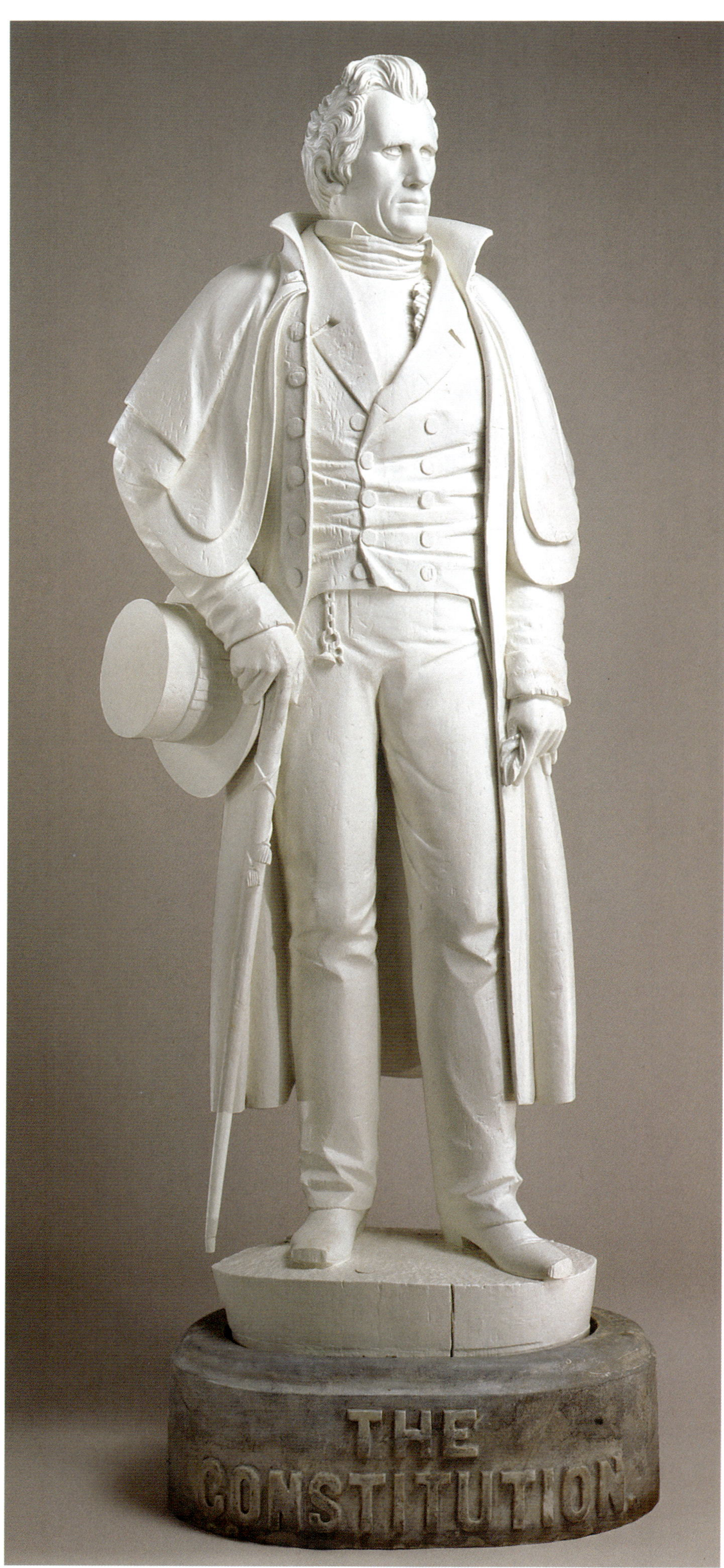

30 William H. Rumney (American, 1837–1927), *Andrew Jackson*, Boston, c. 1860. Painted pine, 78 x 29 x 19 in. (198.1 x 73.6 x 48.3 cm). The Metropolitan Museum of Art, New York. The J. M. Kaplan Fund, Inc. and Mrs. Frederick A. Stoughton Gifts, Harris Brisbane Dick and Louis V. Bell Funds, 1978 (1978.57)

(1809–1891) and William H. Fowle (1813–1862), were the sons of Isaac Fowle, the successor to the Skillin family workshop. Their figurehead of Jackson had a long working life. It remained on the ship until 1874, when it was removed and installed on the grounds of the Philadelphia Navy Yard. It is now in the collection of the United States Naval Academy in Annapolis.[84]

The second example is an over-lifesize statue of Andrew Jackson carved around 1860 by William H. Rumney (1837–1927) (plate 30). The figure was commissioned by Daniel Kelly, a prominent East Boston shipbuilder, as a testament to his admiration for the illustrious general and the populist principals of his presidency. An ardent Democrat, Kelly apparently also enjoyed antagonizing his anti-Jacksonian neighbors by prominently displaying the figure in front of his home. The inscription, "The Constitution," on the statue's marble base surely refers to the two figureheads carved for the frigate, as well as the controversy surrounding the decapitation of Beecher's figure in 1834.[85]

Although the body is somewhat stiffly rendered, the piece has a commanding presence that is further emphasized by a strong, well-modeled face, wavy hair, and a richness in details of costuming. Painted white to simulate marble, it is a faithful likeness of its subject, based on a lithograph of "Andrew Jackson at the Hermitage" done in 1832 by John H. Bufford (1810–1870), which was in turn derived from a portrait by Ralph E. W. Earl (c. 1788–1838) that was completed around 1830.[86] Upon Kelly's death in 1886, his estate was subdivided into small house lots, but the statue remained in place until after 1949.[87]

After mid-century, shipyards in Boston, New York, and other major cities received increasingly strong competition from smaller New England seaports, as previously noted. Rising land values and labor costs in urban areas resulted in higher production expenses and dangerously thin profit margins for builders. Even materials like timber and iron fittings could be secured for lower prices in smaller port towns. Urban shipyards found it difficult to attract orders for new vessels. In February 1868, Donald McKay bemoaned the rapid demise of Boston as a major shipbuilding center: "For myself I have constructed some years 12 ships, while at present I am engaged in building a ship of 1,285 tons, having already spent two months on her, and I can not find a merchant who will buy her at actual cost, not including therein my own services. Within a circuit of five miles, I can count twenty shipbuilding firms which are now idle and have been since the war and most of them built from two to four ships annually before the war."[88]

With the shift away from urban centers, shipyards in places like Bath, Maine, and Mystic, Connecticut, came to the fore. It was not so much that they experienced a major increase in business, than that they more or less sustained their previous level of activity at the expense of the larger seaports. For shipcarvers, commissions for ship work were often sporadic, particularly after the Civil War when wooden shipbuilding continued its steady decline everywhere. As a result, most carving shops along the New England coast accepted a wide range of woodworking jobs.

The diversity of work done by these carvers is illustrated by the Mystic workshop of James Campbell (active c. 1854–1900) and John Colby (1833–1891), as recorded in local newspapers and in the papers of George Greenman and Company,

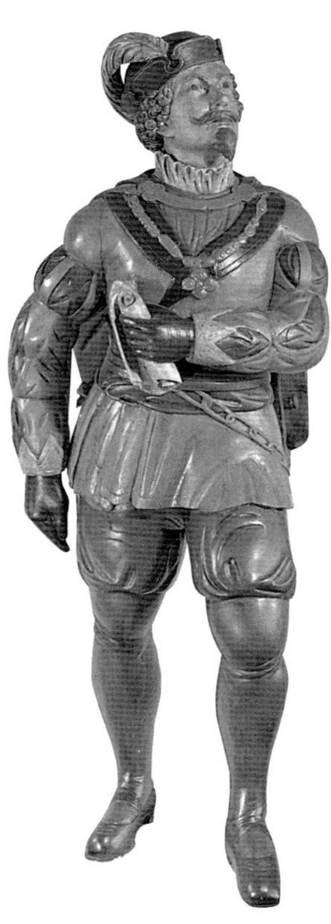

31 *Grandee*, probably New York or Boston, c. 1873. Painted wood, height 72 in. (182.9 cm). Peabody Essex Museum, Salem, Mass. M. R. Coll. (D. M. Little) Charles Darling, 1924

the shipbuilding firm that commissioned the *David Crockett* figurehead from Jacob Anderson.[89] Campbell and Colby were partners from about 1858 to 1877, at a time when Mystic was an important shipbuilding center. In spite of its relatively small size, the town supported seven large shipyards and a number of smaller boatyards. Several fine clippers were built there, as well as many steamships and other types of vessels.

Among the most notable pieces of shipcarving known to have been done by John Colby was a self-portrait for the stern of a schooner named after himself.[90] Another was a figure of a woman playing baseball that he and his partner made for the *Frolic* in 1869. A reporter for the *Mystic Pioneer* noted: "she has a splendid figurehead carved by our artistic townsmen, Campbell and Colby. It is a lady with a bat in one hand in the act of striking a ball which she holds in the other, enjoying a frolic. It is very appropriate."[91]

In addition to figureheads and related shipcarvings, Campbell and Colby created an eight-foot allegorical figure of Justice for the Morgan County Courthouse in Jacksonville, Illinois, and a liberty cap for a liberty pole in Norwich, Connecticut. They also carved and gilded signs and produced ornamental fencing. A few years after they dissolved their partnership, a New London directory listed J. N. Colby and Company as "carvers, gilders and ornamental woodworkers, polishing a specialty, wood turning, jig sawing and fancy scroll work."[92]

Portsmouth, New Hampshire, also benefited from the collapse of the shipbuilding industry in Boston and New York. It had been an important regional center since the colonial era, and as will be recalled, the frigates *Raleigh* and *Congress*, two of the earliest warships commissioned by Congress, were built there. By the mid-nineteenth century, several shipbuilders were active in Portsmouth, including the previously mentioned firm of Fernald and Pettigrew.

As for shipcarvers, only a handful are known to have lived and worked in Portsmouth. William Dearing, the man who worked on the *Congress* in 1799, has already been discussed. Another local carver of note was Woodbury Gerrish (active c. 1850–1875), who is best known for creating a bust of the namesake of the USS *Franklin* when she was being rebuilt in Portsmouth in 1853. His bust replaced one carved by William Rush in 1815, and, while it is not as fine a piece of work, it holds the distinction of being one of the few signed figureheads in existence.[93]

Evidently, Portsmouth could not support more than a few shipcarvers, particularly since local shipbuilders often commissioned figureheads from shops in Boston, Philadelphia, and New York. Several examples have been given in this chapter, from the work of William Rush, who created a figure of Wisdom for the *Congress*, to that of William Mason and the Gleasons. Two New York City carvers, Charles J. Dodge and John L. Cromwell, are also known to have worked for Fernald and Pettigrew.[94]

The figurehead of the ship *Grandee*, built in Portsmouth in 1873, is a fine example of a commission that was probably created elsewhere (plate 31). While its maker is unidentified, it is the type of fanciful historical subject, expertly carved in a realistic style that features period dress, that was a hallmark of the largest urban workshops. Given its date, it was most likely done in New York or Boston.

The best-known carver from the Portsmouth area was John Halley Bellamy (1836–1914), who has become justly famous for his distinctive eagles, which range from small plaques to more complex compositions with shields and draped flags that are over eight feet wide. Many of the plaques were originally done as gifts, while the larger eagles were usually commissions for public buildings and private organizations. His most spectacular piece of work is an eagle figurehead done for the USS *Lancaster* in 1880 that is now at the Mariners' Museum in Newport News, Virginia. Made of blocks of wood that were bolted and screwed together, it has a wingspan of over eighteen feet and weighs more than 3,200 pounds.[95]

Throughout his long career, Bellamy created a wide range of other carved work as well, including architectural ornaments, mounted animal heads, clock cases, and picture frames. A trade card from his Portsmouth shop reads, in part, "John H. Bellamy, Figure and ornamental CARVER, particular attention paid to House, Ship, Furniture, Sign & Frame Carving, GARDEN FIGURES."

North of Portsmouth, several port towns along Maine's rugged coast were important shipbuilding centers during the final era of wooden sailing ships. In the 1870s and 1880s, the most active shipyards in the country were in Bath, but several other places made significant contributions as well. In all, at least thirty-four shipcarvers worked in Maine between 1850 and 1881.[96]

Of them, several worked in Maine's principal city, Portland. Edward Souther Griffin (1834–1928), who operated a shop from 1851 to around 1890, is the best known. Later in life, he noted: "There was a demand for figure-heads in those days, when builders took great pride in their vessels. I made my own designs and many a ship set forth from the Portland wharves bearing my handiwork at the prow or stern."[97] Unfortunately, none of his figureheads is known to survive.

In Bath, Charles A. L. Sampson (1825–1881) was a leading carver from about the mid-1850s until his death. In 1855, he was praised in the local press with a notice that read in part, "We cordially commend this young artist to the public as one who needs only to be judged by his work."[98]

Sampson did his best work in the 1870s, when he carved several full-length figures for Bath shipbuilders. Two are in museum collections and others are known from photographs. The *Belle of Oregon* (plate 32) and the *Western Belle*, which were carved in 1876, are very similar in design.[99] Both represent fashionably dressed women with one arm close to the body and the other extended holding an ear of corn, appropriate since the vessels were primarily intended for the California grain trade. Legs are straight, not striding forward in the more typical pose, resulting in figures that are competently rendered with great attention to details of costuming, but not particularly dynamic or original in conception. They may be portraits, as Sampson is known to have frequently used local women as models. For the *Belle of Bath*, carved in 1877, a "Miss Kelly," daughter of the ship's captain, posed for the figurehead in his workshop.[100]

When Sampson died in 1881, William Southworth (1826–1909) bought his business. Late in life, Southworth estimated that he had carved for more than five hundred ships during his sixty-year career. Not all of these commissions were for figureheads, of course, particularly in the final decades of the century.

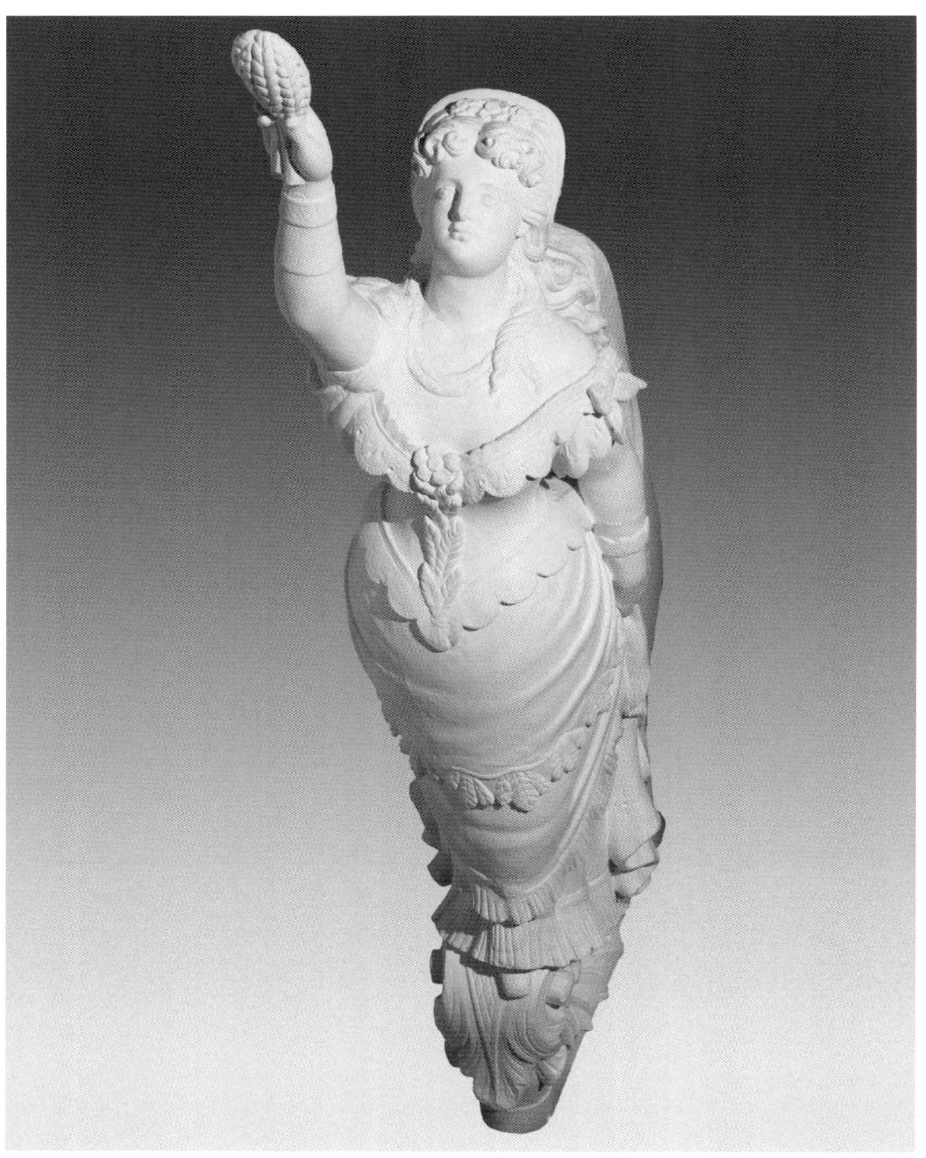

32 Charles A. L. Sampson (American, 1825–1881), *Belle of Oregon*, Bath, Maine, 1876. Painted wood, 76 1/2 x 20 x 26 in. (194.3 x 50.8 x 66 cm). The Mariners' Museum, Newport News, Va.

In 1909, Southworth told a reporter:

> The years that I did most of my work at real ship carving were before I located in Bath for the palmy days were over prior to 1881 . . . the main difference has been that few builders have cared for as elaborate work as used to be called for in the fifties when ships were making money and no expense was spared to make them look right and tight.
>
> There was one time when it was not thought possible for a ship to be fairly completed until she had a figure head as well as the carvings on the stern. . . . There was one long spell when

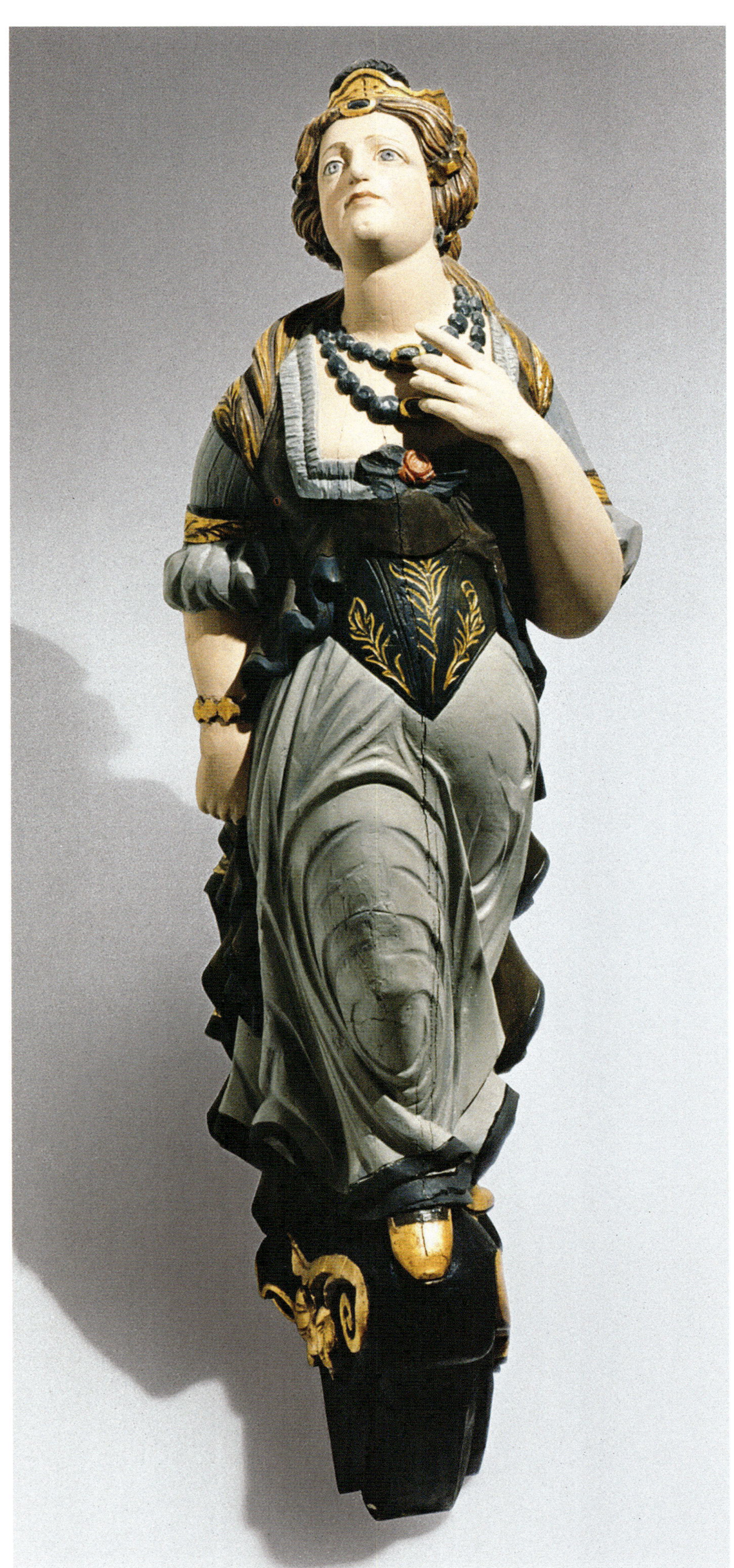

33 Attributed to John Rogerson (Scottish, 1837–1925), *Lady Edmonton*, Saint John, New Brunswick, Canada, c. 1882. Painted wood, 91 x 23 x 19 in. (231.1 x 58.4 x 22.8 cm). The Mariners' Museum, Newport News, Va.

> it seemed as if they all wanted full length figures and they brought good prices too. Take a vessel of 1,000 tons and the price would run from $250 to $400 for the carving, now days if a carver gets a job on one craft amounting to $50 he is doing well. The old days are gone and people do things differently now days.[101]

Among the other Maine carvers who deserve mention is Harvey Counce (1821–after 1880) of Thomaston, who spent his entire life in his birthplace. Besides being credited with most of the carving done for ships built there between about 1840 and 1880, he also did a significant amount of architectural work.[102] Evidently a talented man, his reputation spread beyond his native village. William Southworth was quoted as saying that "Two of the best known carvers in this section in my day were E. S. Griffin of Portland and Harvey Counce of Thomaston."[103]

For those who aspired to be shipcarvers in the generation that followed Southworth, Counce, and Sampson, the future was not promising. Edbury Hatch (1849–1935) of Newcastle, Maine, provides a telling example. Born during the height of the clipper ship era, he entered an apprenticeship with William Southworth in 1865 or 1866. Upon completing his training, he received a glowing recommendation but no offer of employment. Instead, Southworth presented him with a letter that read in part "that Edbury Hatch has served a regular apprenticeship of more than four years with me in the carving business, that he is honest, temperate and industrious. . . . A lack of business is the only reason I do not employ him."[104]

For the next ten years, Hatch found occasional work in Sampson's shop in Bath. He helped carve both the *Belle of Oregon* and the *Belle of Bath* figureheads and kept photographs of them as cherished possessions for the rest of his life.[105] In the early 1880s, Hatch finally gave up shipcarving and moved to Boston, where he became a night watchman in a hotel. Returning to the family home in Newcastle twenty years later, he worked at odd jobs while continuing to carve ship models, picture frames, furniture, and architectural ornaments for himself and his friends and neighbors.[106]

Further north, Canadian shipcarvers were experiencing a similar fate. The port of St. John, New Brunswick, was, like its New England counterparts, a major shipbuilding center for much of the nineteenth century. While several carvers worked there, the best known is John Rogerson (1837–1925), who created a number of distinctive full-length figureheads in the prevailing late-nineteenth-century style.

For this, he received a certain amount of recognition during his lifetime. According to local tradition, in fact, he was once praised in the *London Shipping Journal* as "the best workman on the other side of the Atlantic."[107] This assessment is open to debate, of course, but Rogerson clearly ranks among the best carvers of his day. His full-length figureheads are sturdy women with idealized features, finely arrayed and striding forward in flowing skirts. The piece illustrated here was carved for the *Edmonton*, which was built near Quebec in 1882 (plate 33). It is attributed to Rogerson by comparison with other examples of his work, including a full-length female figurehead in the collection of the New Brunswick Museum. As with Charles Sampson and other late-nineteenth-century carvers, Rogerson's known figureheads show a marked similarity in design and execution.

The close resemblance of figures from workshops like Sampson's and Rogerson's raises the question as to whether or not some sort of template or pattern was used. While it is impossible to make a definitive determination given the lack of evidence, this does not seem to have been the case. As we have seen, carvers often created detailed drawings of proposed figureheads, which were useful in providing clients with an idea of their work. They also used a number of different sources for special commissions, including engravings, photographs, and even live models. The work itself, though, proceeded by hand, guided by an experienced eye and perhaps an outline sketched on the wood. Stylistic similarities in a carver's work were the result of individual preference and force of habit, not a mechanical aid.

Contemporary accounts are rare. One of the best comes from an article that appeared in *Harper's Weekly* in 1892. Quoting the carver that he had visited, the author wrote:

> The first thing to be considered is the shape of the ship's bow and the rake of the bowsprit. On their proportions depends the size of the figure. The original design is drawn on paper with crayons, and in its rough state gives only the slightest suggestion of the finished work. The next step is to pick out the wood. A solid block is chosen, but sometimes two figures are used, and the parts are separately carved and afterwards joined. The length of the average field figure is seven to eight feet. The block is "roughed out" on the floor and then lifted on "horses" where it is finished. The only tools used are chisels, mallets, gauges, and sand-paper. When once started on the figure the paper design is of little use. The carver has to depend most entirely on his eye to get the expression and the proportions. The figure is finished off with sand-paper and gilt. As is everything else, the amount of labor expended depends upon the price. Some figures are finished in a few weeks, and others require months for completion.[108]

Another report noted that the carver marked a centerline on the block of wood and sketched a "profile outline" and "front view" on it as he worked. The author then mentioned that "From four to six days suffice for making the average specimen."[109]

While the size of the figurehead was determined by the size and shape of the bow to which it was to be attached, both carvers and builders allowed some leeway depending upon the desired visual effect. The following excerpt from a letter from S. W. Gleason and Sons to Fernald and Pettigrew written in 1850 demonstrates how the carvers calculated the dimensions of a figure that they wanted to appear lifesize. It also provides evidence of one way in which they adapted artistic conventions to meet their needs. The letter reads in part, "In answer to your question about the size of the figure we would say that we agree with you pretty much, that is to say, we think that the figure should look the size of life after it is on & would have to be in reality 3 or 5 in taller, the standard height among Artists is for a female 5 feet 3 in—suppose we make the figure 5 feet 6 in & the block or scroll as small as possible say 7 in—extreme length of whole 6 feet 1 inch; how will that do?"[110]

The figures were painted upon completion. Generally, a base coat of white lead paint was applied first. They were then either finished in polychrome or white with gold trim. Again, due to a lack of documentation, it is not possible to be certain which treatment was more popular over the course of the eighteenth and nineteenth centuries. The prevailing fashion probably varied at times, and regional preference was no doubt a factor as well. Overall, it is likely that more figures were painted "to life" than done in a classical approach to representation.[111]

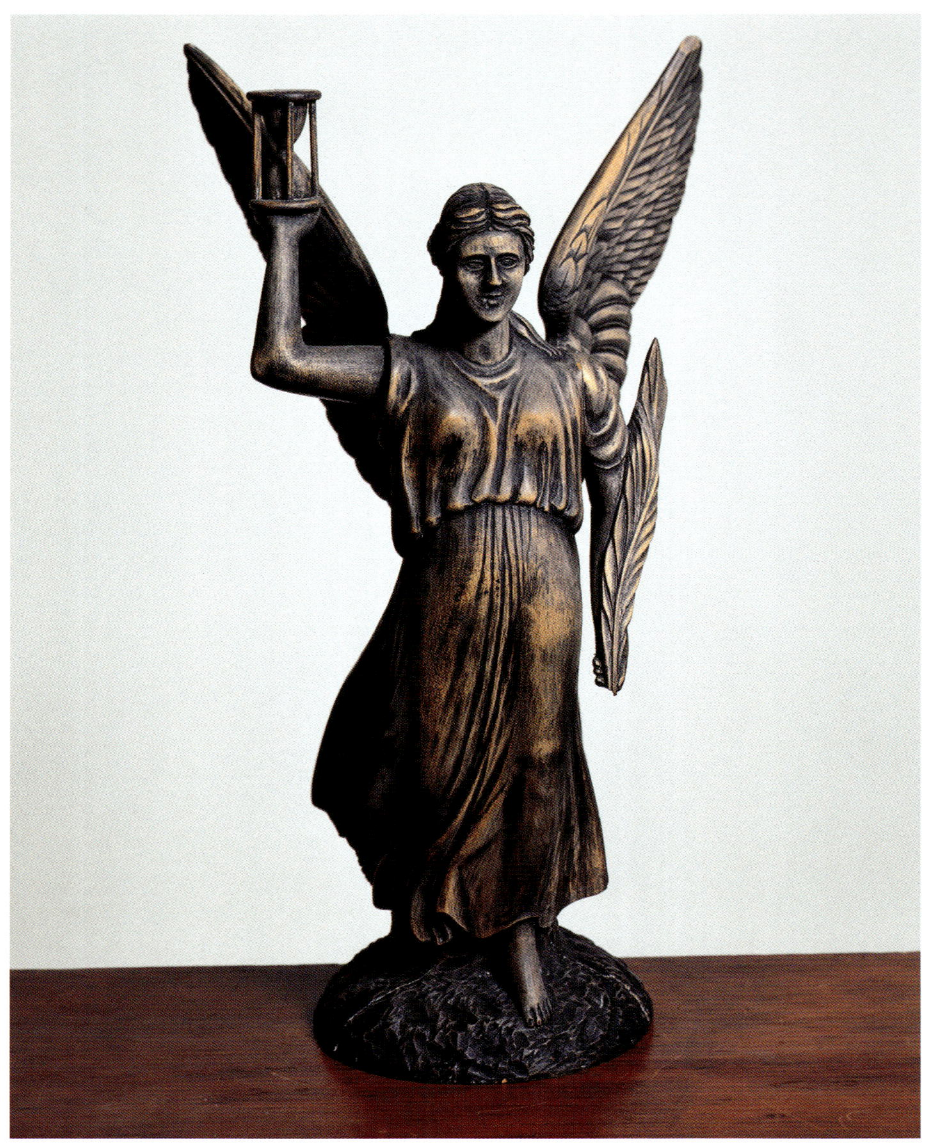

34 *Time*, probably Essex County, Mass., c. 1837. Painted wood, 20½ x 11 x 9½ in. (52 x 27.9 x 24.1 cm). Heritage Museums and Gardens, Sandwich, Mass.

On the other hand, surviving evidence indicates that many New England builders and carvers preferred white figureheads in the second half of the nineteenth century. A review of the clipper *Shooting Star*, written in 1851, described its figurehead: "A full female figure ornaments the bow. She is represented in white vestments, spangled with gilded stars upon her waist; her hair is confined by a gilded zone, in front of which is printed 'Liberty,' and from under which the hair descends loosely over the shoulders—her right foot is advanced, and rests upon a gilded globe."[112]

In another notice, the figurehead of the clipper *Galatea*, built in Charlestown, Massachusetts, in 1854, was reported to be "A full female figure, standing on tiptoe, and robed in vestments of flowing white, fringed with gold, ornaments the bow, and is well designed and very neat."[113] Finally, a recollection from the Maine shipcarver William Southworth confirms that these two examples were not just random occurrences. Shortly before his death in 1909, he told a reporter that "The figureheads were all about painted white, unless the character represented required more gaudy colors, most of them were white though."[114]

IN ADDITION TO CREATING FIGUREHEADS and stern decorations for sailing ships, carvers found opportunities on the newer types of vessels that increasingly replaced them after mid-century. The great paddle-wheel steamers that plied inland water routes after 1840 or so offered a number of possibilities for ornamental work. Designed to attract a prosperous middle-class clientele, they featured opulent cabins with carved architectural detail and plush furnishings. While their straight-stemmed bows, flat bottoms, and shallow draft precluded the use of figureheads, many of the river steamers displayed full-length figures or eagles on their decks or on top of a central pilothouse.

In addition to deck figures, related types that can be attributed to shipcarvers on stylistic grounds attest to the versatility and skill of their makers. One such piece is an allegorical figure of Time, thought to have been made for a hearse in Essex County, Massachusetts, around 1837 (plate 34).[115] Holding an hourglass and quill to mark the passage of time and the deeds of men, the figure surges forward in a typical figurehead pose. The carver has delineated the female form under the flowing drapery in a manner that is consistent with contemporary sculptural technique. While the arm holding the hourglass is a bit stiff, the figure transmits a dynamic sense of movement that emphasizes the passage of time. One of the most notable features of the piece is its exuberant, deeply carved wings that billow out from the shoulders, balancing the curve of the lower body and the windblown drapery that extends back behind the figure. Surely her creator was as familiar with eagles as he was with the other popular types in the shipcarver's repertoire.

Naturally enough, another one of these was the sailor himself. As in England, representations of sailors, or "Jack Tars," as ordinary seamen were often called, were used for a variety of purposes, particularly as shop signs for nautical instrument makers and tobacconists. Three figures from the third quarter of the nineteenth century provide an interesting comparison in possible approaches to the interpretation of the seafaring man. The first is a relatively realistic tobacconist

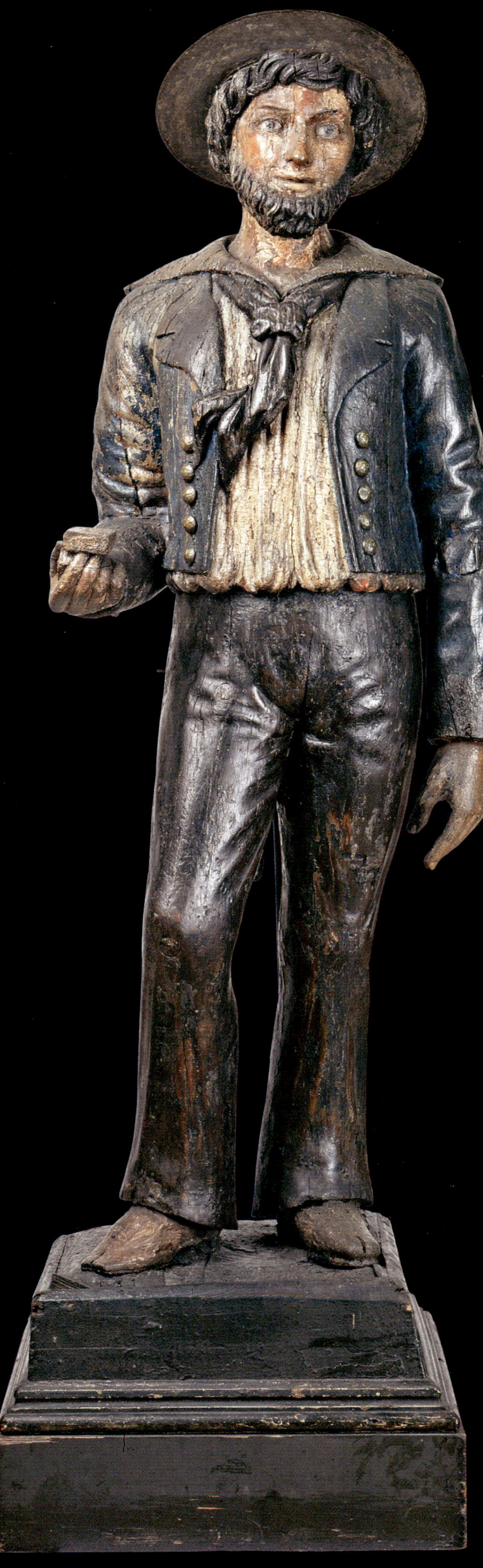

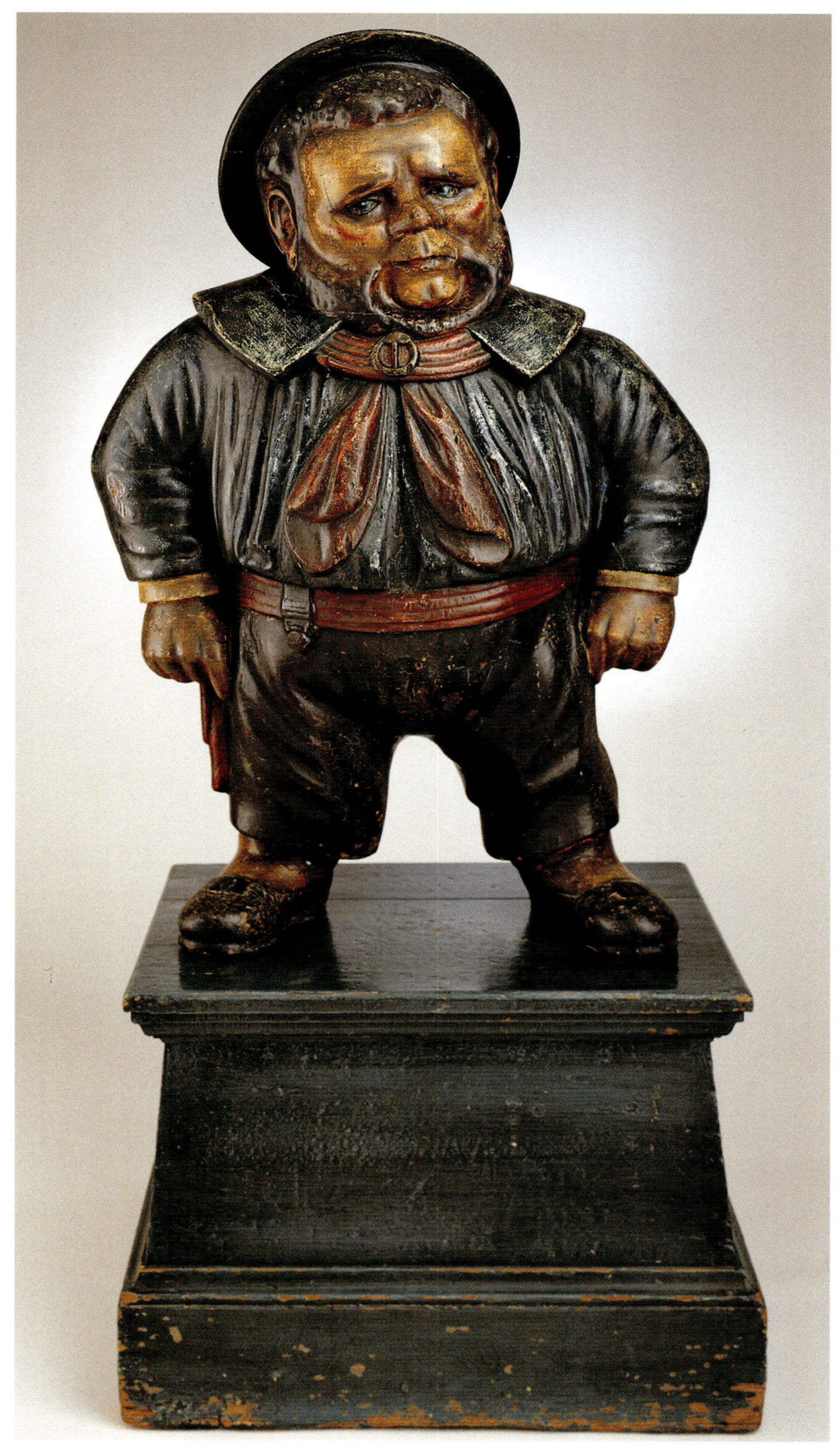

35 (OPPOSITE) *Sailor*, New York City, c. 1860. Painted wood, 75 x 25 x 12 in. (190.5 x 63.5 x 30.5 cm). The New-York Historical Society, New York (1937.1400)

36 (RIGHT) *Jack Tar*, northeastern United States, c. 1865. Painted wood, 61 x 29½ x 24 in. (154.9 x 74.9 x 61 cm). © Shelburne Museum, Shelburne, Vt.

figure that was probably carved in New York City (plate 35). Holding a package of tobacco in his right hand, he strikes a relaxed pose while he casually offers his wares.

In contrast, the second example is a rotund contemporary with a quizzical look on his face (plate 36). A caricature of everyone's favorite Jack Tar, he is standing still for a moment, but seems somewhat uncomfortable as the object of the viewer's gaze. He was likely derived from a popular print. A nearly identical chalkware figure that was recorded in the Index of American Design provides support for this conjecture.[116]

The third sailor is the liveliest of the group, as he tips his hat to passersby or perhaps prepares to dance a jig (plate 37). The sense of movement is enhanced through a verticality emphasized by long legs and a diagonal formed by the figure's curving arms. As with his counterparts, he is skillfully carved with great attention to details of costuming, in this case a fairly accurate rendering of an American merchant seaman's outfit of around 1845.[117] On the other hand, the individualized handling of his facial features, including his receding hairline and prominent cheekbones, differentiates him from the generalized, smooth planes of the first figure's face and the fleshy caricature of the second's.

As for other figures, a *Sailor with Binnacle*, a housing for a ship compass that was made between about 1851 and 1860 for the clipper *N. B. Palmer*, is a rare variation on the theme (plate 38). According to oral tradition, he was removed from the deck of the ship after making several voyages to the Far East because crew members were uncomfortable with his gaze, claiming that his eyes followed them around the deck during night watch. He then served for many years as a shop sign for T. S. Negus and Company, nautical instrument makers on Water Street in lower Manhattan.[118]

Another fine example of the type is a *Man with Spyglass* that was carved around 1850 (plate 39). Probably used as a ship chandler's sign, the gentleman represents a merchant or shipowner striding forward as he surveys the distance through his glass. This sense of movement gives him a dynamic presence that marks him as an exceptional work. He has, in fact, become something of an icon of American folk art over the years.

A final piece from earlier in the century that has achieved a similar status is the famous *Little Navigator* (plate 40). The stocky little figure is a highly simplified form with rather shallow carving and generalized features. As such, he relates directly to traditional English nautical figures such as the one noted by Charles Dickens in *Dealings with the Firm of Dombey and Son* that was discussed in the previous chapter.

Carved around 1810, the figure was first used as a nautical instrument maker's sign by James Fales of Newport, Rhode Island, and later by his son, James, Jr., a watch and clockmaker in New Bedford, Massachusetts. Late-nineteenth-century evidence suggests that he may have been created by Samuel King (1749–1820), a versatile man who was both a nautical instrument maker and a painter of portraits and miniatures. King was Washington Allston's first teacher and may have given lessons to a young Gilbert Stuart.[119] If he did create this piece, then the strength of his stylization marks him as a talented carver as well.

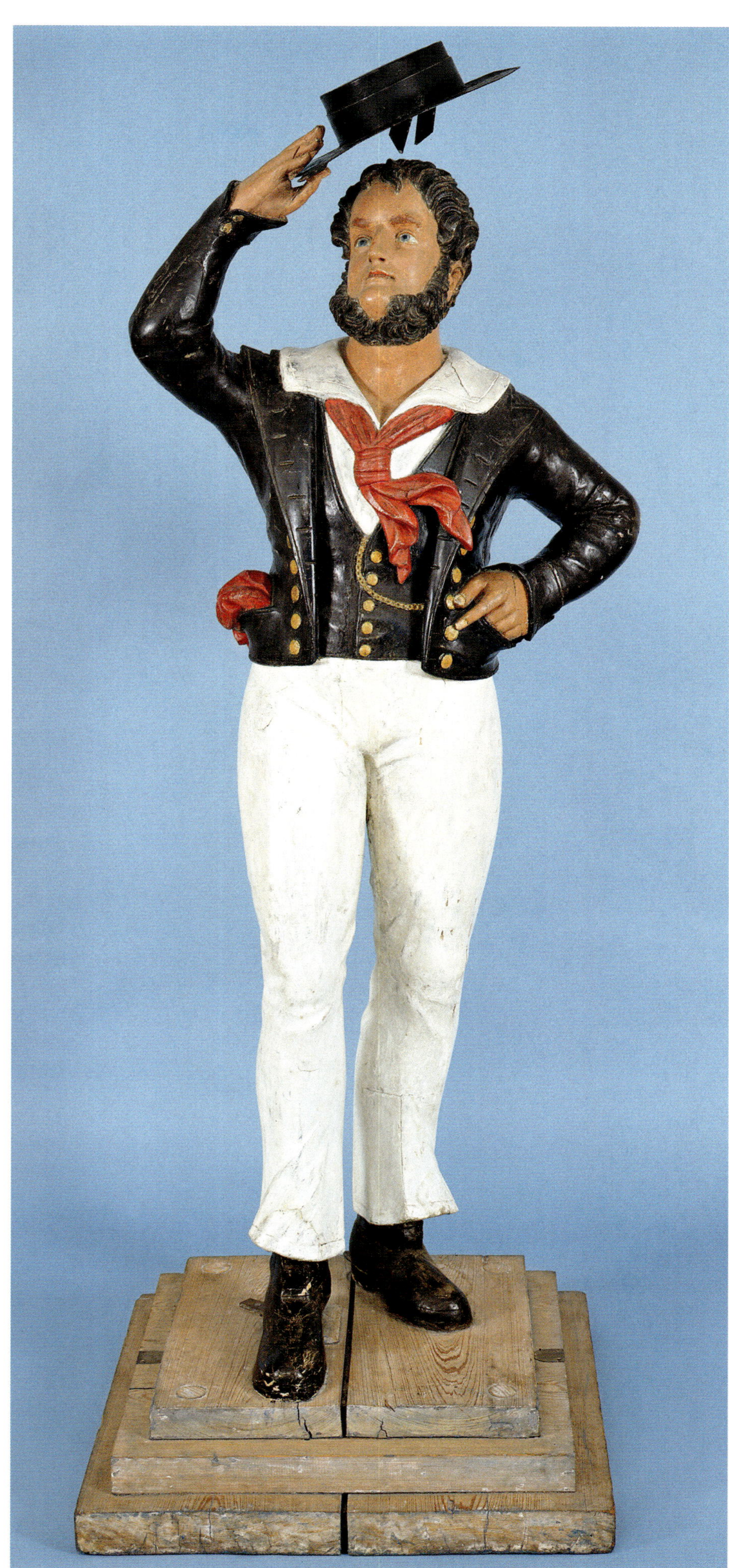

37 *Jack Tar*, northeastern United States, c. 1845. Painted wood, height 86 1/2 in. (219.7 cm). J. Welles Henderson Collection

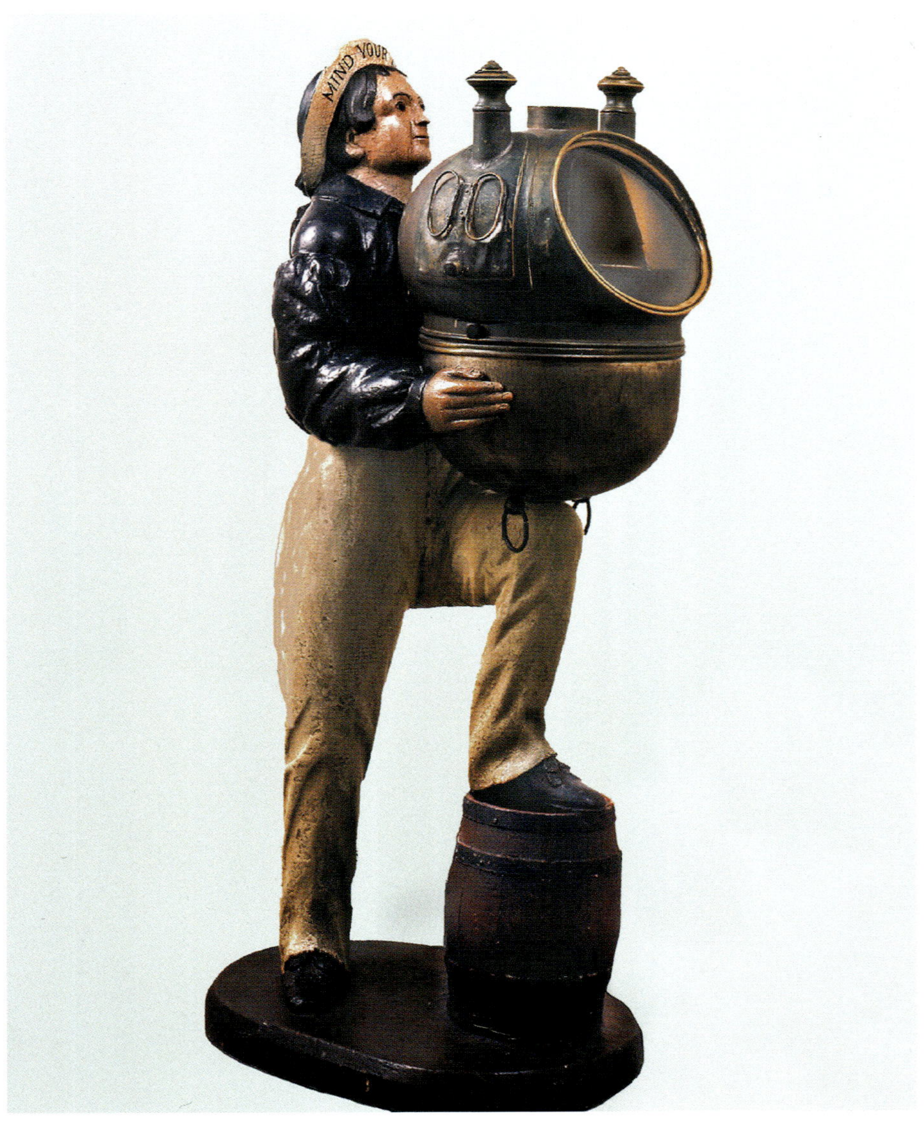

38 *Sailor with Binnacle*, New York, 1851–65. Painted wood, brass, and glass, 55 x 18 x 25 in. (139.7 x 45.7 x 63.5 cm). Museum of the City of New York. Bequest of J. S. Negus, II (63.178.1)

A photograph of the shop of James Fales, Jr., around 1870 that shows the *Little Navigator* above the doorway speaks volumes about the place of traditional carved wooden signs in nineteenth-century America (plate 41). The information transmitted by the pocket watch, rifle, and navigator is direct and immediately understandable, while at the same time visually richer than the utilitarian painted and lettered signboard that is visible to the left. Everyday objects such as these resonate with personal meaning. The depth of possible associations with the viewer's own experience that is embodied in carved and figural shop signs relates them to the symbolic function of figureheads and helps to explain their popularity in an era of general literacy when they were no longer necessary on a practical level.

The widespread use of carved wooden figures in a variety of circumstances in the eighteenth and nineteenth centuries demonstrates their continued cultural

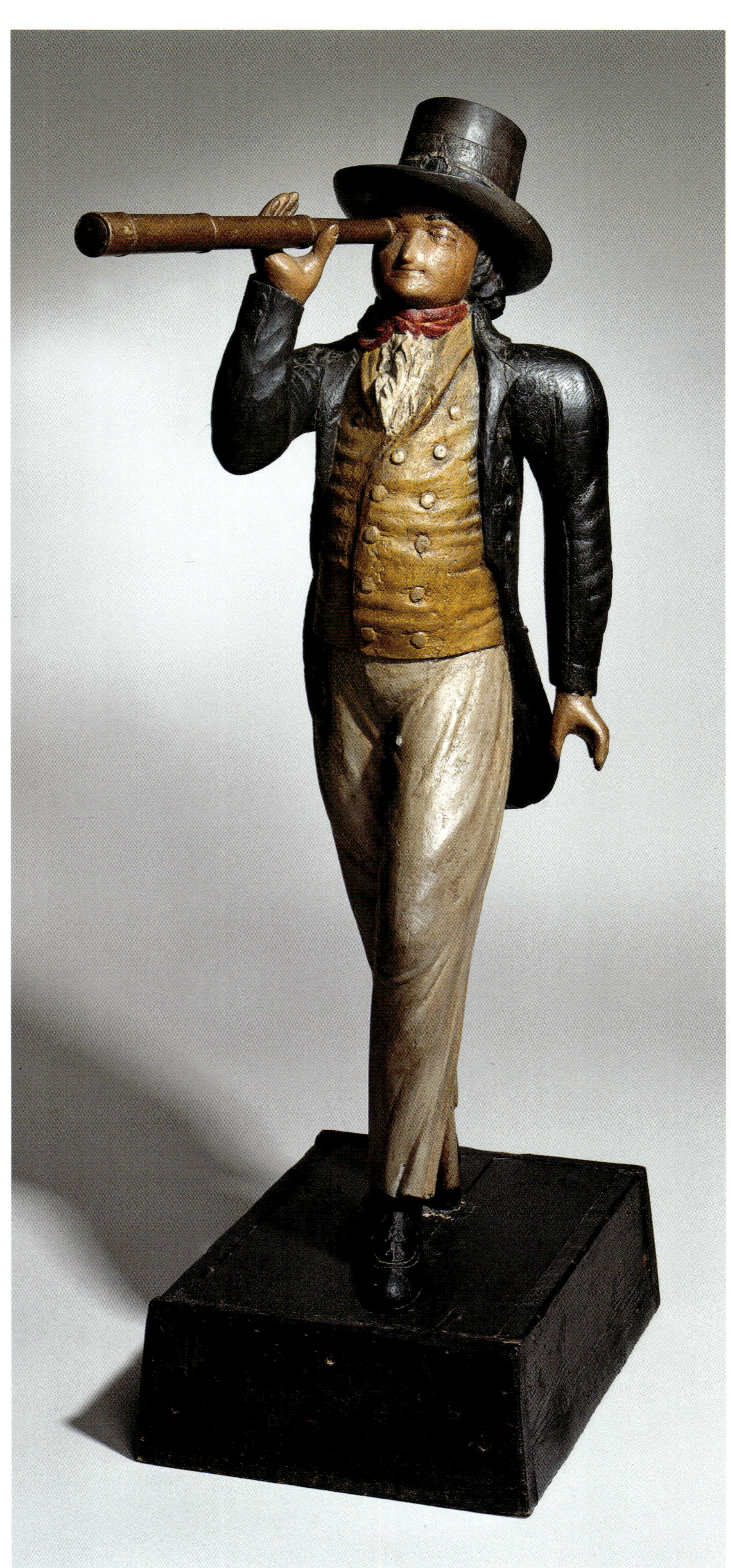

39 *Man with Spyglass*, New England, c. 1850. Painted wood, 49 x $14^1/_2$ x $26^1/_4$ in. (124.4 x 36.8 x 66.7 cm). Mystic Seaport, Conn.

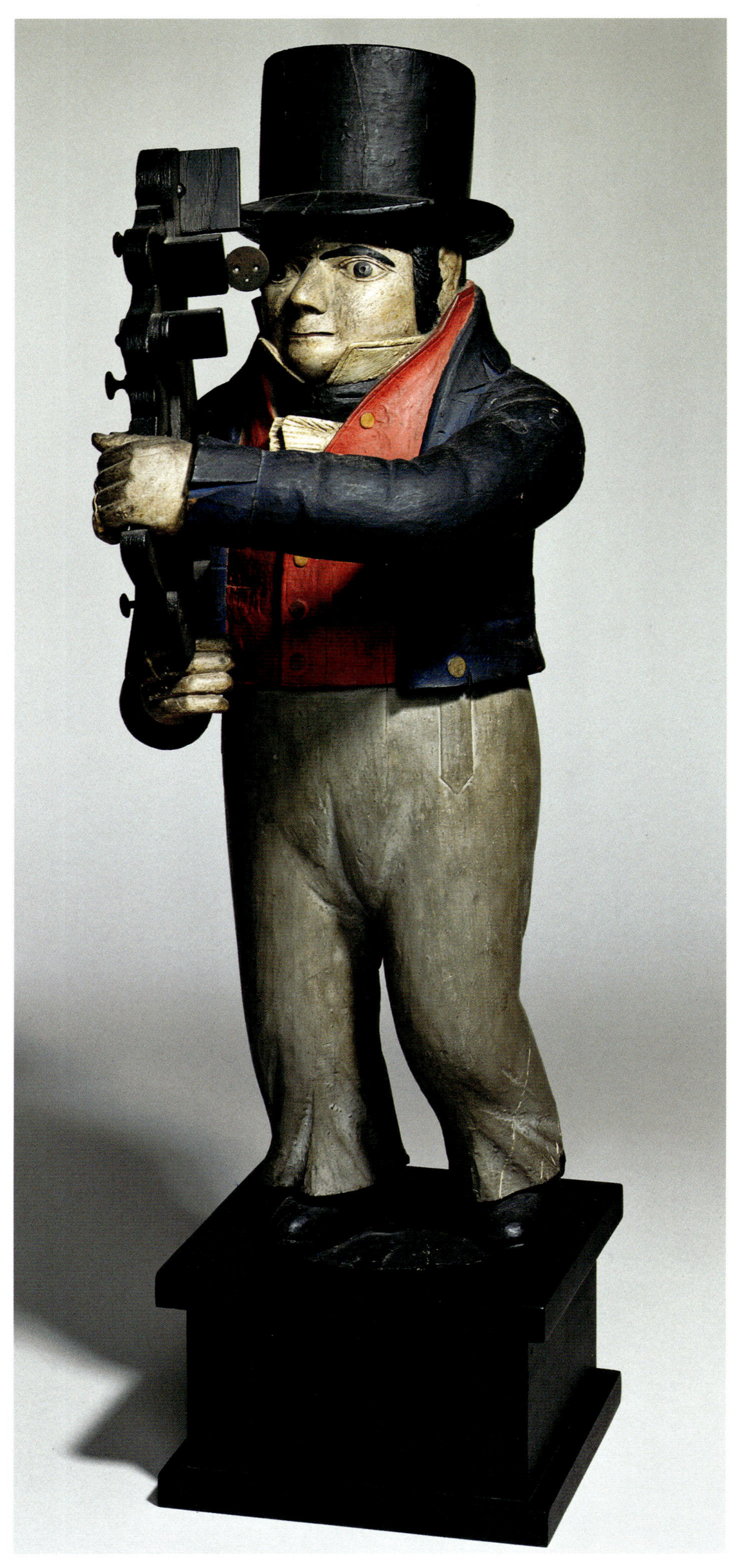

40 Probably Samuel King (American, 1749–1820), *The Little Navigator,* Newport, R.I., c. 1810. Painted wood, 24 x 8 x 11 1/2 in. (60.9 x 20.3 x 29.2 cm). The New Bedford Whaling Museum, Mass.

significance. As figureheads, stern figures, commemorative civic sculpture, garden statuary, or shop signs, they simultaneously played symbolic, ceremonial, and commercial roles to varying degrees. The figures themselves were often interchangeable or at least readily adaptable to any of these desired purposes. The men who created them were the inheritors of a tradition that has been traced from Renaissance Europe to Victorian America. Although their art was doomed to extinction with the passing of the wooden-hulled sailing ship in the second half of the nineteenth century, shipcarvers continued to collectively exercise their talents and training for as long as possible in a final burst of creativity seen particularly in shop and cigar-store figures.

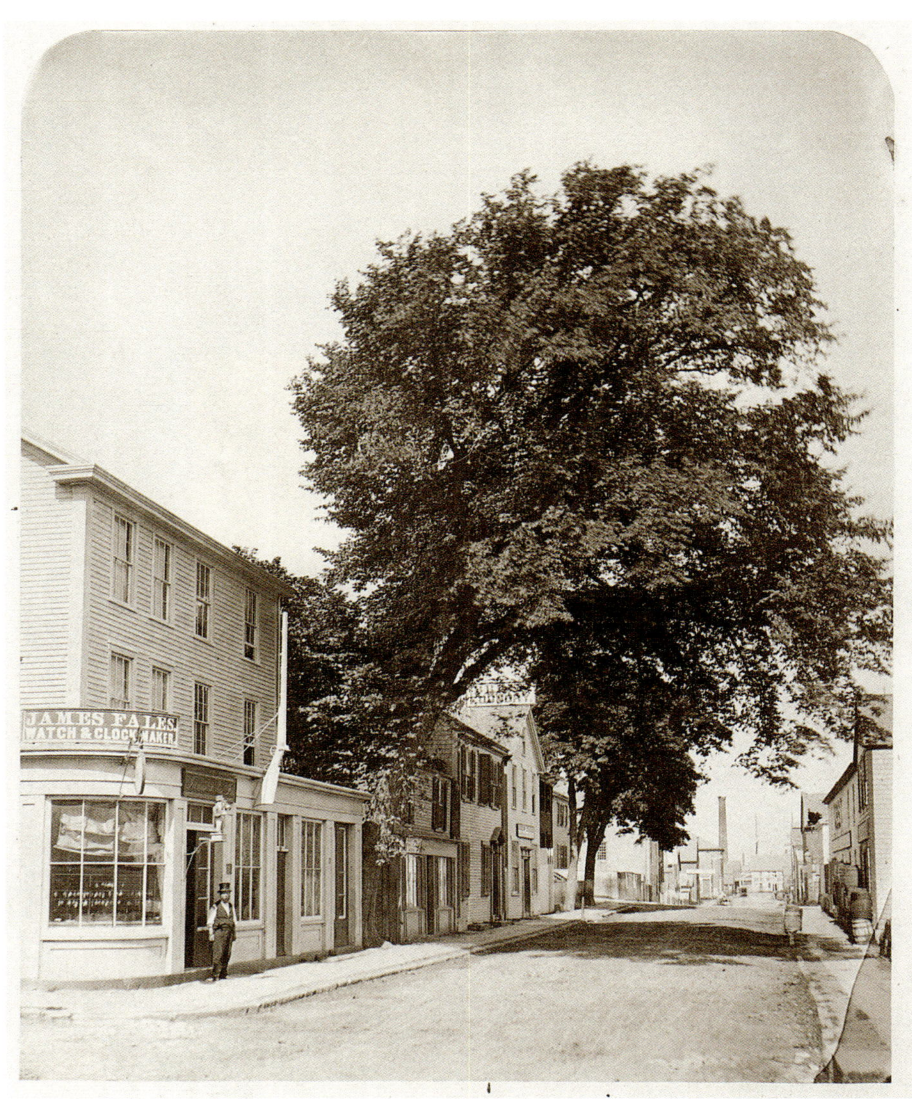

41 *Watch and Clockmaking Shop of James Fales, Jr.*, New Bedford, Mass., c. 1870. Photograph in the collection of The New Bedford Whaling Museum, Mass.

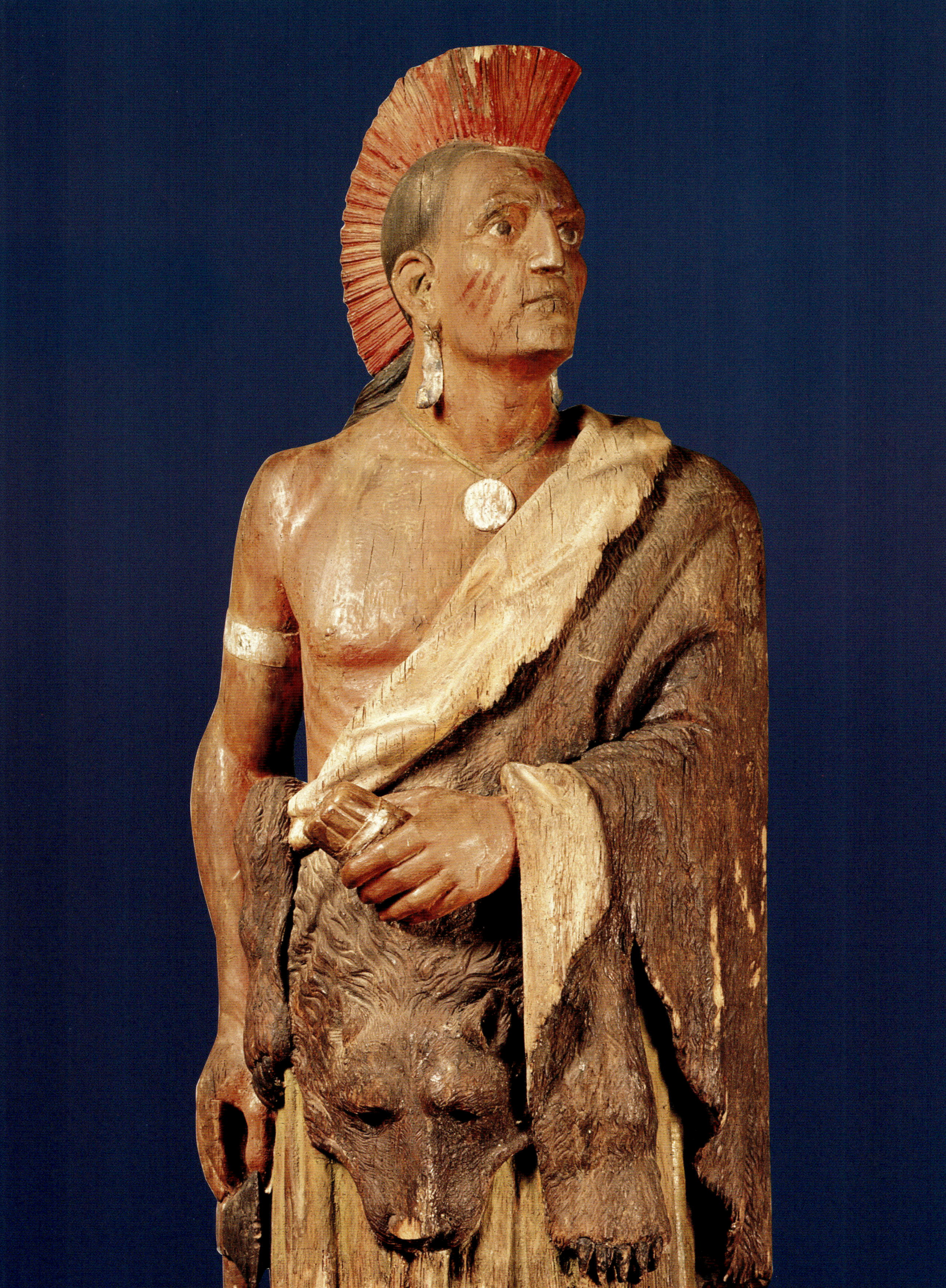

CHAPTER 3 WOODEN INDIANS AND NOBLE SAVAGES

ON MARCH 22, 1856, just four months after Henry Wadsworth Longfellow's poem "Hiawatha" was first published, the clipper *Minehaha* was launched at Donald McKay's East Boston shipyard. Its figurehead, carved by "Mr. Gleason," represented the celebrated English actress Julia Bennett Barrow as Minehaha, as she currently appeared in costume when giving readings from the poem in Boston and Salem. Among the guests at the "entertainment" held at McKay's home following the launch were the poet himself, Mrs. Barrow, General John S. Tyler, and "Col. Adams." After a series of remarks and well wishes for the success of the ship and its owner, Mrs. Barrow recited passages from the poem. Throughout the evening, "Both [Longfellow and Barrow] were complimented by sentiments which elicited the warm applause of the company."[1]

Besides affording a glimpse of a fashionable Boston social event, this anecdote highlights some important aspects of the relationship between art, commerce, and shipcarving in mid-century America. Shipbuilder, poet, and actress gathered to celebrate an important community event—the launching of a new ship—and were united in their mutual appreciation of their various accomplishments. McKay no doubt wished to honor Longfellow's poem and Barrow's interpretation of it through his choice of Minehaha as the name of his clipper, but he must also have calculated that their popularity with the press and public would bring the maximum amount of favorable publicity to his new commercial venture. His prestige and that of his ship would be increased by association with these well-known celebrities, both of whom in turn benefited from the accolades bestowed upon them by Boston's leading shipbuilder and the other prominent citizens who had gathered that night.

At the center of the story is the image of the American Indian, in this case a figurehead that is also a theatrical portrait and a fictitious literary character.[2] Each of these types of representation of the Indian was popular at the time, and when used in combination, they were all the more effective in capturing public attention. This was particularly true in the East, which was not only the center of American commerce and culture, but was also an area where the "Indian problem" had already been settled. Far from the warfare and displacement that was taking place further west, easterners could more comfortably contemplate the Indian's imagined past and uncertain future than could those who were in closer contact with independent Native communities that were still resisting the encroachment of soldiers and settlers.

White America expressed its ambivalent feelings about Indians in a variety of ways in the nineteenth century, most of which had evolved from European precedents. The image of the American Indian continued to function as a national symbol of sorts, for example—a role that it had played since the earliest days of

42 Detail of plate 47

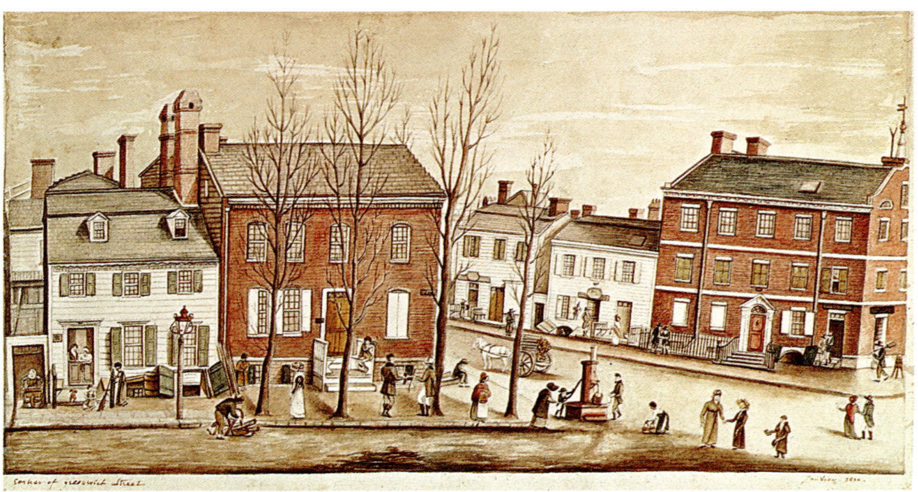

43 Baroness Hyde de Neuville (French, c. 1779–1849), *Corner of Greenwich Street, January 1810*, 1810. Watercolor on paper, 7 5/16 x 13 1/16 in. (18.5 x 33.3 cm). I. N. Phelps Stokes Collection, Miriam and Ira D. Wallach Division of Art, Prints, and Photographs, The New York Public Library, Astor, Lenox, and Tilden Foundations

European discovery and conquest. As discussed earlier, the figure of the Native American was used by Europeans to represent the New World by the mid-sixteenth century. Indians embellished maps, prints, ceramics, textiles, and anything else inspired by the theme of America or the four continents. American colonists adopted the convention and made it their own, as graphically illustrated by the Boston Tea Party of 1773, during which a group of disgruntled merchants and patriots disguised themselves as Indians in order to protest British policy. By the early nineteenth century, other idealized images were competing for the title of national symbol, most notably the closely related personifications of the Goddess of Liberty and Columbia. Nevertheless, the figure of the American Indian maintained its symbolic importance through several stylistic changes and an increasing number of applications.[3]

As noted, English tobacconists were among the first to capitalize upon the image of the Native American. Black boys and Virginians, in reality highly fanciful combinations of Indians and Africans, were meant to represent the inhabitants of the New World and advertise shops that dispensed the "Indian weed." The extent to which this type of figure was used in the American colonies is unknown, although it is reasonable to assume that merchants employed them in some of the larger port towns. The earliest visual evidence of the use of a tobacconist Indian in America appears in a watercolor of the corner of Greenwich and Dey Streets in New York City, done by the Baroness Hyde de Neuville (c. 1779–1849) in January 1810. The painting shows a small Indian figure prominently displayed outside a tobacco shop, the second building from the right (plate 43).[4]

As for figures themselves, the oldest known example of an American cigar-store Indian is a piece with a long history in Albany, New York, that is usually dated around 1810 (plate 44). A representation of it that appeared in an advertisement for Caldwell and Solomons Tobacco and Snuff Store in the November 17, 1817, issue of the *Albany Gazette and Daily Advertiser* documents its existence (plate 45). In 1823, the figure was repainted by Ezra Ames, who recorded in his account book that he charged "Mr. Solomon" for "painting an Indian statue."[5]

It is entirely likely that the figure was carved several decades earlier than 1810, though, as it is executed in a generally Baroque style more typical of the eighteenth century. The deeply carved tunic and cape, along with the prominence of details of costuming and accessories give it a Rococo exuberance that was out of date by the early nineteenth century. It may be a late example of the style, or it may have been featured in the Caldwell and Solomons advertisement because it was a well-known local landmark that had been on the streets of Albany for many years.

Because Neoclassicism, the most up-to-date mode in America in the first decades of the nineteenth century, was primarily concerned with ancient Greece and Rome, and the virtues of "calm grandeur and noble simplicity" as defined by the eighteenth-century German art historian, Johann Winckelmann, the image of the American Indian was less appropriate in and of itself, unless modified to conform to this emphasis on Old World classicism. This was easily accomplished in the fine arts, and the Indian did in fact figure into Neoclassical philosophy as the stoic, moral Noble Savage who lived a simple life close to nature, just as the ancient Greeks were imagined to have done.

The famous story of Benjamin West (1738–1820) and his first encounter with the *Apollo Belvedere* is a case in point. While probably apocryphal, the anecdote is nonetheless significant for what it reveals about contemporary attitudes. Shortly after arriving in Rome, West was supposedly taken to see the statue by Cardinal Albani and a group of his friends. Upon viewing it, the artist remarked that it reminded him of a Mohawk warrior. His hosts were at first shocked that he found a resemblance between this sublime icon of classicism and a foreign savage, but after learning of the rustic nobility and pastoral virtues of the Mohawks, they agreed that it was an apt comparison.[6]

West used American Indians in several of his paintings, but none is more appropriate for our purposes than his *Penn's Treaty with the Indians* of 1771–72 (plate 46). The moment depicted in this Neoclassical composition is one in which the leaders of two different races meet in harmony to forge an agreement that will benefit both and allow for the peaceful and orderly development of the promised land of Pennsylvania. Although a Native American artist would have no doubt interpreted the scene quite differently, West's image resonated through American culture for decades, as seen in Edward Hicks's paintings by the same name. In all, Hicks (1780–1849) painted thirteen versions of *Penn's Treaty with the Indians.* He probably based his picture on an engraving by John Hall, published by John Boydell of London in 1775.[7]

Elements of Neoclassicism profoundly affected the depiction of nineteenth-century cigar-store Indians, although they were rarely incorporated without some modification. One of the finest examples of this is *Chief Black Hawk*, believed to have been carved in New York City around 1848 for J. C. Baumberger, the Swiss consul in Louisville, Kentucky (plate 47). The piece stood in front of three different cigar stores in Louisville until purchased by a New York real-estate developer in 1926.[8] In his pose and togalike costume, this highly individualized carving of a nineteenth-century Indian warrior transmits the distinct impression of a Roman senator. On the other hand, his scalp lock and the catamount pelt draped over his shoulder are contemporary features that provide him with a more modern identity.[9]

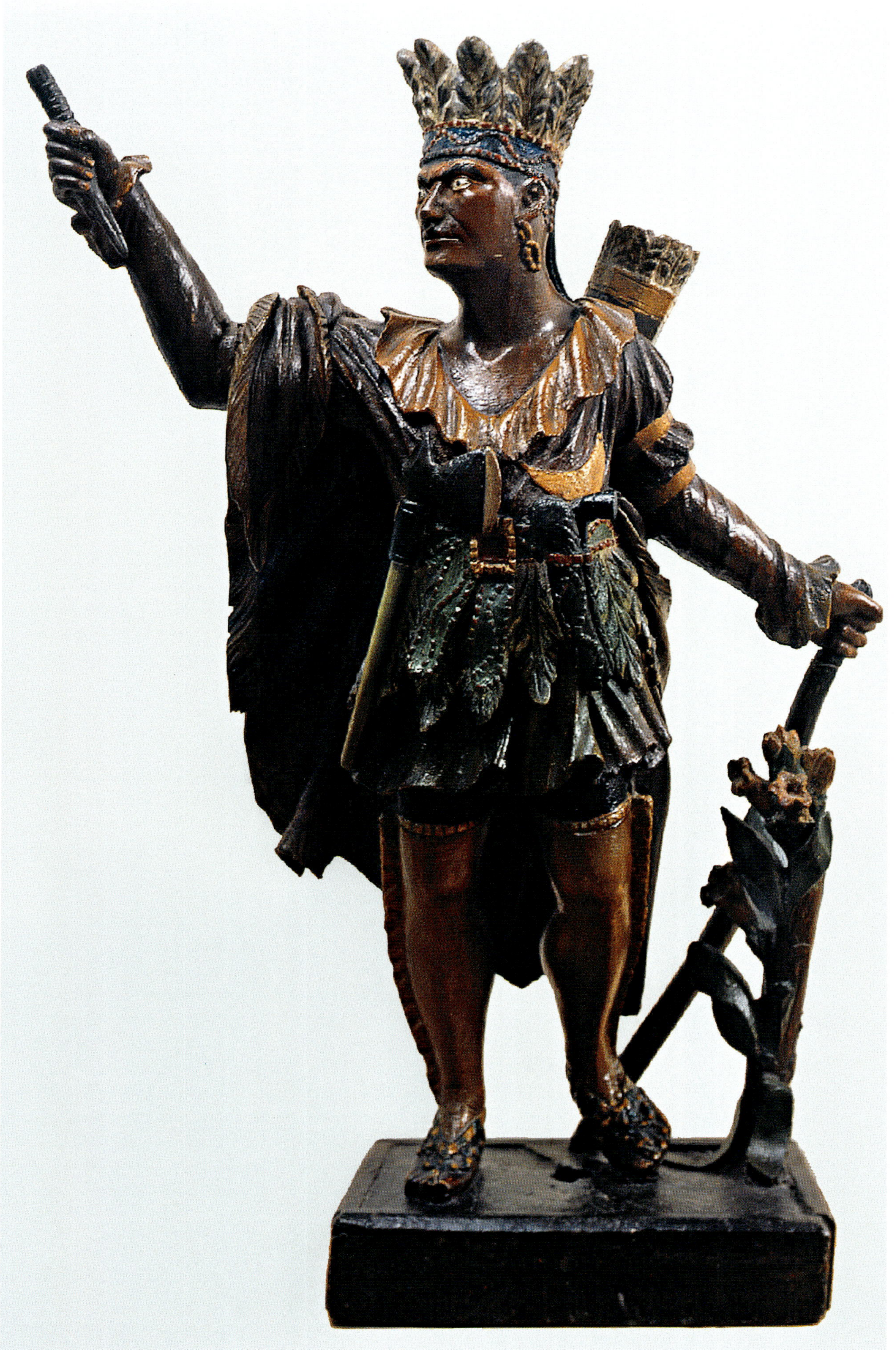

44 (OPPOSITE) *Indian*, probably Albany or New York, c. 1810. Painted wood, 31 3/4 x 21 1/2 x 16 in. (34.3 x 54.6 x 40.6 cm). Private collection

45 (BELOW) Advertisement for Caldwell and Solomons Tobacco and Snuff Store, *Albany Gazette and Daily Advertiser*, 17 Nov. 1817

Gods and goddesses in a modified Neoclassical style were also popular subjects at the time, as seen in a figure of *Mercury*, carved around 1830 and attributed to William Rush (plate 48). The figure stood in front of John Foble's Tobacco Store in Cambridge, Maryland, from about 1830 to 1926, when it was given to the Maryland Historical Society in Baltimore. As the patron of commerce and messenger of the gods, Mercury is an appropriate choice for a tobacconist's sign. Then again, the store owner may have simply wanted a distinctive figure carved in the latest style. The details of *Mercury*'s costume are crisply rendered, while the attention to anatomical details seen in the musculature of the neck and legs mark it as the work of a master like Rush. Compared to the Albany Indian discussed above, its shallower and more realistic carving illustrates an important stylistic development that we have also seen in figureheads of the period.

As up-to-date as Mr. Foble may have wished to be, however, by the time he placed his *Mercury* in front of his shop, a new stylistic and philosophical trend that had been circulating in intellectual circles in Europe for several decades was challenging Neoclassicism's dominance and gaining wide currency in America. Known generally as Romanticism, it is particularly important to this discussion because it radically altered the popular conception of the American Indian, introducing new elements into literary and artistic characterizations of the Noble Savage.

Whereas the imaginary Indian of the eighteenth century was a combination of the ancient stoic of Neoclassicism and the natural, rational man of Enlightenment philosophy, his nineteenth-century counterpart gained the more emotional and melancholic personality of a romantic hero on an inevitable course of destruction due to forces beyond his control. If the Indian had previously stood apart from the decadence of Western civilization and offered a model for its salvation, he was now caught in its clutches, a hapless victim of progress and one of the last remaining members of a vanishing race.[10]

The figure of the American Indian was in fact central to the development of the literary and artistic genres of Romanticism. His role can be traced to the first stirrings of the movement, as seen, for example, in Benjamin West's *Death of General Wolfe* (1770; National Gallery of Canada, Ottawa) and Joseph Wright's *Indian Widow* (1785; Derby Museum and Art Gallery, Derby, England), both of which fuse elements of Neoclassicism and Romanticism in dramatic, emotionally charged canvases.[11]

As for literature, Alexander Pope's *An Essay on Man* of 1733–34 provides an important early point of reference. While Pope was an eighteenth-century Humanist and not a Romantic, his poem incorporated certain motifs and imagery that have a definite romantic tinge to them. A stanza from epistle 1, part 3, is particularly significant, as its opening lines achieved widespread recognition in England and America, becoming one of the most frequently quoted characterizations of the American Indian until the end of the nineteenth century. They read:

> Lo! the poor Indian, whose untutored mind
> Sees God in clouds, or hears him in the wind;
> His soul proud Science never taught to stray
> Far as the solar walk or milky way;[12]

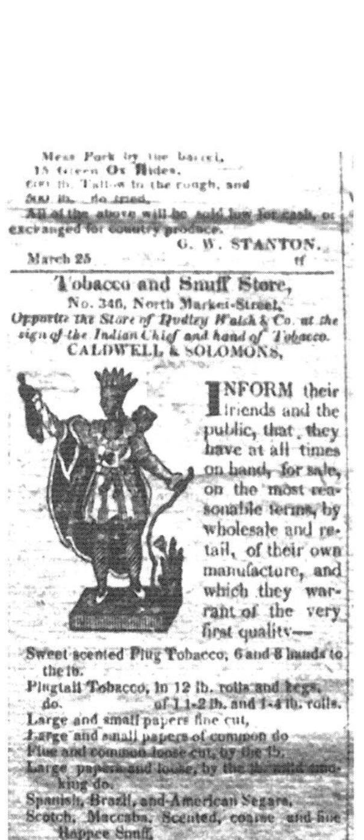

Mess Pork by the barrel,
15 Green Ox Hides.
exchanged for country produce.
G. W. STANTON.
March 25 tf

Tobacco and Snuff Store,
No. 346, North Market-Street,
Opposite the Store of Dudley Walsh & Co. at the sign of the Indian Chief and hand of Tobacco.
CALDWELL & SOLOMONS,

INFORM their friends and the public, that they have at all times on hand, for sale, on the most reasonable terms, by wholesale and retail, of their own manufacture, and which they warrant of the very first quality—

Sweet scented Plug Tobacco, 6 and 8 hands to the lb.
Pigtail Tobacco, in 12 lb. rolls and kegs,
do. of 1 1-2 lb. and 1-4 lb. rolls.
Large and small papers fine cut,
Large and small papers of common do
Fine and common loose cut, by the lb.
Spanish, Brazil, and American Segars,
Scotch, Maccaba, Scented, coarse and fine Rappee Snuff,
Ladies Twist,
Carrot Tobacco, and North West Twist,
Chocolate, Pearl Barley, Split Pease, and Cocoa Shells
April 20

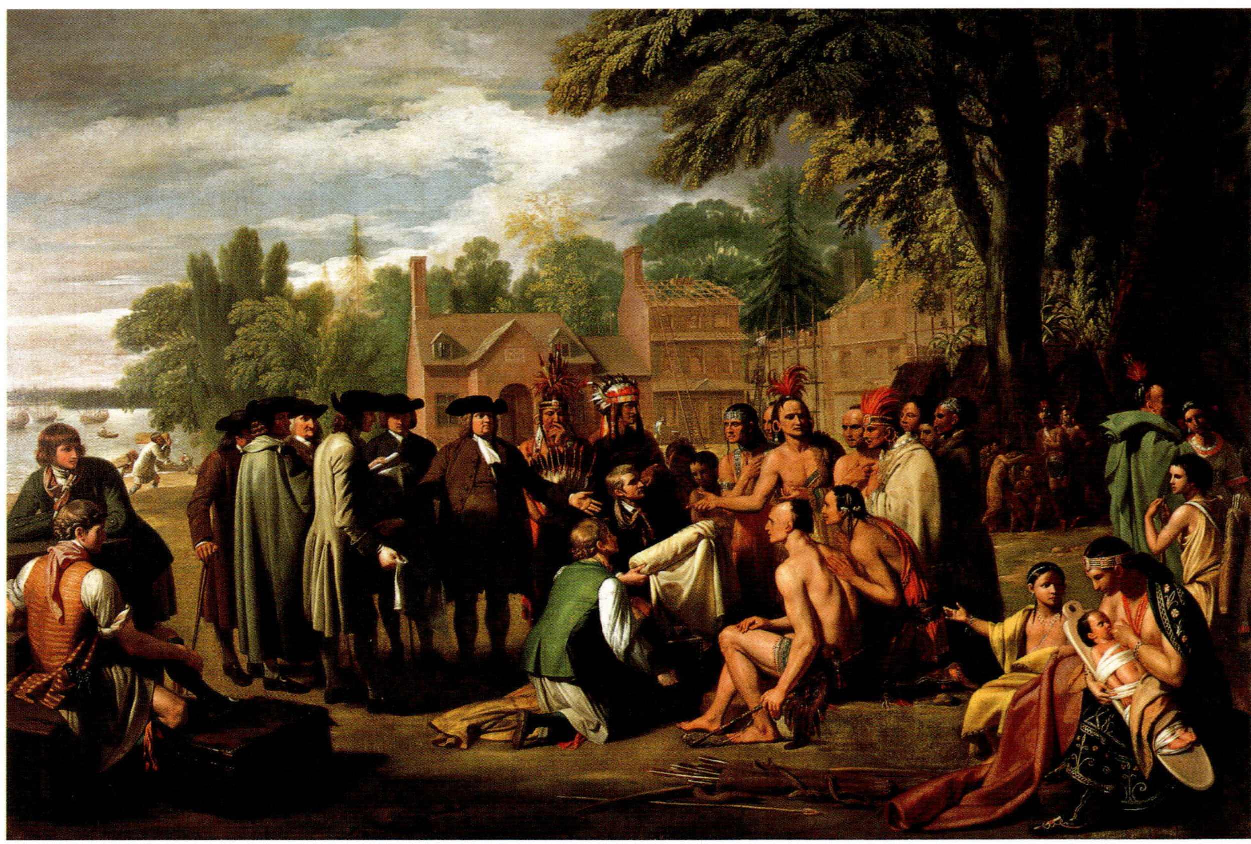

46 Benjamin West (American, 1738–1820), *Penn's Treaty with the Indians*, 1771–72. Oil on canvas, $75^{1}/_{2}$ x $107^{3}/_{4}$ in. (191.8 x 273.7 cm). Pennsylvania Academy of the Fine Arts, Philadelphia. Gift of Mrs. Sarah Harrison (The Joseph Harrison, Jr. Collection)

The first phrase, "Lo! the poor Indian," was so ubiquitous, in fact, that many cigar-store Indians were nicknamed "Lo," and the reference appeared in the titles of a number of articles about them.

In the United States, the poems of Philip Freneau were the first to develop the image of the romantic Noble Savage and his tragic destiny. Among them were "The Prophecy of King Tammany" (1782), "The Dying Indian" (1784), and "The Indian Burying Ground" (1788).[13] Underlying these and other works was the image of the rational, enlightened savage who began to sense his fate and the futility of resistance in the face of the onslaught of a superior civilization. As he did, he became an object of compassion, nostalgia, and sentimentalism, the perfect vehicle for romantic sensibilities.

This new definition of the Indian proved to be very appealing to European and American audiences, particularly after the appearance in 1801 of François-René de Chateaubriand's *Atala*, which is perhaps the single most influential work in the popularization of the romantic conception of Noble Savage. Set in the Mississippi River Valley in the late seventeenth century, it is the story of two star-crossed lovers, Chactas, a member of the Natchez tribe, and Atala, the Christianized, half-Indian daughter of a chief of their sworn enemies, the Muscogee. Escaping torture and certain death, Chactas and Atala journey through mysterious forests and primeval landscapes to reach the Mission of the friendly Père Aubry, only

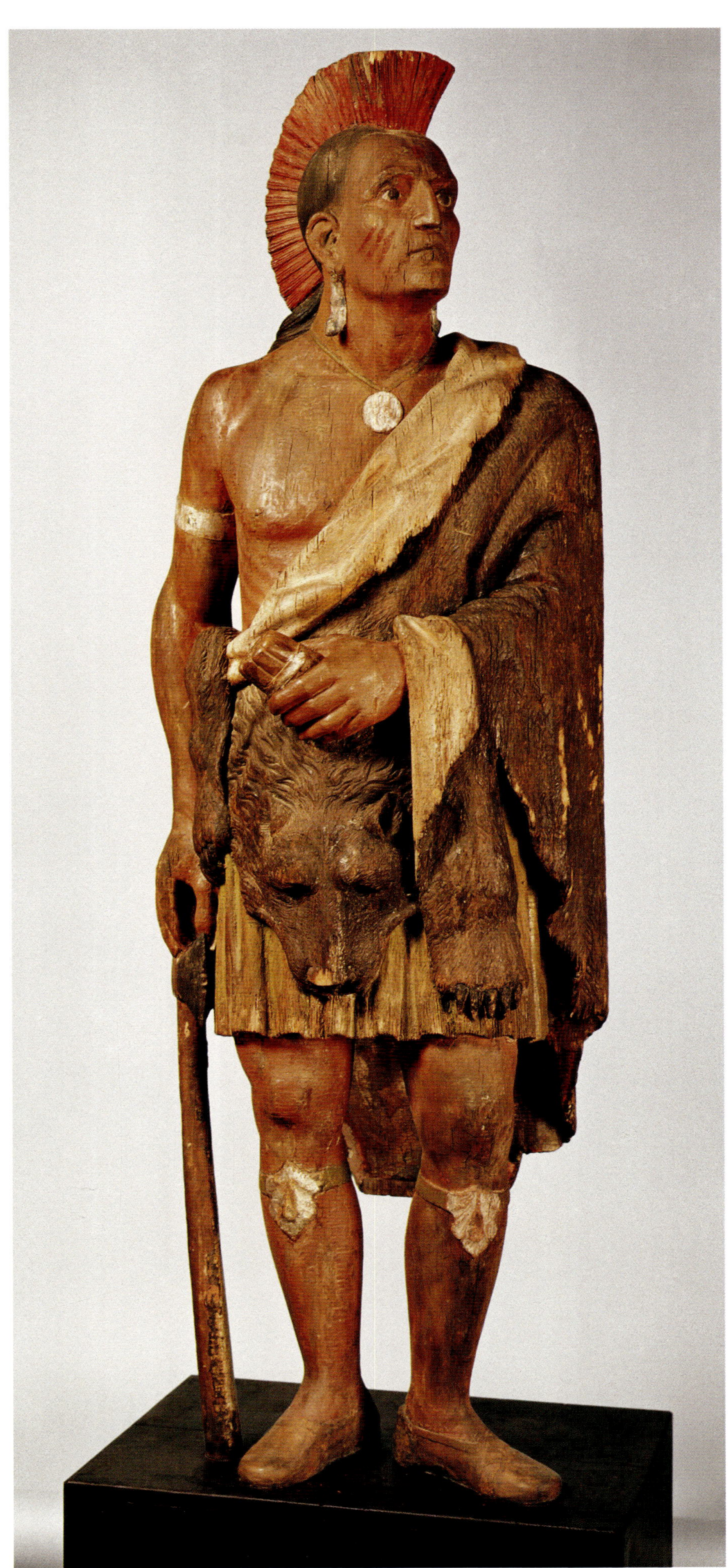

47 *Chief Black Hawk*, probably New York, c. 1848. Painted wood, $80^{1}/_{2} \times 26^{1}/_{2} \times 19$ in. (204.5 x 67.3 x 28.2 cm). Heritage Museums and Gardens, Sandwich, Mass.

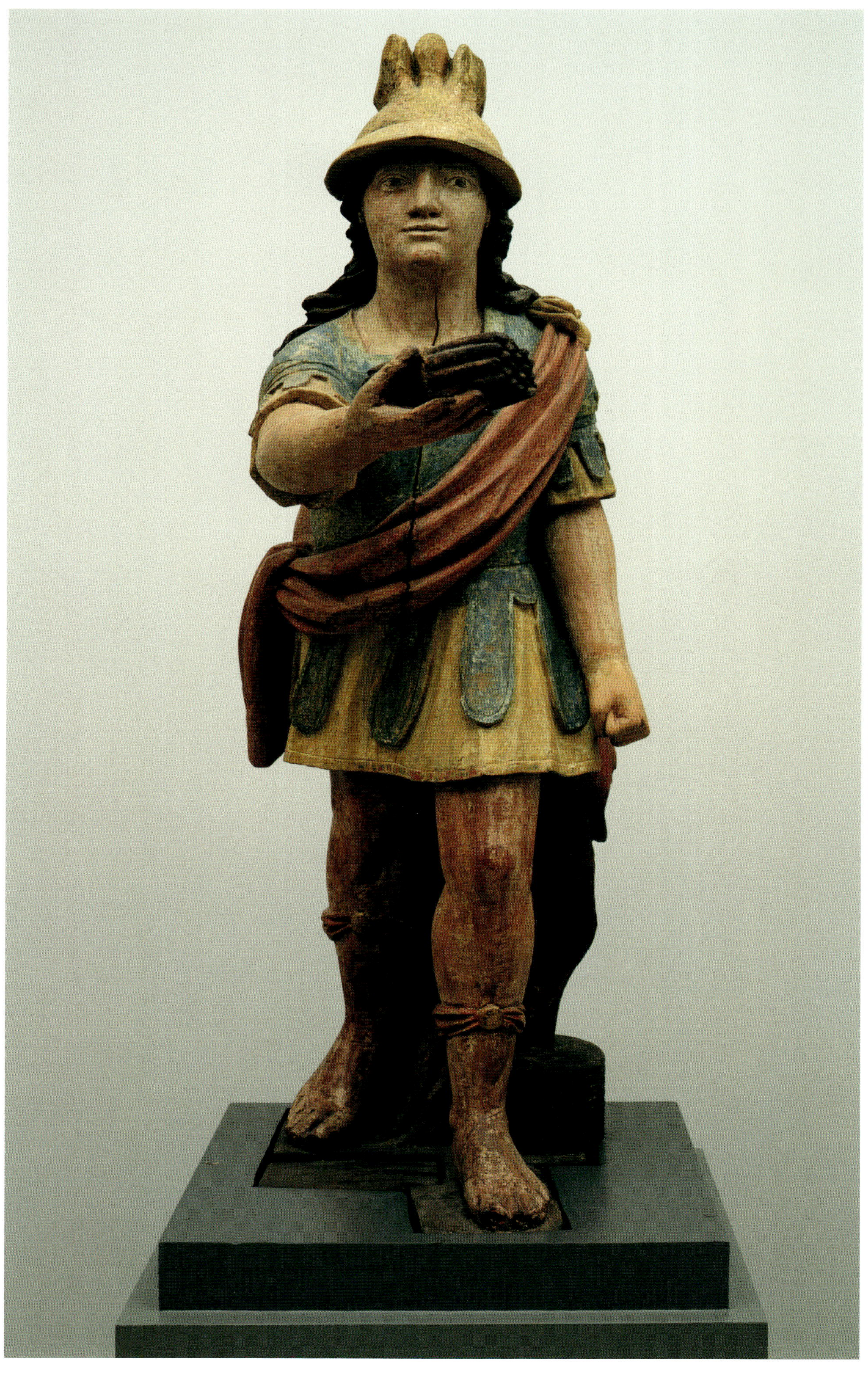

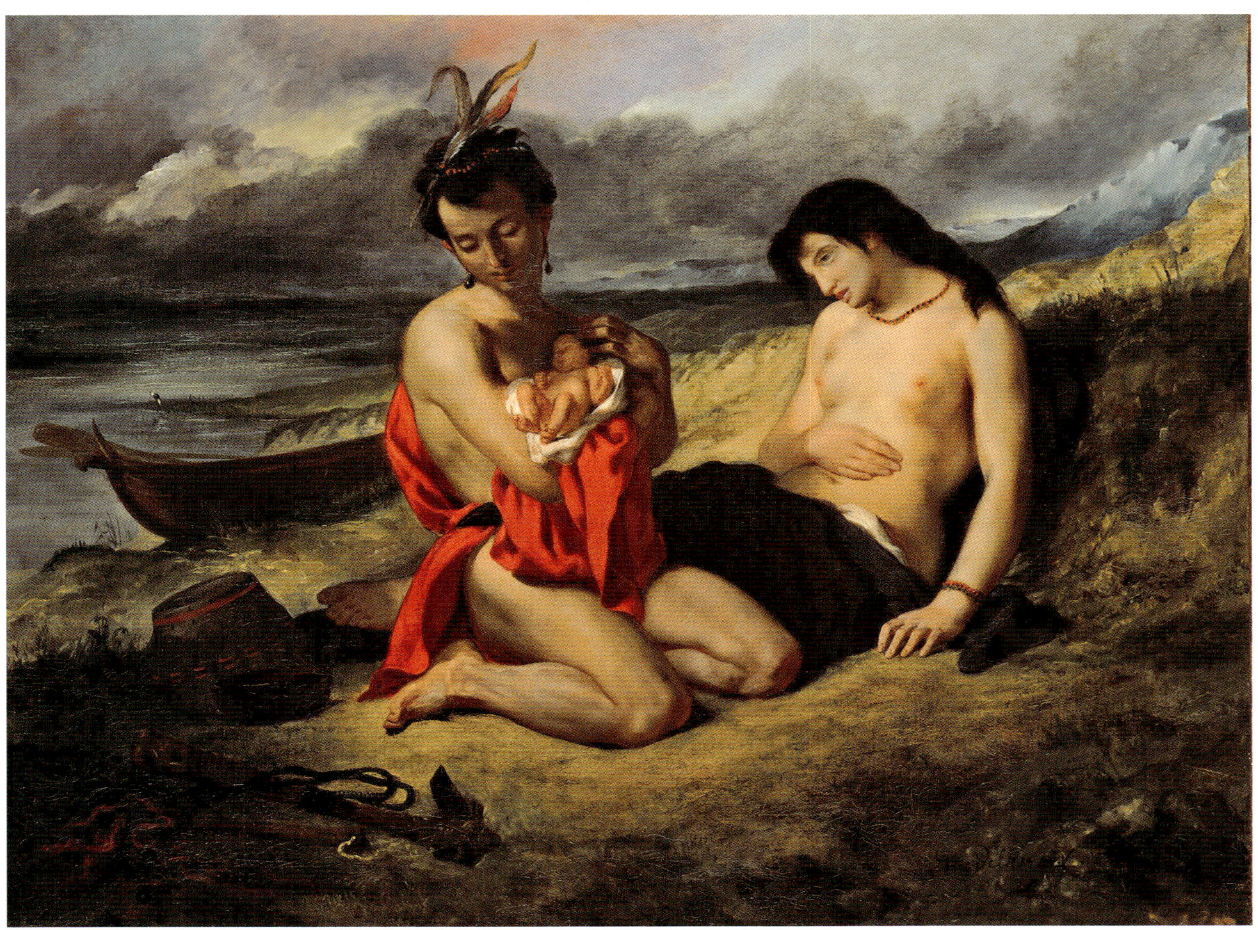

48 (OPPOSITE) Attributed to William Rush, *Mercury*, Philadelphia, c. 1830. Painted wood, 38 x 10½ x 15 in. (96.5 x 26.7 x 38.1 cm). The Maryland Historical Society, Baltimore

49 (ABOVE) Eugène Delacroix (French, 1798–1863), *The Natchez*, 1824–35. Oil on canvas, 35½ x 46 in. (90.1 x 116.8 cm). The Metropolitan Museum of Art, New York. Purchase, Gifts of George N. and Helen M. Richard and Mr. and Mrs. Charles S. McVeigh and Bequest of Emma A. Sheafer, by exchange, 1989 (1989.328)

to have Atala reveal that she has poisoned herself in order to avoid temptation and fulfill a vow of chastity taken as her mother's dying wish.[14] The novel was an immediate success and went through eleven editions between 1801 and 1805, while also inspiring countless imitators and a long line of paintings, prints, and statues based on its most touching moments.[15]

The most famous of these is undoubtedly the painting *The Burial of Atala* (1808; Musée du Louvre, Paris), by Anne-Louis Girodet-Trioson (1767–1824), which depicts a classicized Chactas and hooded Père Aubry lowering an angelic Atala into her grave. Another well-known depiction is *The Natchez*, of 1824–35, by Eugène Delacroix (1798–1863) (plate 49). In this case, the artist based his painting on an episode found in the story's epilogue, in which the scene shifts to the present day, that is, the late eighteenth century. The narrator tells of his encounter with an Indian couple at Niagara who are lamenting the death of their newborn child. They provide the details of Chactas's later life and Père Aubry's martyrdom at the hands of the Cherokee. The reader is also informed that they are the last of the Natchez, the sole survivors of a once-proud tribe.[16]

This theme of the American Indian as a member of a vanishing race became a dominant one that was repeated countless times throughout the nineteenth century. Although at first more popular in Europe, it had gained wide acceptance in the eastern United States by mid-century, not long after the first reservations had been created and the official policy of removal to the West had taken effect. For many white Americans, the Indian was a figure of curiosity and nostalgia, and what better way to indulge sentimental notions and perhaps assuage underlying feelings of guilt than to cloak him in the mysterious aura of a fallen romantic hero? As the original inhabitant of the New World, he was, after all, the perfect vehicle for expressing nationalistic sentiments in a country that was searching to establish its identity and distinguish itself from Europe. No longer a direct threat, the Indian was a picturesque detail that evoked visions of the primeval bounty of the promised land of America. An editorial that appeared in 1856 in the American art journal *Crayon* expressed several of these ideas:

> It seems to us that the Indian has not received justice in American art. . . . It should be held in dutiful remembrance that he is fast passing away from the face of the earth. Soon the last red man will have faded forever from his native land, and those who come after us will trust to our scanty records for their knowledge of his habits and appearance. . . . Seen in his primitive garb, the wild, untamed denizen of an unknown country, he is a sublimely eloquent representative of the hidden resources, and the mental solitude of the uncivilized wilderness.

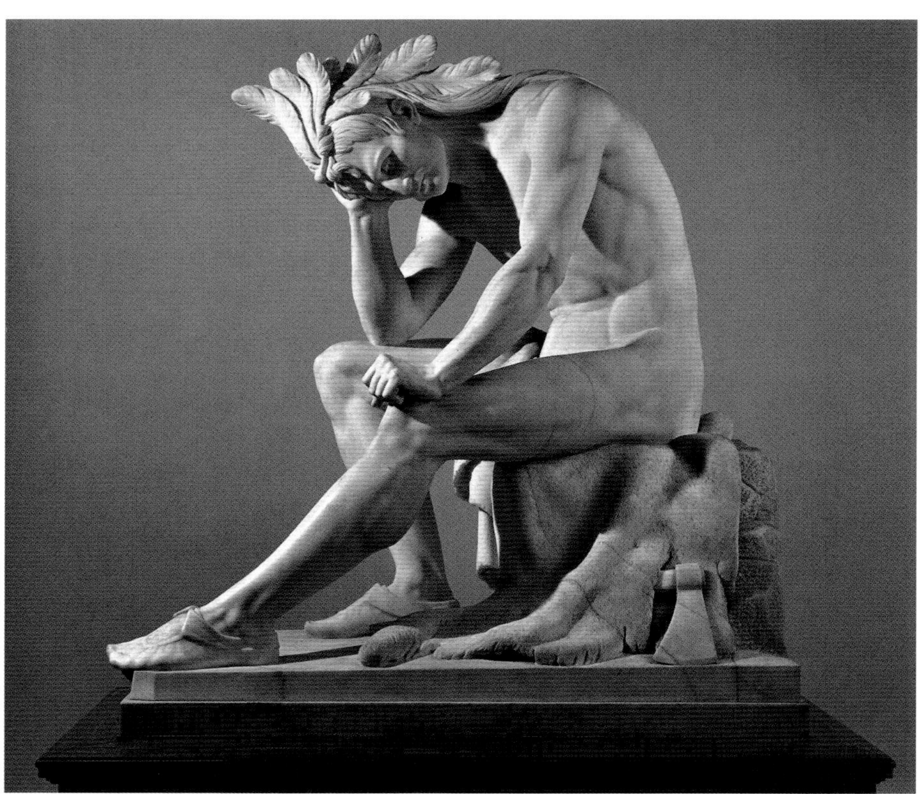

50 Thomas Crawford (American, 1813–1857), *Dying Chief Contemplating the Progress of Civilization*, 1856. Marble, height 55 in. (139.7 cm). The New-York Historical Society, New York (1875.4)

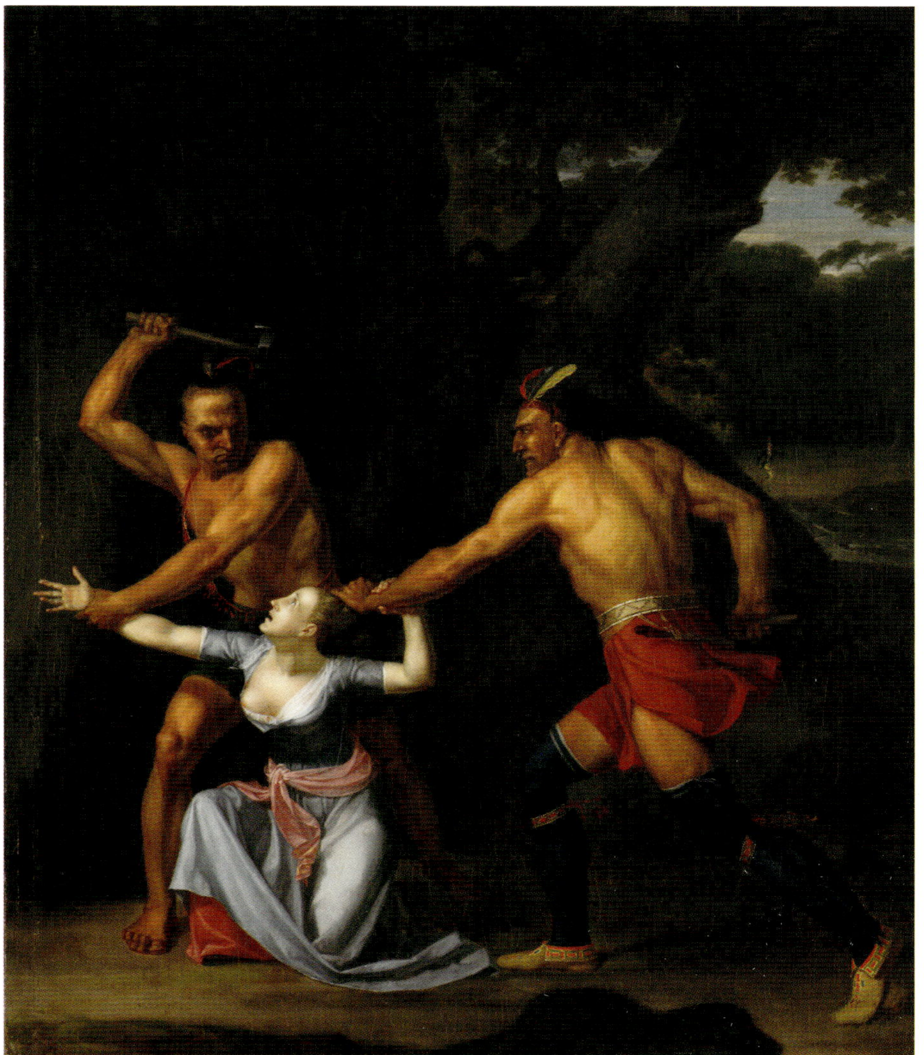

51 John Vanderlyn (American, 1775–1852), *The Murder of Jane McCrea*, 1803–4. Oil on canvas, 32 1/2 x 26 1/2 in. (82.5 x 67.3 cm). Wadsworth Atheneum, Hartford, Conn. Purchased by the Wadsworth Atheneum

> The Indian, reposing at night by his campfire, or seen in the energy of his fiercest fight, sulking behind logs and trees, stealthily tracing his enemies' path in the leaves and bushes, grouped in council or roving in solitude—in all these positions, and in hundreds of others, is eminently picturesque and interesting. As an accessory in landscape, the Indian may be used with great effect. He is at home in every scene of primitive country. Picture them marching "Indian file," winding silently along through the light and shade of some grand old primitive forest.[17]

The writer has presented us with a catalogue of stereotypical images of the imaginary Indian. In another section of the essay, he considers the many visual possibilities presented to artists by the colonial Indian wars. While discussing King Philip's War, he describes the chief as "the solitary warrior, in an open clear-

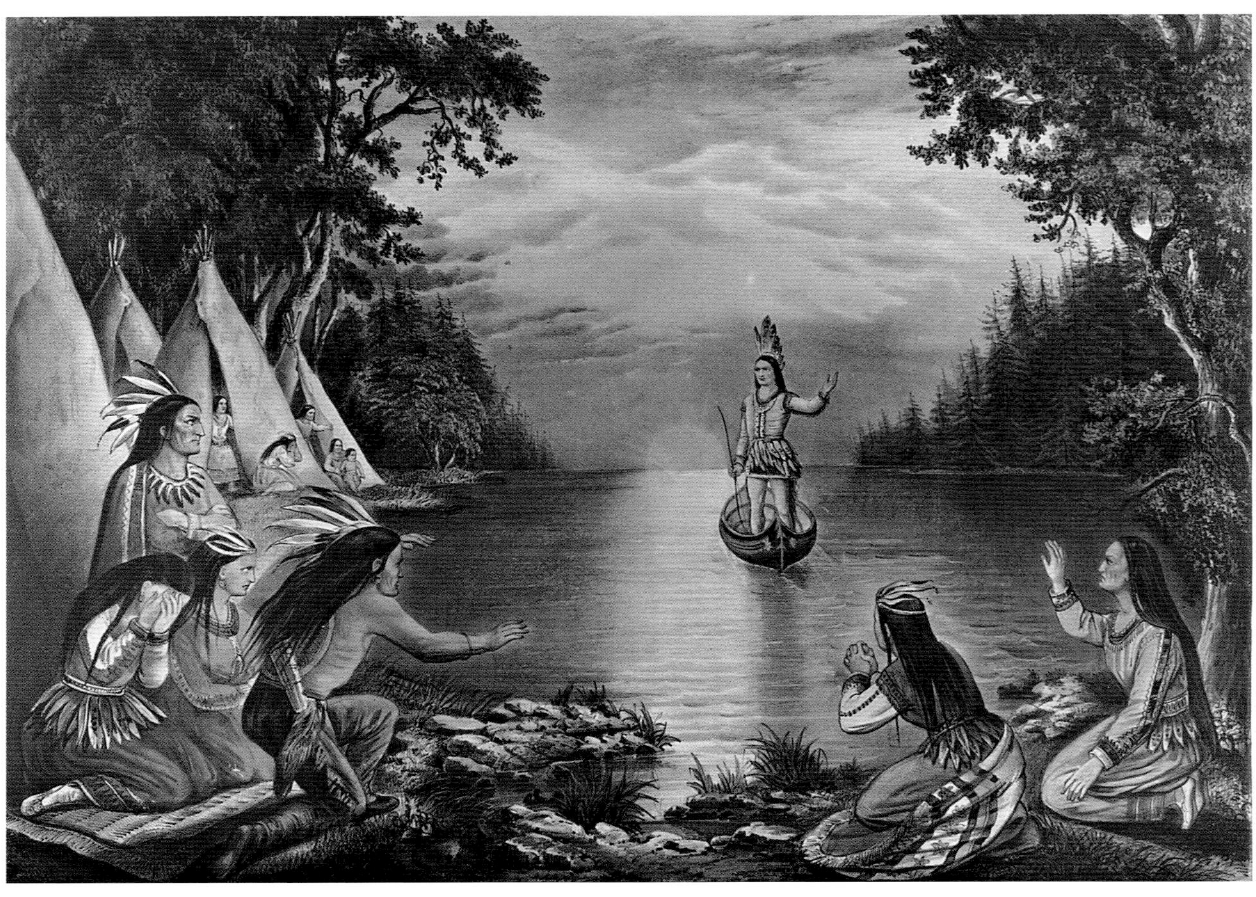

52 *Hiawatha's Departure*, 1868. Lithograph, 15 x 20 1/2 in. (38.1 x 52 cm). Published by Currier and Ives, New York. Museum of the City of New York. The Harry T. Peters Collection (56.300.81)

ing, seated on a stump, his face buried in his hands, brooding over the fallen fortunes of his country." This motif of the melancholic Indian chief seated with his chin supported by a bent arm is the nineteenth-century Noble Savage par excellence. It was used in a wide range of literary and visual representations, including Thomas Crawford's *Dying Chief Contemplating the Progress of Civilization*, which was designed for the Senate pediment of the United States Capitol and completed in 1856, the same year that the *Crayon* article was published (plate 50). The image has a long history in Western art, and can ultimately be traced to the seated angel in the 1541 engraving *Melancholia I* by Albrecht Dürer.[18]

As suggested in the passage from the *Crayon*, however, the Noble Savage was only one-half of the equation. His counterpart, the "ignoble savage" or bad Indian, was the treacherous warrior "sulking behind logs and trees" and engaged in his "fiercest fight." He was the terrifying presence of the frontier, the bloodthirsty demon who attacked isolated cabins and lay in wait for defenseless travelers. In the safety of a comfortable eastern home, his exploits could send a romantic chill up the spine of a reader, or serve as intellectual justification for the government's Indian policy. He, too, could be found in a variety of melodramatic guises, from a caricature of a degraded savage to an idealized conception of dangers of the primeval forest. As for the latter of these, *The Murder of Jane McCrea* of 1803–4 by John Vanderlyn (1775–1852) is certainly one of the most influential images of the bad Indian in American art (plate 51).

The painting is based upon an incident that occurred in upstate New York in the summer of 1777. Jane McCrea, a Tory from New Jersey, was being escorted through the woods near Lake George by a party of Indians on her way to meet her fiancé, a young British officer serving under General John Burgoyne. At some point, they met another group of Indians, a dispute broke out, and she was killed and scalped. The event was widely publicized and quickly seized upon by politicians and the press as a prime example of the atrocities committed by Indian mercenaries in British service. The ensuing controversy resulted in a major propaganda coup for the American cause, while the fact that the victim was an English sympathizer was conveniently forgotten.[19]

Originally commissioned by Joel Barlow as an illustration for his epic poem *Columbiad*, Vanderlyn's picture is a highly idealized conception of the actual incident, a fashionable Neoclassical composition with a strong dose of melodramatic Romanticism. The physiques and poses of the Indians are based on several antique precedents, while Miss McCrea is suitably exposed and vulnerable enough to evoke sympathy from even the most hard-hearted viewer. Painted in Paris, the picture was a great success at the annual Salon of 1804 and brought widespread recognition to the young American artist. It was then sent to New York, where it seems to have been received somewhat less enthusiastically.[20] Nevertheless, it was the first in a long series of nineteenth-century interpretations of the subject, some of which were based on Vanderlyn's painting, while others were derived from different sources. Paintings, prints, broadsides, and bookplates all celebrated this famous Revolutionary War incident.[21]

The point to be made here is that by the early nineteenth century, even representations of the bad Indian, presumably based on the dangerous foe who was still active on the Western frontier, were often highly romanticized in contemporary art and literature. Entire genres were based on the fictions of the good and bad Indian, an updated version of the eternal struggle between good and evil. The Noble Savage and his counterpart were useful for a variety of artistic, philosophical, and political purposes and were readily employed across a wide spectrum of issues and ideas.

In fact, the image of the good and bad Indian infused nineteenth-century American culture. While solid citizens like tobacco-store owners and shipcarvers may not have read the *Crayon* or kept up on the latest art from Paris, they were certainly familiar with Longfellow's *Hiawatha* and other representations of American Indians in popular literature and art.[22] Schoolchildren memorized passages from the famous poem, while adults devoured the novels of James Fenimore Cooper, whose *Leatherstocking Tales* of the 1820s, 1830s, and 1840s were international best-sellers. Cooper's characterizations of Hawkeye, the woodsman, Chinagachook and Uncas, the last of the Mohicans, and Magua, the evil Huron, became household names to generations of Americans.

Prints depicting Indian themes were also widely distributed. In 1858, for example, Currier and Ives published the first in a series of seven Hiawatha prints that were issued over a ten-year period. *Hiawatha's Departure*, which first

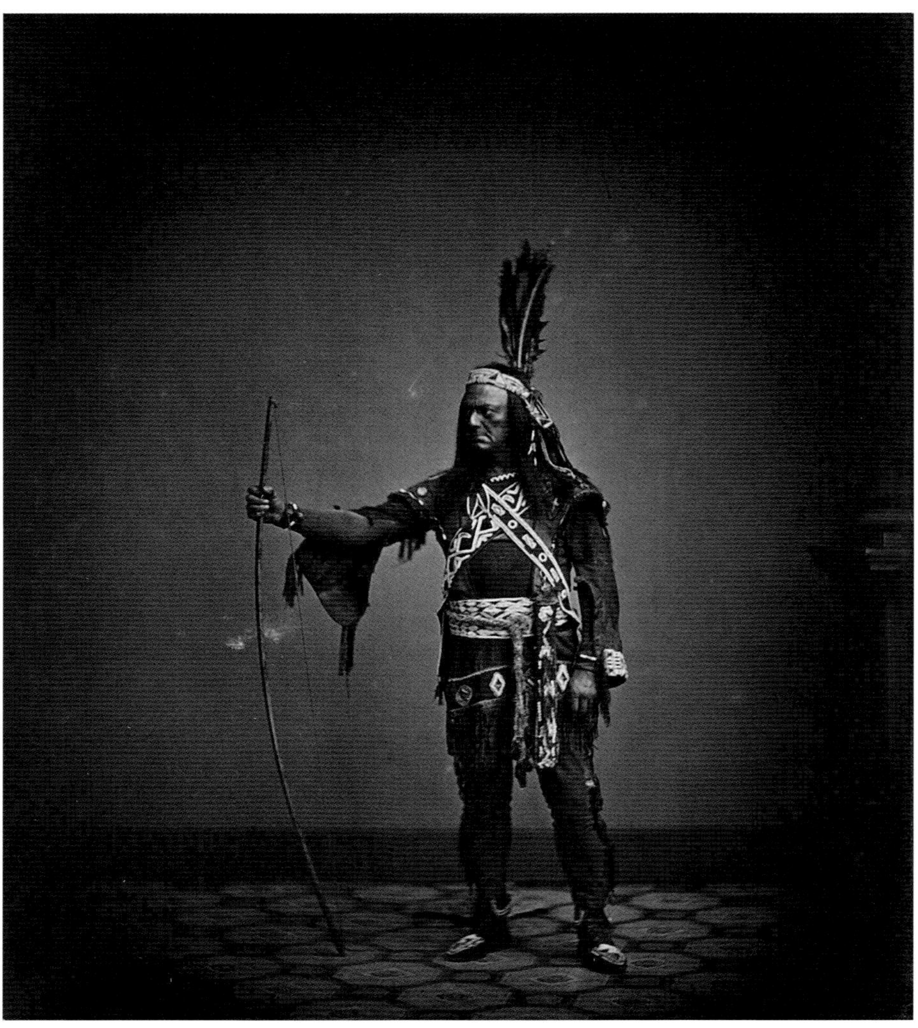

53 Mathew Brady (American, 1823–1896), *Edwin Forrest as Metamora*, 1861. Modern albumen silver print from glass-plate negative, 20 x 17 in. (50.8 x 43.2 cm). National Portrait Gallery, Smithsonian Institution, Washington, D.C. Gift of The Edwin Forrest Home

appeared in 1868, is particularly relevant to this discussion (plate 52). Standing in his canoe, the hero bids farewell to his people as he embarks on his final journey westward to the land of the setting sun. Viewers would have recognized the symbolism of the image, as well as the obvious allusion to American Indians as a vanishing race being forced to the West by the inexorable march of civilization.[23]

Another venue in which the Noble Savage made a frequent appearance was the theater. Indian melodramas were very popular in the East, and leading tragic actors found the figure of the Native American to be a perfect vehicle for wrenching emotions from eager audiences. One of the first such plays was a romantic tale of Pocahontas entitled *The Indian Princess; or, La Belle Sauvage: An Operatic Melo-Drame*, written by James Nelson Barker in 1808.[24]

The most successful and longest-running Indian play was John Augustus Stones's *Metamora; or, The Last of the Wampanoags*. In November 1828, the famous actor Edwin Forrest offered a sum of five hundred dollars and a part share for "the best tragedy, in five acts, of which the hero, or principal character, shall be

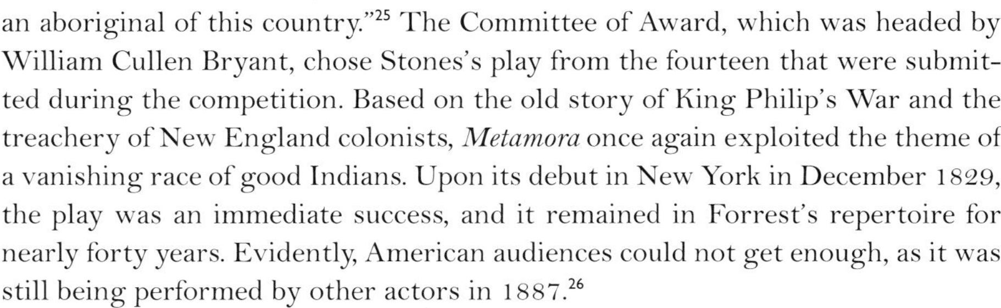

an aboriginal of this country."[25] The Committee of Award, which was headed by William Cullen Bryant, chose Stones's play from the fourteen that were submitted during the competition. Based on the old story of King Philip's War and the treachery of New England colonists, *Metamora* once again exploited the theme of a vanishing race of good Indians. Upon its debut in New York in December 1829, the play was an immediate success, and it remained in Forrest's repertoire for nearly forty years. Evidently, American audiences could not get enough, as it was still being performed by other actors in 1887.[26]

Forrest's characterization of *Metamora* inspired other works of art in a number of different media, including a theatrical portrait by Frederick Agate that was exhibited at the National Academy of Design in New York in 1833 and a photograph by Mathew Brady (1823–1896) taken in 1861 (plate 53). It also inspired at least one carver, as evidenced by a well-executed figure of the actor in costume that has "Metamora" inscribed on its base (plate 54). Although the original purpose of the piece is not known, it most likely served as a theater or shop sign.[27]

Another distinctive cigar-store figure rendered in the Noble Savage mode is a piece known as the *Breneiser Chief* (plate 55). Probably made in New York or Philadelphia, it stood in front of the tobacco shop and cigar manufactory of Charles Breneiser and Sons of Reading, Pennsylvania, for about seventy years.[28] Boldly carved, the figure is particularly notable for its details of costuming such as the sun disk that he wears around his neck, as well as the definition given to anatomical features in the chest and neck areas. The tobacco leaves in his left hand identify his purpose, but his pensive, faraway look indicates that his mind is not on his work. Even though he is not seated in the more traditional pose of the vanishing American, by resting his bent arm on a staff and his chin in his hand, the figure clearly references the familiar image of the solitary warrior contemplating the inevitable extinction of his race.

As for his counterpart, the bad Indian was one of the most popular of all cigar-store figures, particularly if he was represented as brandishing a raised tomahawk in a menacing gesture (plate 56). Contemporary accounts indicate that the type was a standard for much of the nineteenth century, even more common than some of the comely female figures that were generally rendered in the good Indian mode. A newspaper article about the production and popularity of cigar-store figures that first appeared in the *New York Sun* in 1886 quoted a carver as saying: "Oh, of course styles change, but the genuine old roving redskin with a bad eye and ugly-looking tomahawk in his hand is the stand-by—that is, in the majority of the eastern and middle states. . . . The plain old war-whoop savage of the plains is the only chap you can bank on as steadily trustworthy. Indian maidens do very well, but not so well as the fine old gore-drinking warriors, with feathers and meat axes."[29] Working within the prevailing stereotypes, then, the carvers responded to public demand by creating any number of variations on the theme of the bad Indian.

The example illustrated here is attributed to John L. Cromwell (1805–1873), one of the leading New York shipcarvers of his generation. For over thirty years, Cromwell operated shops in New York City's maritime district and is known to have completed a number of important shipcarving commissions. He actively

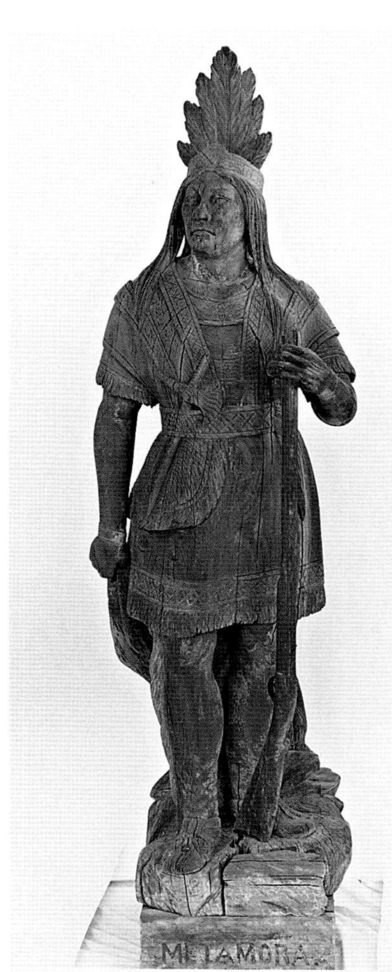

54 *Metamora*, probably Philadelphia, c. 1860. Painted wood, 78 x 20 x 22½ in. (198.1 x 50.8 x 57.1 cm). Brandywine River Museum, Chadds Ford, Pa. Gift of Mr. and Mrs. Harry G. Haskell, 1979

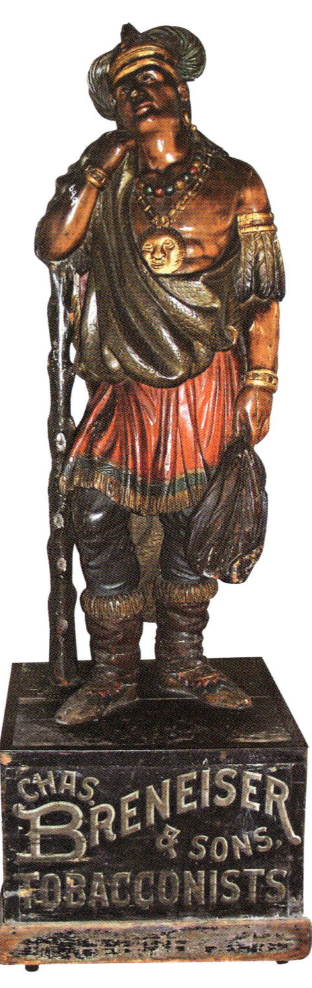

55 *Breneiser Chief*, probably New York or Philadelphia, c. 1860. Painted wood, height 78 in. (198.1 cm). Historical Society of Berks County, Reading, Pa.

diversified his business as well, not only by producing shop figures, but also by being one of the first shipcarvers to create decorations for circus wagons, a line of work that became an increasingly important source of income for many carvers as the century progressed.[30]

A photograph of the piece illustrated in plate 56 was published in 1948. The author noted that a previous owner claimed that it had been in his family's possession since 1857 and that many years earlier Cromwell's son had identified it as his father's work.[31] Assuming that this account is accurate, it represents a rare and significant piece of evidence that establishes the importance of Cromwell's role in the development of shop-figure carving in New York. The figure shows many typical features of a new type of work that was produced in New York City after mid-century.

The 1840s and 1850s were decades of innovation in American figure carving, as previously noted. In response to the emergence of the clipper ship and its distinctive bow, shipcarvers developed a new style of figurehead with a horizontal thrust and dynamic presence that matched the fast and sleek vessels. As stern carvings, taffrails, and other types of ship decoration were greatly reduced or eliminated altogether, the figurehead became the focus of the carver's creativity, resulting in some of the finest examples of the art ever produced in this country. It was perhaps inevitable that this burst of activity would influence other aspects of the shipcarver's repertoire as well. Shop and cigar-store figures are a case in point. While the older types of counter and half-lifesize figures continued to be popular, the carvers also began to produce a new kind of figure that quickly captured the public imagination and transformed a time-honored tradition into a Victorian fad.

Certainly, cigar-store Indians were already in widespread use in America by this time. A rare reference to their popularity appears in *Big Abel and the Little Manhattan*, a humorous tale written by Cornelius Mathews that was published in 1845. In it, a descendant of Henry Hudson and a member of the tribe that once inhabited the island walk the streets of New York to determine whether white men or Indians are the rightful owners. Upon seeing a cigar-store Indian in front of a store, Little Manhattan claims all the tobacconist shops with similar figures as his own, at which point, "Big Abel staggers at the recollection that the town is held in every part by such as these."[32]

By merging the tradition of lifesize or larger figureheads with that of the generally smaller shop figures, mid-century carvers created an imposing sculptural form that was readily adaptable to the rapidly expanding and increasingly competitive American business environment. In this they were again following English precedent, as full-size representations of Scotsmen had been used as tobacconist signs since the eighteenth century. The British figures were relatively few, however, compared to the burst of creativity that was about to ensue on this side of the Atlantic.

A comparison of three figures that were probably made within a few years of one another in the mid-1840s illustrates some of these stylistic developments. The first piece stood in front of the Maltzberger cigar store in Reading, Pennsylvania, from 1847 to 1928 (plate 57). By tradition, John Maltzberger pur-

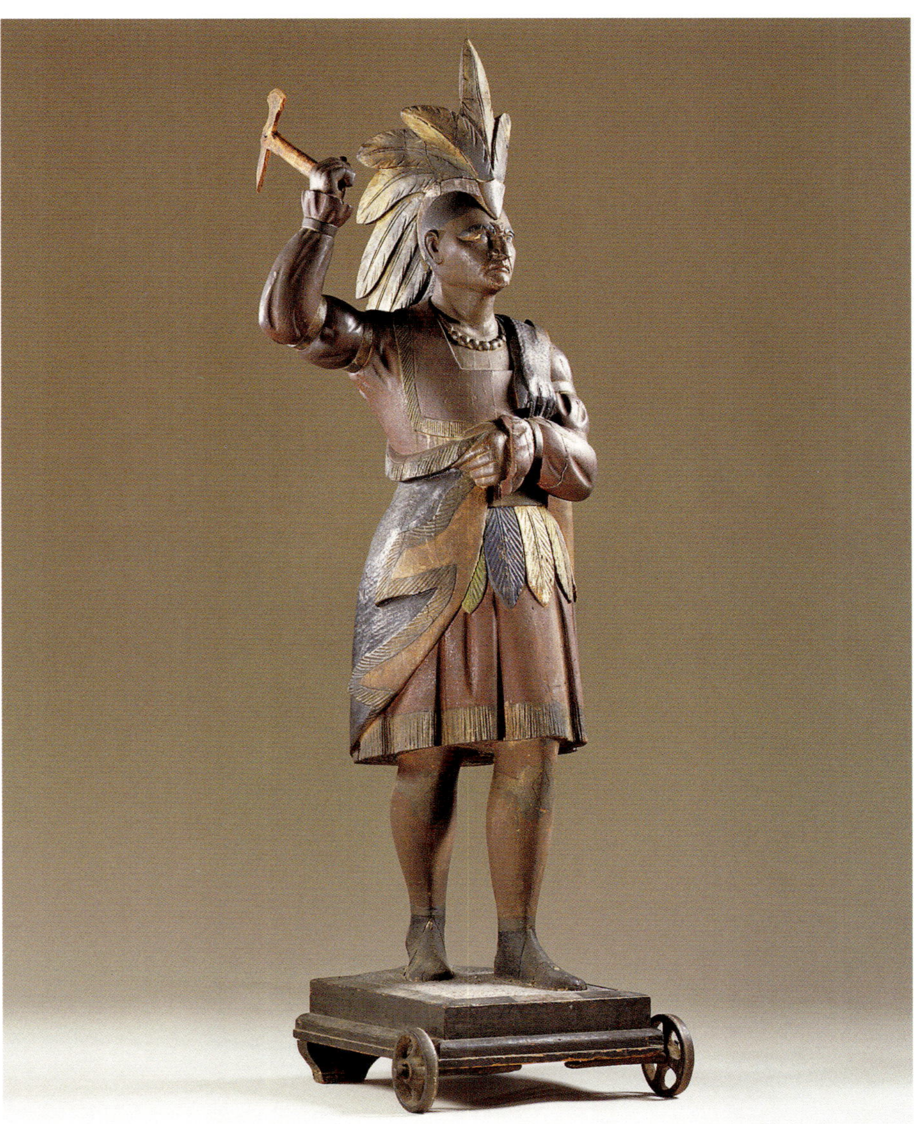

56 Attributed to John L. Cromwell (American, 1805–1873), *Indian*, New York, c. 1855. Painted wood, 81 x 25 x 25 in. (205.7 x 63.5 x 63.5 cm). Private collection

chased it from a New York City carver when he opened his shop.[33] Although it has been repaired and repainted over the years, it is still a fine example of its type. The raised right leg and the right arm that crosses the chest close to the body are reminiscent of figureheads of the period.

The second figure is closely related stylistically and in a better state of preservation, although nothing is known of its history (plate 58). Both pieces feature details that relate them to eighteenth- and early-nineteenth-century print sources. This is seen particularly in the flattened plumed headdresses, and in the tightly wrapped, thin bundle of tobacco leaves held by the *Maltzberger Indian*. In addition, the grouping of tobacco coils, cigars, and boxes at their feet are typical of earlier graphic representations of Indians used for trade cards and tobacconists' advertisements.

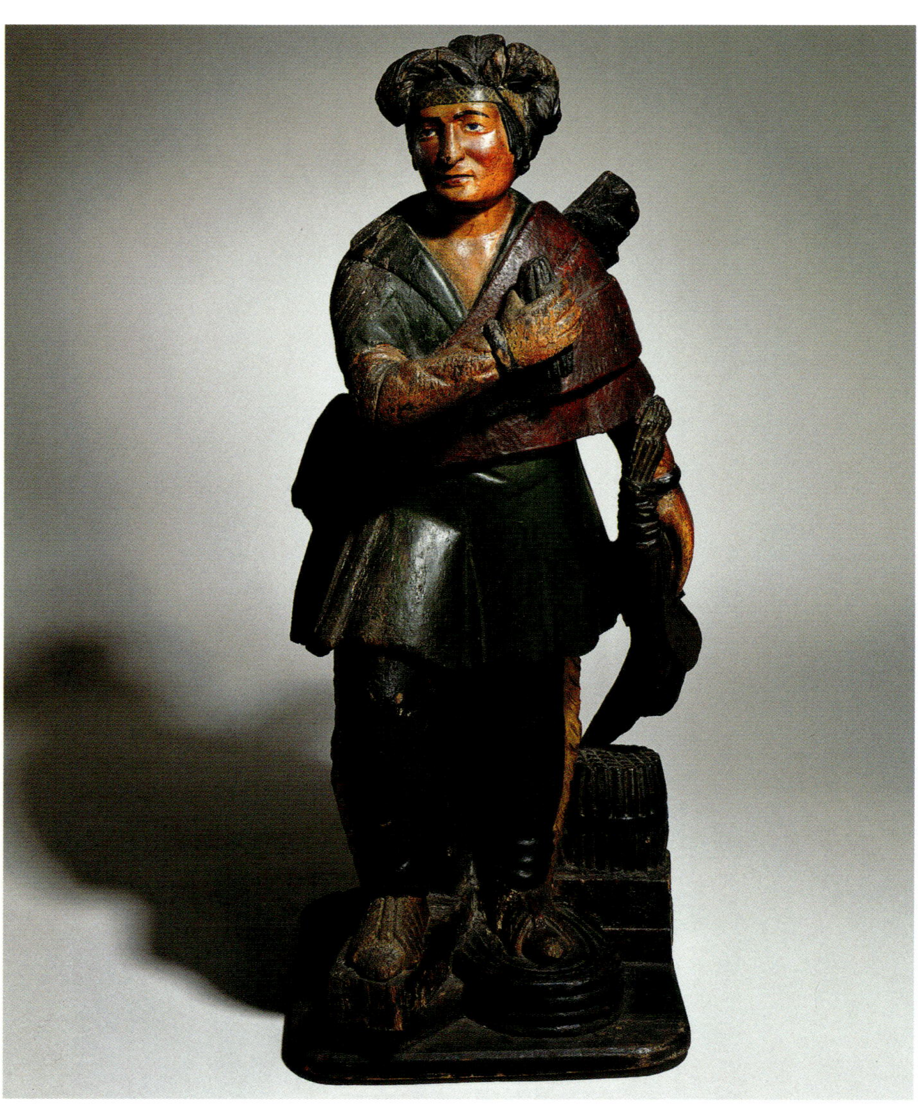

57 *Maltzberger Indian*, probably New York, c. 1845. Painted wood, 44 x 16 x 19 in. (111.7 x 40.6 x 48.2 cm). Historical Society of Berks County, Reading, Pa.

The third example has a long history in New York City (plate 59). It was probably purchased in the mid-1840s by David McAlpin for his tobacco shop on Catherine Street. In 1866, he moved it to his tobacco store and factory on East Tenth Street. Then, when the McAlpin Hotel opened in Herald Square in 1919, it was placed in a prominent location in the lobby. It was finally donated to the Museum of the City of New York in 1934.[34] The figure shares some general similarities with the two discussed above, particularly the plumed headdress that covers its head and the stack of coiled tobacco and boxes upon which it rests its arm. Overall, though, it is more characteristic of the new type of figure that would be produced until the end of the century. Its costuming and the details of necklaces, knotted sash at the waist, and the distinctive banded sleeve are all features that would be repeated by carvers for decades to come. The *McAlpin Indian* also bears a greater resemblance to the standard mid-century representation of

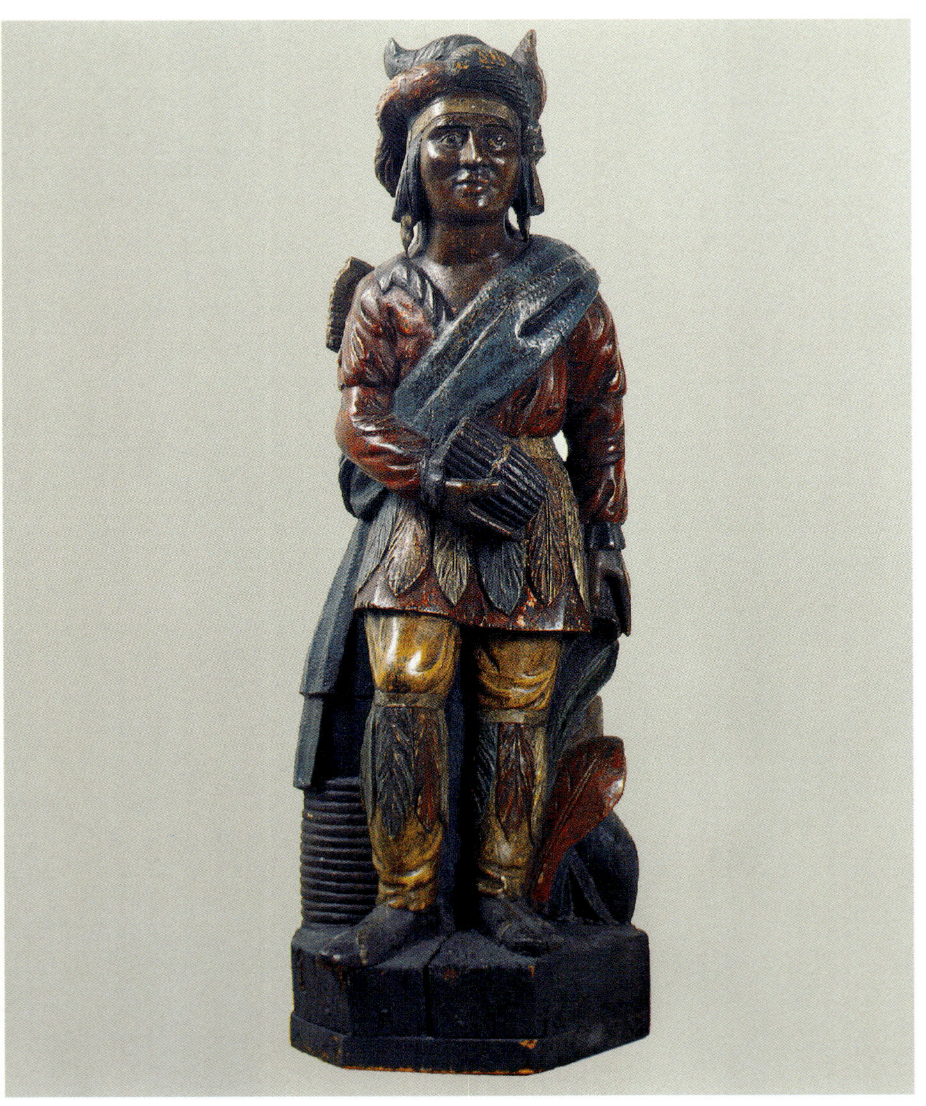

58 *Indian*, probably New York, c. 1845. Painted wood, 44 x 12 x 10 in. (111.7 x 30.5 x 25.4 cm). Mark Goldman/Mom's Cigars Collection, New York

the imaginary Indian seen in the popular press than do the other two. In addition, at nearly lifesize, it has a more commanding presence.

The *McAlpin Indian*, then, marks the emergence a new type of cigar-store figure, one that came to be known as a "show figure." Due to a lack of documentation, it is impossible to determine just how innovative it was in the mid-1840s. It may have been more typical than it currently appears, but in any event, it establishes an approximate date for the beginning of what can best be described as the New York City show-figure style.

One of the best surviving examples from later in the century is illustrated here, a female Indian with the words "S. A. Robb. Carver. 114 Centre St." incised on the top-front edge of its base (plate 60). The piece is in a fine state of preservation, retaining most of its original carved detail and paint surface. It may have spent much of its working life indoors, possibly in a store window, and therefore

59 (BELOW) *McAlpin Indian*, New York City, c. 1845. Painted wood, height 62 in. (157.5 cm). Museum of the City of New York. Gift of Charles W. McAlpin (34.249)

60 (OPPOSITE) Incised on base: "S. A. Robb. Carver. 114 Centre St.," *Indian*, New York, 1888–1903. Painted wood, 71½ x 15 x 21 in. (181.6 x 38.1 x 53.3 cm). Penny and Allan Katz Collection

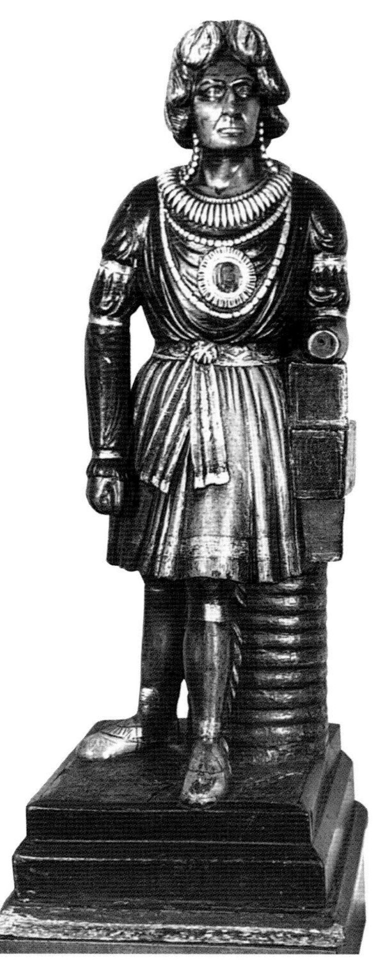

escaped the exposure to the elements and other types of wear and tear that led many figures to be routinely repainted. The fact that the paint is brighter in areas that would have been protected from the sun lends credence to this thought. The figure's expressive face and cross-legged pose give it a casual, almost jaunty, air that is much more lifelike than many of its more static contemporaries.

Among the identifying stylistic traits that it shares with the Cromwell figure and the *McAlpin Indian* are the generally shallow carving overall and the emphasis on smooth planes. The idealized handling of the face is typical as well, as is the costuming, most notably the pronounced skirtlike effect that was probably derived from the tunic of Neoclassical representation. Other important details include the banded sleeves, knotted sash or row of tobacco leaves at the waist, and painted bands below the knees. Two other standard New York show-figure features seen on the Robb and Cromwell pieces are the rows of vertically scored fringe at the bottom of the skirt and elsewhere, and the headdress of multicolored, shaded feathers.

Starting with John Cromwell and some of his contemporaries, three generations of New York shipcarvers worked in this manner, producing thousands of figures that are largely variations on a relatively small number of themes. With the exception of special commissions, upon which the carvers often indulged their imaginations in highly individualized conceptions, the majority of figures were created using a standard repertoire of poses, expressions, and accessories. This is not to say that they were either devoid of originality or indistinguishable from one another. The number of combinations of the various elements was seemingly endless, and the best carvers imparted an individualized touch to their work. Even in the case of the most popular types of figures, no two pieces were exactly alike.

The figure illustrated in plate 60 came from the workshop of Samuel Anderson Robb (1851–1928), the most successful member of the last generation of New York City shipcarvers who made show figures. Robb is also the best-known New York carver today. Because his workshop was the largest and most active of its kind in the 1880s and 1890s, he and some of his employees were interviewed on several different occasions by reporters who were curious about the history of a craft that was by that time recognized as being on the verge of extinction. In addition, scholar Frederick Fried collected a significant amount of information from Samuel Robb's daughter, Elizabeth, before she died in 1967. As a result, Robb's career is among the best documented of any American shipcarver.

Born in New York in 1851, Samuel Robb was probably apprenticed to Thomas V. Brooks in 1864.[35] Brooks was another successful shipcarver who, as we will see, played a central role in the development of the show-figure business. After serving his term in Brooks's shop, Robb went to work carving figures for William Demuth, a tobacco-products distributor who was also instrumental in promoting the show-figure fad. At the same time, Robb undertook some formal instruction in the fine arts. He received a certificate in perspective drawing from the Free Night School of Science and Art at the Cooper Union in 1872 and then studied at the National Academy of Design, where he was enrolled in the antique class from 1867 to 1875 and the life class from 1869 to 1875.[36]

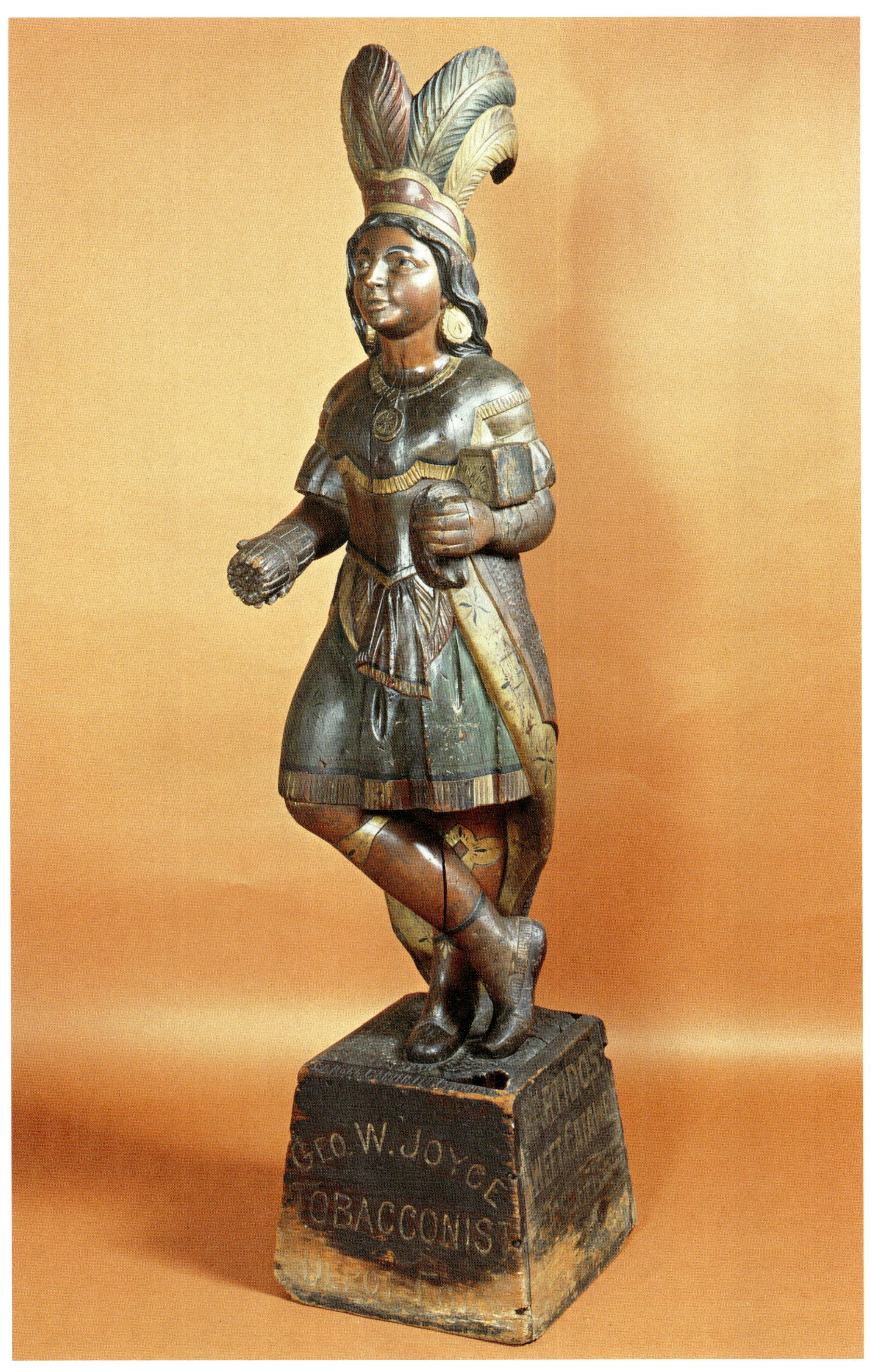
GEO. W. JOYCE
TOBACCONIST

In 1876, Robb opened his first shop at 195 Canal Street. He continued to supply figures to Demuth, but also developed a successful business of his own. By the early 1880s, he was the leading shop-figure carver in the city. In 1888, he moved his workshop to 114 Centre Street, where he remained until 1903.[37]

A rare photograph of the interior of Robb's Canal Street workshop that was taken around 1879 further documents the New York show-figure style (plate 61). Robb can be seen on the right. To the left of him and along the wall behind him are several Indian figures in various stages of completion. All show the typical features of the type. The use of bold colors and strongly shaded feathers on the pieces that have been painted is particularly notable. Though faded with time, this color scheme is still evident on a number of surviving examples, including a figure that is marked "S. A. Robb. Carver. 195 Canal St. NY" in the usual spot on the top-front edge of the base (plate 62). The address confirms that the piece is more or less contemporary with those in the photograph. Comparing it to them indicates that this solid, well-carved Indian with an idealized Anglo-American face represents a popular type that was produced in large numbers.

Another marked example is an Indian woman with a chubby child looking over her shoulder. Carved in the best New York style, it features an idealized female face and many of the now-familiar details of costuming seen in related types (plate 63). The piece lost most of its paint surface some time ago, making it something of a study of the carver's art. The top-front edge of the base is incised "S. A. Robb Manu'f. 195 Canal St."

A third piece that can be confidently attributed to Robb's shop is a large and imposing male figure wearing an eagle headdress and holding a large pipe in its right hand (plate 64). The headdress, gold breastplate, and other details of costuming identify it as vaguely Mexican, based on contemporary conceptions of an Aztec warrior. A similar figure appeared on a trade card that advertised Robb's Centre Street shop.[38]

Because of their incised markings or through comparison with other marked examples, figures such as these are frequently identified as the work of Samuel Robb himself. As tempting as this attribution might be, it ignores both the complexity of the workshop system in which they were made, as well as some of the recorded facts about the contributions of other carvers. One of the best pieces of evidence comes from an article about a visit to Robb's shop that appeared in the *New York Times* in 1890. In it, the reporter discussed a number of notable shop and circus figures to be seen in the New York area. He then added that "Nearly all of these figures came from Robb's shop, and many of them are Thomas White's handiwork."[39]

Born in New York City, Thomas J. White (1825–1902) probably apprenticed with John L. Cromwell. Following the economic depression of 1855, he moved to Boston, where he worked with William H. Rumney, who created one of the Andrew Jackson figures discussed in the previous chapter (see plate 30). White returned to New York around 1866, and by 1870, had entered a brief partnership with Thomas V. Brooks. He then went to work for William Demuth. When Samuel Robb opened his Canal Street shop in 1876, White joined him, beginning a relationship that lasted for more than twenty years.[40] He can be seen standing next to Samuel Robb in the center of the photograph of Robb's shop.

Thomas V. Brooks (1828–1895), White's partner in 1870 and probably Samuel Robb's master in the 1860s, was another major player in the shop-figure business. Brooks, too, was born in New York City and apprenticed to John Cromwell. In 1848, he opened a shop on South Street, and the next year entered a brief partnership with another carver, Thomas Millard, Jr. Around 1855, Brooks began supplying figures to Edward Hen, a tobacco-products distributor who marketed them nationally. He continued to operate his shop in New York until 1880 or 1881, when he moved to Chicago in search of new opportunities. For the next fifteen years, he maintained shops in both cities, though he spent most of his time in Chicago.[41]

Thomas Millard, Jr. (1803–1870), who was Brooks's partner in 1849 and 1850, also made a major contribution to the development of the New York show-figure style. A contemporary of John Cromwell, Millard was born in Connecticut, the son of a shipcarver from Philadelphia.[42] In the early 1850s, he began producing shop figures for James Chichester, another tobacco-products supplier with an active business. He moved to Brooklyn in 1855, and for most of the rest of his career, worked for other carvers instead of maintaining his own shop.[43]

Among the other shipcarvers who were involved in the shop-figure business were Nicholas Collins (active c. 1871–90) and John W. Anderson (1834–1904), both of whom were about ten years younger than Brooks and White. Collins holds the distinction of being one of five men—along with Cromwell, Brooks, White, and Millard—to be mentioned by name in the *New York Times* in 1890 as "prominent figures in the early history of the art."[44] Unfortunately, however, his relationship to the other, better-known carvers has not been established. It is known that he operated a shop on South Street in New York's maritime district

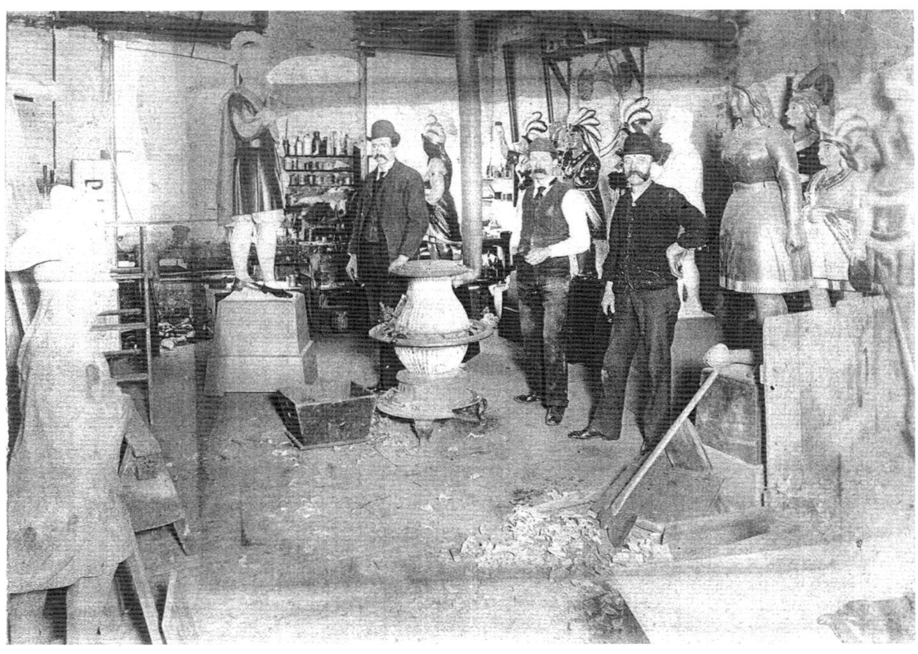

61 Workshop of Samuel Anderson Robb (American, 1851–1928), 195 Canal Street, New York, c. 1879. Photograph. The Frederick and Mary Fried Folk Arts Archives, National Museum of American History, Smithsonian Institution, Washington, D.C.

62 (RIGHT) Incised on base: "S. A. Robb. Carver. 195 Canal St. NY," *Indian*, New York, 1876–88. Painted wood, 77 x 19 x 22 in. (195.6 x 48.3 x 55.9 cm). The New-York Historical Society, New York (1930.16)

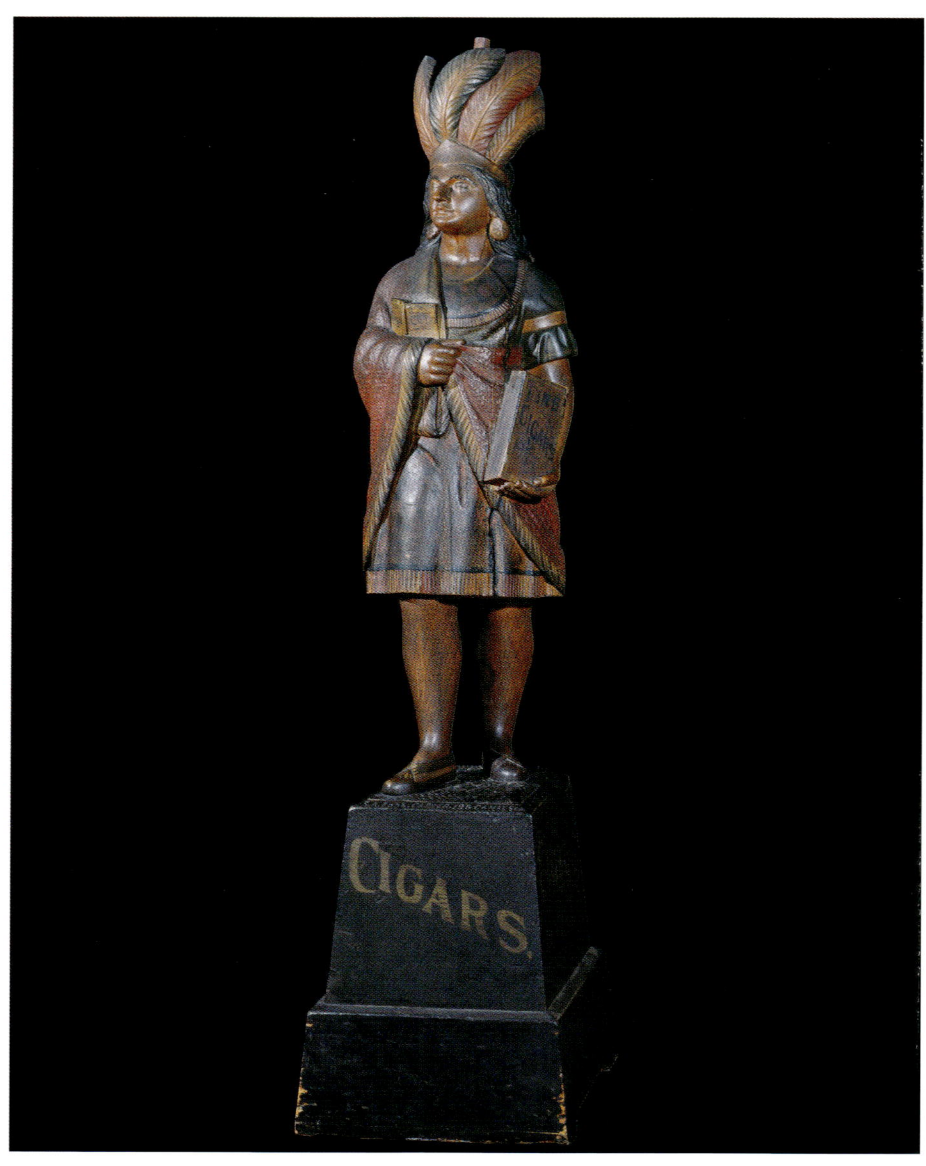

in the 1870s, and that he had a number of partners over the years.[45] Perhaps he was one of the several carvers who chiefly hired themselves out to other shops. If so, the nature of his contributions to the development of the show-figure business may never be clear.

63 (OPPOSITE) Incised on base: "S. A. Robb Manu'f. 195 Canal St.," *Indian and Child*, New York, 1876–88. Painted wood, 80 x 22 x 18 in. (203.2 x 55.9 x 45.7 cm). Museum Village, Monroe, N.Y.

John Anderson is an example of a mid-century shipcarver who concentrated on figureheads and other types of ship work, but who also produced shop figures. He was the son of Jacob S. Anderson, who created the figurehead for the *David Crockett* discussed in the last chapter (see plate 27). Jacob died prematurely in 1857, when his son was barely beyond the apprentice stage of his career. Rather than close the family shop, Jacob's wife, Jane, took over the business, an unusual arrangement in a profession dominated by men. In the 1860 Products of Indus-

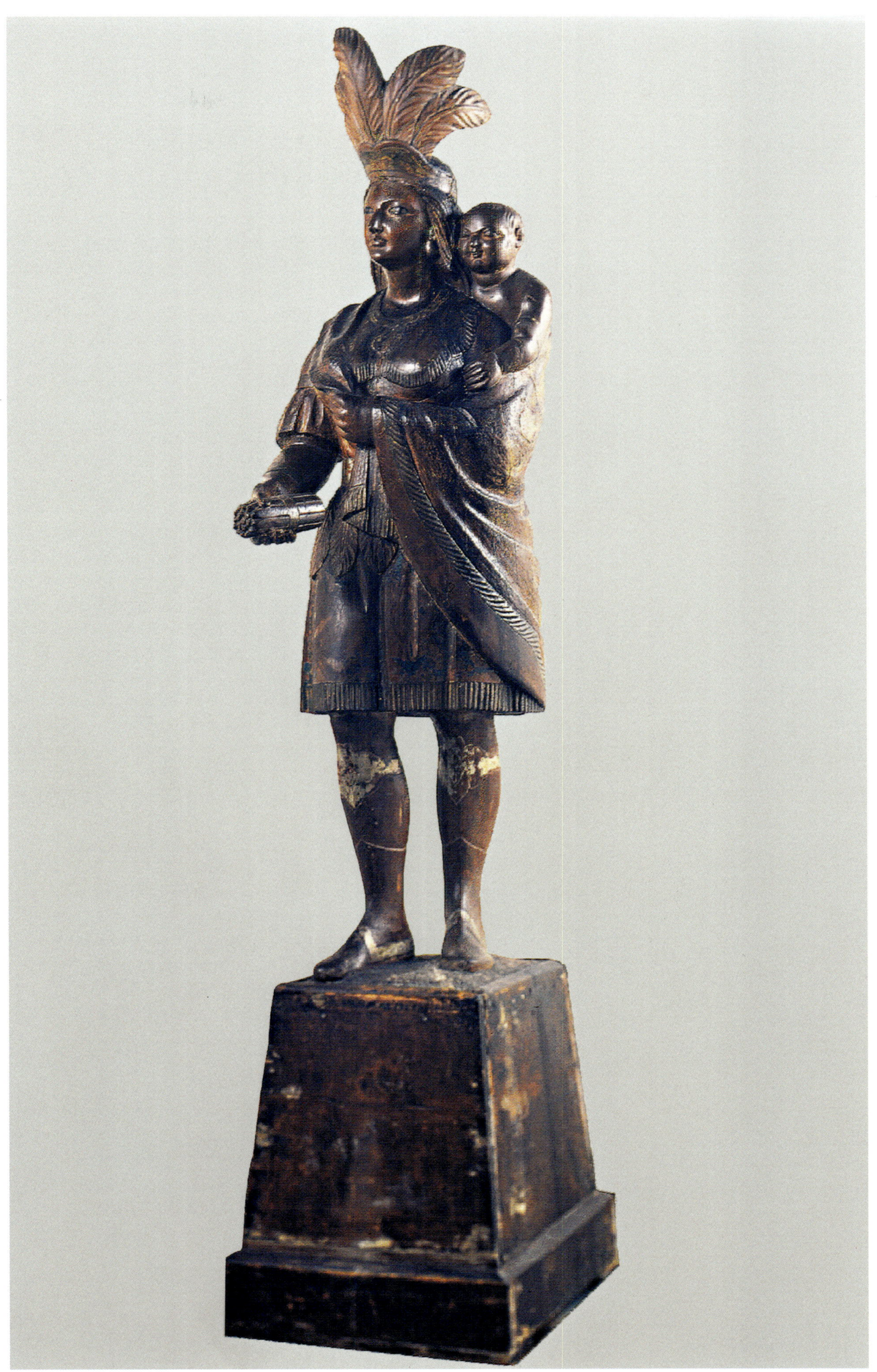

64 Attributed to Robb workshop, *Indian with Pipe*, New York, c. 1880. Painted wood, 78 x 22 x 22 in. (198.1 x 55.9 x 55.9 cm). The Eleanor and Mabel Van Alstyne Collection of American Folk Art, National Museum of American History, Smithsonian Institution, Washington, D.C.

try Schedules of the Federal Census, she listed herself as "agent, widow of Jacob S.," in charge of a shop with one employee, presumably her son.

By 1870 John had assumed control, and his shop was one of the most active in Manhattan. As with Nick Collins, the extent of his involvement in the show-figure business is not known, although he listed his products as "Figure Heads," "Cigar Signs," and "Ornaments" in the 1870 Federal Census. In addition, he advertised in 1881 that he had "Ornamental Figures for Cigar Stores Constantly on Hand."[46] He was also distantly related to Samuel Anderson Robb.

Another carver who deserves recognition is Thomas Brooks's son, James (1869–1937), particularly because he was one of the last traditional shipcarvers to practice the craft. By 1889, he was a partner with his father, listing himself as "sculptor" in the Chicago business directory. He returned to New York City around 1890 to manage the family shop there. After the Chicago shop was sold in 1895, he operated out of his home in Brooklyn under the name of the Standard Show Figure Company.[47] Still other carvers who should be mentioned are Charles Robb (1855–1904) and Clarence Robb (1878–1956), Samuel's brother and son, respectively. Both worked in the Centre Street shop, with Charles assuming an important enough role to be listed on the firm's trade card for several years.[48]

The intent of these brief biographical sketches is to demonstrate the extent to which the shop-figure carving business in New York was dominated over the course of three generations by a small group of men who were bound by master-apprentice relationships and numerous short-lived partnerships. A few additional names could be mentioned and still others remain unrecognized, but all in all, it is clear that, at any one time, there were never more than a handful of journeymen and master shipcarvers working in New York City, or in any American city for that matter. Theirs was a highly skilled profession that required innate talent and many years of specialized training. Although the prevailing daily wage was relatively high, work was often sporadic even in the best of times, and so few who entered the trade as apprentices remained in it for their entire careers. As a journalist explained in 1889:

> Twelve to fourteen years of apprenticeship is said to be necessary to make a competent workman, and that accounts for the scarcity of good hands, for the wages are low, and the demand limited.
>
> The carvers are paid four dollars a day, but the work is unsteady, and only a poor average is made at the end of the year, as orders come and go irregularly, and a workman may call every day for a month, and find no figure in the embryo stage of an order. . . . Owing to the scarcity of employment, the carvers may be said not to work much.[49]

It is true that these comments were made at a time when shop figures were past the point of their greatest popularity and shipcarving was rapidly becoming a lost art. Certainly, times had been better for New York carvers, particularly from about 1830 to 1880, during the period that the boom years of wooden shipbuilding overlapped with the height of the show-figure fad. Still, shipcarvers

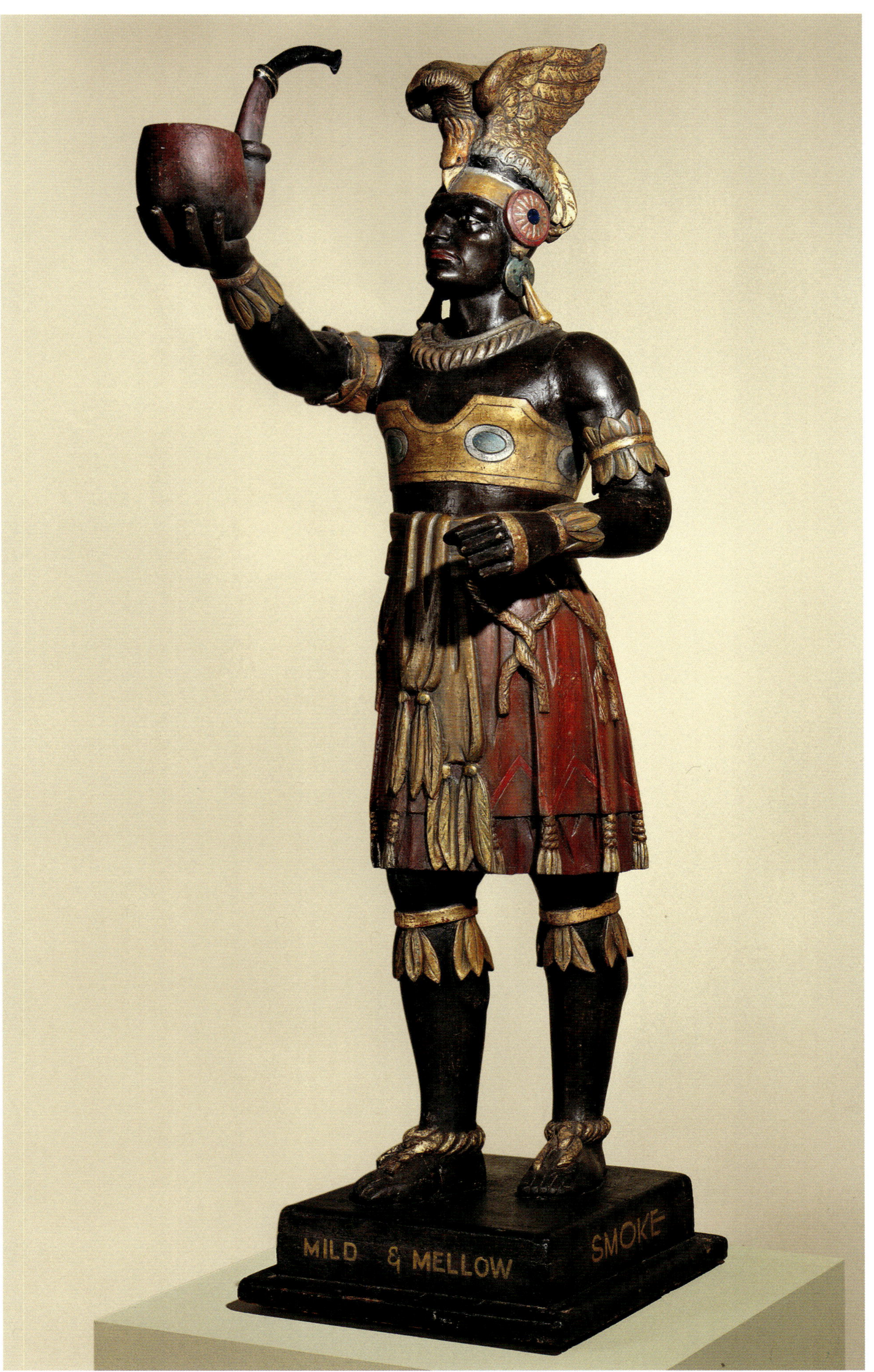
MILD & MELLOW SMOKE

were never numerous. As an unidentified carver was quoted as saying in an article that appeared in the *New York Sun* in 1886, "There never was over a dozen carvers here in New York at one time. There are not over six here now."[50]

With these thoughts in mind, the history of the show-figure business in New York City during its heyday can be reconstructed to some extent. The process is aided considerably by information contained in the Products of Industry Schedules of the Federal Census.[51] In 1850, around the time that large, characteristic type of figure that has been labeled the New York show figure emerged, four leading carvers are listed—Jacob Anderson, John L. Cromwell, Charles J. Dodge, and Thomas V. Brooks. Their shops were close to one another on South Street in the maritime district of the old Seventh Ward.[52] As mentioned in the last chapter, Anderson's shop was the largest, with an average of seven employees producing "various Figures" valued at $6,000. The other three were similar to one another in size. Cromwell listed five employees and figures worth $3,000; Dodge, four employees and carving worth $3,250; and Brooks, four employees and figures worth $4,500.

While all of these carvers probably created show figures, Cromwell's shop appears to have been the center for many of the most important developments in the 1840s, as both Thomas Brooks and Thomas White were likely apprenticed there. As noted, Cromwell was actively diversifying his shipcarving business by 1850, taking in orders for decorative work for circus wagons as well as shop figures.

His contemporary, Thomas Millard, who was not listed in the 1850 Schedules, was also increasingly concentrating on show figures. He may have been included as one of Brooks's employees in the census, because their business addresses were the same in New York Directories in the early 1850s. In any case, after interviewing Samuel Robb in 1890, a reporter wrote: "It appears that the first man to introduce carved figures as tobacconist's signs was a certain Chichester. They were carved by one Tom Millard. This was about forty years ago."[53] Clearly, either Robb was misquoted or misinformed about the origins of his art, but the fact that he linked Millard with a type of figure that was gaining popularity around 1850 provides good evidence for his contribution to their development.

Anderson and Dodge were probably still concentrating on figureheads and ship work at the time. Dodge listed his product as "ship carving" in the Schedules, for example, while both Cromwell and Brooks listed theirs as "various carved figures." Dodge is known to have produced shop figures, however, although the extent of his involvement with them is unclear. In 1883, a journalist noted: "Old Jim Crow, a famous figure cut forty years ago by Charley Dodge—now dead and gone—was in the Canal Street shop for repairs not long ago. A new foot was put on, a missing ear supplied, a piece chipped out of the cheek was replaced, the hat was reconstructed, and Old Jim Crow emerged as good as new. The figure is now doing service in an up-town hotel."[54]

More than twenty years younger than these men, Thomas Brooks had just recently established his own shop when the 1850 census was taken. His brief partnership with Millard in 1849 and 1850 has already been mentioned. With this experience in hand, he went on to become the single most innovative and influential shop-figure carver of his generation. The testimony comes from the carvers themselves. One is recorded in the 1880s as saying: "The father of the business is Brooks of Chicago. He left here some years ago. I remember him forty years ago."[55] At about the same time another carver was interviewed in "a shop on Canal Street," a likely reference to Samuel Robb's workshop. He said: "The image business is not what it was a few years ago . . . because we have lost old Daddy Brooks. Ah, old Daddy was the boss carver, and he taught about all the carvers we have here. That's why we call him Daddy. He used to be down in West Broadway somewhere. Now he is in Chicago, and he took a lot of boys out with him—that is he took three or four."[56]

By the late 1850s, after Cromwell had turned over much of his business to him, Brooks had become the dominant force in the trade. Jacob Anderson was dead, Charles Dodge was apparently devoting most of his time to his duties as a tax commissioner, and Thomas White was in Boston.[57] For a time Brooks had little serious competition. In the 1860 Schedules, he is listed in the Sixth Ward as the proprietor of a shop with six employees, producing one hundred figures worth $4,000. Significantly, he listed himself as a "Carver & Gilder" and not a "Ship Carver," which would seem to indicate the extent to which he was diversifying his shop. He also gave two business addresses in the New York City Directory for that year: 117 Canal Street, in the Sixth Ward, and 256 South Street, in the Seventh Ward.

In comparison, the next largest shop in the 1860 Schedules was that of "M'Laren & Lawlor," which had three employees producing six figures and "repairing." Nothing else is known about these two men. As mentioned above, Jacob Anderson's widow, Jane, was also listed as an "agent." The family workshop had one employee, probably John, producing four figures valued at $250 and "repairing" worth $450.

Brooks apparently employed several of the best carvers in his shop, including Thomas White after his return to New York around 1866. It seems reasonable to assume that many of the elements of the New York show-figure style were established in Brooks's shop in the 1850s and 1860s. An old photograph of a standing chief probably made by Brooks is illustrated here (plate 65). Known to the carvers as a "scout" because it holds its right hand to its brow, the piece shows many typical features. The photo was once owned by Samuel Robb and has "Brooks" lightly penciled on its reverse.[58]

The demand for wooden figures remained strong throughout the 1870s. Brooks was listed in the 1870 Schedules in the Seventh Ward in partnership with Thomas White, as "Brooks & White—Carvers," with a product of "Figure Heads" and "Cigar Figures" valued at $2,800. Curiously, however, the shop recorded only one man and one youth under sixteen as employees. In addition, no entry for a shop on Canal Street or thereabouts could be located, although research was hampered by several pages in the Schedules that were virtually illegible. While these mysteries will probably never be solved, evidence of Brooks's prominence reappeared in the New York City Directory for 1872, where he advertised that he was a "Show Figure and Ornamental Carver" who had "From 75 to 100 Figures always on hand."[59]

Two other shops were located close to Brooks and White in the Seventh Ward in the 1870 Schedules: "J. W. Anderson" and "Wm. Demuth & Co." In charge of

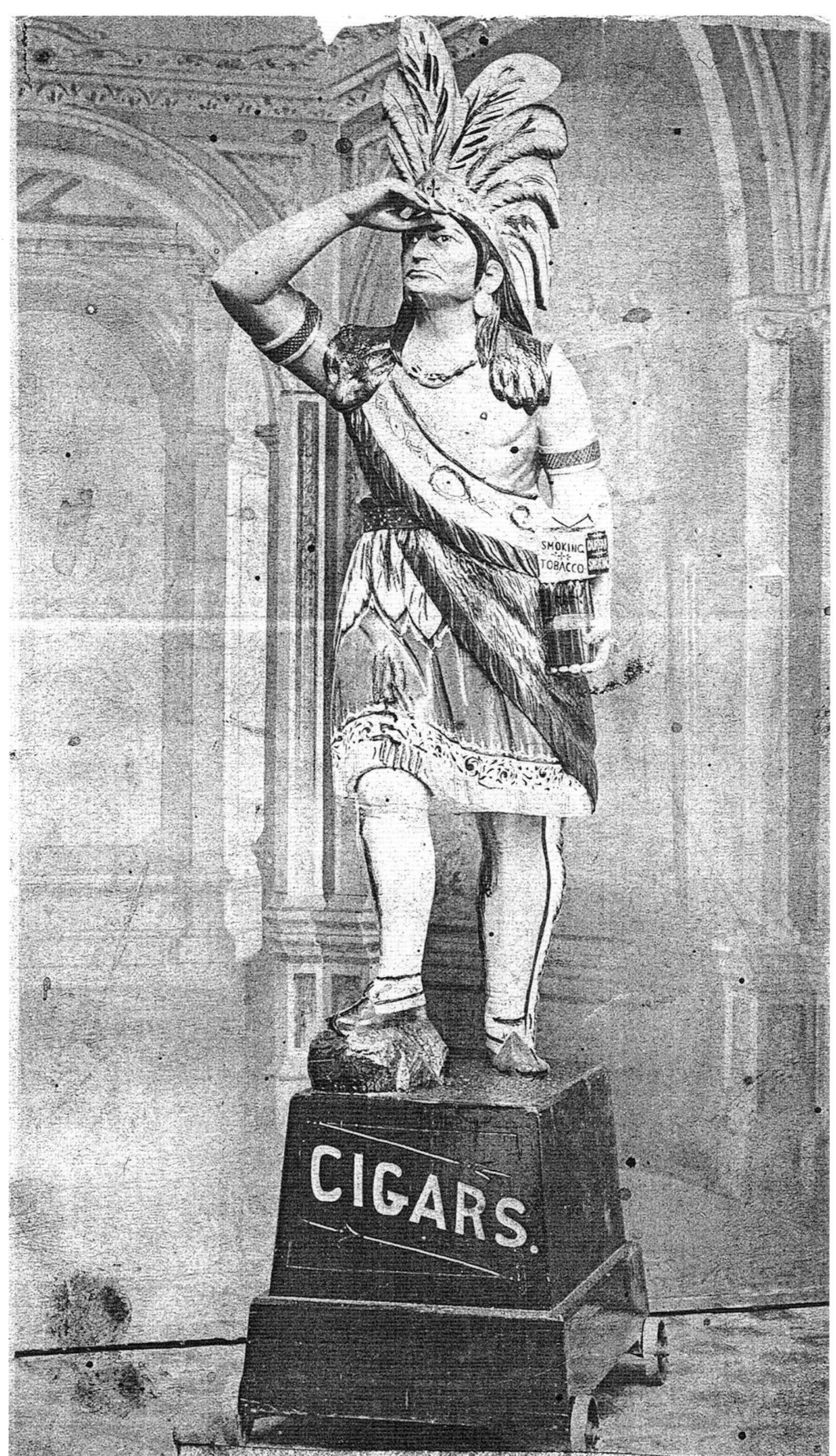

65 Attributed to Thomas V. Brooks (American, 1828–1895), *Indian.* Photograph. The Frederick and Mary Fried Folk Arts Archives, National Museum of American History, Smithsonian Institution, Washington, D.C.

the family shop by this time, John Anderson was listed as a "Ship & Ornamental Carver" with two employees who produced "Figure Heads," "Cigar Signs," and "Ornaments" valued at $5,000. The Demuth workshop had two employees, one of whom was undoubtedly nineteen-year-old Samuel Robb. It produced 120 show figures worth $4,000.

The final chapter of the story belongs to Robb. As discussed, he became the undisputed leader in the New York show-figure business after Brooks moved to Chicago around 1880.[60] This is confirmed by the 1880 Schedules, although the surviving records are organized differently than they had been in previous decades. Businesses are grouped by type, not location, and "Wood Turning" and "Carving" shops are listed on the same page without an indication of their particular specialty. The information is therefore somewhat less useful for comparative purposes.

The only recognizable name gleaned from that year is Samuel A. Robb.[61] Significantly, he was listed as having ten employees, the largest number recorded for a carver on any of the Schedules. With Thomas White as a mainstay, and with Charles and Clarence Robb and several other unidentified carvers working with him at times, Robb's shop continued to be the primary source for New York show figures until the demise of the tradition at the turn of the twentieth century.

Regardless of their size, all of the workshops operated in a similar fashion. The only significant difference was the degree of specialization of tasks resulting from the number of men and boys employed at any one time. The larger shops comprised one or two master carvers, a few apprentices, and some itinerant journeymen carvers who were engaged on a daily or weekly basis, depending upon the number of orders to be filled. Other master carvers worked alone, with or without an apprentice. A good example of this appeared in the 1850 Schedules, where a John Wheeler was listed as a "Ship Carver" with one employee, presumably himself, producing "various ship carving" valued at $923.

In either case, the work proceeded in a traditional manner, as it had for generations. The preferred material was white pine, usually three- to seven-foot sections of masts purchased at spar yards in the maritime district. First an outline of the desired figure was sketched on the log or "stick," as the carvers called them. "While the carving is mostly done by the eye, chalk or pencil lines are drawn on the log for general contour," a reporter noted at the time.[62] For the more popular types that were often repeated, a paper or cardboard pattern was used as a guide. Then the "chopping" began. The most complete description of the carving process was recorded in a *New York Times* article that appeared in August 1890. Due to its importance, it is quoted here at length:

> The wood used is generally white pine, which is bought in logs of various lengths at the spar yards. The artist begins by making the roughest kind of an outline—a mere suggestion of what the proportions of the figure are to be. In this he is guided by paper patterns. The log is blocked out with the axe into appropriate spaces for the head, the body down to the waist, the portion from there to the knees, the rest of the legs (which are at

> once divided,) and the feet. In its present embryo state the figure to be is not very apparent to the eye. The feeling for form in the chopped block is so very elementary as to have complete suggestiveness only for the practiced artist.
>
> A hole is now bored into each end of the prepared log about 5 inches deep. Into each of these holes an iron bolt is placed, the projecting parts of which rest on supports, so that the body hangs free. The carver now goes from the general to the particular. The surface of the wood soon becomes chipped up by the chisel, and the log generally takes on more definite form. Then, when the figure is completely evolved, the finishing touches are put on with finer carving tools. Detached hands and arms are made separately and joined on to the body by screws. Then the various portions of the figure are appropriately painted, the whole is set upon a stand running on wheels, and it is ready for delivery.[63]

In the larger shops, three or four people were engaged in different parts of this process. It was the master carver who first roughed out the form with an ax, cutting to within "half an inch of the lines" established by his chalk marks, as another account explains.[64] A second man, probably a journeyman, finished the body with a mallet and chisels, leaving only the face for the master to complete. An apprentice then smoothed the entire surface with sandpaper, and someone else painted it. Estimates for the amount of time required to complete a figure vary significantly in the few surviving accounts. One stated that "For the ordinary six foot Indian a foot per day is good carving, and painting and finishing runs at the same speed making twelve days in all."[65] Another set the time at four or five days: "A man can rough this out in one day. For that he gets $4. Another man for $2 goes over it with a chisel to take out the gouge marks, but doesn't touch the face, which the other man leaves perfect 'cept for the sandpaper. A boy at 75¢ a day does the sandpaperin'. Then it's ready for the painter who can polish it off in a day."[66]

In all, then, the carving was a cooperative effort that required a significant amount of specialization if it were to be done quickly and efficiently enough for the shop to turn a reasonable profit. The master's hand was evident in each piece, however, because he was the man responsible for the overall form and detailing of the most important area: the face. He was also in charge of the entire process, supervising the work of his apprentices and journeymen. "Sometimes a workman gets on a spree and would turn out a monstrosity, but for the sharp eye of the master," a journalist noted in 1889.[67]

66 Incised on base: "Robb Manu'f'r. 114 Centre St. NY," *Indian*, New York, 1888–1903. Painted wood, 79 x $24\frac{3}{4}$ x $25\frac{3}{4}$ in. (200.7 x 62.9 x 65.4 cm). The Eleanor and Mabel Van Alstyne Collection of American Folk Art, National Museum of American History, Smithsonian Institution, Washington, D.C.

Those who were closely involved in the trade recognized and appreciated the individual touch of the best carvers. New and successful types of figures were quickly borrowed and adapted by competing shops, and, as we have seen, a general stylistic consistency developed among several of the master carvers, particularly in New York City. Each maintained a signature style, however. Late in his life, James Brooks responded to an article on cigar-store figures that appeared in *Scribner's Magazine* in 1929. Besides correcting what he believed to be the author's errors, he offered identifications for some of the illustrations. "Chiseling

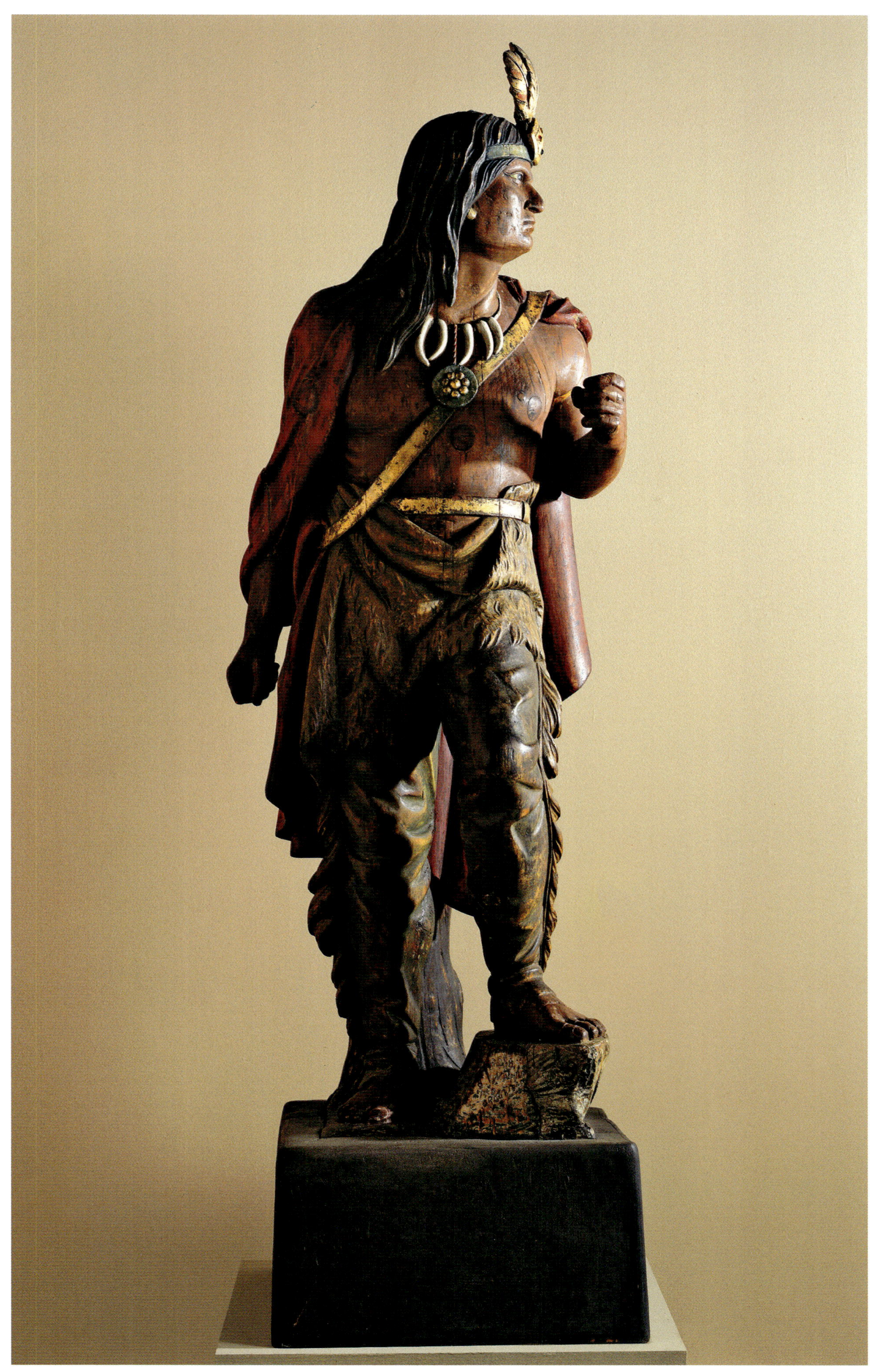

on wooden Indians is to Mr. Brooks like handwriting to the rest of us and he recognized some of the pictured braves in October *Scribner's* as the handiwork of old friends," the article's author noted.[68] Unfortunately, he did not record any of Brooks's attributions.

A powerful figure of a chief with a bear-claw necklace that is incised "Robb Manu'f'r. 114 Centre St. NY" illustrates the distinctive approach of the most accomplished carvers (plate 66). The figure originally had a bow in his right hand and an arrow in his left. The pose is well articulated, with the weight convincingly shifted to the right leg as the figure looks to the left. The emphasis on the realistic handling of an ideal subject follows the prevailing trend in contemporary sculpture, revealing the influence of Robb's study of fine art models. Metal versions of this figure were exhibited by William Demuth and Company at both the Philadelphia Centennial Exposition in 1876 and the World's Columbian Exposition in Chicago in 1893.[69]

Another notable figure, in this case certainly a unique work, is a *Seated Indian*, smoking a long pipe and holding a typical bunch of cigars in his left hand (plate 67). Probably made by a New York City shipcarver, it was done for a cigar store on Montague Street in Brooklyn Heights, either in 1863 when the shop opened or in 1877 when a new owner took over the business. It remained a local landmark until 1930, when it was acquired by the Long Island Historical Society (now the Brooklyn Historical Society).[70] The carver paid much attention to the realistic rendering of details of costuming and facial expression, resulting in an air of solemn dignity that is rarely surpassed in cigar-store figures. The piece is also notable for the rendition of a rustic Adirondack chair, a type that was then coming into vogue.

It has been suggested that the *Seated Indian* is the work of Charles Dodge.[71] The piece is not marked, however, nor does any documentation exist connecting it to a particular workshop. This is not to say that it could not have been made by Dodge, but rather that there is not enough information to make a definitive judgment. James Brooks's knowledge followed him to the grave in 1937. With his death, the direct link with the last generation of New York shipcarvers was severed.

Frederick Fried interviewed Samuel Robb's daughter Elizabeth in the 1960s, and she supplied him with important biographical information and photographs that have helped reconstruct the nature of her father's business. She was not a shipcarver herself, nor was she familiar with the work of any of her father's contemporaries. Samuel Robb was the only man who marked his figures with any consistency, but while it is often assumed that he personally carved all those that he marked, it must be remembered that Thomas White worked alongside him for over two decades. It is therefore likely that the Robb name incised on the base of a number of surviving figures is a shop mark rather than an identification of artistic authorship, particularly since different face types are in evidence. Throughout the long history of the art in Europe and America, it was never customary for a shipcarver to sign his work.

The problems of attributing a specific figure to a particular carver are illustrated by a comparison of three pieces of the type that is often ascribed to John Cromwell (plates 56, 68, and 69). As discussed earlier, a few distinctive male fig-

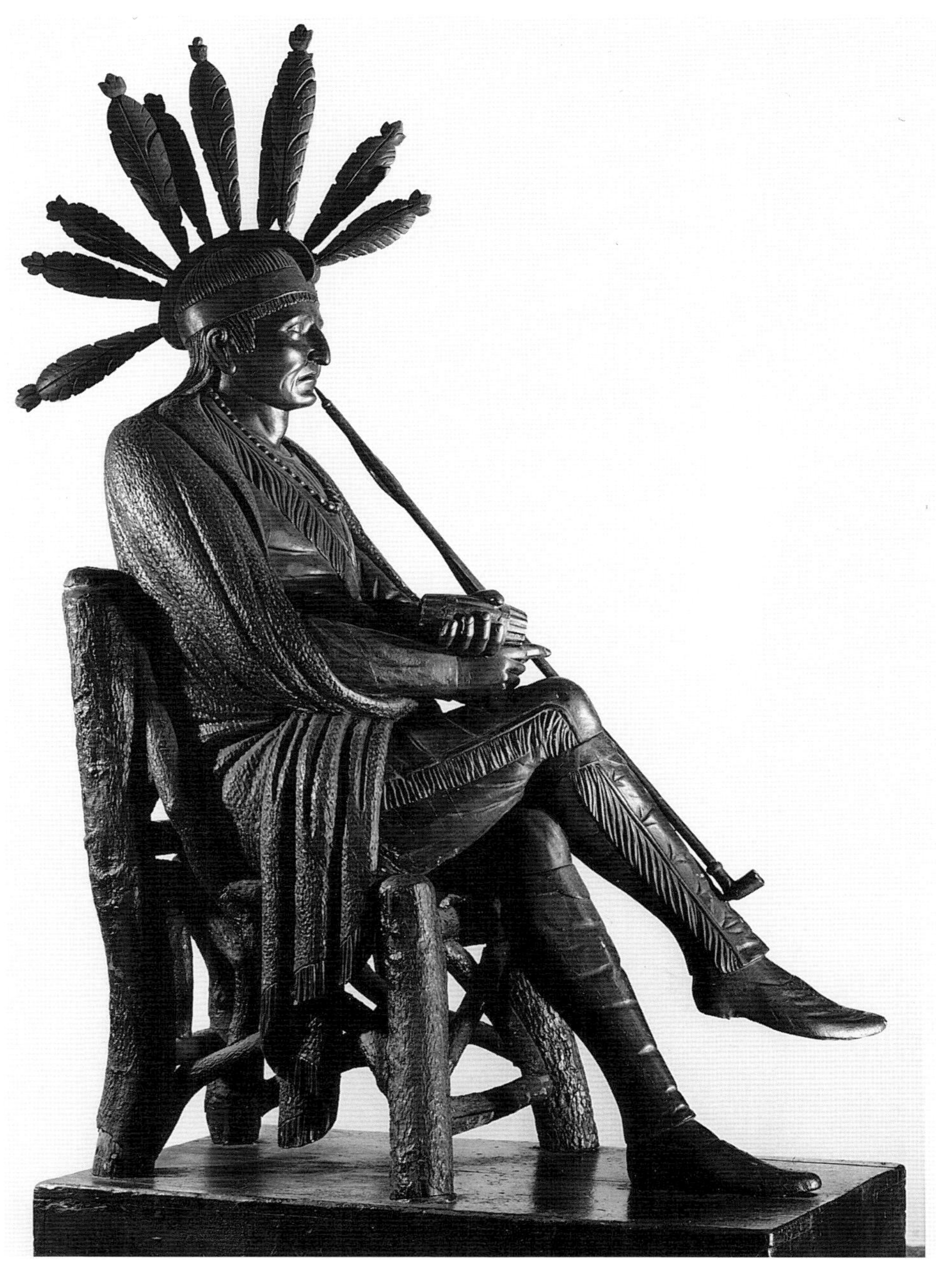

67 *Seated Indian*, New York, c. 1863–77. Painted wood, 75 x 27³/₄ x 42¹/₂ in. (190.5 x 70.5 x 107.9 cm). Brooklyn Historical Society, New York

ures with scalp locks and raised tomahawks have been convincingly identified as Cromwell's work. The three examples shown here share a number of similar features, including pose and some details of costuming. Upon closer examination, though, several differences are evident as well. The most obvious are the arrangement of the legs—that is, whether the right or left is forward—and the treatment of the faces. Given the importance of faces and the amount of attention that master carvers paid to them, this difference alone provides strong evidence that they are not all from the same shop. These visual observations are confirmed

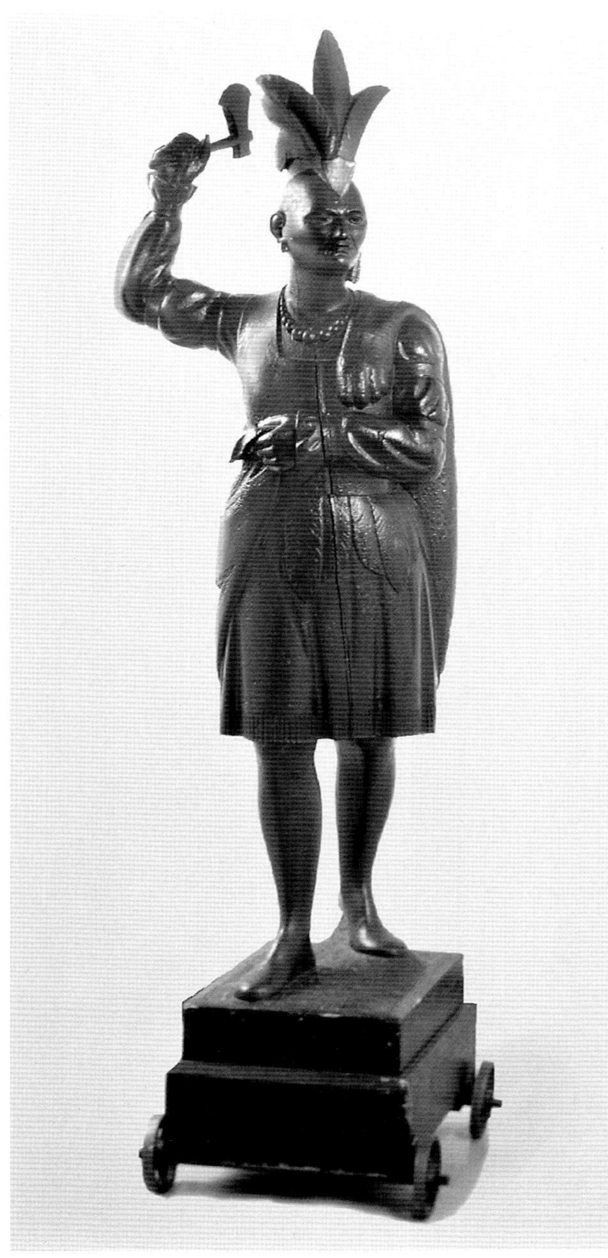

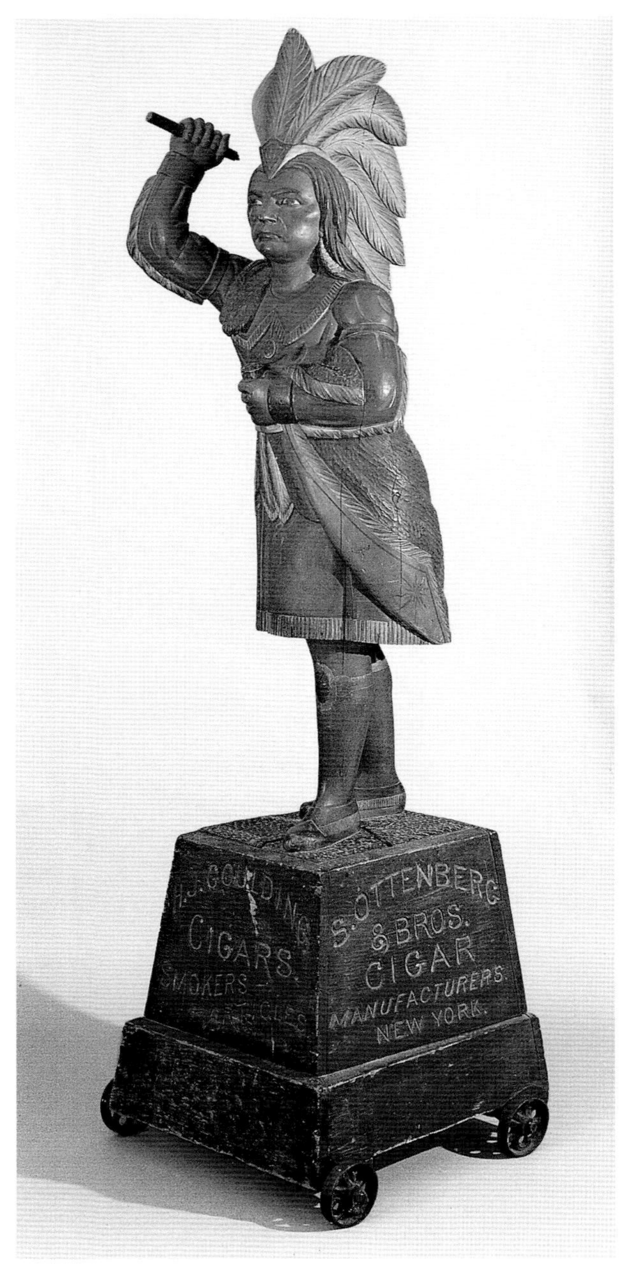

68 (ABOVE, LEFT) Attributed to John L. Cromwell, *Indian*, New York, c. 1855. Painted wood, 81 x 25 x 25 in. (205.7 x 63.5 x 63.5 cm). Mark Goldman/ Mom's Cigars Collection, New York

by one final detail. The piece shown in plate 69 has "Robb 114 Centre St. N.Y." inscribed on its base.

Evidently, then, although few examples can be attributed to John Cromwell with any certainty, it was a very popular type of figure that was carved with a significant amount of stylistic consistency in several New York City workshops over the course of three or four decades. As the central players in the development of the New York show-figure style, Cromwell, Brooks, White, and Robb probably all made them. A final comparison strengthens the case.

Around 1890, Charles Brown (1846–1917) carved an Indian chief in a war bonnet (plate 70). Brown was a New York shipcarver who began advertising in city directories about 1870. A fine example of its type, the chief is crisply carved, with a precise, if somewhat shallow rendering of costume details. Brown paid particular attention to the face and headdress, cutting expressive lines around the eyes and mouth that give the figure the impression of a certain age and stature.

While it shares some features with other contemporary cigar-store figures, the chief is not stylistically related to the work that was being produced in Robb's shop at the same time. In fact, if the piece could not be positively documented as Brown's work, it would be difficult to determine if it was made in New York or in some other East Coast seaport. Even though he was working only a few blocks away from them, Brown was obviously not very closely connected to the succession of carvers who produced the majority of show figures that were so widely distributed around the country.

NEW YORK CITY REMAINED the most influential center of show-figure production throughout the last quarter of the nineteenth century, particularly after the tobacco-products retailer William Demuth established a system of national distribution through catalogue sales in the 1870s. (Demuth's role will be considered in the next chapter.) Elements of the New York show-figure style spread in other ways as well. As discussed, Thomas White worked in Boston from 1856 to about 1866, while Thomas Brooks moved to Chicago around 1880 and opened a successful shop that received orders from throughout the Midwest.

Brooks and White were by no means the first or only carvers to relocate. Following the itinerant nature of their profession, other New York shipcarvers, including some who had no doubt apprenticed with Cromwell, Brooks, or Robb, traveled to other towns in search of opportunity. Pierre Gaspari, a prominent Baltimore tobacconist who was once called "the town's foremost dealer in wooden Indians," is recorded as saying that in 1864 he hired a "man from New York to make figures."[72] He also claimed that for a time he had a "manufacturing branch" in New York, which probably means that he had some sort of business arrangement with one particular workshop.[73]

As a principal port for the export of tobacco and a major shipbuilding center, Baltimore was a logical place for a flourishing figure-carving business. The frigate *Constellation* was built there in the 1790s, with a figurehead carved by William Rush. The city was also the home of the famous Baltimore clippers, predecessors of the mid-century ocean clippers that were built between about 1800 and 1825. Brewington identified fifteen shipcarvers active in Baltimore from the late eighteenth century to the end of the nineteenth, and this was admittedly an incomplete list. The first known carver was John Brown, who trained with Rush and was working from about 1789 to 1804. At mid-century, James Randolph and two men both named James Mullen were the leaders.[74] It is not known how many of these carvers made shop figures, but several must have been engaged in it at one time or another. Pierre Gaspari once estimated that there were approximately eight hundred figures on the streets of Baltimore in the

69 (OPPOSITE, RIGHT) Incised on base: "Robb 114 Centre St. N.Y.," *Indian*, New York, 1888–1903. Painted wood, 81 x 20½ x 23 in. (205.7 x 52 x 58.4 cm). Albany Institute of History and Art. Gift of James Hazen Hyde

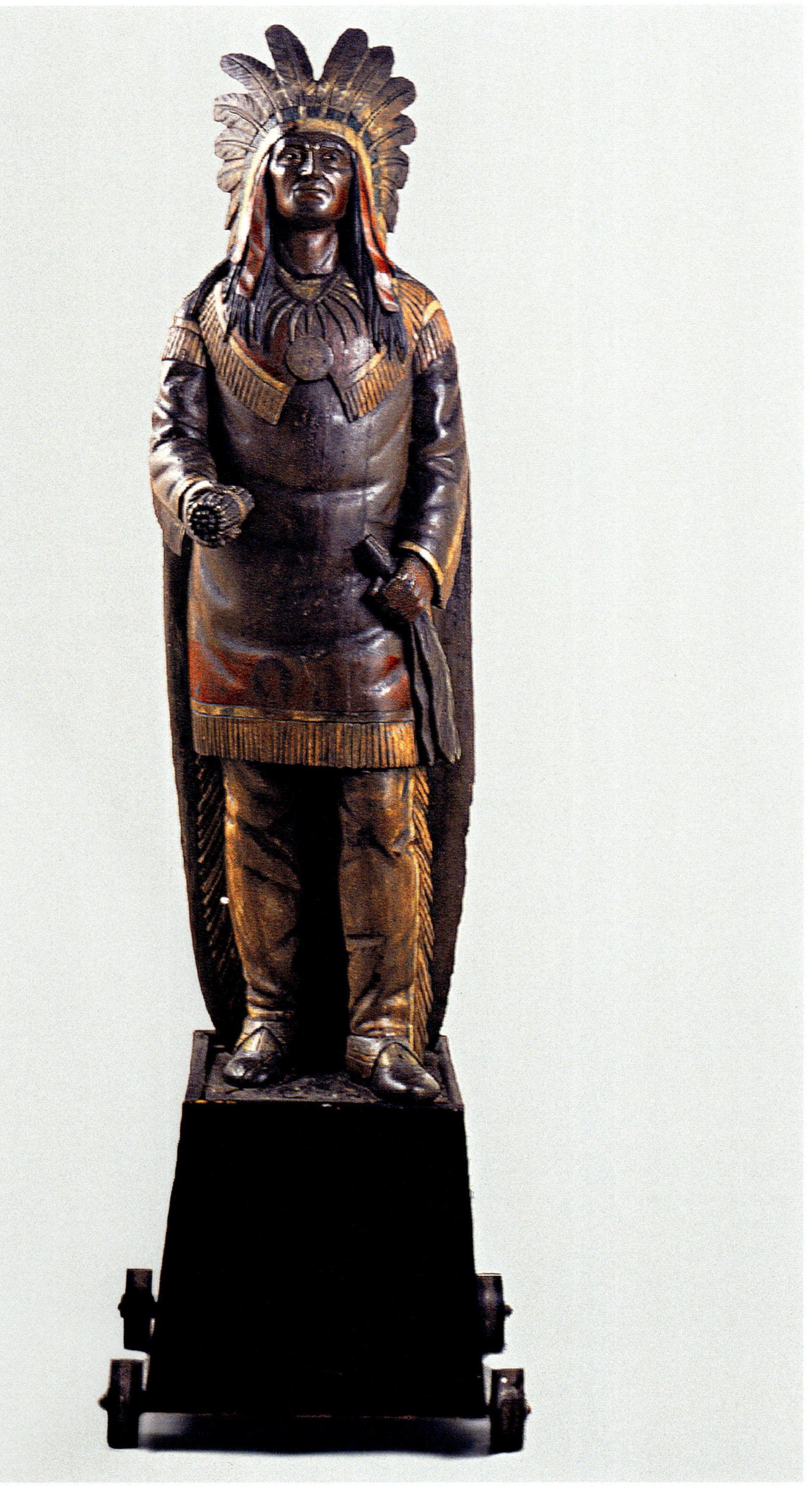

1870s. At the height of his business, he carried a stock of almost two hundred, and "sold figures in many other towns and cities."[75]

The best-known figure carver in Baltimore in the second half of the nineteenth century was John Philip Yaeger (1823–1899), a German immigrant who settled there in 1847. The nature of his training is not known, but before long he was operating one of the most successful shops in the city. In 1853, he advertised in the Baltimore Directory as a "plain, ornamental, and fancy carver" specializing in "architectural and ship work" and "moulds for castings and sculpture." He also carved altars and interiors for local churches.[76] His most distinctive cigar-store figure is a nearly lifesize representation of a girl or woman holding a bunch of cigars in her right hand and tobacco leaves in her left (plate 71). The model for the piece was his eighth child, Eva Isabelle, wearing a favorite cap and dressed in a vaguely Germanic outfit with a large heart on the bodice.[77] Otherwise, the overall design of the figure follows many of the conventions of the typical cigar-store Indian, resulting in a unique stylization and a highly individualized conception.

Throughout the nineteenth century, many other carvers worked in American towns and cities, filling local demand for shop figures of all shapes and sizes. Some, like Yaeger, were professional woodcarvers, while others were carpenters, furniture makers, or self-taught artists who only occasionally may have fashioned human images from wood. Given the lack of documentation and all the work that has long since disappeared, it is impossible to reconstruct much of what they accomplished. Following is a selective survey of some of the more distinctive figures that have survived and some of their makers, intended to highlight the fact that their efforts rivaled those of their better-known New York contemporaries in diversity and quality of carving, if not in quantity of production.

As one of the earliest shipbuilding centers in the nation, Philadelphia also supported generations of shipcarvers. The career of the most influential of them, William Rush, has already been considered. Brewington lists an additional twenty-five Philadelphia shipcarvers, beginning with Robert Mullard, who was active from about 1708 to 1722, and ending with Samuel Sailor, who operated several shops from about 1858 to 1885.[78] Of them, only Rush and Sailor are known to have carved shop figures, the latter's sole documented contribution being a lifesize representation of a ship's officer holding a sextant that served as a sign for Riggs and Brother's nautical instrument and watch shop for nearly one hundred years.[79] Another carver, James Brown, maintained a shop from about 1883 to 1902, advertising that he supplied "garden ornaments, steamboat eagles, figures, church ornaments, pompeys, and cigar Indians." Finally, an Austrian cabinetmaker named Francis (or Fritz) Decker is also known to have created some figures in Philadelphia in the 1880s and 1890s.[80] His work was quite distinctive in that it was made of small blocks of wood that were glued together and carved, a technique that was fairly common among European cabinetmakers but very rare here.

70 Charles Brown (American, 1846–1917), *Indian Chief*, New York, c. 1890. Painted wood, 72 x 20 x 22 in. (182.9 x 50.8 x 55.9 cm). Mark Goldman/Mom's Cigars Collection, New York

This paucity of information about shop-figure carvers in Philadelphia is all the more curious in light of the fact that they were as popular there as they were in any other major American seaport. An article that appeared in the *Philadelphia Times* in December 1892 stated: "Fifty or sixty years ago the carving of these tobacco signs was a recognized business in this city. One of the principal carvers, as is well known, was William Rush, who afterwards became noted as a sculptor of wood of considerable ability. . . . There is not now in Philadelphia any man, so far as the writer can determine, who makes a business of carving these wooden figures."[81]

Perhaps he should have checked the city directory for James Brown's listing. In any event, when he inquired of a retailer in one of the larger tobacco shops how he could acquire a figure, he was told that "there was a firm in New York who, in connection with the manufacture of pipes, also carved cigar store figures, and . . . 'Most of our ship carvers here in this city will get you one up to order.'"[82]

This quote could also have come from Boston, which, as discussed, was the earliest shipbuilding center in America and continued to support a significant number of shipcarvers until the end of the nineteenth century. Brewington identified forty-one carvers active in Boston from the 1660s to the 1890s, a total that was surpassed only by New York City.[83] The careers of several of these men have already been considered, but, while many of them must have made cigar-store figures, no surviving examples can be attributed to Boston shops with any certainty. It should be remembered, however, that Thomas White worked on Commercial Street in the maritime district from 1856 to about 1866.

Nearby Gloucester, Massachusetts, had several shipyards of its own from the early colonial period through the nineteenth century. The town is of particular interest here because of a unique figure attributed to a shipcarver named David R. Proctor (plate 72). Nothing is known of Proctor other than the fact that he was active in both Gloucester and Belfast, Maine, from at least 1856 to 1866. The figure stood in front of Mancell's Cigar Store in Gloucester from about 1855 to 1910.[84] A finely carved piece, it is clothed in a hairy pelt belted at the waist, a rare feature shared by only one or two other known examples. The overall effect relates this imaginary Indian to the much older European tradition of the "wild man," probably inspired by some as yet unidentified print source.

Newburyport was another important port town on the Massachusetts coast, north of Boston. The Revolutionary War frigate *Hancock* was built there in the 1770s, as were many other vessels throughout the eighteenth and nineteenth centuries. A finely carved tobacconist Indian with a local history has survived in a good state of preservation (plate 73). Over lifesize, the figure features a number of notable details, including an ornate belt and sash, arm- and wristbands, feathered headdress, and fringed leggings. Probably done around 1880, it stood in front of Kelleher's Smoke Shop until about 1914.[85] While its maker remains unidentified, he was evidently aware of the prevailing show-figure style. The figure could have been made in Newburyport, since the town supported some talented shipcarvers over the years, but more likely it was carved in an urban shop that specialized in such work, probably in either New York or Boston.

71 John Philip Yaeger (German, 1823–1899), *Tobacconist's Figure*, Baltimore, c. 1879. Painted wood, height 56 1/2 in. (143.5 cm). The Maryland Historical Society, Baltimore

Three members of the Wilson family were the most prominent shipcarvers in Newburyport in the nineteenth century. The brothers James (1825–1893) and Albert (b. 1828) Wilson may have been active around the time that the Indian figure was carved, when they would have been in their mid-fifties to early sixties. It was their father, however, who gained the most widespread recognition. Joseph

Wilson (1779–1857) was born in Marblehead and moved to Newburyport in 1798, where he did ship and architectural carving for over fifty years. His best-known work was done for a celebrated eccentric and self-styled aristocrat, "Lord" Timothy Dexter, who peopled his property with painted figures of famous individuals and biblical characters mounted on fifteen-foot pedestals and ornate arches. In all, Wilson created over thirty-seven representations of such luminaries as George Washington, Thomas Jefferson, Benjamin Franklin, William Pitt, Napoleon Bonaparte, Adam and Eve, King Solomon, and, of course, Timothy Dexter himself. Wilson also carved their columns and at least four triumphal arches. The resulting display was a local marvel and tourist attraction until it was destroyed by a hurricane in 1815.[86]

Little evidence of shop-figure carving is available for the many coastal towns north of Newburyport. Given the number of shipcarvers who operated in Maine and the diversity of work that they produced, however, it is reasonable to assume that several of them were commissioned by local merchants to create figures at one time or another. Hopefully, more information will be forthcoming in the future.

Canada supported several shipbuilding centers besides St. John, New Brunswick, of course, which was considered in the last chapter. Quebec City was the earliest, but active shipyards also operated in several locations along the St. Lawrence River, particularly in Montreal, as well as in smaller ports on the Great Lakes. Just as their counterparts in the United States, shipcarvers produced a wide range of work, from figureheads and shop signs to architectural and church decorations. The Catholic Church was the major patron from the earliest days, and due to its strong influence, religious statuary remained a mainstay for carvers for years after orders for shipcarving fell off towards the end of the nineteenth century.

The French workshop tradition was brought to Quebec early in its colonial history, with the introduction of a guild of master woodworkers-sculptors, known as the Brotherhood of Saint Anne, around 1650.[87] In addition, academically trained sculptors were contracted by the Church to come to Quebec from France for various commissions in the seventeenth and early eighteenth centuries. Before long, a strong sculptural and woodworking tradition had been established. Jean (1622–1686) and Pierre (1629–1681) Levasseur, for example, came to Quebec from Paris in 1651. At least twenty-two of their descendents worked as ornamental carvers, carpenters, carriage-makers, and sculptors over the course of four generations. The most influential workshop was no doubt that of the Baillairgé family, Jean (1726–1805), François (1759–1830), and Thomas (1791–1859). François studied in Paris for three years from 1778 to 1781, where he absorbed elements of French Neoclassicism that he then transmitted to the architecture and wooden sculpture of Quebec.[88]

The two best-known French-Canadian figure carvers in the nineteenth century, Jean-Baptiste Côté (1834–1907) and Louis Jobin (1845–1928), were trained in the Quebec tradition. Côté probably apprenticed with Louis-Thomas Berlinguet (1789–1863), a leading sculptor and architect, while Jobin worked with Berlinguet's son, François-Xavier (1830–1926). In both cases, their course of instruction included drawing, drafting, and carving techniques, as well as the study of the principles of architecture.[89] Jobin later recalled that much of the work that he and

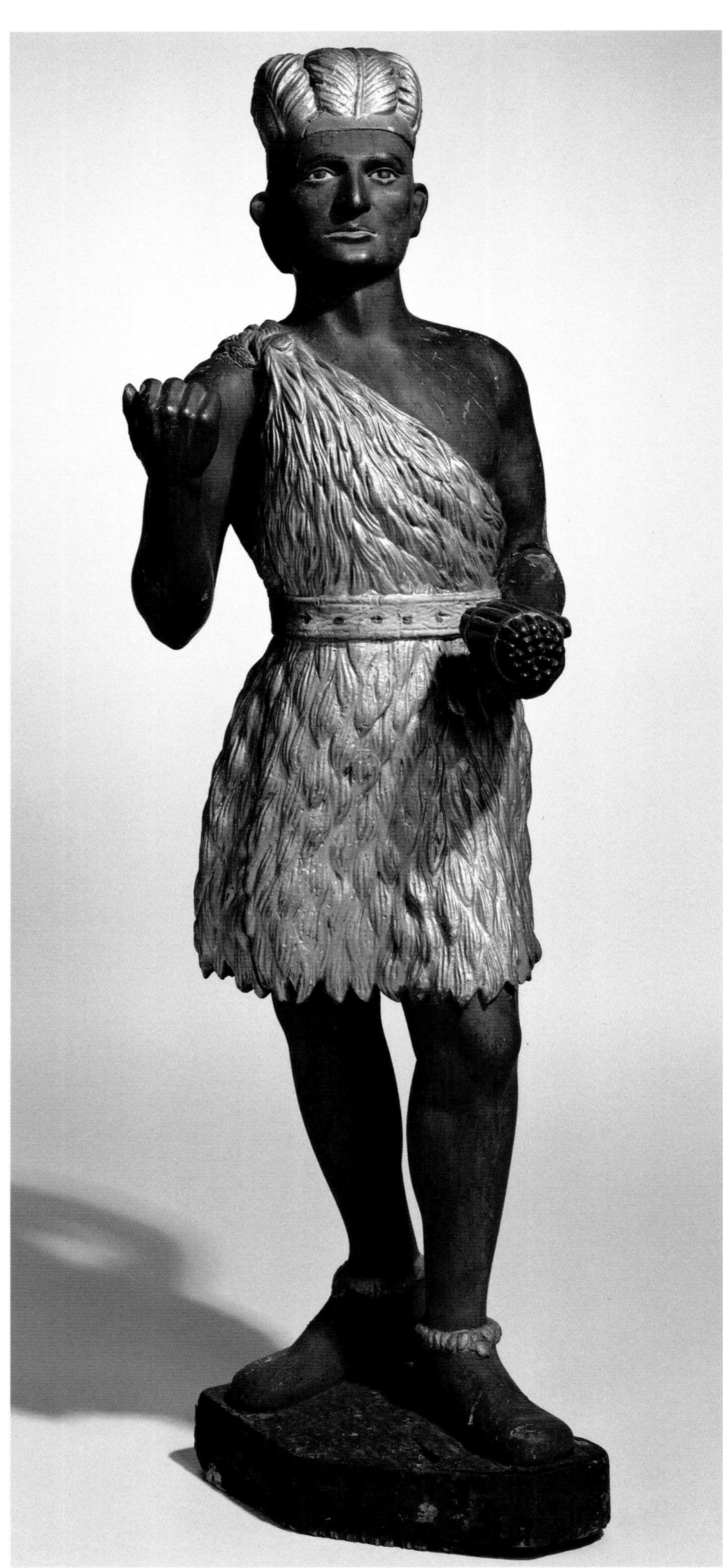

72 Attributed to David R. Proctor (American, active c. 1856–66), *Indian*, Gloucester, Mass., c. 1855. Painted wood, $55^{1}/_{2}$ x 17 x 17 in. (141 x 43.2 x 43.2 cm). Peabody Essex Museum, Salem, Mass.

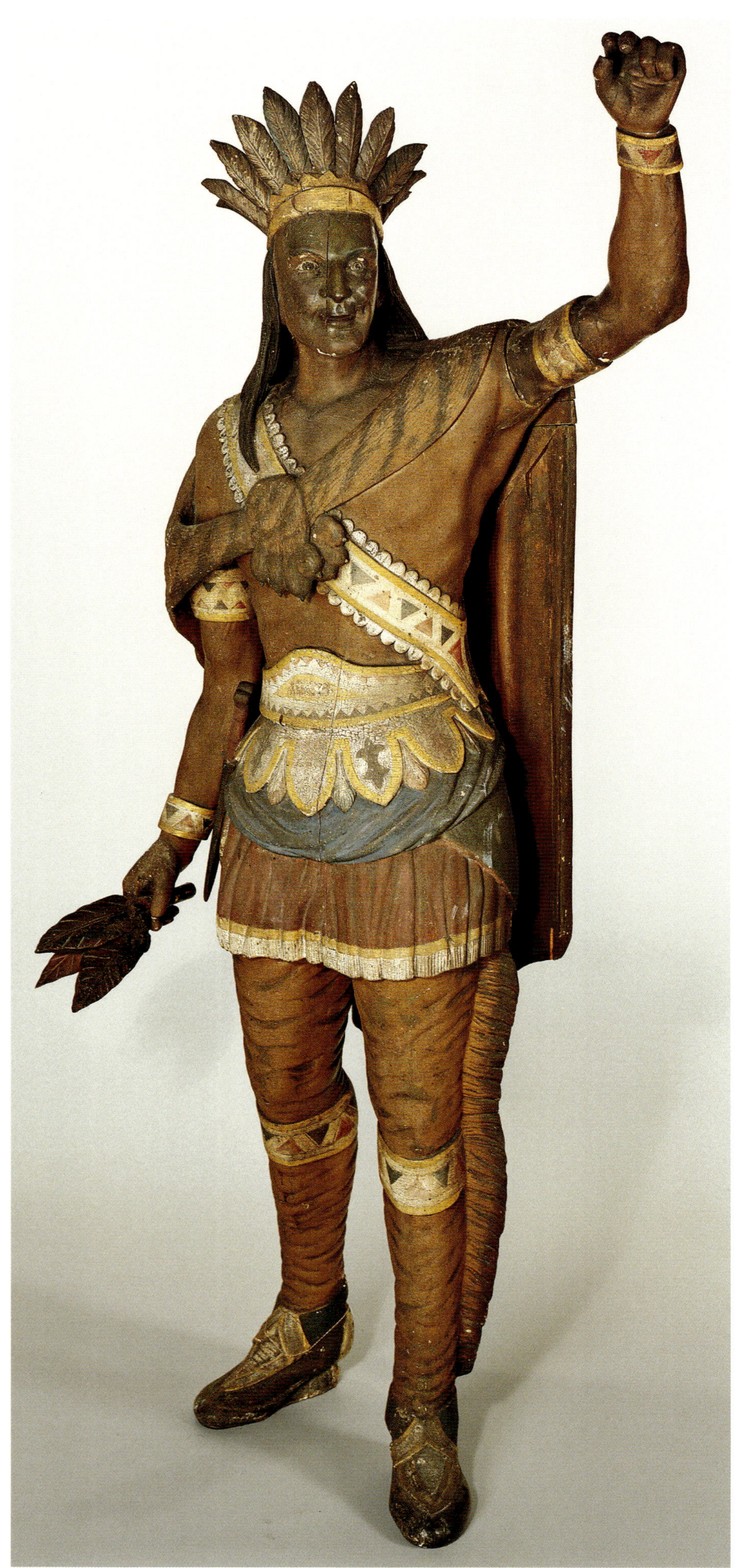

73 *Indian*, probably New England or New York, c. 1880. Painted wood with gold leaf, $71^{1}/_{2}$ x 21 x 20 in. (178.6 x 52.7 x 50.2 cm). Hood Museum of Art, Dartmouth College, Hanover, N.H. Gift of the Class of 1930

his fellows did at the time was maritime. "In those days it was all figureheads," he told a journalist in 1922.[90]

Côté briefly pursued architecture after he finished his apprenticeship, but by the mid-1850s he had established a shipcarving workshop in his old neighborhood of Saint Roche on the St. Charles River, where his father was a ship carpenter and foreman of a local shipyard. Throughout the 1860s, he also created over five hundred woodcut illustrations, primarily caricatures for satirical newspapers. With the decline of shipbuilding in Quebec after 1870, he increasingly focused on religious statuary and reliefs for churches and individual patrons, as well as shop and garden figures and commemorative sculpture.[91] An Indian figure that he carved around 1880 for Joseph Goulet's tobacco store in Saint Roche is in the collection of the Museé du Québec. Among the finest surviving examples of his work is a large statue of Johannes Guttenberg, modeled after a bronze by David d'Angers (1788–1856) in Strasbourg, France (plate 74).

Commissioned by the Society of Printers and Typographers of Quebec, Côté's *Guttenberg* was featured on a parade car in the Saint John the Baptist celebration, which was held during the "Convention nationale" of 1880. A major gathering of French-Canadian interests in Quebec with strong patriotic and religious overtones, the convention culminated in a spectacular parade of some twenty-five floats and eighty elaborate banners representing more than forty organizations and trade unions.[92] In this, the parade was a part of a venerable tradition descended from religious processions, which paralleled similar events in the United States that included the work of American carvers like William Rush and the Skillins.

Côté also supervised the construction of the float for the Society of Saint John the Baptist of Quebec—the most important one in the parade—and carved a figure of the saint for it. His colleague and competitor Louis Jobin was responsible for all or part of four floats, including statues of Saint Cecilia for the musicians' society and Ceres for an agriculture float sponsored by the farmers of Ancienne-Lorette (both now in the collection of the Musée du Québec).

Jobin is also known today for a distinctive type of tobacconist's Indian. After completing a three-year apprenticeship in 1868, he went to New York City, where he worked for an English sculptor and woodcarver named William Boulton (active c. 1860–1874), who had specialized in marble before coming to the United States. He was then employed by some German carvers, one of whom may have been Simon Strauss (active c. 1866–d. 1897). While in New York, Jobin fashioned figures of all types and sizes and became particularly proficient in roughing out forms.[93] Judging by his later work, the shop figures that he learned to make followed the prevailing show-figure style that was then reaching the height of its popularity.

Returning to Canada in 1870, Jobin settled in Montreal and opened his own shop. He later recalled that in addition to carving religious figures and altars, "above all I made signs. . . . I created a hanging sheep, to represent a tailor; female savages to represent tobacco; various types of savages, even little Negroes."[94] After five years in Montreal, he relocated to Quebec City, where he operated a successful carving business until 1896, when his shop was destroyed by fire for the second time in twenty years. He then moved to Ste-Anne-de-Beaupré, a small town twenty miles to the northeast on the St. Lawrence River. The site of

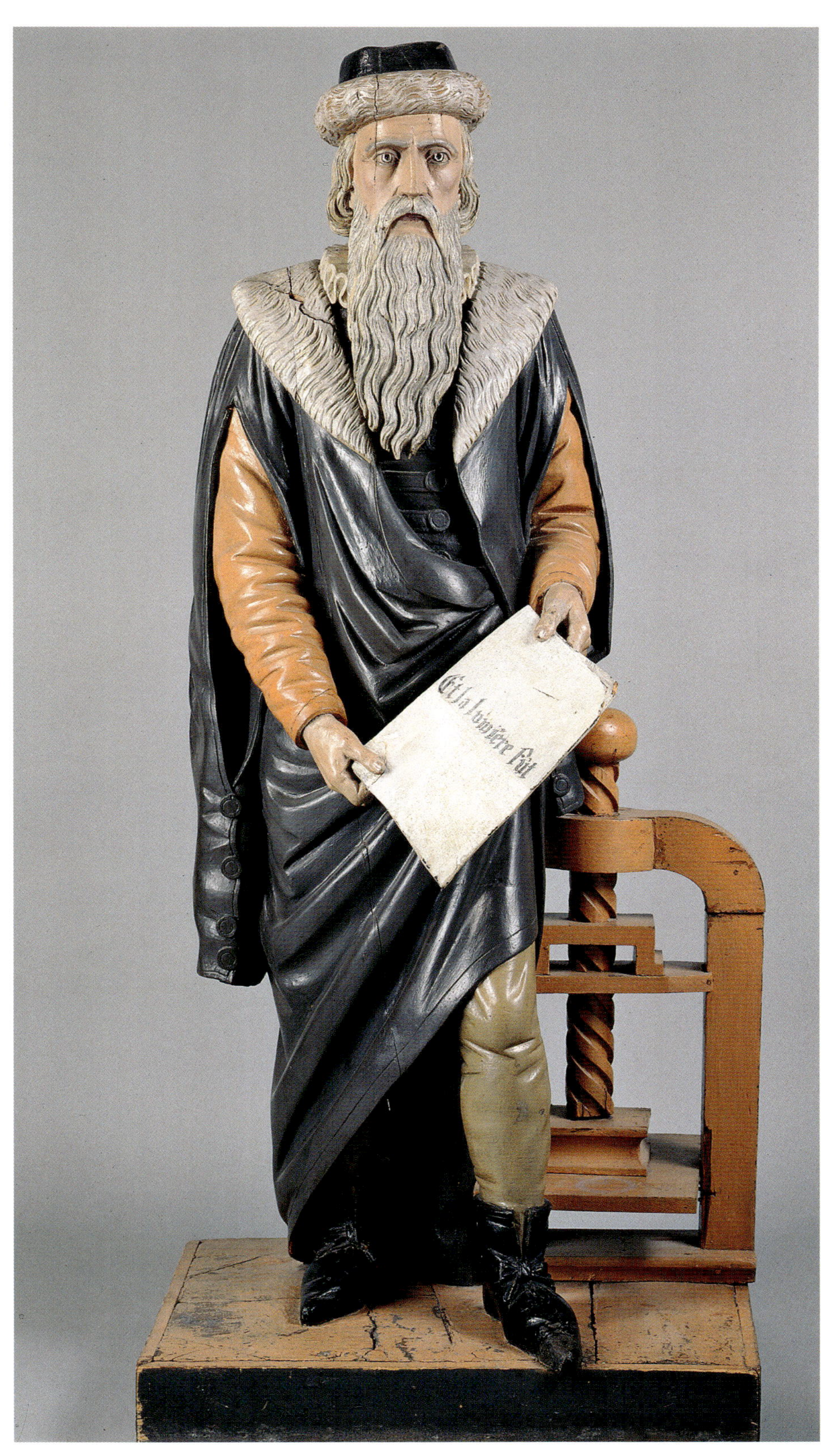

74 Jean-Baptiste Côté (Canadian, 1834–1907), *Johannes Guttenberg*, Quebec, 1880. Painted wood, height $78\frac{1}{2}$ in. (199.4 cm). Musée national des beaux-arts du Québec (38.58)

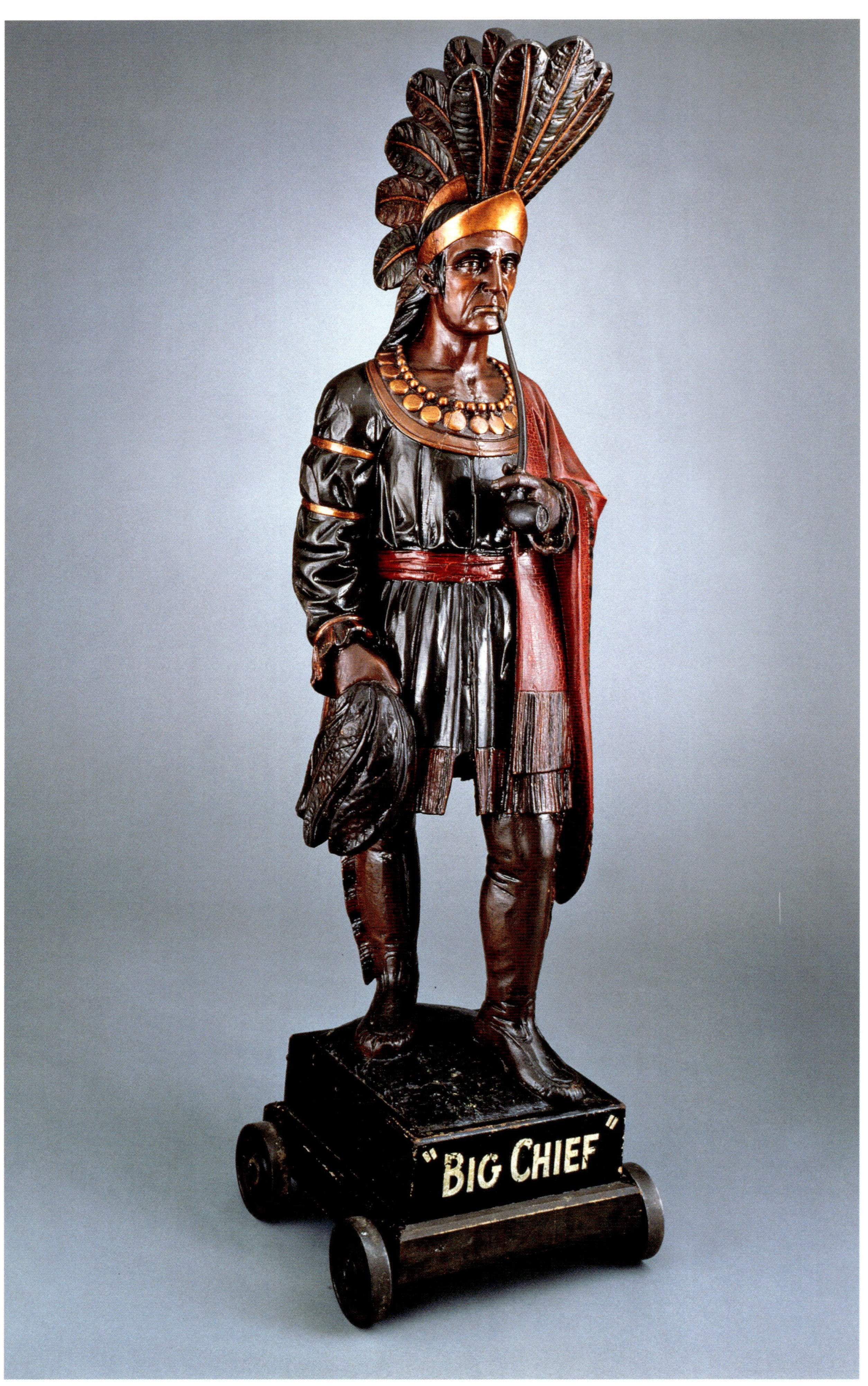
"BIG CHIEF"

75 (OPPOSITE) Attributed to Louis Jobin (Canadian, 1845–1928), *Indian*, Quebec, c. 1885. Painted wood, 79 x 22 x 20 in. (200.7 x 55.9 x 50.8 cm). © Shelburne Museum, Shelburne, Vt.

reported miracles that dated back to the early colonial era, Ste-Anne was and still is a popular destination for pilgrimages. Jobin primarily fashioned saints and votive carvings for visitors and other patrons until his death in 1928.[95]

Over the course of his long and productive career, Jobin carved approximately one thousand figures. Wooden statuary sheathed in lead for exteriors was something of a specialty. His most ambitious work is undoubtedly *Our Lady of the Saguenay*, an Immaculate Conception, twenty-five feet high, that was installed at Cape Trinity on the Saguenay River in 1881. Done from three huge blocks of pine and sheathed in lead, it was a monumental ex-voto commissioned by a man who believed that his life had been miraculously saved after his carriage broke through the ice on the river.[96]

Jobin's surviving cigar-store figures are particularly notable (plate 75). All share a similar pose, sharply modeled face, large feathered headdress, and several costuming details, including fringed tunic, leggings, and shawl draped over the

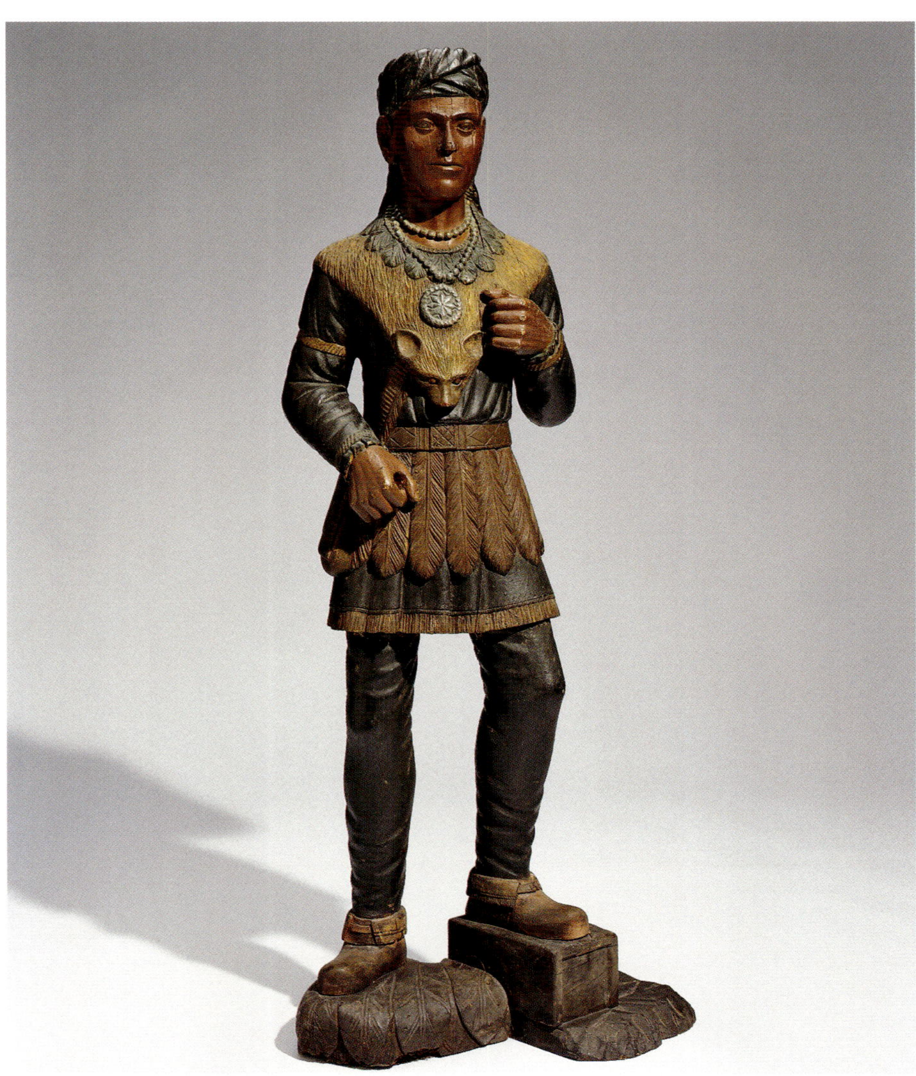

76 (RIGHT) Attributed to Julius Melchers (Prussian, 1829–1909), *Fur Trapper*, Detroit, c. 1865. Painted wood, 46 x 19 x 12½ in. (116.8 x 48.3 x 31.7 cm). Fenimore Art Museum, Cooperstown, N.Y.

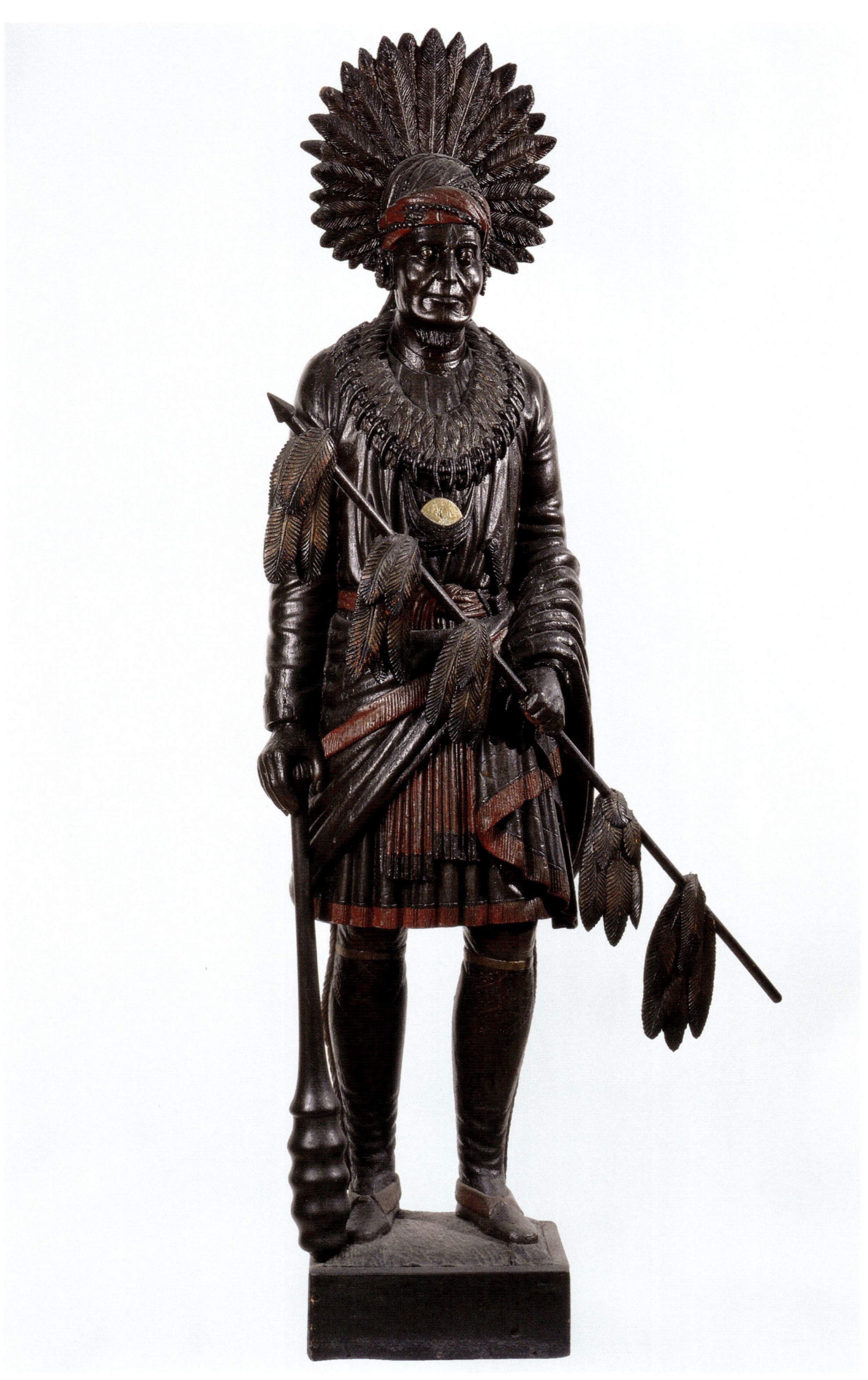

77 (OPPOSITE) Attributed to Julius Melchers, *Keokuk*, Detroit, c. 1870. Painted wood, height 92 in. (233.7 cm). The New-York Historical Society, New York (1956.86)

left shoulder and arm. Other accessories differ, such as the pipe seen in the piece illustrated here, but the general stylistic consistency of his work is reminiscent of the practice of some of the New York shipcarvers whom he might have known as a young man. Like them, Jobin developed the individualized touch of a master carver within the context of the larger show-figure tradition.

Besides Jobin, Côté, and some of the American shipcarvers already discussed, the best-known nineteenth-century carver is undoubtedly Julius Melchers (1829–1909), a German sculptor and woodcarver who settled in Detroit in 1855. His reputation is well deserved, as he was certainly a master of the art. Because he was recognized in his lifetime for his many contributions to his adopted city, several articles were written about him in Detroit newspapers beginning in 1899, including two interviews. This information provides a fairly complete record of both his career and his workshop practices.

Trained in traditional German woodcarving techniques, Melchers was not a shipcarver, although he did maritime work after he settled in Detroit. By and large, European craft traditions were more specialized than those in North America, and while generations of shipcarvers worked in German ports on the North and Baltic Seas, Melchers was not one of them. Born in Soest, Prussia, he was apprenticed to a sculptor and master woodcarver who taught him to be a carver of architectural, religious, and commemorative sculpture in wood and certain types of stone. As a young man with revolutionary sympathies, he was forced to flee Prussia during the Revolution of 1848. He first went to Paris and then, in 1851, to England, where he modeled decorations for the famed Crystal Palace. A year later, he sailed for New York City, finally moving to Detroit in 1855.[97]

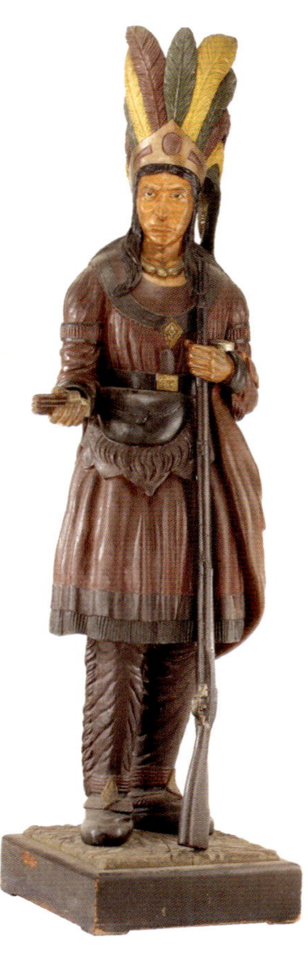

78 (BELOW) Arnold Ruef (American, active c. 1870–90), *Seneca John*, Tiffin, Ohio, c. 1870. Painted wood, height 81 in. (205.7 cm). Henry Ford Museum, Dearborn, Mich.

Once there, Melchers joined a growing German community and quickly became involved in a number of social activities and local organizations. He soon found, however, that his specialized carving skills were not much in demand.[98] A resourceful and enterprising type, Melchers diversified. He opened a workshop that for almost forty years produced a wide range of architectural sculpture, church carvings, patterns for decorative castings, maritime work, and shop figures. Melchers also conducted classes in drawing and modeling, and so made a major contribution to Detroit's fledgling artistic community. His efforts were later recognized by a local journalist: "It may be said without exaggeration that out of Julius Melchers' studio and his Sunday morning classes came much of Detroit's artistic development during the succeeding 35 years. Practically all the well known artists who have come out of Detroit, and some of them are world-famous, had their early instruction and their basic ideals of art out of the Melchers school."[99] Included among them was his most famous student and son, the painter Gari Melchers (1860–1932).

While he never considered them to be an art form that was truly worthy of his talents, Melchers produced many shop figures for local merchants. He is also known to have supplied tobacconists throughout Illinois and neighboring states. As he explained to a reporter in 1899:

> Then I carved more Indians. I bought a lot of old masts at the old Clark drydock. There's no timber like an old mast for carv-

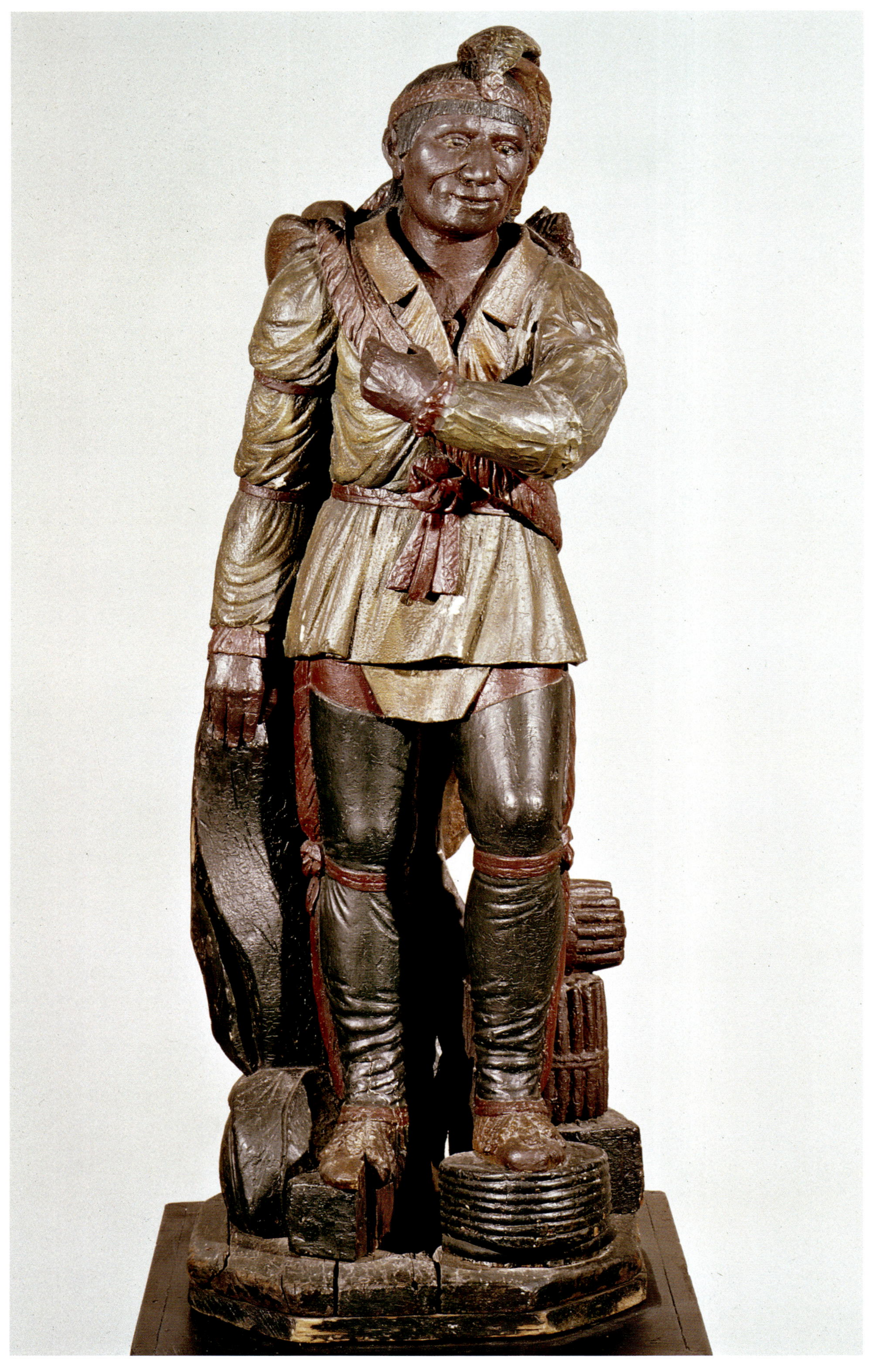

79 (OPPOSITE) *Trapper Indian*, eastern United States or Canada, c. 1850. Painted wood, height $42^{3}/_{4}$ in. 108.6 cm). Abby Aldrich Rockefeller Folk Art Museum, Colonial Williamsburg Foundation, Williamsburg, Va.

> ing. It is straight-grained, and so thoroughly seasoned with its many years of exposure on the deck of a ship that there is no danger of its cracking. I carved all sorts of Indians. Big Indians, little Indians, chiefs, and Indian queens. Sometimes the images represented real characters but they were oftener ideal figures. I made Blackhawks, Pontiacs, Hiawathas and Pocahontases. The first Hiawatha I carved was for Daniel Scotten when he brought out his Hiawatha brand of fine cut. But I made Indians only when there was a lack of other work, or to keep my apprentices employed. I made the models, and they cut out the images. They liked this work as it gave them practice in the study of figures.[100]

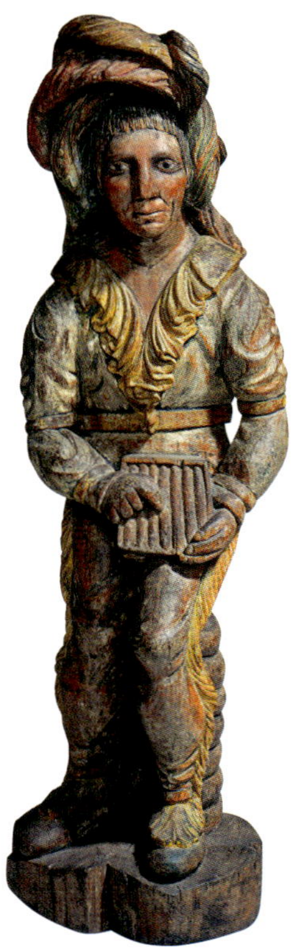

80 (ABOVE) *Trapper Indian*, northeastern United States or Canada, mid-nineteenth century. Painted wood, 38 x 10 x $9^{1}/_{4}$ in. (96.5 x 25.4 x 23.5 cm). The Eleanor and Mabel Van Alstyne Collection of American Folk Art, National Museum of American History, Smithsonian Institution, Washington, D.C.

Not only were shop figures a welcome source of income, then, but they also proved to be a useful means of instruction. Unlike shipcarving workshops in the eastern seaports, in which master carvers, journeymen, and apprentices usually cooperated in making a single figure, Melchers apparently allowed his assistants and apprentices to complete an entire piece under his supervision. This helps account for some of the variations seen in figures that have been attributed to him over the years.

Melchers's best figures are sensitively rendered, with a naturalism that is quite convincing. A *Fur Trapper* attributed to him has several conventional features, including a feathered skirt, catamount pelt, and left leg supported by a box, but is nevertheless far from typical (plate 76). The masterful carving seen in the handling of form, as well as in the modeling of the face and other details, is particularly notable. Another outstanding piece that has been attributed to his hand is a figure of Keokuk (plate 77), a leader of the Sauk tribe in the first half of the nineteenth century and a contemporary of Black Hawk, the Sauk chief mentioned earlier. Perhaps based on an as yet unlocated print source, it is a tour de force of realistic carving that was probably a special commission, given the detailed treatment that it received. The entire surface is precisely worked, with individual elements carefully subordinated to the whole.[101]

Julius Melchers was just one of many German-born carvers who created shop figures in the United States in the second half of the nineteenth century. John Philip Yaeger of Baltimore was another. In spite of a number of contemporary references to German craftsmen working here, most of them remain unidentified. The same can be said for many of the other European-trained carvers who immigrated to the United States and set up workshops in cities and towns throughout the country. Of the many distinctive shop figures made outside the major East Coast seaports, few surviving examples can be documented to specific carvers. Moreover, even when one can be linked to its maker, often little more is known about him than his name and address.

A figure known as *Seneca John* that was made around 1870 is a case in point (plate 78). The piece was carved by Arnold Ruef (active c. 1870–90) of Tiffin, Ohio, with the help of his son, Peter. According to an article that appeared in the *Cleveland Plain Dealer* in 1928, it stood in front of John Dehmer's cigar store in Tiffin for many years. Evidently a well-known local landmark, it was also called

"The Tiffin Tecumseh" by townspeople.[102] The two nicknames are unrelated. Tecumseh (c. 1768–1813) was a legendary Shawnee chief who formed a powerful pan-Indian alliance and helped defeat American attempts to invade Canada during the War of 1812. He was not a member of the Seneca Nation of upstate New York, nor was his surname John. From this we can assume that, as is often the case, the Ruef figure was not originally intended to represent a particular individual, and that the names accrued to it over time.

A skillful piece of carving, the figure has understandably attracted much attention over the years. Ruef was evidently a trained carver, but where and when he received his instruction is impossible to say. He may have apprenticed with a shipcarver in an eastern port before moving to Ohio, or may have worked with a European-trained carver in some midwestern city. The mystery will probably never be solved, but the figure remains a testament to the high quality of work that was produced in many smaller American towns.

Among the other distinctive figures by unidentified makers that deserve mention are two that are both known as *Trapper Indians* (plates 79 and 80). The first has been the subject of much speculation since its public debut at the landmark exhibition of folk sculpture held at the Newark Museum in 1931. A finely carved piece with a remarkably expressive face, it is sensitively rendered in the best nineteenth-century fashion. The coils of tobacco and bunches of cigars that surround the figure's feet and legs link it to work that was done before about 1850. It has been suggested that the clothing resembles that worn by Indians in the Southeast, but the piece could have been carved in any one of a number of cities or towns in the eastern United States or Canada.[103]

The second *Trapper Indian* is a more stylized rendition with some striking features that mark it as a one-of-a-kind work. The headdress of plumes or feathers is similar to some examples that have been discussed earlier, but in this case, it is exaggerated to the extent of being out of scale with the rest of the figure. The costume is an unusual combination of what appears to be a ruffled shirt and fringed buckskin leggings. The various elements indicate that the figure was carved outside of the major shipcarving centers in the United States, and that it is possibly of French-Canadian origin.

Its handling suggests the work of a self-taught carver, one of the many men not trained in either Anglo-American shipcarving or European woodcarving traditions who fashioned figures for local markets, often in smaller inland towns and rural areas. Throughout the eighteenth and nineteenth centuries, carpenters, cabinetmakers, and part-time woodworkers in all parts of the country produced shop figures on demand or for personal enjoyment. Little can be said about common training or techniques of these generally unidentified artists, other than what can be inferred from their work. They represent a diverse collection of individuals who usually operated independently of one another, often creating unique, one-of-a-kind pieces patterned after those produced in the seaport shops. In all, they produced far fewer figures than shipcarvers, and again survival rates are low. As a result, their work is extremely rare today. Their artistry speaks for itself, however, and among the surviving examples are some of the most dynamic and engaging pieces of American folk sculpture.

81 Attributed to Job (dates unknown), *African-American Indian*, Freehold, N.J., mid-nineteenth century. Painted wood, 46 x 16 1/4 x 12 1/4 in. (116.8 x 41.3 x 31.1 cm). Fenimore Art Museum, Cooperstown, N.Y.

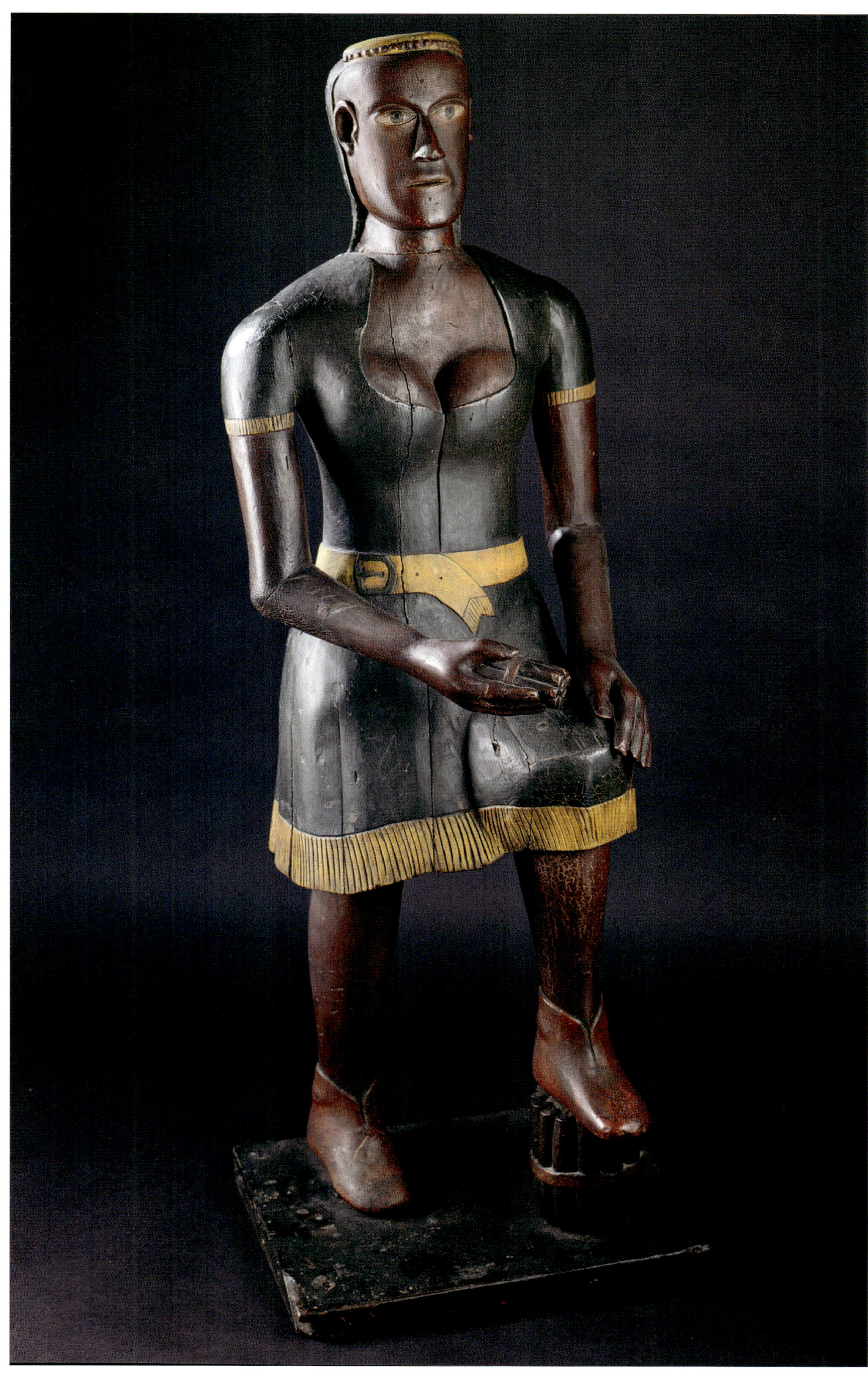

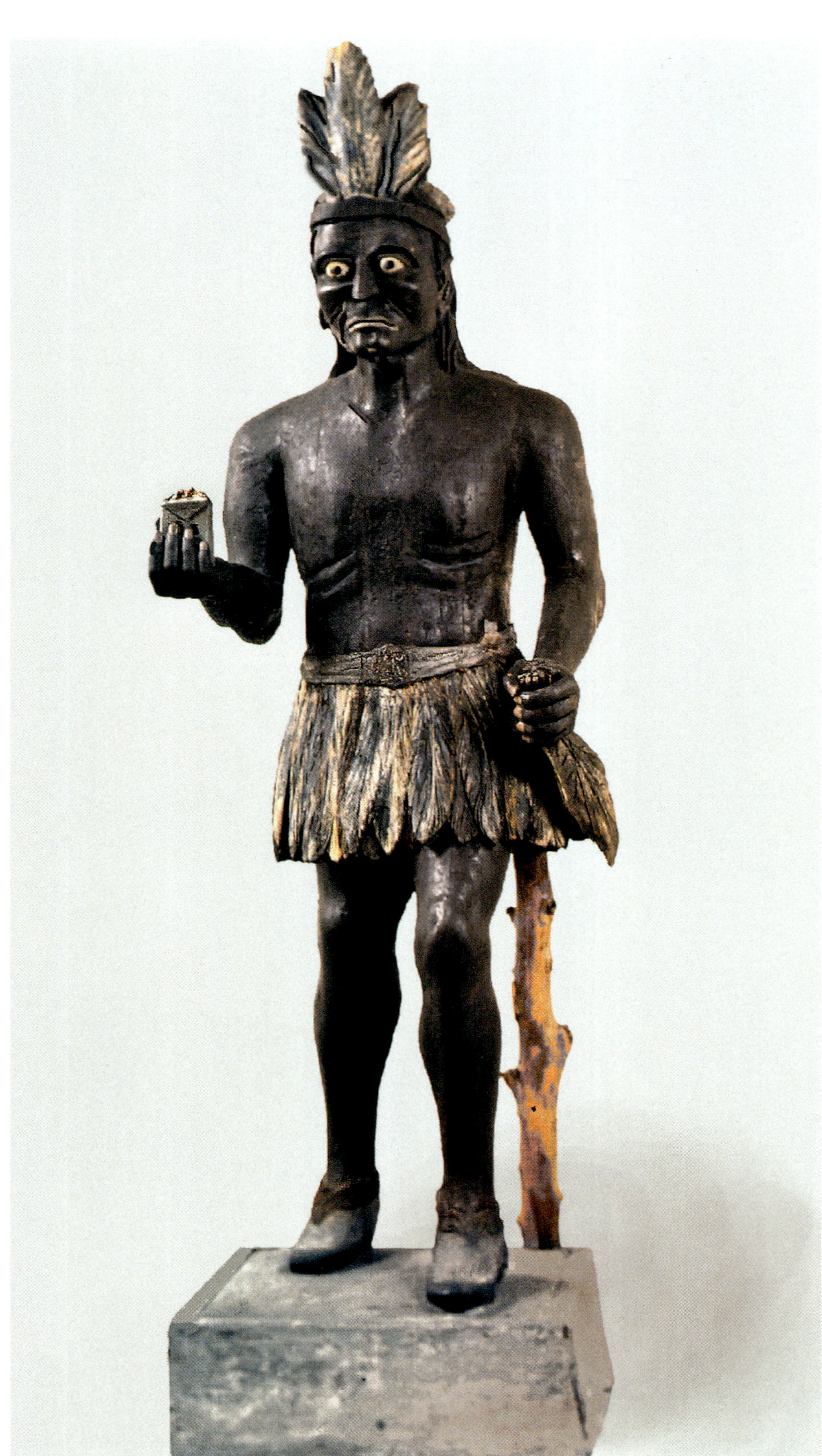

82 *Indian*, eastern United States, c. 1875. Painted wood, 82 x 26 x 24 in. (208.3 x 66 x 60.9 cm). General Cigar Holdings Collection, New York

One of the most distinctive of these is a figure of a woman thought to have been carved in Freehold, New Jersey, around mid-century by an African-American named Job (plate 81).[104] Powerfully stylized, it has an abstracted presence, stripped of ornamentation and yet presented in a typical pose with the left leg raised and supported by a bunch of cigars. The carver was obviously aware of the show figures being made some forty miles to the north in New York City. This is particularly evident in his treatment of the two bunches of cigars and the use of scored fringe at the bottom of the skirt and on the sleeves. In addition, the revealing cut of the dress is a rare but not unique feature among urban figures, designed to catch the eye of male customers. In this case, the result is a highly individualized interpretation combining an eroticized body with a bold, masklike face that has been noted for its formality and an "iconic intensity"[105] suggestive of African sculpture.

Another powerful, if somewhat disquieting, figure by an unidentified self-taught carver is a large and imposing representation of a male Indian, possibly of southern origin (plate 82).[106] Its massive upper body and head, combined with a short feathered skirt and thin legs, give it a sense of being slightly off-balance. This probably suited the carver's intentions, for the figure is evidently a caricature with strong racial overtones. Its dark, almost naked body, straining neck, and face with prominently bulging eyes and light-colored lips present a parody of the stereotypical Indian, suggesting a minstrel figure in blackface. In this way, it is a stark reminder of the conflicting feelings toward American Indians in a society that placed this image alongside that of the Noble Savage. The derogatory portrayal of this grotesquely comic figure contrasts sharply with that of the stoic warrior who gallantly accepts his cruel, but inevitable fate in the grand scheme of the progress of civilization.

With this figure, we have moved a considerable distance from Donald McKay's East Boston shipyard and the figurehead of *Minehaha* with which the chapter began. The discussion has ranged from the network of seaport shops that were the major figure-carving centers, through small-town America and its skilled woodcarvers, to the vital self-taught tradition that flourished alongside and in response to the old craft workshops. The common denominator has been the image of the American Indian, a representation that infused American society throughout the eighteenth and nineteenth centuries as national symbol, tragic hero of romantic musings, object of derision, and commercial emblem. While none of this has much to do with the reality of Native American life, it does reflect the importance of the Indian presence in the United States and the extent to which it helped shape the American psyche. In the sheer numbers produced and diversity of types represented, shop and cigar-store figures tell a complicated tale of the imaginary Indian as a fundamental part of the American experience.

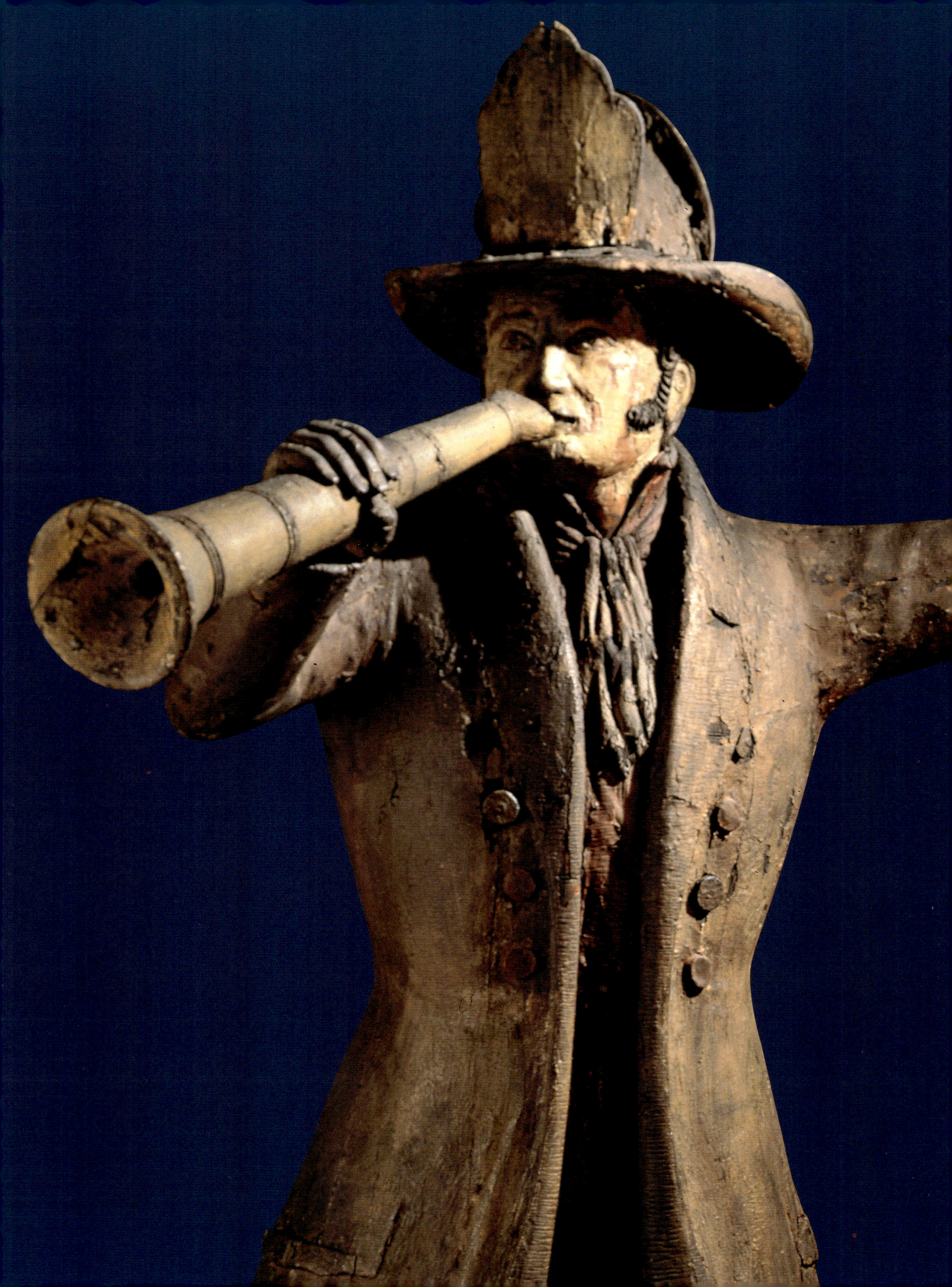

CHAPTER 4 SHOW FIGURES

Caricature and Stereotypes

83 (OPPOSITE) Detail of plate 112

SOMETIME AROUND 1850, a figure of Father Diedrich Knickerbocker, the personification of old Dutch New York made famous by Washington Irving, was placed in a niche on the exterior of Knickerbocker Hall on the northwest corner of Twenty-Third Street and Eighth Avenue in New York City (plate 84). A dapper gentleman dressed in colonial attire and standing about three feet tall, he was used as a sign for the Knickerbocker Stage Line, which occupied the building until it was demolished in 1867. He can be seen behind one of the company's horse-drawn buses in a contemporary view of Knickerbocker Hall (plate 85) by William Seaman (active c. 1840s–60s).[1]

In his costume, size, and traditional associations, *Father Knickerbocker* represented an older type of figural sign that was rapidly losing favor even as he was assuming pride of place on Knickerbocker Hall. Just like the cigar-store Indians that were considered in the last chapter, he and his kind were being rendered obsolete by more up-to-date characters carved in the mid-century show-figure style.

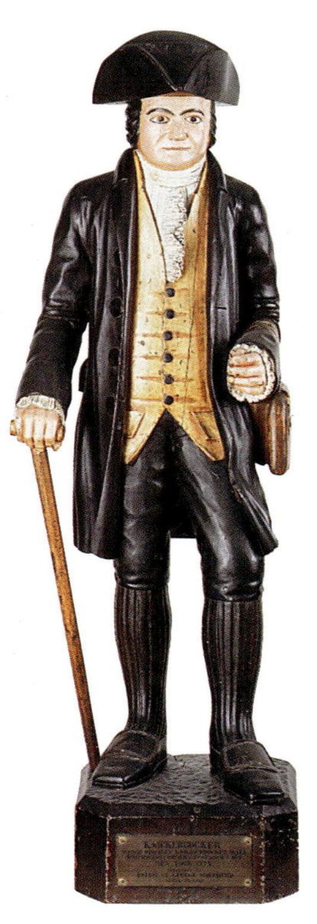

84 (ABOVE) *Father Knickerbocker*, New York, c. 1850–69. Painted wood, 36 x 12 x 9 1/2 in. (91.4 x 30.5 x 24.1 cm). The New-York Historical Society, New York (1912.22)

The ubiquitous Indian and his familiar counterparts, the Highlander, Turk, and sailor, were part of an old tradition. As we have seen, painted signboards, wooden figures, and hanging three-dimensional images of shoes, gloves, hats, and the like had been employed by merchants and tradesmen for centuries. By the mid-nineteenth century, however, the accelerating pace of American life and the increasingly competitive business environment that accompanied it had affected a significant change. An emerging national popular culture engaged the public's attention, whether it was the latest fashion, theatrical performance, or political event. The carvers responded to these trends by creating new types of figures, which shopkeepers found advantageous in their efforts to outdo one another to attract customers. An emphasis on change and variety began to replace the older concepts of familiarity and traditional association that had dominated earlier forms of marketing and advertising.

Reflecting on the popularity of shop figures during the past half-century or so, a reporter wrote in 1890:

> Time changes and so does the popular taste. At first the red man ruled the market almost completely. Then came a heavy sprinkling of other figures—fiery Scotchmen, English officers with small fatigue caps or high bearskins, and heavy swells of ante-bellum times and the war period, with marvelously wide pantaloons and waving mutton chop whiskers, ogled simpering Dolly Vardens with short-cut skirts, bustles, and hats tilted for-

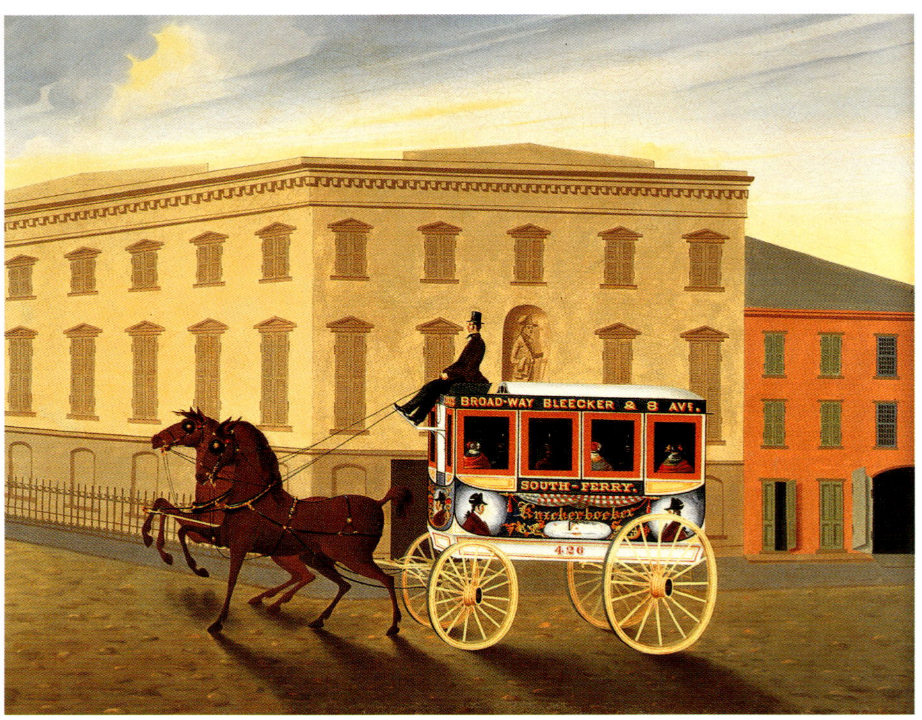

85 William Seaman (active c. 1840s–60s), *Knickerbocker Stage Line Omnibus*, c. 1850. Oil on canvas, 28 3/4 x 36 in. (73 x 91.4 cm). The New-York Historical Society, New York (1912.8)

> ward over the eyes. Then came grave Turks, gorgeous sultanas, and columbines with alarmingly short skirts. Punch, with rubicund nose and protuberant chin, was a favorite figure. There was also the conventional plantation "nigger," with striped pantaloons and a great expanse of shirt collar.[2]

Some of these characters and the stereotypical attitudes that they represent are already familiar, while others are more obscure. All of them will be encountered in one form or another in this chapter.

By the mid-1850s, the shop-figure tradition had reached the dimensions of a fad, and New York City had become the leading center for production and distribution. New figures were being continually introduced, and the number and types of businesses that displayed them increased dramatically. In 1871, New York tobacco-products distributor William Demuth advertised that he had a "Large and Varied Assortment of Wooden Show Figures which we are constantly manufacturing for all classes of business, such as Segar Stores, Wine & Liquors, Druggists, Yankee Notions, Umbrella, Clothing, Tea Stores, Theatres, Gardens, Banks, Insurance Companies, &c" (plate 86).[3]

Demuth and a few other distributors were, in fact, a principal reason for the rapid expansion of popularity of show figures. Assuming the role of middlemen and promoters, they employed shipcarvers to make figures that they then added to their inventories and displayed in their stores. They also took custom orders and commissions from their clients and shipped the figures throughout the country. Their increasingly sophisticated marketing techniques made New York show figures readily available on a national basis, thereby further stimulating demand.

Although the surviving evidence is somewhat scarce, the first of these innovative entrepreneurs appears to have been James Chichester, a tobacconist who opened a shop on New York's Water Street in 1837 and relocated in 1848 to the Bowery between Bayard and Canal Streets, not far from the old Bowery Theatre. In the early 1850s, he began carrying a line of shop figures made by Thomas Millard, who, as will be recalled, was later credited by Samuel Robb as being one of

WM. DEMUTH & CO.,
No. 403 BROADWAY, N. Y.,
IMPORTERS AND MANUFACTURERS OF
SEGARS AND SMOKERS' ARTICLES
WOODEN FIGURES.

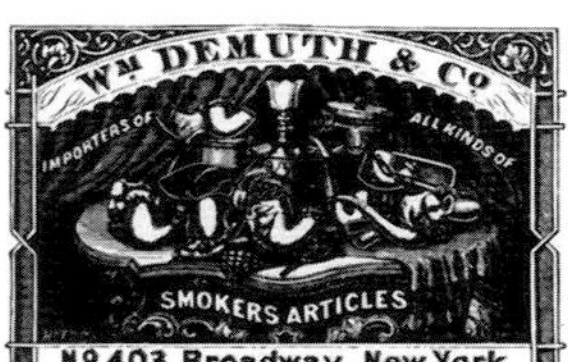

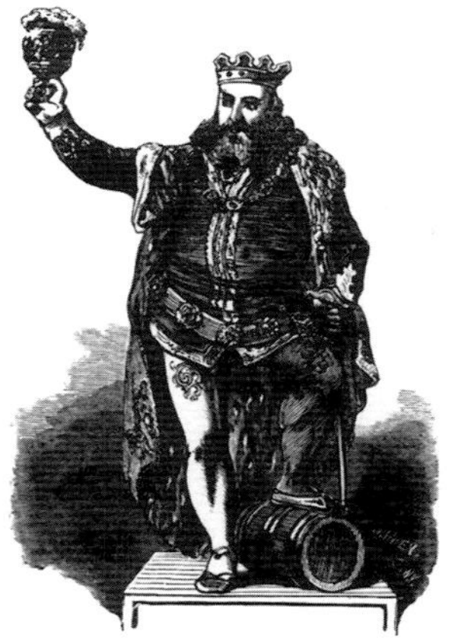

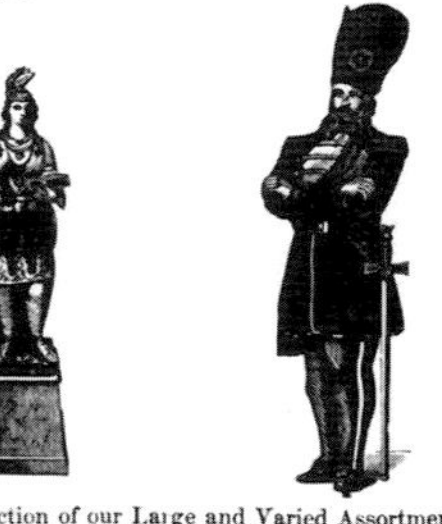

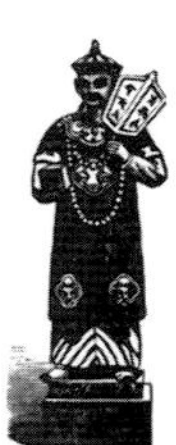

WE would respectfully solicit from the Public generally an Inspection of our Large and Varied Assortment of

WOODEN SHOW FIGURES,

which we are constantly manufacturing for all classes of business, such as

SEGAR STORES, WINE & LIQUORS, DRUGGISTS, YANKEE NOTIONS, UMBRELLA, CLOTHING, TEA STORES, THEATRES, GARDENS, BANKS, INSURANCE COMPANIES, &c.

Before we commenced Manufacturing Show Figures, their use was almost entirely confined to Tobacconists, who displayed before their Stores a figure of what by a great stretch of imagination might have been recognised as an Indian—the workmanship of which, to say the least, was not very artistic.

Since then we claim not only to have Manufactured Figures which are both carved and painted in a manner which cannot be excelled, but also to have introduced a number of entirely new and original designs for same, to which we are constantly making additions to suit many other classes of trade (as stated above) besides the Tobacco.

But although our Figures invariably gave full satisfaction, still we wished to make a greater improvement in the line, and by the use of some more durable substance than Wood, thus prevent cracking, which will sometimes occur in Wooden Figures, especially when exposed to the climate of our Southern States.

For this purpose, after incurring a heavy outlay for Designs, Moulds, &c., we commenced the Manufacture of our New

METAL SHOW FIGURES,

(being the first parties in the country to introduce same), which have now been before the public for over two years, during which time we have sent large numbers to all sections of the country without ever having received the slightest word of complaint in regard to them.

We claim for these Figures the following qualities: that they are durable, and as light as wooden figures; are designed and executed in a highly artistic manner; and can be furnished at comparatively low prices.

We are constantly receiving orders for Statues and Emblematic Signs, and can furnish same, of any required design, to order, with promptness.

WILLIAM DEMUTH & CO.,
403 BROADWAY, New York.

M. Thalmessinger & Co., Stationers, 308 Broadway, N. Y.

86 Advertisement for William Demuth and Company, New York, c. 1871. Lithograph. National Museum of American History, Smithsonian Institution, Washington, D.C.

the most influential carvers of his generation.[4] The venture proved to be quite successful, prompting Chichester's shop to be later remembered as "the wooden Indian store."[5] He does not seem to have expanded his business much beyond New York City, however. Evidently content with the local trade, he left it to others to exploit the marketing potential on a national scale.

At about the time that Chichester opened his first shop, a young German immigrant named Edward Hen arrived in New York. An ambitious man and legendary eccentric who reportedly wore the same cloak for over twenty-six years, Hen established a tobacco- and novelty-supply business on Liberty Street around 1840. Before long, he was one of the leading tobacco-products distributors in the city, amassing a considerable fortune through years of hard work, frugality, and shrewd investments. He was also adept at marketing his products, becoming the first to offer New York show figures on a national basis.[6] An advertisement that appeared in 1856 read, "Edward Hen, importer of French & German fancy goods, also smoker's articles, clay pipes, of all kinds, real and imitation meerschaums, hookas, and other Turkish waterpipes, adapted for one or more smokers, amber, meerschaums, horns & china segar tubes, tobacco & snuff boxes, segar cases, matches, Turkish tobacco, walking canes, show figures, Indians, &c &c."[7]

Hen's principal source for figures was Thomas Brooks, the most influential carver at the time. The relationship proved to be profitable for both men, with Brooks supplying Hen for over twelve years.[8] By the late 1860s, Hen's shop was overflowing with figures on display, creating what one long-time cigar-maker later remembered as "the largest congress of wooden braves the world has ever seen or ever will see."[9] By including the figures as a standard line of merchandise that could be shipped throughout the country, Hen vastly expanded the market for New York work. His business was instrumental in establishing New York City as the center for the production of show figures, as well as a model for a young employee who eventually became his successor, William Demuth.[10]

Born in Germany, Demuth immigrated to the United States in 1851 at age sixteen. He was working as a clerk for Hen by 1860, and three years later left to establish his own business as a direct competitor. By the end of the decade he was one of the leading tobacco-products distributors in the country. Pipes were a particular specialty, but he also offered a complete line of "segars and smokers' articles." His marketing strategies were even more aggressive than those of Edward Hen. He sent salesmen across the country and set up elaborate displays in the major national expositions and industrial fairs, including the World's Colombian Exposition in Chicago in 1893. As his reputation spread and business expanded, he became a wealthy man.[11]

Following in Hen's footsteps, Demuth also offered show figures as a part of his standard line. Both Samuel Robb and Thomas White worked for him, and other carvers may have as well. Robb began carving for Demuth in the late 1860s, soon after he completed his apprenticeship with Thomas Brooks, and continued to supply him with figures after he opened his own shop in 1876. White entered Demuth's employ a few years later, in 1872 or 1873, after he had ended his brief partnership with Brooks.[12] Since White then joined Robb in the Centre Street shop, it can be assumed that he, too, continued to carve for Demuth, albeit less directly.

As show figures became a larger part of his business, Demuth introduced some important innovations. Around 1868, he approached Moritz J. Seelig, another German immigrant who operated a foundry in Williamsburg, Brooklyn, with the idea of casting figures in zinc. The results of their initial experiment were encouraging, and before long, Demuth was offering a line of metal figures along with the more familiar wooden ones.[13] In 1869, the American Institute of the City of New York, a group organized to promote agriculture, manufacturing, and the "useful arts," awarded Demuth a medal for his entry of "Eight Metal and Wood Figures for Stores" at their Annual Fair.[14] Soon thereafter, he produced the flyer that is illustrated in plate 86. Then, in 1875, he issued an illustrated catalogue featuring thirty zinc figures that could be ordered in different sizes, or in the case of Indians, as either male or female. In it, Demuth stated:

> After a number of years' experience in the manufacture of Wooden Figures, we were induced to make use of a more durable material, and thus remove a difficulty unavoidably adherent to wood; its cracking from exposure to climatic changes; and, under heavy expenditures for designs, moulds, etc., we commenced the manufacture of our Metal Show Figures. During a period of over seven years we have shipped large numbers to all sections of the country; they have resulted in giving the fullest satisfaction to our patrons, and the sale of Metal Figures is now far exceeding that of wooden ones. Their advantages are evident; made in zinc, they combine strength with beauty; they are as light as wooden figures, and considering their everlasting durability, far cheaper.[15]

Evidently, his national market was well established by this time, and zinc figures were rapidly gaining popularity. They would continue to do so, but judging by the significantly larger number of wooden figures that have survived, Demuth's claim that sales of metal figures were "far exceeding that of wooden ones" would seem to be something of an exaggeration.

While it might seem that cast-metal figures had little to do with the old wooden Indians, the new process was actually not as large a departure from tradition as it first appears. Initially, the same men who made wooden figures were engaged to carve the models from which the zinc figures were cast.[16] The resulting metal figures closely resembled their wooden counterparts in many ways. The shipcarver's hand can be detected in both the general contours and detailing of the finished piece.

One such example is a type that was known as *Rising Star*, which was listed as no. 62 in Demuth's 1875 catalogue (plate 87). The treatment of her face, hair, and costume is consistent with the New York show-figure style as defined in the last chapter. She is also interesting as a sort of composite figure that combines elements of a cigar-store Indian with the short skirt of another type that was called a "Theatrical" (plate 88). This wooden figure could have been used by a theater or vaudeville hall, since she does not hold a bunch of cigars like her zinc counter-

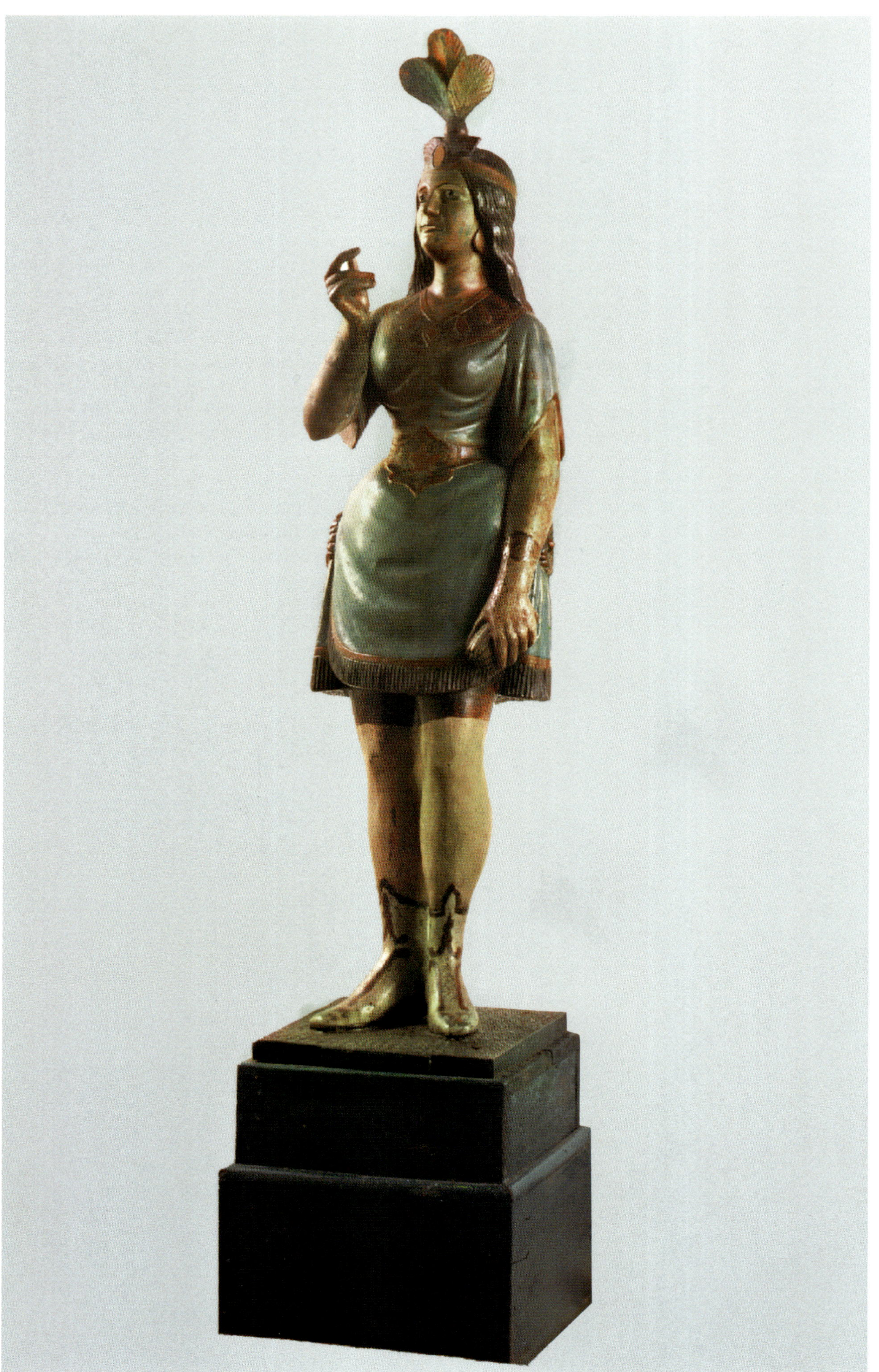

87 (OPPOSITE) Plate on base: "Wm. Demuth & Co.," *Rising Star,* New York, c. 1880. Painted zinc, 79 x 18 x 18 in. (200.6 x 45.7 x 45.7 cm). General Cigar Holdings Collection, New York

88 (BELOW) *Theatrical Figure,* probably New York, c. 1880. Painted wood, height 61 in. (154.9 cm). Private collection

part. She could also have served as a cigar-store figure, however, and an old photograph in a private collection shows a "Theatrical" very similar to plate 88 in front of a tobacco shop. Overall, the stylistic similarities between the two figures are quite striking. Both feature racy costumes designed to attract the attention of male patrons. They certainly qualify as "columbines with alarmingly short skirts," as quoted above, rendered marginally acceptable by their somewhat dubious professions as actresses and performers.

In creating these ladies, the carvers were not only responding to male fantasies but were also reflecting aspects of the shared artistic and cultural imagination seen in all show figures, Indian and non-Indian. As in the case of the Noble Savage, the images were based on contemporary perceptions, mirroring the attitudes, opinions, and prejudices of mainstream culture. A fundamental concept underlying their portrayal is the Victorian notion of the anthropological type. One of the principal concerns of the new social science of anthropology was the systematic classification and ordering of humanity through observation and inductive reasoning, in much the same way as the older and more-established natural sciences of botany and biology. Closely related were two so-called sciences: physiognomy, the belief that an individual's character was indicated by facial fea-

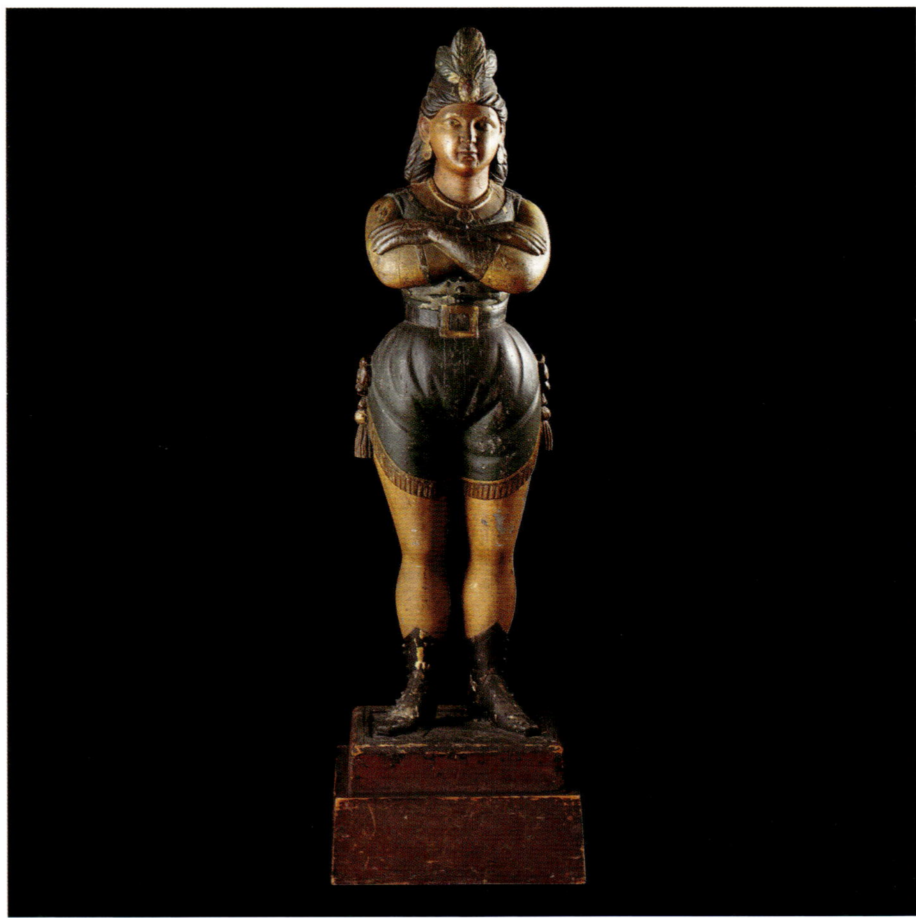

tures and forms of the head and body, and phrenology, in which character was read through the shape of the skull. Physiognomy, in particular, was almost universally accepted, and its academic practitioners believed themselves to be employing a scientific system of classification that was as legitimate as the methods used by botanists and zoologists.[17]

While it was primarily a means of distinguishing one individual from another, physiognomy also provided a rationale for grouping people who shared certain physical characteristics. Blurring distinctions between class, race, and type, it aided anthropologists and other students of humanity in their efforts to organize mankind according to a hierarchical, Darwinian scheme that assigned specific intellectual and moral identities to physically distinctive individuals and groups.

On a popular level, certain physical and personality traits were commonly used to define characteristics for entire classes of people. The attributed traits might be regional, as with the shrewd Yankee and the genteel southerner, or ethnic, as with the scrappy Irishman and the swarthy Italian, or racial, as with the inscrutable Chinaman and the happy Negro. Identifying contemporary types and applying generalized, stereotypical identities to them was considered to be an appropriate way to characterize and differentiate humanity, particularly in mainstream Anglo-American society, which tended to reserve the most flattering traits for itself.

Following is a survey of many of the most popular types represented by show figures, along with commentary intended to provide identifications and contextual background. Due to low survival rates and a lack of documentation for many of the figures, as well as the enormous amount of literature on ethnic and gender stereotyping, a complete treatment of the material would not be a feasible undertaking. Instead, the discussion will highlight the remarkable diversity of figures carved and cast in the second half of the nineteenth century, and attempt to demonstrate the major artistic trends and social historical issues that informed their creation.

From our vantage point today, the stereotypical images in show figures range from the relatively benign to the egregious. By and large, representations of exotic foreign types fall in the former category. The Turk is a case in point. While never totally out of fashion, he experienced something of a comeback as a show figure in the second half of the nineteenth century. One of the finest examples is a lifesize *Turk* that closely resembles an illustration of a figure listed as no. 40 in William Demuth's 1875 catalogue (plate 89). Carved in a realistic style, his face, turban, and long, flowing beard are sensitively rendered, while his impassive stare gives him an air of remoteness appropriate to his origins in a faraway land. He is also notable for his long-stemmed pipe, an original accessory that is rarely encountered.

The *Turk*'s impressive stature is matched by that of a monumental *Sultana* that has survived intact with an original paint surface that shows almost no evidence of retouching (plate 90). Her many details, including a jeweled and feathered turban, fringed sash around her waist, and basket of cigars and tobacco boxes cradled in her left arm, make her an exceptional example of a New York City show figure. Finally, these two figures bear comparison to a remarkably stylized countersize *Turk* that was probably done by a self-taught carver (plate 91). The smooth planes and generalized but sure carving of this stocky little figure illustrate the range of interpretations of the theme at the time.

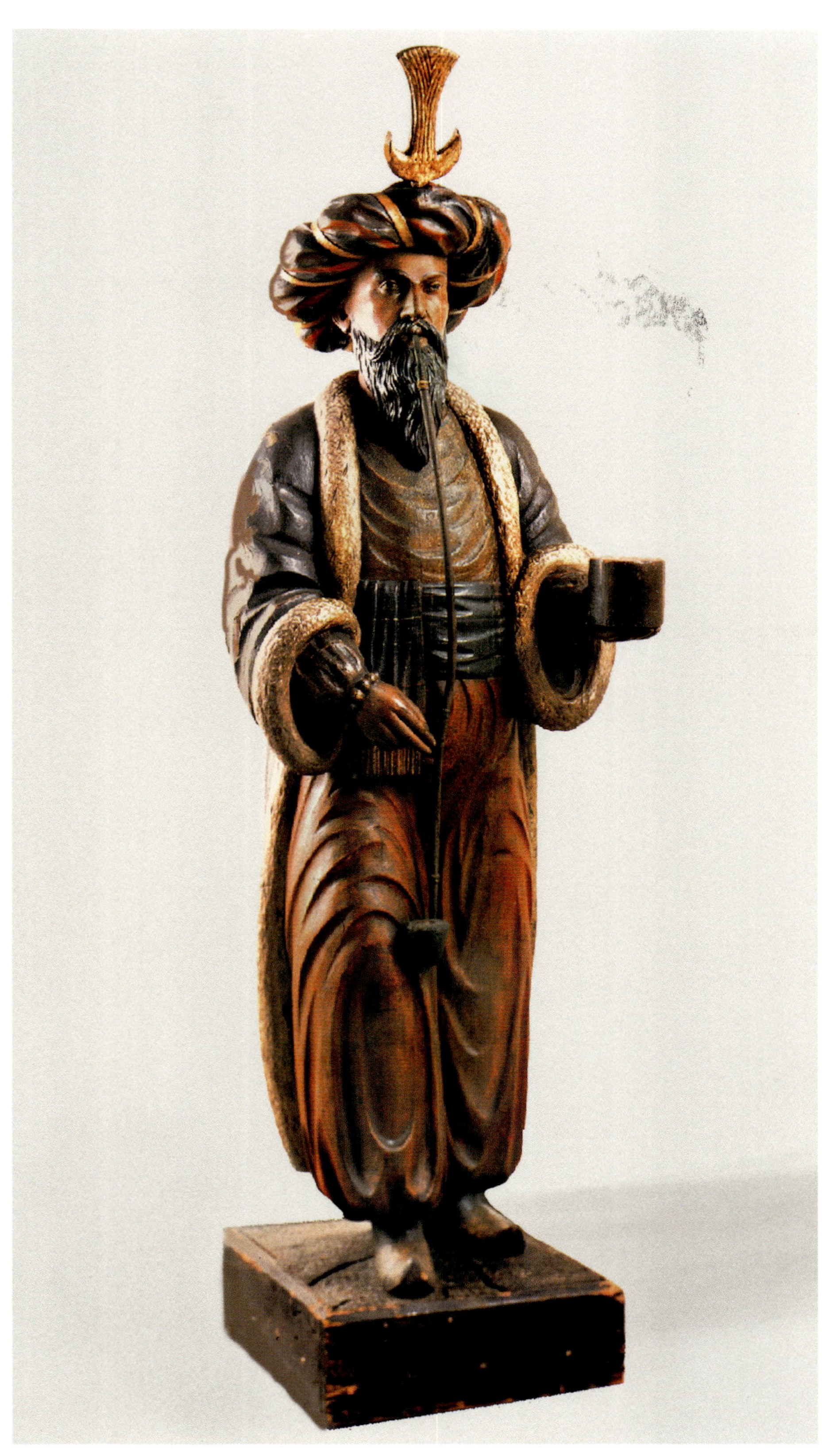

89 Probably workshop of Samuel Robb, *Turk*, New York, c. 1880. Painted wood, 78 x 27 x 27 in. (198.1 x 68.6 x 68.6 cm). The Zipkin Family Collection

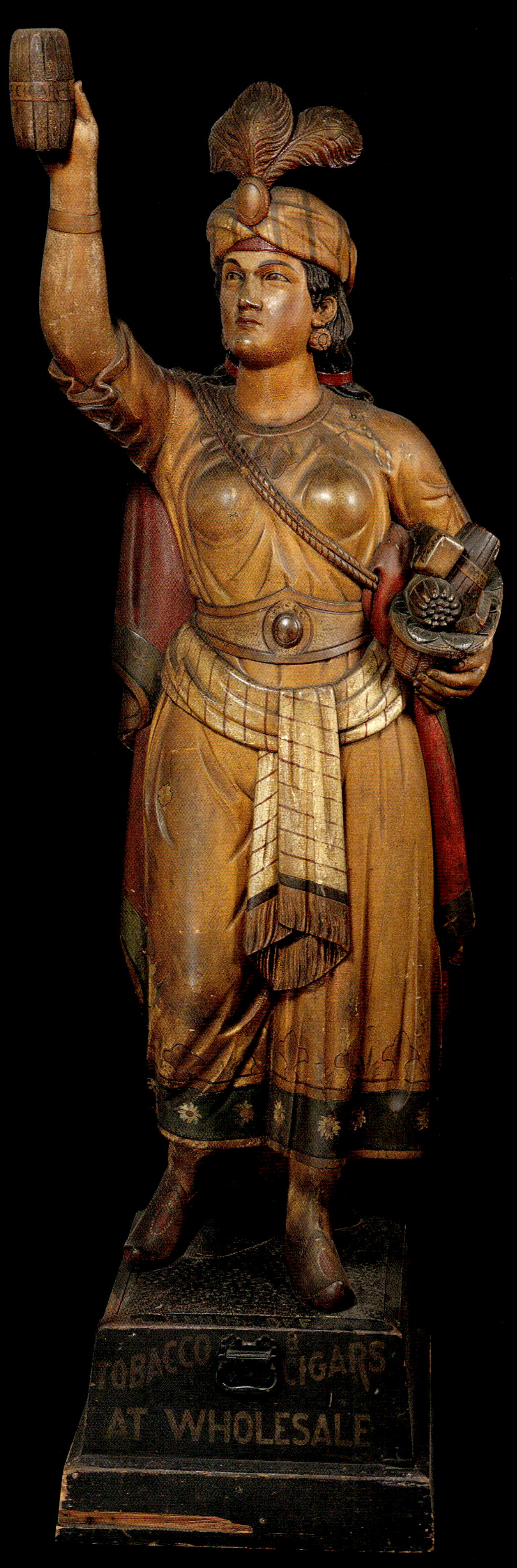
TOBACCO & CIGARS
AT WHOLESALE

90 (OPPOSITE) Probably workshop of Samuel Robb, *Sultana*, New York, c. 1880. Painted wood, 86 x 26 1/2 x 28 in. (218.4 x 67.3 x 71.1 cm). American Folk Art Museum, New York. Promised gift of Ralph Esmerian (P1.2001.349)

Another traditional type with a long history, the Highlander, is represented here by a striking figure in regimental uniform (plate 92). As will be recalled, Highlanders were much more popular in England, where they were commonly identified with snuff shops throughout the eighteenth and nineteenth centuries. This American version remains true to his origins, then, as he prepares to take a pinch of snuff.

Rarer still in the United States is his female counterpart, the Highland Lassie (plate 93). While this example has a long history in Reading, Pennsylvania, she was probably carved in New York City.[18] The handling of her face and skirt are particularly telling. With a few modifications in costuming, she could easily be an Indian maiden.

Tea-store figures with generalized Chinese features constitute a third category of exotic foreign types. Although they seem to have been relatively popular in the nineteenth century, few have survived.[19] One of the finest examples is a figure of a woman wearing a layered costume and gold-beaded necklace highlighted through a carefully restored paint surface (plate 94). She stands in a modest pose with downcast eyes, appropriate for a dignified representative of the mysterious Orient.

With the exception of the stylized little *Turk*, these figures mix elements of realism and idealism to varying degrees. Costumes and accessories, although not

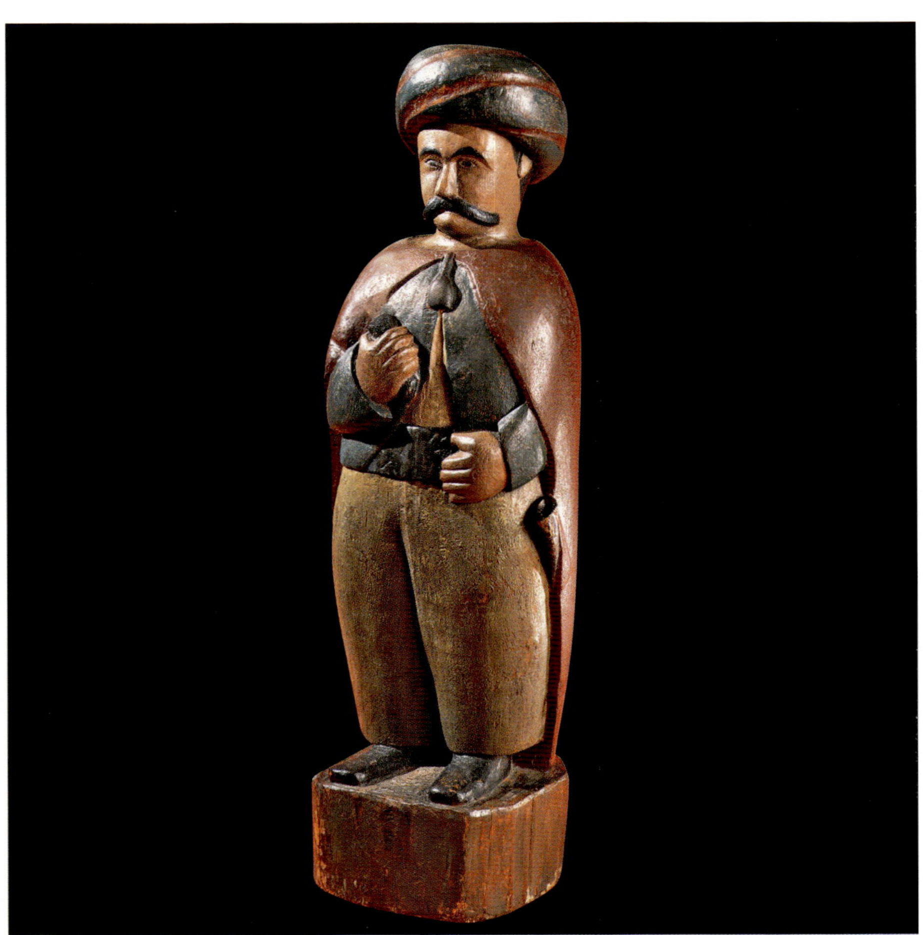

91 (RIGHT) *Turk*, possibly Monmouth County, N.J., c. 1880. Painted wood, height 32 in. (81.3 cm). Abby Aldrich Rockefeller Folk Art Museum, Colonial Williamsburg Foundation, Williamsburg, Va.

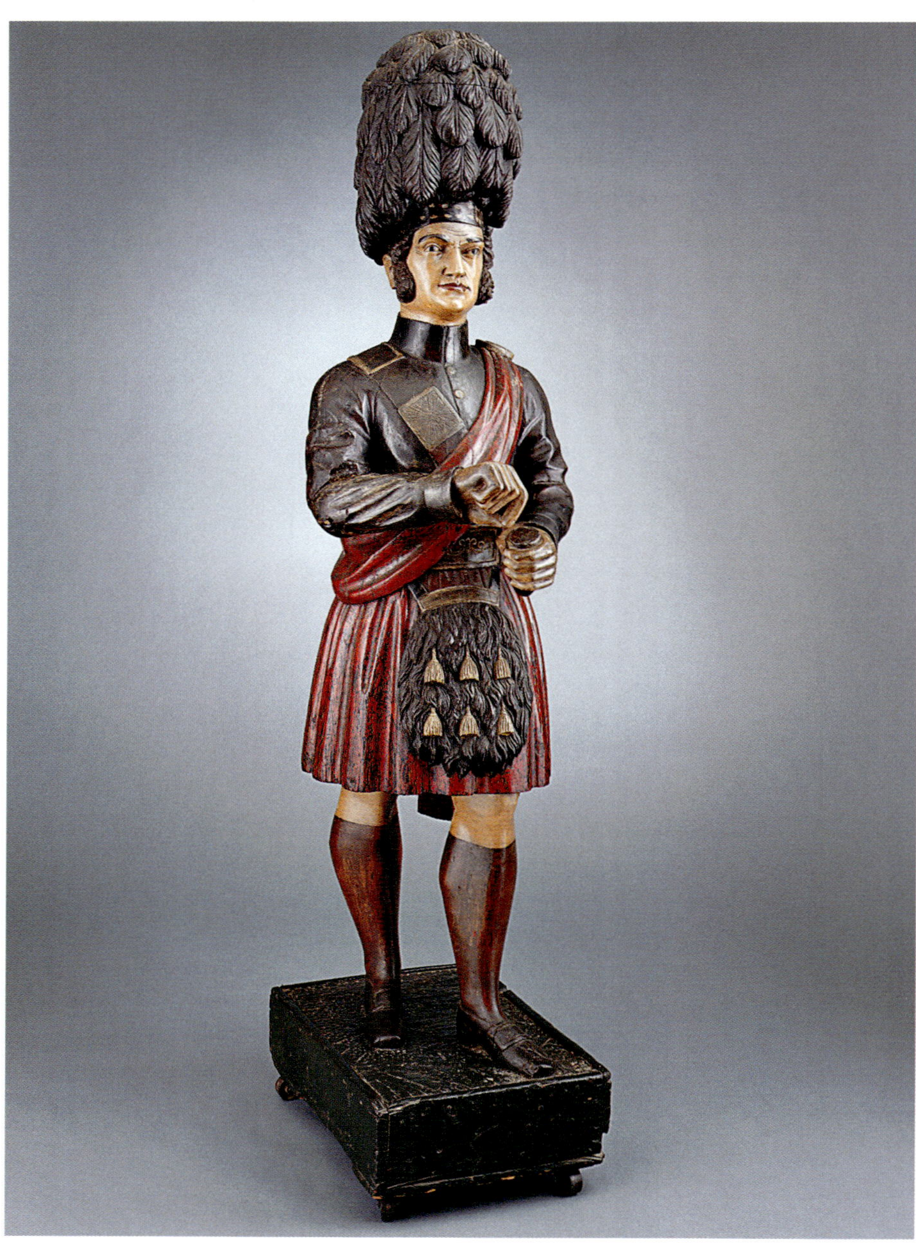

92 *Highlander*, probably New York, c. 1875. Painted wood, 88 x 21 x $25^{1}/_{2}$ in. (223.5 x 53.3 x 64.8 cm). © Shelburne Museum, Shelburne, Vt.

historically accurate, were carved in a realistic style that was intended to convince the viewer of their veracity. On the other hand, their generalized faces rendered in smooth planes and regular features crossed into the realm of idealized beauty. As discussed, this was also the case with many figureheads and Indian show figures.

In approaching their work in this way, the carvers reflected one of the major artistic dialogues in the nineteenth century. By the time that show figures were at the height of their popularity, realism was generally considered to be the most appropriate style for commemorative statues and public sculpture, which became

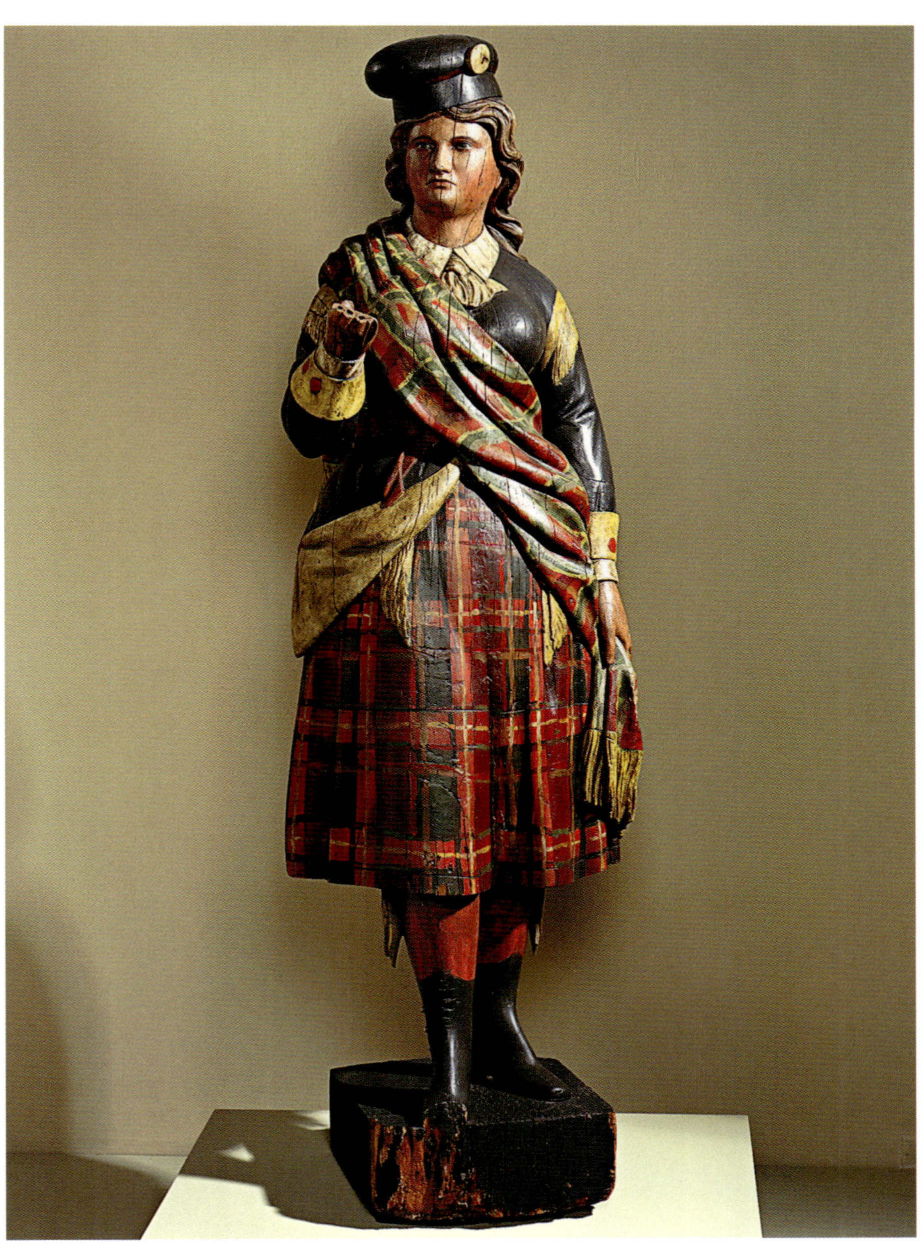

93 *Highland Lassie*, probably New York, c. 1875. Painted wood, 71 x 21 x 19 in. (180.3 x 53.3 x 48.2 cm). Historical Society of Berks County, Reading, Pa.

particularly evident in the many Civil War memorial groups commissioned throughout the country that featured soldiers in contemporary uniforms. In the private sphere, however, opinions varied and the arguments often grew heated. To some, realism in painting and sculpture was fidelity to Nature and the transcription of human events and natural beauty. To others, it was merely copying, a tedious enterprise not worthy of a true artist.

In the other artistic camp were those who favored older forms of idealism like Neoclassicism, the eighteenth-century conception of absolute beauty that lingered long into the nineteenth, particularly in the popular marble sculpture created in Italy. In addition, more modern forms of idealism were evident in many of the new painting styles, such as the bucolic and spiritualized canvases of George Inness (1825–1894) and his French and American Barbizon contemporaries. Again, to some, this was the only True Art, while to others it was either old and lifeless, as in the case of Neoclassicism, or misdirected, incomprehensible, and not worthy of the name, as with modern art.

While the men who carved show figures did not participate directly in this intellectual and stylistic debate, their work was certainly influenced by it.[20] Reviewing new developments after about 1860, a reporter noted: "Meanwhile, the spirit of realistic art entered more and more into the work of the sign sculptors. The wooden Indians grew better, quite artistic in some instances. Even the half nude was attempted with success. . . . [Thomas] White even went into ideal statuary to such an extent as to produce a 'Greek Slave' and 'Adam and Eve' in wood."[21]

The *Greek Slave* was undoubtedly the most famous piece of American sculpture in the nineteenth century (plate 95). Modeled in 1841–43 in Florence by the expatriate sculptor Hiram Powers (1805–1873), it was the first full-length nude sculpture to be successfully exhibited throughout the United States. Its acceptance was largely due to its critical acclaim in Europe and because its subject related to the Greek War for Independence, a cause célèbre on both sides of the Atlantic. The statue depicts a virtuous young Christian girl who has been abducted by the Turks and is about to be sold in a slave market in Constantinople. She is therefore nude through no fault of her own. Dubious audiences were assured of her virginal purity by the faultless white marble and by an aggressive marketing campaign that solicited commendations from respected clergymen, one of whom wrote that she was "clothed all over with sentiment, sheltered, protected by it from every profane eye."[22] Considered by many critics to be the height of Neoclassical sculpture, it had a major impact in the United States. In all, it was reproduced in six full-size versions, several busts, and numerous other smaller editions in marble and ceramic.[23]

Unfortunately, no trace of Thomas White's wooden *Greek Slave* has survived. Other attempts at "ideal statuary" in wood and zinc have, however, providing some examples of the carvers' approach to the subject. One is a figure of a *Woman with Dove*, a sweetly contemplative piece that shows late Neoclassical tendencies in both its subject and execution (plate 96). Probably used as a garden or architectural figure, she may originate from eastern Massachusetts. The half-nude subject in wood is extremely rare, even in as modest a pose as this, indicating that the piece was almost certainly a special commission. Stylistically it appears that she was done by a shipcarver who had a reasonably good understanding of the nude, which he may have acquired through the study of prints or sculpture that could be seen in places like the National Academy of Design in New York City or the Pennsylvania Academy of the Fine Arts in Philadelphia.[24]

Another figure that was probably a special commission as well is a captivating rendition of idealized beauty (plate 97). She was also most likely used as a garden or architectural figure, although her present condition suggests that she has been protected from the elements for most of her existence. The profusion of flowers in the cornucopia and wreath along with the roses in her hair make her allegori-

94 Chinese Woman, probably New York, c. 1875. Painted wood, height 63 1/4 in. (160.6 cm). Henry Ford Museum, Dearborn, Mich.

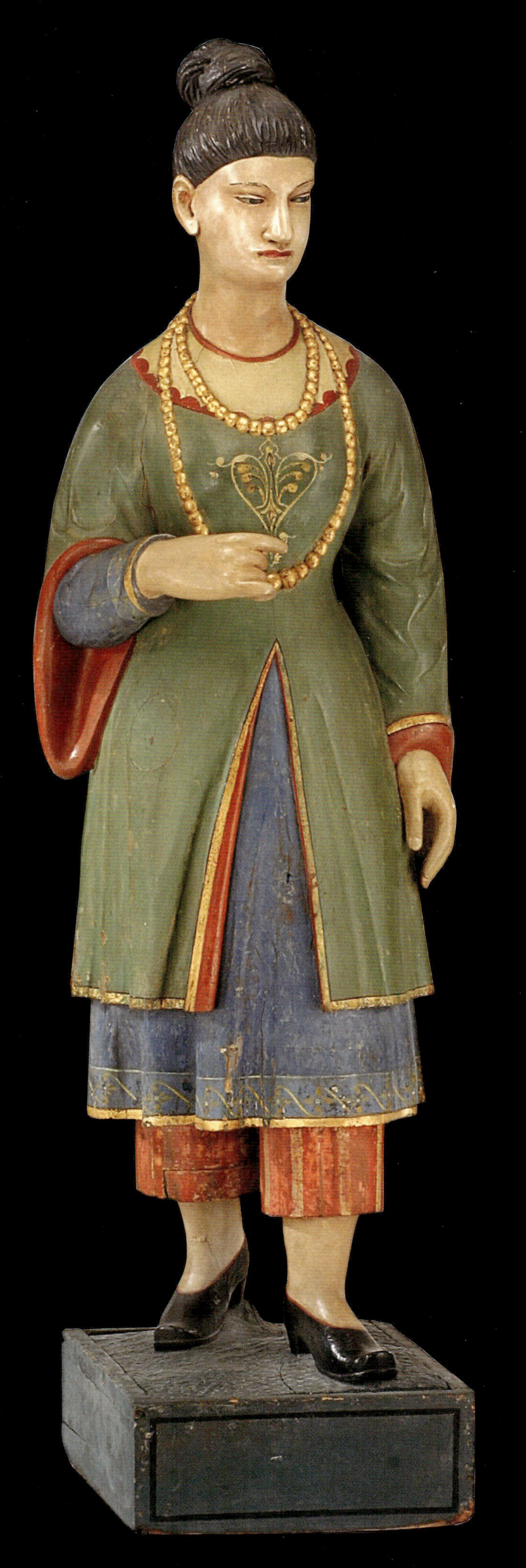

cal references somewhat mysterious. She could represent Flora, the Roman goddess of flowers, who was usually portrayed with a cornucopia of blossoms that she scattered over the earth. Given her youth and beauty, she might also have been intended to personify Spring, particularly if she was originally part of a series of the four seasons. Then, too, she could represent Love or Beauty, ideals that were commonly associated with roses.

The ancient image of Flora became quite popular in the early nineteenth century due to the revival of interest in flower symbolism, otherwise known as the "language of flowers." Starting in Napoleonic France, a seemingly endless number of gift books, dictionaries, and emblem books gained a huge audience on both sides of the Atlantic. Books like Charlotte de Latour's *La Langage des Fleurs* of

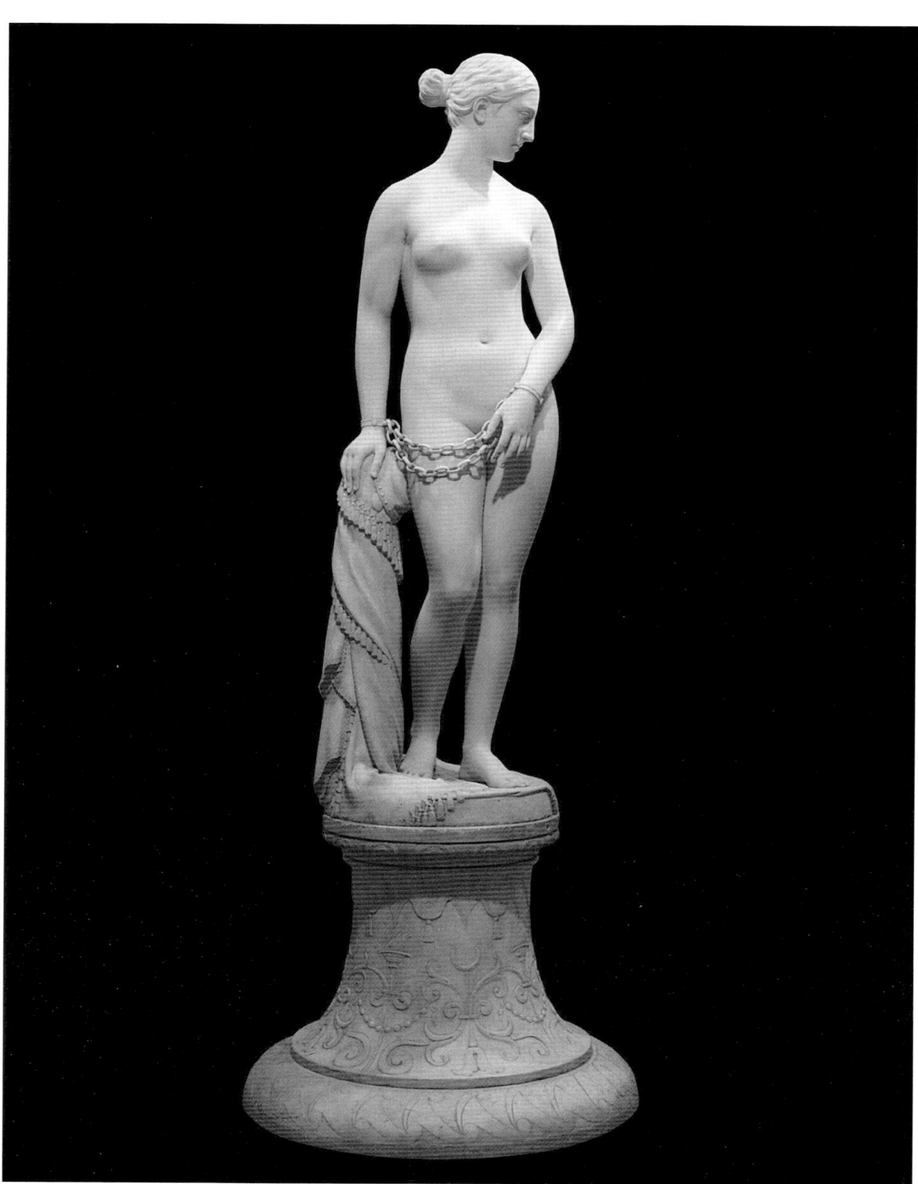

95 (RIGHT) Hiram Powers (American, 1805–1873), *The Greek Slave*, 1849–50. Marble, 65 1/4 x 21 x 18 1/4 in. (165.7 x 53.3 x 46.4 cm). Yale University Art Gallery, New Haven, Conn. Olive Louise Dann Fund

96 (OPPOSITE) *Woman with Dove*, possibly Mass., 1850–90. Painted wood, 58 x 15 1/2 x 15 1/2 in. (147.3 x 39.4 x 39.4 cm). The Eleanor and Mabel Van Alstyne Collection of American Folk Art, National Museum of American History, Smithsonian Institution, Washington, D.C.

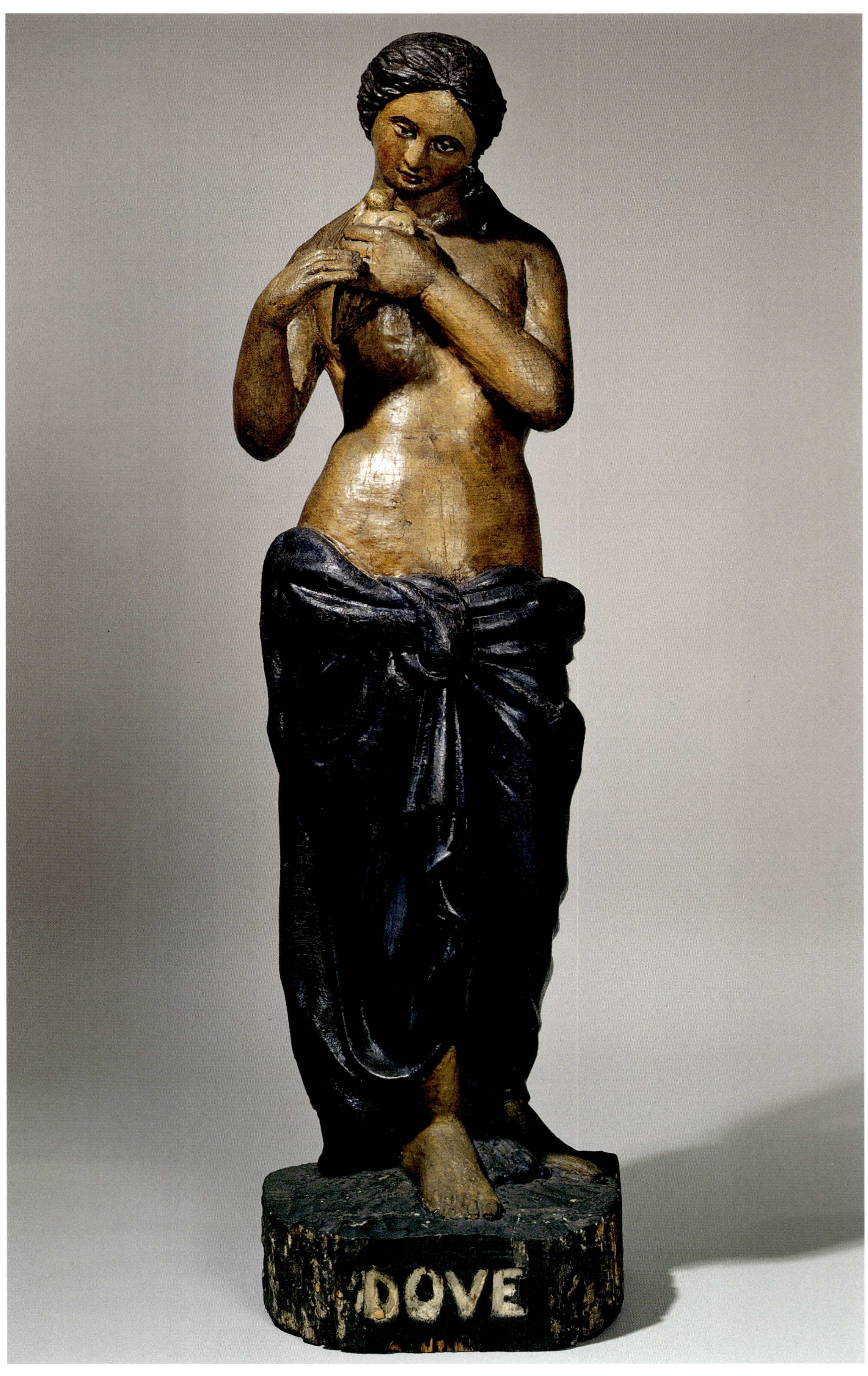
DOVE

1819 and Elizabeth Wirt's *Flora's Dictionary* of 1829 became international best-sellers, inspiring all sorts of related visual imagery, from prints to ceramic statues. In the United States, language of flower books reached a high point of popularity in the 1840s and 1850s, and they maintained their appeal until the end of the century.[25] The Victorian language of flowers was a language of love, a means of expressing sentiments through delicate and beautiful objects. In this case, the figure's exposed leg rendered her too sensual for a church, but her resemblance to a traditional Madonna suggests that she was created by one of the many European-trained carvers who immigrated to the United States in the mid-nineteenth century.[26]

IN ADDITION TO REALISM AND IDEALISM, another mode of artistic representation that strongly influenced figure carving in the second half of the century was caricature. Widely used in prints, books, magazines, and newspapers, it was a popular way to inject humor into many of the standardized stereotypical images of the day. In this, artists and publishers were again following English and European precedent, as seen especially in the work of eighteenth-century artists such as William Hogarth (1697–1764) and other social and political satirists. In both England and America, caricatures of prominent people and important political events could be quite ruthless and devastatingly funny, at least to those who agreed with the point of view expressed in a particular cartoon or illustration. While caricature in shop figures is less politically charged, it is just as inclusive in its range of targets.

The most popular and widely read American satirical magazine in the last quarter of the nineteenth century was *Puck*, published in New York by Joseph Keppler between 1877 and 1918. The magazine's masthead featured an image of Puck, complete with top hat and oversized pen in hand. Its contents included cartoons, humorous articles, editorials, poems, and jokes, all of which provided sly commentary on recent political and social events. The well-known trademark descended from medieval English folklore, where a puck was widely believed to be a type of evil spirit. By Shakespeare's time, he had assumed a gentler guise, as best known in the mischievous sprite of *A Midsummer Night's Dream*.

Two statues of Puck commissioned by Keppler from the German-born sculptor Henry Baerer (1837–1908) can still be seen on the Puck Building on Houston Street in New York City.[27] As a cigar-store figure, Puck was particularly popular in the late 1870s and early 1880s, and to a lesser extent until the end of the century (plate 98). There was also a brand of cigars by the same name. Caspar Buberl (1834–1899), a Czechoslovakian-born sculptor best known for his Civil War memorial groups, modeled a Puck around 1875 that William Demuth offered in zinc.[28] The rare wooden version from Samuel Robb's shop that is shown here was based on Buberl's figure. He has lost the bottom half of his pen, but otherwise is a fine likeness of his namesake.

Another popular fictitious character of ancient lineage was Punch, a traditional clown figure identified by his humpback, hooked nose, and mischievous leer (plate 99). His most immediate source of inspiration was the well-known puppet in the Punch and Judy shows that delighted nineteenth-century audiences

97 *Allegorical Figure: Flora*, probably New York, 1840–80. Painted wood, 54 x 17 x 18 in. (137.1 x 43.2 x 45.7 cm). American Folk Art Museum, New York. Promised gift of Ralph Esmerian (P1.2001.353)

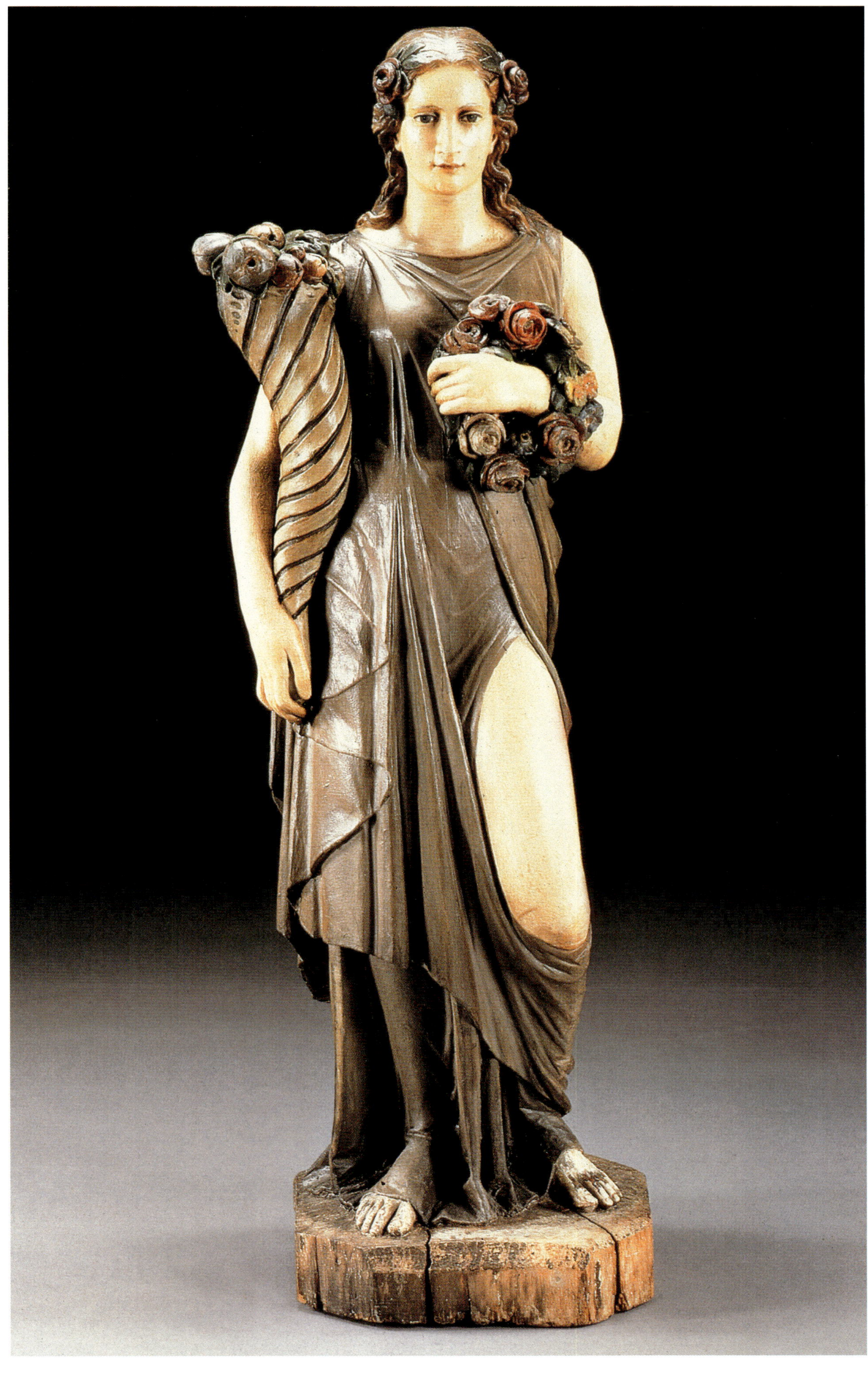

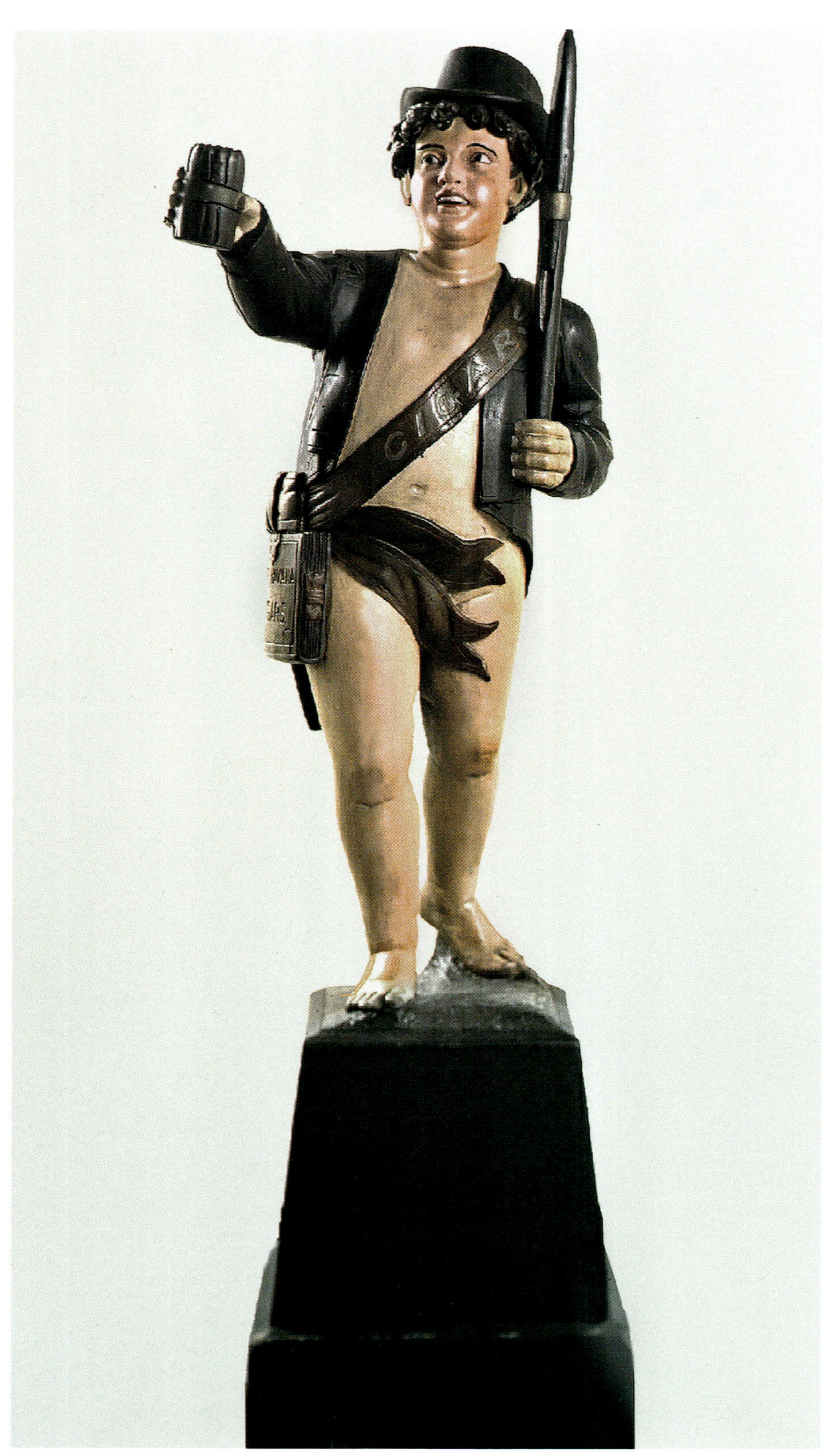

98 Incised on base: "Robb Manu'f'r. 114 Centre St. NY," *Puck*, New York, 1888–1903. Painted wood, $75\frac{1}{2}$ x 24 x 30 in. (191.8 x 60.9 x 76.2 cm). The Hudson River Museum, Yonkers, N.Y. Gift of Mr. Simon S. Klein and Mr. M. J. Witson (25.566)

throughout the United States and England. As with Puck, he, too, had a brand of cigars named after him, and was particularly popular as both shop figure and cigar in the 1870s and 1880s.[29] Nevertheless, Punch himself was much older than any of these nineteenth-century sources. In his traditional English guise of Punch or Punchinello, he had been popular since at least the late seventeenth century. From there, he can be traced through France to Renaissance Italy, where Polichinelle, later Pulcinella, was a comic figure in the Commedia dell'Arte. His ultimate progenitor is Maccus, a humpbacked, hooked-nose character from the Atellanæ, an ancient form of Roman satirical drama.[30]

More medieval in conception was Gambrinus, otherwise known as King Lager (plate 100). As seen here, he was usually portrayed holding a frothy mug and sword, bedecked in some sort of armor or military regalia befitting his royal station. King Gambrinus was a mythical character, possibly Flemish in origin, who was celebrated as the inventor of beer. Naturally enough, he was a popular sign

99 *Punch*, possibly New York or New Jersey, c. 1880. Painted wood, 68 x 24 x 26 in. (172.7 x 60.9 x 66 cm). Mercer Museum, Doylestown, Pa.

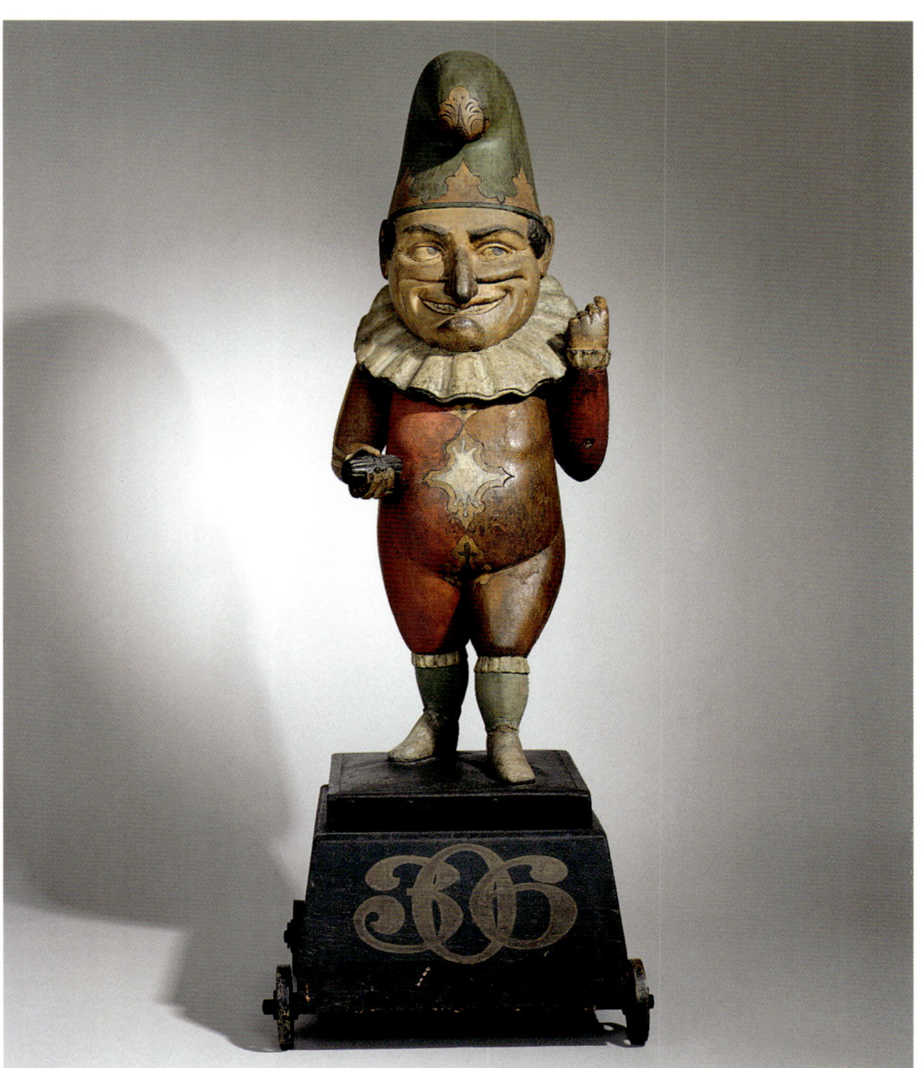

for beer halls and saloons in the last quarter of the nineteenth century.[31] Few of his kind have survived, however, and today he is very rarely encountered.

As traditional figures, Puck, Punch, and Gambrinus retained their old associations while being updated as show figures. In order to maximize their appeal to contemporary audiences, the carvers emphasized their humorous elements to a large extent, particularly in the case of Punch. Even so, they did not quite enter the realm of caricature, which was generally reserved for more modern subjects.

The increasingly rapid pace of modern urban life was the subject of much social commentary. Many observers decried the loss of traditional values, citing increased materialism and the accumulation of wealth, the depersonalized and uprooted nature of city life, and the undue attention paid to the latest fads and fashions as evidence of moral and spiritual decay. Others celebrated the era's new ideas, rapid change, and advances in technology and industrialization as progress that was benefiting the entire country. Finally, a third group took the middle ground, accepting the new developments with a nostalgic look backward to what was perceived as a simpler and more honest past. In short, the discussion was essentially the same as that which is endlessly debated in the media today.

What was new was the emergence of a national popular culture beginning in the second quarter of the nineteenth century. As the Industrial Revolution truly took hold in the United States, a wide range of social and economic factors conspired to usher in the first phase of the modern era. Industrialization and the introduction of processes of mass production significantly increased the supply of consumer goods and made them affordable to many members of the growing middle class. New publishing technologies and greater public demand resulted in less expensive newspapers, dime novels, and magazines that specialized in art, literature, and fashion. Improvements in transportation, from better roads and horse-drawn conveyances to the development of railroads and steamships, promoted travel and communication, as well as the wider distribution of many of these new goods and services. At the same time and certainly in part due to these developments, social mores also began to change, most evidently in the gradual loosening of some of the old restrictions regarding public forms of entertainment, gender roles, and interaction between the sexes.

All of this gave artists, writers, and other social commentators grist for the mills of caricature. Popular stereotypes were given a contemporary twist and achieved international recognition. A favorite was the Girl of the Period, which became a symbol of modern urban life as well as a caricature of the vain, fashionable young woman of the time (plate 101). Satirized and celebrated on both sides of the Atlantic, she was a fashionplate image for an increasingly fashion-conscious era. As one disapproving English writer noted in the *Saturday Review* in 1868:

> The girl of the period is a creature who dyes her hair and paints her face, as the first articles of her personal religion; whose sole idea of life is plenty of fun and luxury; and whose dress is the object of such thought and intellect as she possesses. Her main endeavor in this is to outvie her neighbors in the extravagance of fashion. No matter whether, as in the time of crinolines, she

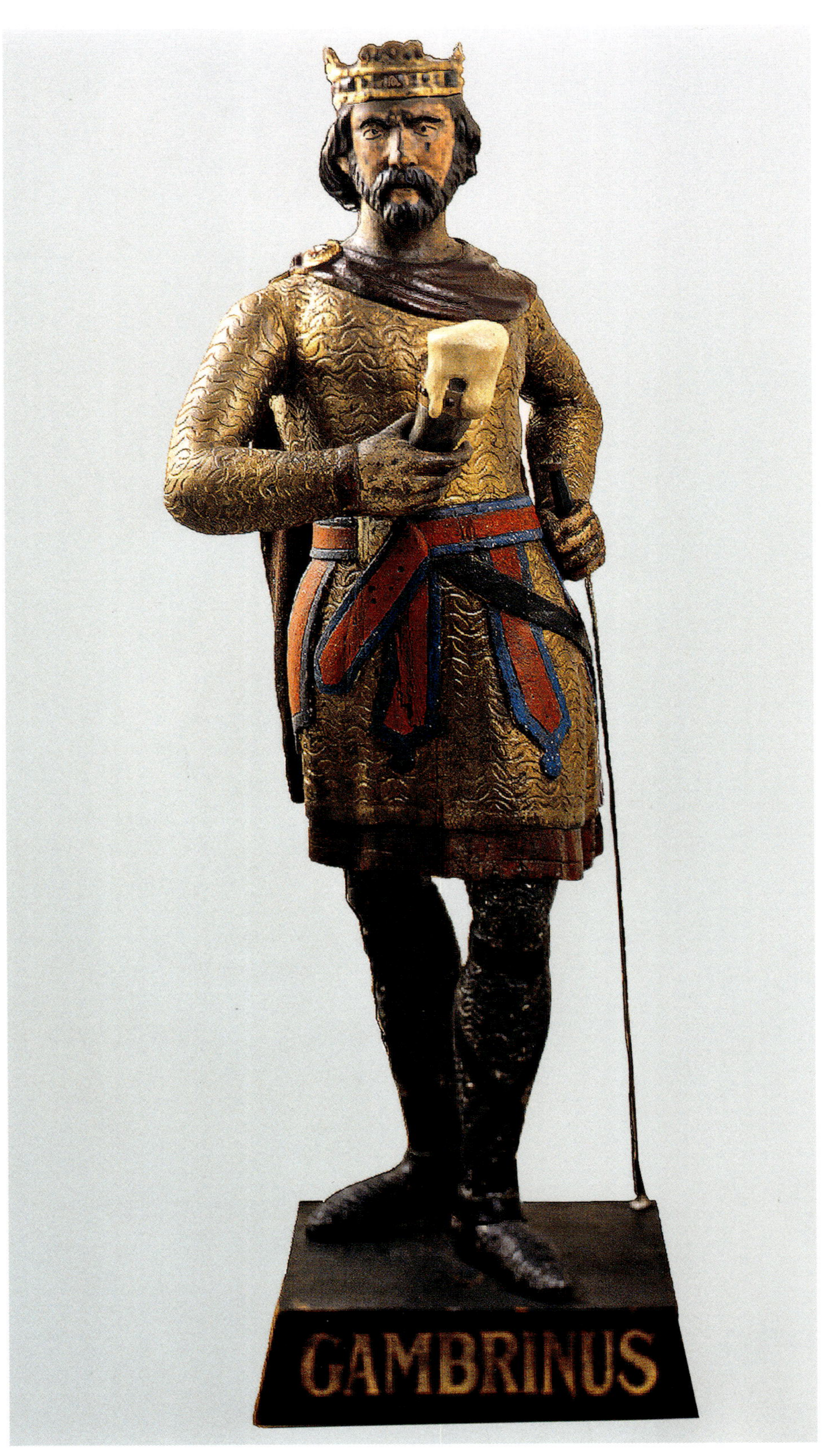

100 *Gambrinus, King Lager*, northeastern United States, c. 1880. Painted wood, 64 x 20 x 21 in. (162.5 x 50.8 x 53.3 cm). Mark Goldman/Mom's Cigars Collection, New York

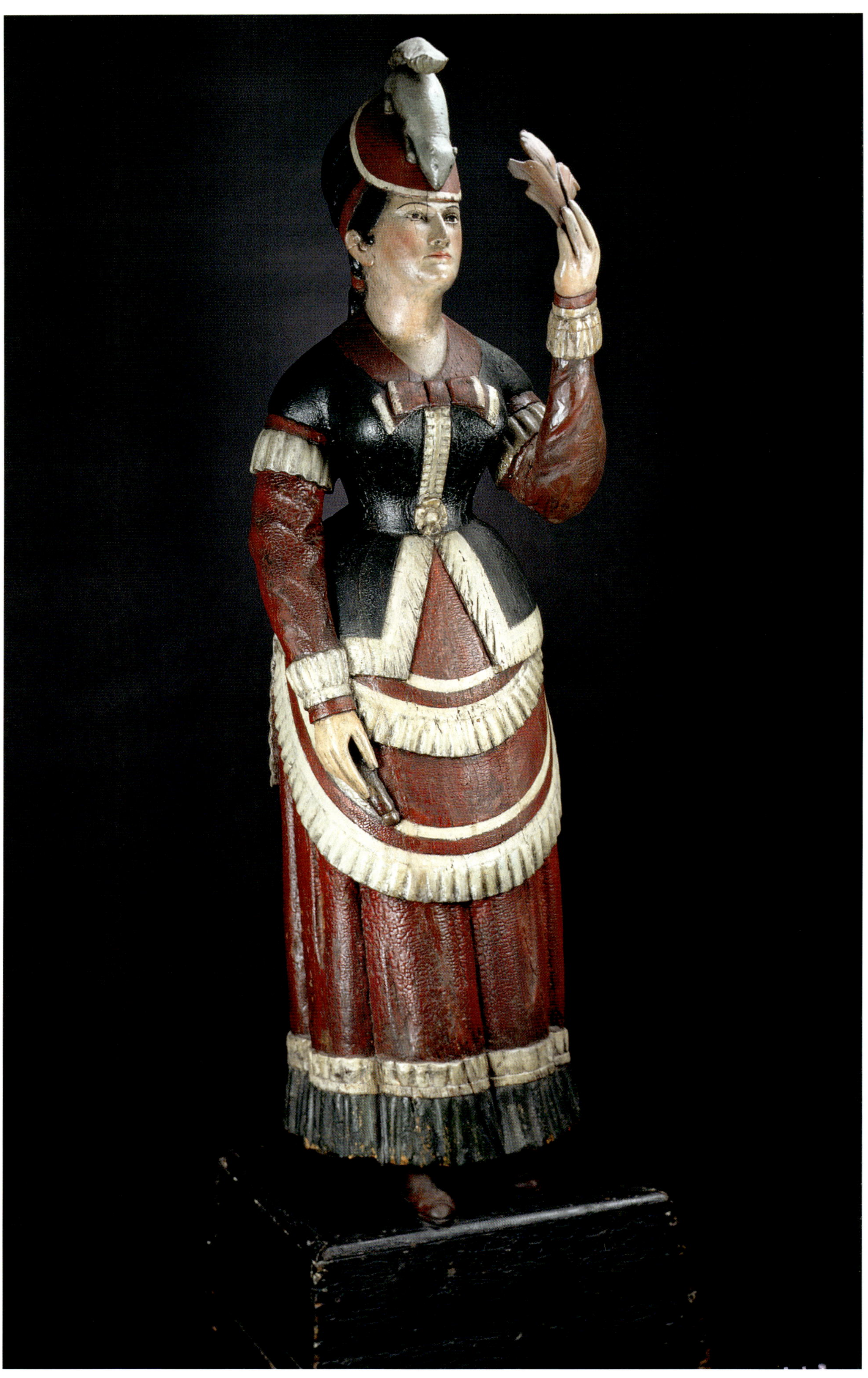

> sacrifices decency, or, as now, in the time of trains, she sacrifices cleanliness; no matter either, whether she makes herself a nuisance and an inconvenience to every one she meets. The girl of the period has done away with such moral muffishness as consideration for others, or regard for counsel and rebuke. . . . she is far too fast and flourishing to be stopped in mid-career by these slow old mortals.
>
> This imitation of the *demi-monde* in dress leads to something in manner and feeling, not quite so pronounced perhaps, but far too like to be honourable to herself or satisfactory to her friends. It leads to slang, bold talk, and fastness; to the love of pleasure and indifference to duty; to the desire of money before either love or happiness; to uselessness at home, dissatisfaction with the monotony of ordinary life, and horror of all useful work; in a word, to the worst forms of luxury and selfishness, to the most fatal effects arising from want of high principle and absence of tender feeling.[32]

A few months later, the American magazine *Nation* published a review that condemned this rather vicious commentary as "a wanton exaggeration in the interest of sensationalism." Its author had a broader target in mind, noting that:

> A young girl given up to dress is certainly a very flimsy and empty creature, and there is something truly ignoble in the incessant effort to gratify and stimulate the idle taste of a host of possible "admirers." But between this sort of thing and the sort of thing described by the Saturday Reviewers there is a very wide gulf—a gulf made by that strong conservative element in the feminine nature of which the writer in question seems to have so little notion. . . . The whole indictment represented by this volume seems to us perfectly irrational. It is impossible to discuss and condemn the follies of "modern women" apart from those of modern men. They are all part and parcel of the follies of modern civilization, which is working itself out through innumerable blunders. . . . We are all of us extravagant, superficial, and luxurious together. It is a "sign of the times." Women share in the fault not as women, but as simple human beings.[33]

Modern woman, then, is symptomatic of modern times. Both writers see these developments as lamentable, although the author of the article in the *Nation* blames modern men as much as, if not more than, women for the current state of affairs.

101 *Girl of the Period*, New York, c. 1870. Painted wood, 68 x $24^1/2$ x 22 in. (172.7 x 62.2 x 55.9 cm). Fenimore Art Museum, Cooperstown, N.Y.

Either way, it was evident that the old social order was changing. Many women were moving away from domesticity of hearth and home, forsaking their traditional roles as wives and mothers for the public realm. Some chose to pursue professional careers instead of marriage, while others asserted their independence in different ways. The woman suffrage movement came of age in the United

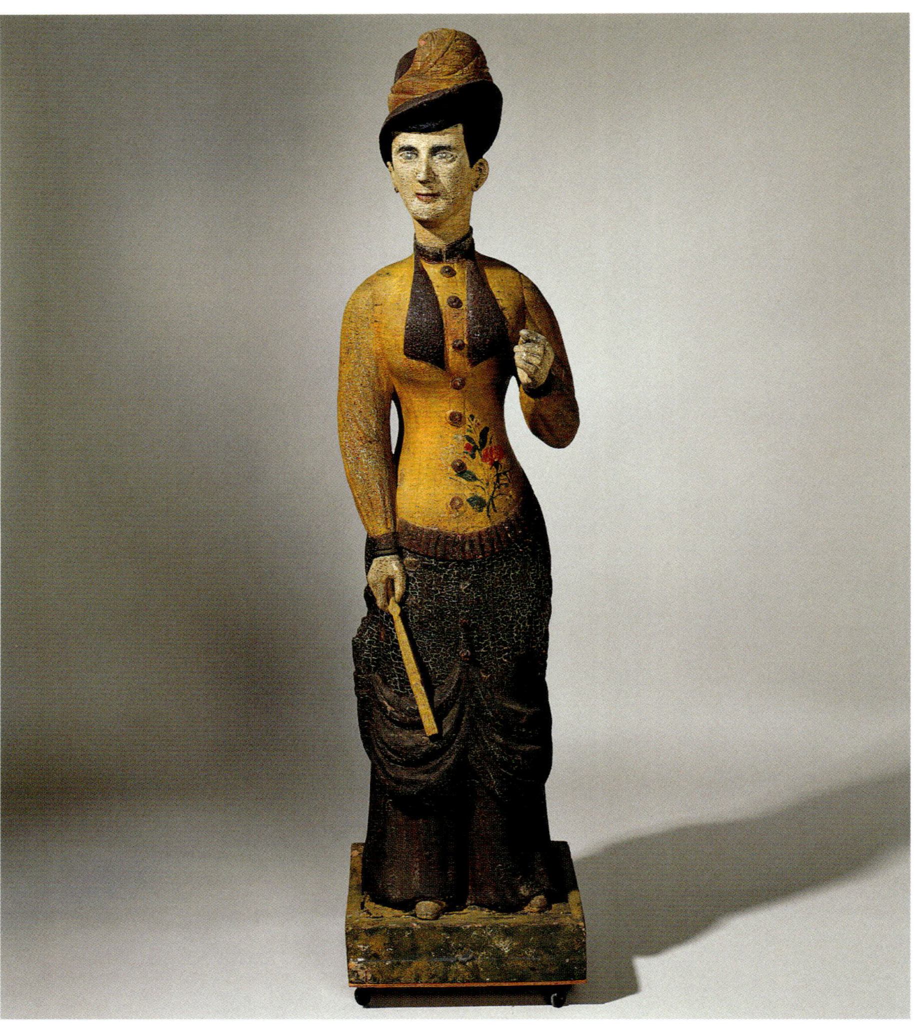

102 *Milliner's Figure*, northeastern United States, c. 1875. Painted wood, height 62 1/2 in. (158.7 cm). The Eleanor and Mabel Van Alstyne Collection of American Folk Art, National Museum of American History, Smithsonian Institution, Washington, D.C.

States in 1848, for example, with the first Women's Rights Convention in Seneca Falls, New York. Later in the century, single women were living alone or sharing apartments in American cities in such numbers that a new term, "bachelor girl," had entered the vocabulary.[34] Traditionalists, both male and female, were unsettled by these developments, leading to torrents of public criticism such as this.

The Girl of the Period was also known as a Dolly Varden, after a character in *Barnaby Rudge*, a Charles Dickens novel first published in 1841. Set in the 1770s and 1780s, the story featured the independently minded and thoroughly modern Miss Varden, the daughter of a well-to-do locksmith. As a show figure, the Girl of the Period first emerged in the mid-1860s and remained popular for several decades.[35] She could be adapted to a variety of purposes but was most frequently used as a sign for a tobacconist, milliner, or dressmaker, depending upon her accessories. Generally depicted with the "Grecian bend," an exaggerated forward lean emphasized by her corset and bustle, she often sported a squirrel hat, reflecting the popularity of small animals, stuffed and skinned, as articles of fashion.

Squirrel hats achieved particular notoriety when they were worn by Lydia Thompson and her British Blondes in a burlesque review entitled the "Girl of the Period" that caused a sensation in New York in the late 1860s. According to one reviewer, her troupe owed most of its success to "the free exhibition of legs."[36] The show figure seen here is similar to an illustration, complete with squirrel hat, that appeared as no. 51 in William Demuth's 1875 catalogue.

More sedate perhaps, but just as fashionable is a lovely figure holding a fan (plate 102). A highly individualized piece, she may have been modeled after an actual woman and probably served as a shop sign for a milliner or dressmaker.[37] She is particularly distinctive due to her old paint surface that features a floral motif near her waist.

103 *Dude*, probably New York or Chicago, c. 1880. Painted wood, 84 x 22 x 28 in. (213.3 x 55.9 x 71.1 cm). Heritage Museums and Gardens, Sandwich, Mass.

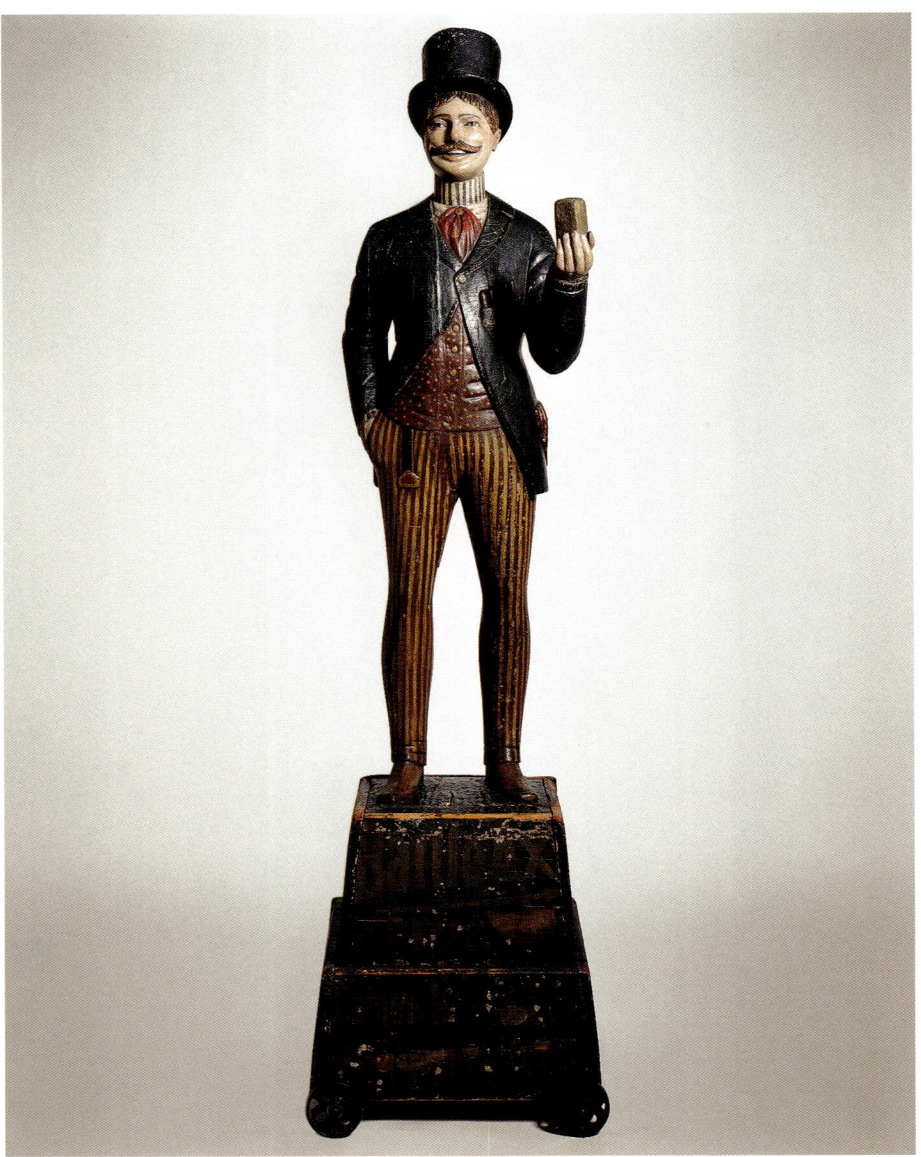

The Girl of the Period had a male counterpart in the Dude, another caricature of a contemporary urban type that was popular in many parts of the country (plate 103). As a carver explained in 1886: "When you get away out west there is quite a run of just such flash Bowery girls as I am painting up here now. Dudes had quite a go for a while. I have got fully twenty-five dudes planted around in Brooklyn and New York now, though dudes are on the wane."[38]

The *Dude* illustrated here stood in front of a tobacco shop in Emporia, Kansas, for many years. With his tight pants and jacket, striped collar, and watch fob, he is the perfect image of the city slicker. A slightly disreputable character, he was also known as a Sporting Dude, and more recently, as a Race Track Tout.[39] The bold use of paint, which in this case has been carefully restored, is especially important in creating the overall effect.

104 Probably Thomas J. White (American, 1825–1902), *Captain Jinks*, New York, c. 1880. Painted wood, 81 1/2 x 19 in. (207 x 48.2 cm). Private collection

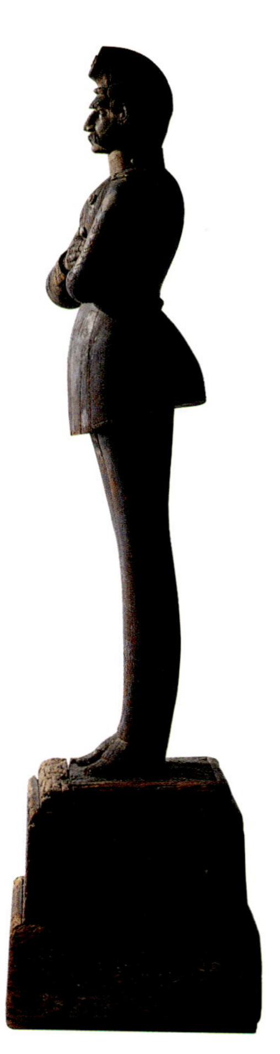

Closely related to the *Dude* was the erstwhile military man, *Captain Jinks* (plate 104). His name derives from "Captain Jinks of the Horse Marines," a popular song composed by T. Maclagan in the early 1860s that satirized vain soldiers who lived beyond their means and seemed more interested in parading in fancy uniforms than serving in the military.[40] It remained a hit for several decades, at a time when it was fashionable for young men to enlist in the National Guard and participate in elaborate drills, which to some observers seemed primarily intended to impress the young women in the audience. This figure could be a portrait of Samuel Robb. According to Robb's daughter, Thomas White created a figure of him in uniform soon after he enlisted in the New York State National Guard in 1879.[41] It retains an exceptional amount of carved detail and an old weathered surface with the remnants of what is probably the original paint surface.

Another well-known fictional character who inspired interpretations in a variety of media was Colonel Sellers, a character from *The Gilded Age*, written by Mark Twain and Charles Dudley Warner in 1873 (plate 105). An eternal optimist and self-promoter, Colonel Mulberry Sellers was a parody of the era's overly enthusiastic entrepreneurs who were continually developing new schemes to enrich themselves. The Colonel himself invested in numerous enterprises that eventually failed, always declaring that he saw "millions in it," a phrase that is painted on the left side of the base. The figure is thought to have been used as an apothecary-shop sign in Sellersville, Pennsylvania.[42] Its stylized form indicates that it was probably done not by a shipcarver, but rather by a talented local craftsman. No doubt it represents the Colonel hawking one of his favorite products, "Beriah Seller's Infallible Imperial Oriental Optic Liniment and Salvation for Sore Eyes—the Medical Wonder of the Age." Twain also adapted his novel for the stage, and the play successfully toured the country for a number of years. This figure may in fact represent the actor John T. Raymond in his role as Colonel Sellers, based on a small statue of Raymond done by the sculptor Jonathan Scott Hartley (1845–1912).[43]

Among the other actors immortalized in wood was George Washington Lafayette Fox, a famous pantomimist who created the clown character of Humpty Dumpty, which became one of his most successful stage roles. A figure of Fox in costume was placed in the lobby of the Olympic Theatre in New York during the play's long run that began in 1867. Another, or possibly the same, image stood

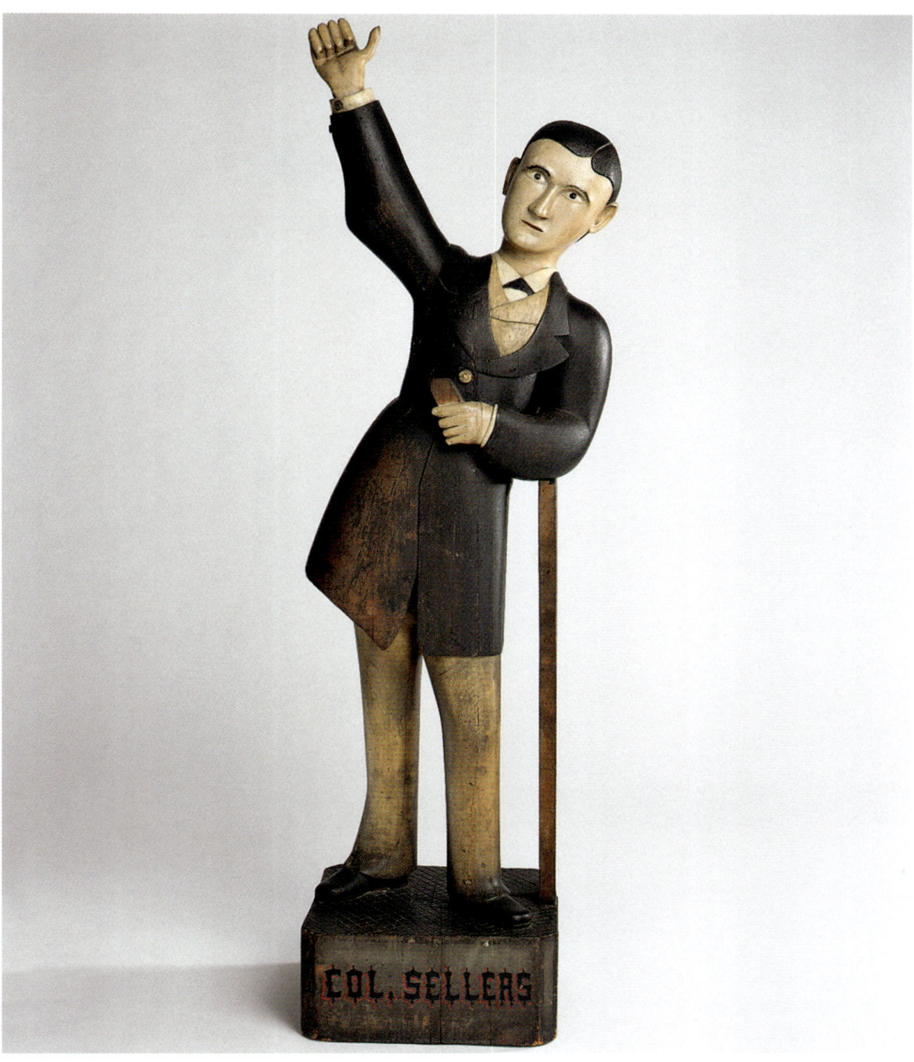

105 *Colonel Sellers*, possibly Sellersville, Pa, c. 1875. Painted wood, 52 x 10½ x 12 in. (132.1 x 26.7 x 30.5 cm). Fenimore Art Museum, Cooperstown, N.Y.

on the sidewalk outside the Broadway Theatre during Fox's last appearances in October and November 1875.[44]

A cigar-store figure that may have been carved in Philadelphia is remarkably similar to an existing photograph of Fox, from the ornate frills on the costume to its central medallion (plates 106 and 107). Even the pose is the same. The only significant differences are the words "Geo. W. Child—Generously Good" that surround the medallion on the figure's chest and "J. Wertheimer" within the smaller circle at the center. Founder and publisher of the *Philadelphia Ledger*, George W. Child was a well-known philanthropist who, among other honors, had a cigar named after him.[45]

While stage portraits were quite common as paintings in the eighteenth and nineteenth centuries, they were much rarer as shop figures. The celebrated Shakespearean actor Edwin Forrest is known to have been carved in at least two roles, as Metamora, which was discussed in the previous chapter, and as Mark

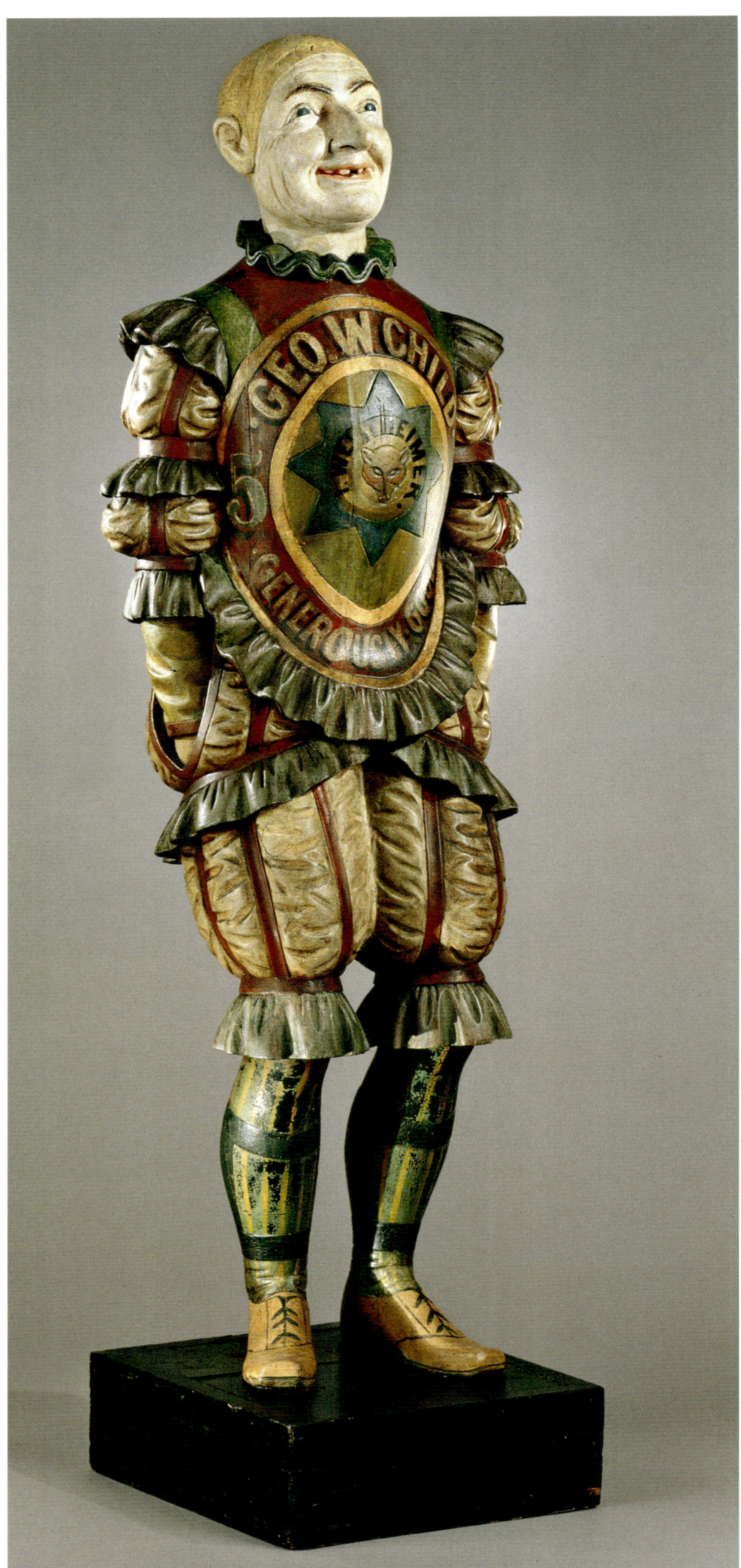

106 (RIGHT) *George L. Fox as Humpty Dumpty*, possibly Philadelphia, c. 1870. Painted wood, height 72 in. (182.9 cm). Abby Aldrich Rockefeller Folk Art Museum, Colonial Williamsburg Foundation, Williamsburg, Va.

107 (OPPOSITE) *George L. Fox as Humpty Dumpty*, New York, c. 1865. Photograph from the bequest of Evert Jansen Wendell, The Harvard Theatre Collection, The Houghton Library, Harvard University, Cambridge, Mass.

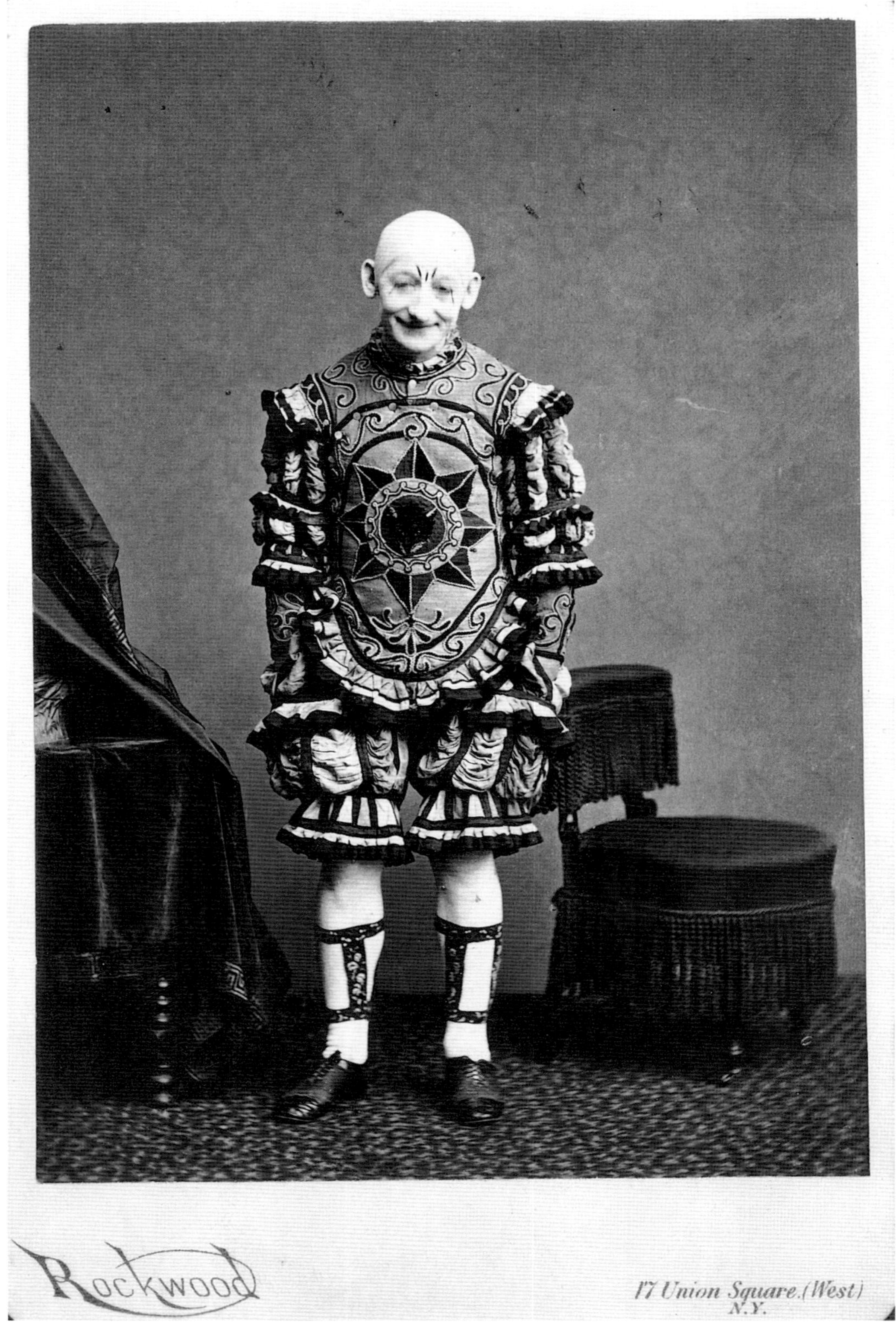
Rockwood
17 Union Square (West)
N.Y.

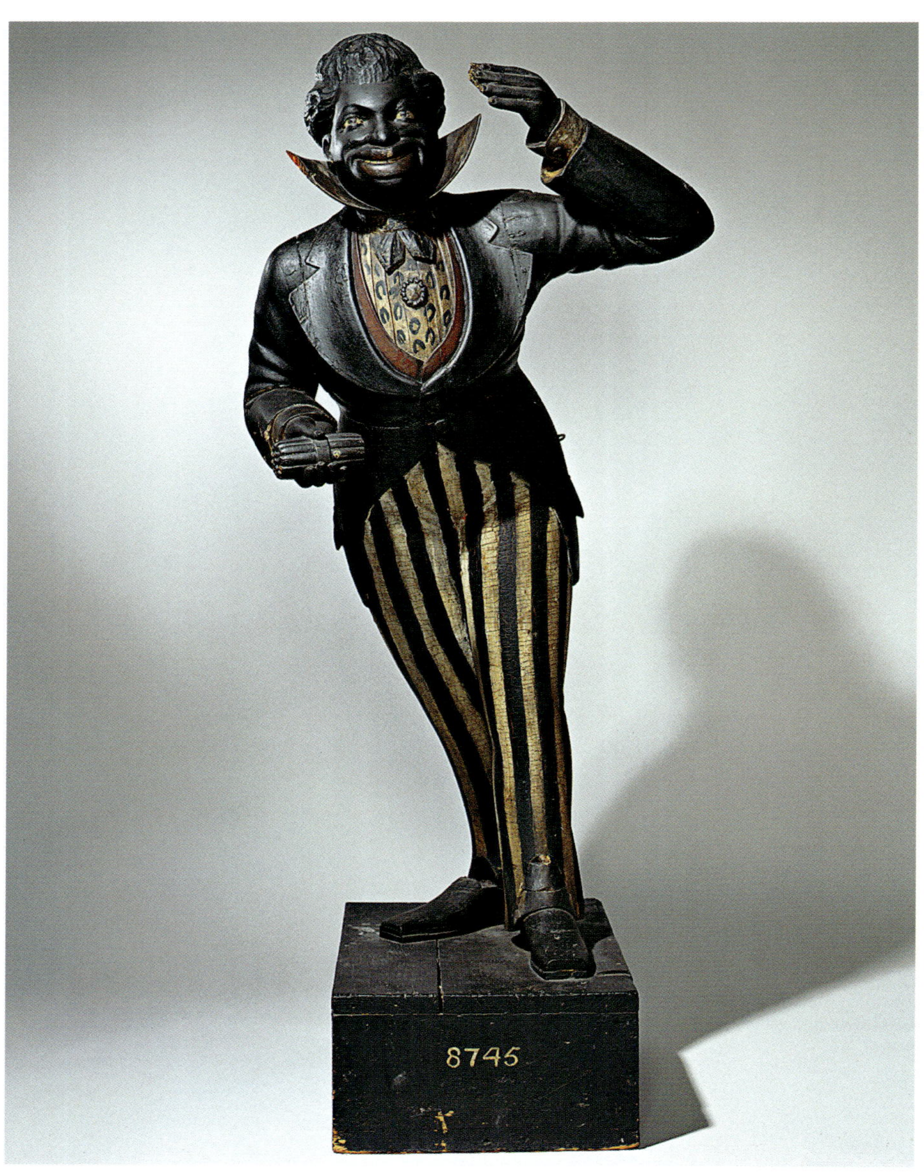

108 *Black Man*, eastern United States, c. 1875. Painted wood, 61 x 27 x 29 in. (154.9 x 68.6 x 73.6 cm). Mercer Museum, Doylestown, Pa.

Anthony.[46] Other contemporary references are few and far between. It is therefore even more remarkable that another figure of George W. L. Fox, done by a different carver, is owned by the Heritage Museums and Gardens, Sandwich, Massachusetts.[47] Given the low survival rate of show figures in general, these two examples attest to Fox's widespread popularity and name recognition, while also demonstrating the extent to which carvers succeeded in capturing an accurate likeness of their subject.

Besides identifiable stage personalities like Fox, Raymond, and Forrest, other more generic types of performers were popular as show figures. Examples of the mildly titillating representations of actresses and acrobats that graced theater entrances and lobbies have already been considered. Minstrel figures were

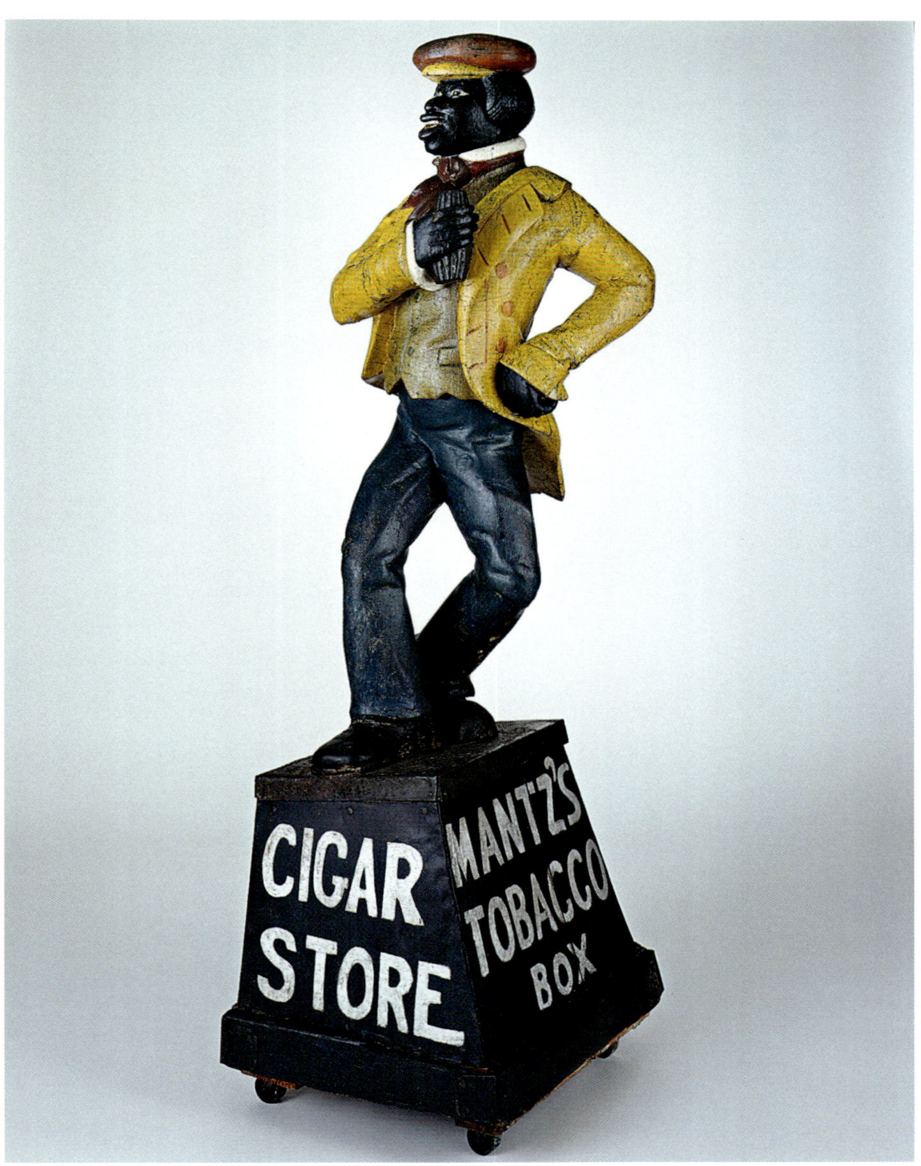

109 *Mantz's Minstrel*, eastern United States, c. 1875. Painted wood, 76 x 21 x 24 in. (193 x 53.3 x 61 cm). © Shelburne Museum, Shelburne, Vt.

another favorite, derived from the popular touring shows that featured white actors and musicians in blackface. Some were carved with exaggerated black facial features, while others were closer to representations of whites dressed as blacks. In all cases, they played upon one of the most common racist notions in white society, the belief that blacks were natural musicians and mimics. As such, African-Americans were considered ideally suited to be entertainers. American minstrel shows were largely based on this supposition.[48]

Of all the stereotypes presented by shop and cigar-store figures, these images are certainly the most derogatory. Reflecting the widely held racist views of mainstream white culture, the imaginary black man was generally characterized as the happy Negro, the smiling servant in northern households or the field

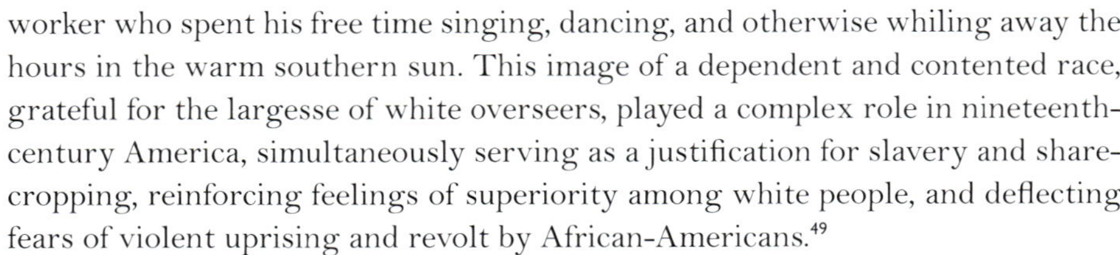

worker who spent his free time singing, dancing, and otherwise whiling away the hours in the warm southern sun. This image of a dependent and contented race, grateful for the largesse of white overseers, played a complex role in nineteenth-century America, simultaneously serving as a justification for slavery and sharecropping, reinforcing feelings of superiority among white people, and deflecting fears of violent uprising and revolt by African-Americans.[49]

The image of the black minstrel proved to be irresistible to white audiences, both on stage and in front of shops. Fictitious and exaggerated physical features and dress that fit the popular minstrel stereotype dominated the portrayal of most African-American figures (plate 108). A few of the more thoughtful and sympathetic white observers clearly recognized this fact. In 1892, a Philadelphia journalist noted:

> The tobacconist's wooden negro was invariably sculptured after the most extravagant Ethiopian minstrel pattern. He was generally dressed in a light-blue coat, swallow-tail cut, yellow breeches, and top boots, a style not usually affected by colored gentlemen in real life. His head, if covered at all, was dignified with a tall, steeple-crowned hat, and as for his collar, nothing so outrageous as his could really have been manufactured to meet an existing demand.[50]

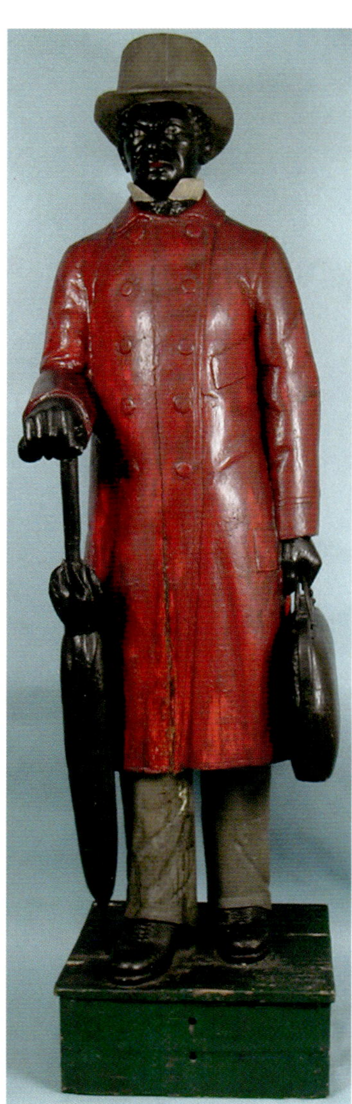

110 *Reverend Campbell*, probably Chicago, c. 1880. Painted wood, height 96 in. (243.8 cm). Fenimore Art Museum, Cooperstown, N.Y.

Overt racism became more intense and virulent after emancipation. The slavery system that kept blacks in bondage also defined their place in society before the Civil War. After the Emancipation Proclamation of 1863, white society was haunted even more by the nightmare of insurrection and the possibility that African-Americans might challenge its paternalistic authority. Images that expressed notions of racial inferiority were an effective and popular means of reinforcing the status quo that denied blacks access to social and economic opportunities (plate 109).

Even those representations of African-Americans that appear somewhat dignified were frequently accompanied by derogatory associations. A figure of Reverend Campbell is one such example (plate 110). For many years Reverend Campbell was the minister of an African-American church on the estate of the famous detective, Allen Pinkerton, in Onarga, Illinois. The story goes that on a trip to Chicago, Pinkerton was struck by the uniform of a black porter at the hotel in which he was staying. He purchased one like it and presented it to Reverend Campbell upon his return home, telling him that all the black ministers in Chicago wore similar outfits. The minister was supposedly so taken with it that he wore it to church every Sunday for the next ten years and preached with his hat on. When he died, Pinkerton commissioned a figure of the beloved minister in his porter's uniform, complete with top hat, umbrella, and briefcase.[51]

This not-so-subtle tale again plays upon notions of gullibility and ignorance, reinforcing the subservient role assigned to African-Americans as a legacy of slavery. In much the same way as the Noble Savage stereotype operated on the

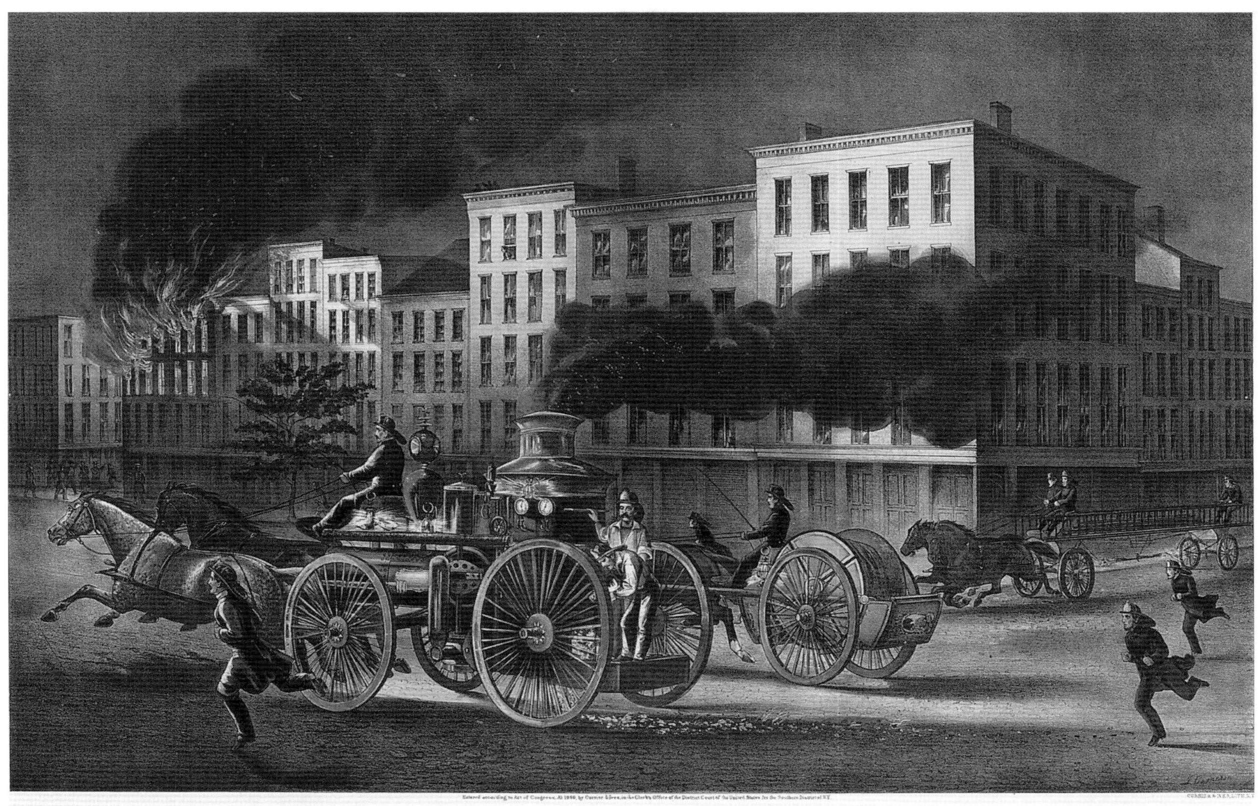

111 *The Life of a Fireman, The Metropolitan System*, 1866. Lithograph, 17 1/2 x 26 3/4 in. (44.4 x 67.9 cm). Published by Currier and Ives, New York. Print Collection, Miriam and Ira D. Wallach Division of Art, Prints, and Photographs, The New York Public Library, Astor, Lenox, and Tilden Foundations

representation of the American Indian, a seemingly positive image is subverted by a subtext of otherness. Show figures and related carvings like *Reverend Campbell* conveyed powerful, if sometimes contradictory, messages that resonated deeply throughout nineteenth-century America.

IT WILL COME AS NO SURPRISE to learn that in the public arena of visual representation, whites fared better than their black and Indian counterparts, both as individuals and groups. Caricatures like the Dude and the Girl of the Period were common, but just as popular were idealized images of local and national heroes. Among them, perhaps none was more collectively celebrated than firemen. Seen as men of action and heroic types, they were widely admired for their readiness to risk life and limb to protect their communities. Men from all walks of life joined volunteer companies in cities and towns throughout the country. In the larger urban areas, professional firefighters were a prominent feature by the Civil War era. Volunteers and professionals alike were the subject of much attention, and their courageous deeds were frequently recorded in art and literature. Two of Currier and Ives's most popular series, for example, were entitled "The Life of a Fireman" and "The American Fireman," groups of six and four prints issued between 1854 and 1866, and in 1858, respectively (plate 111).[52]

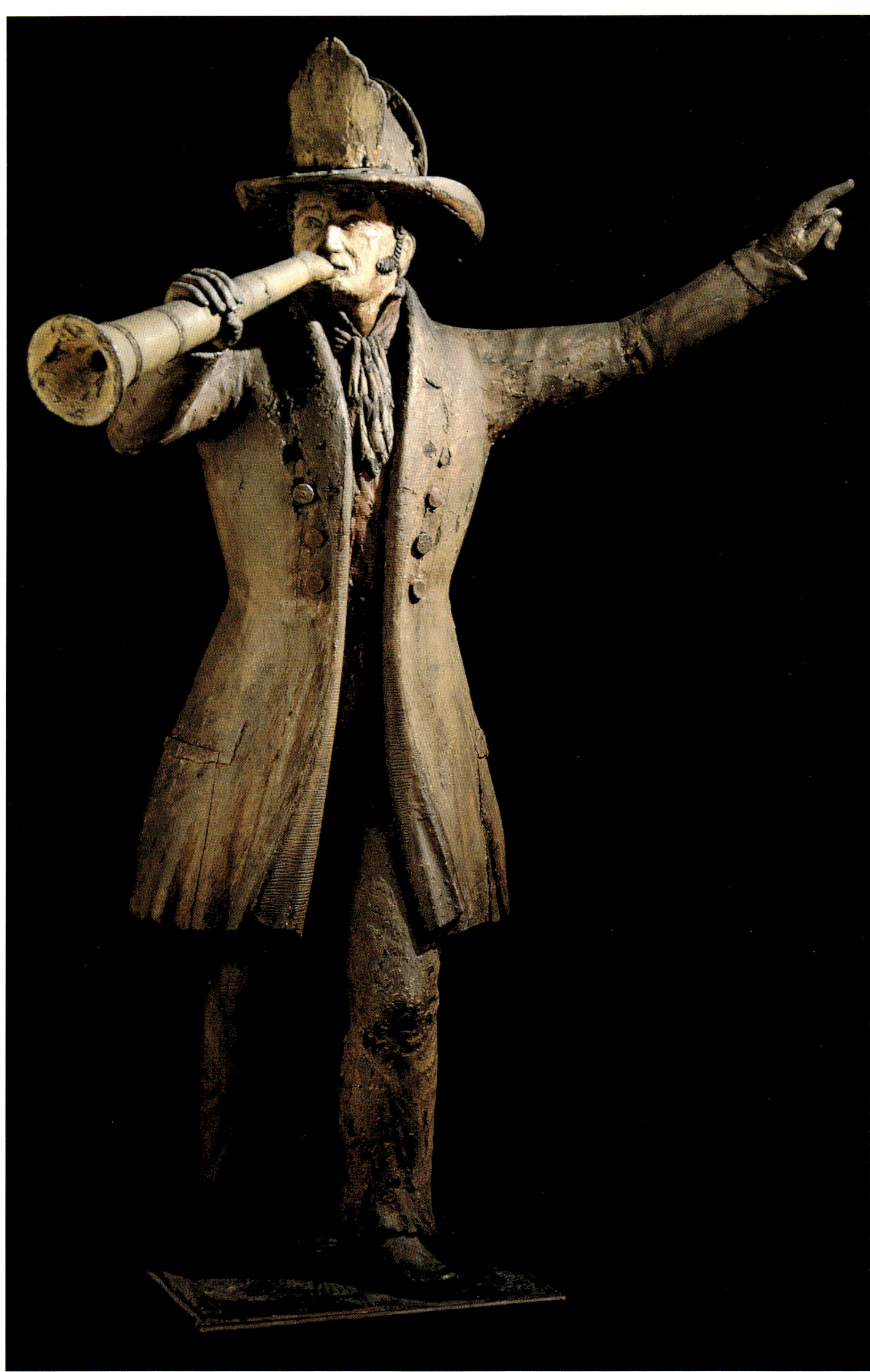

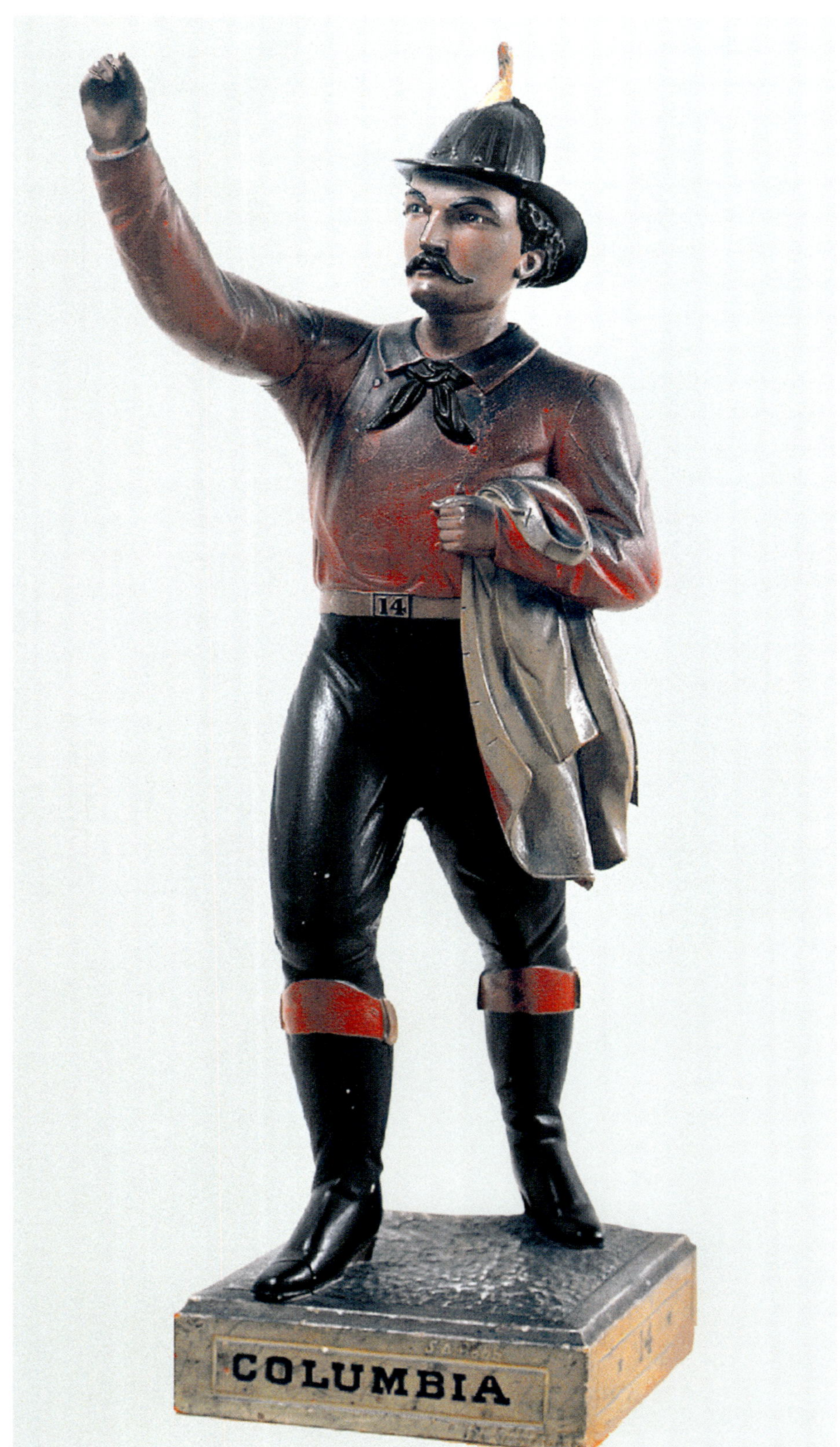

112 (OPPOSITE) *Harry Howard*, New York, c. 1860. Painted wood, height 91 in. (231.1 cm). The New-York Historical Society, New York (1937.328)

113 (RIGHT) Incised on base: "S. A. Robb, 195 Canal St.," *Volunteer Fireman*, New York, 1876–88. Painted wood, 35 x 11 x 19 in. (88.9 x 27.9 x 48.2 cm). New York City Fire Museum, New York

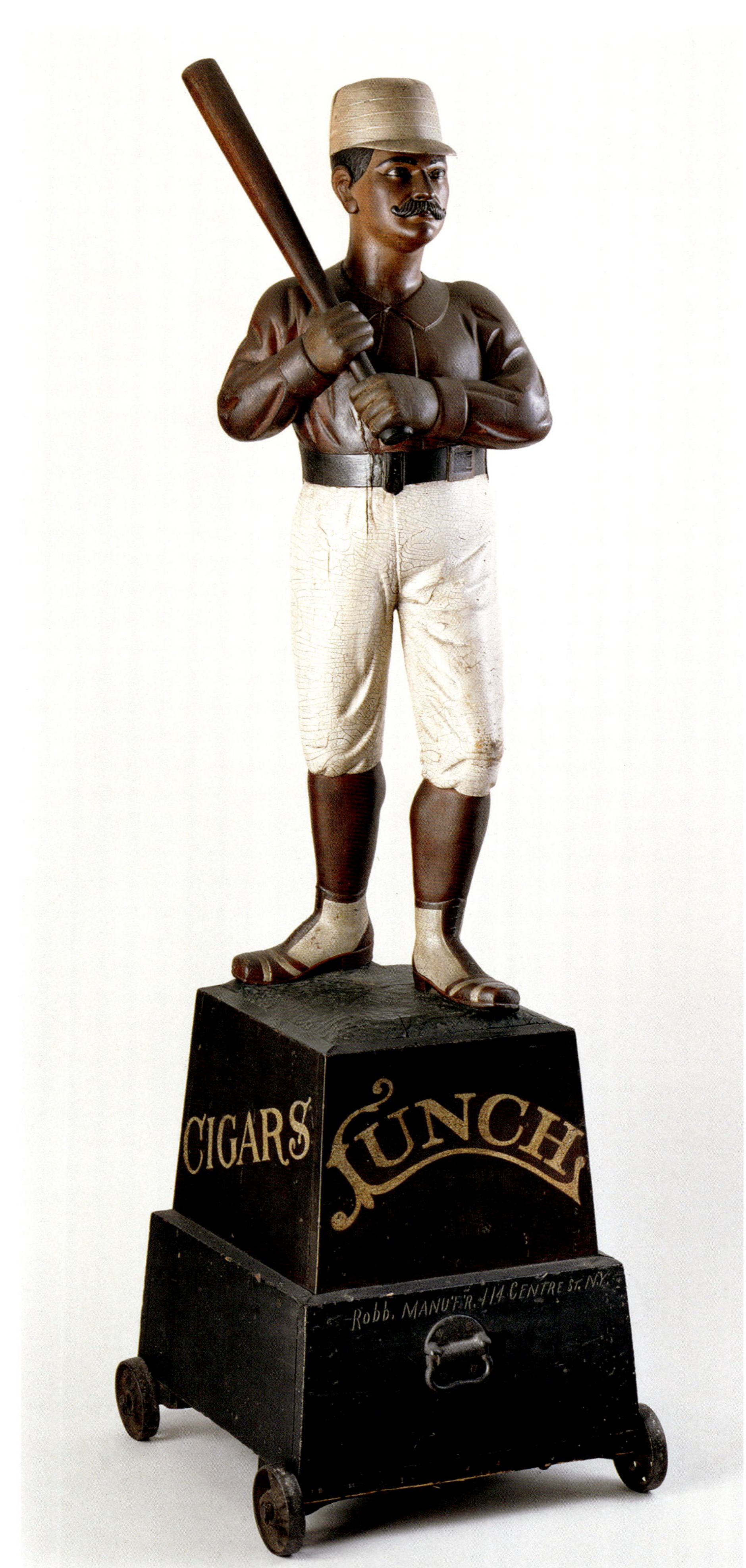

114 Incised on base: "Robb. Manu'f'r. 114 Centre St. NY.," *Baseball Player*, New York, 1888–1903. Painted wood, 76 x 21 3/4 x 21 3/4 in. (193 x 55.2 x 55.2 cm). American Folk Art Museum, New York. Promised gift of Millie and Bill Gladstone (P4.1999.1)

In addition, the firemen themselves often commissioned paintings and sculpture to commemorate important personalities and events, or to identify their companies. This is particularly true of the many wooden figures of firemen that were created, including a monumental statue of Harry Howard (plate 112). Chief Engineer of the New York City Volunteer Fire Department from 1857 to 1860, Howard was honored by his fellows by having his portrait carved in wood and placed on a pediment on top of Firemen's Hall on Mercer Street. Poised in an attitude of leadership, the figure holds a fire horn in his right hand while gesturing a command with his left, the perfect image of a dramatic popular hero.[53]

Another expressively carved figure has "Columbia 14" painted on its base (plate 113). It is incised "S. A. Robb. 195 Canal St.," which is particularly significant because it establishes that the piece is, in fact, a commemorative figure carved fifteen or twenty years after the Columbian Engine Company 14 had

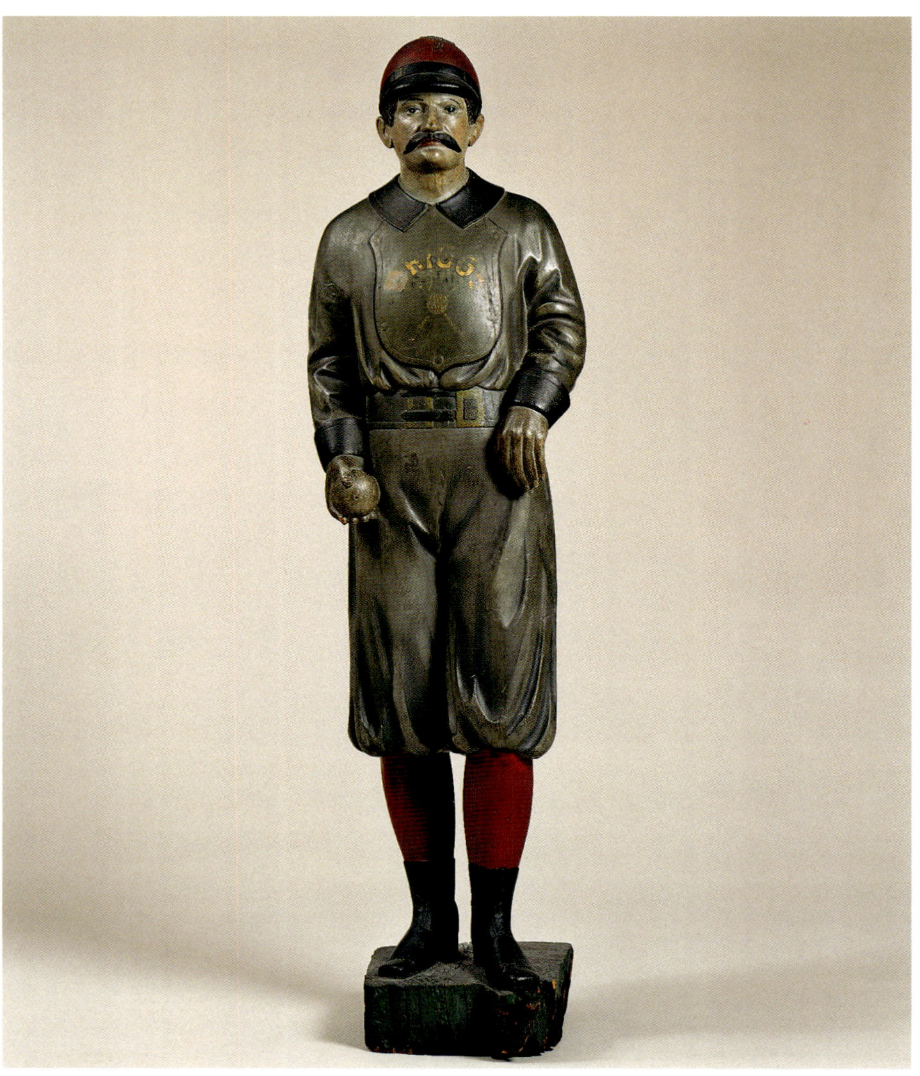

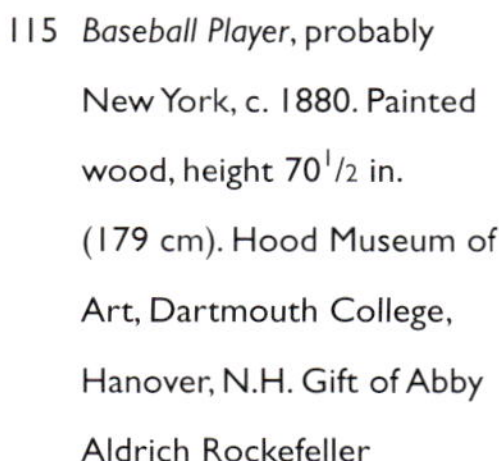

115 *Baseball Player*, probably New York, c. 1880. Painted wood, height 70½ in. (179 cm). Hood Museum of Art, Dartmouth College, Hanover, N.H. Gift of Abby Aldrich Rockefeller

ceased to exist. As will be recalled, Robb had a workshop on Canal Street between 1876 and 1888. Nevertheless, the figure is wearing a uniform that was typical of New York City volunteer companies around 1860. Professional firefighting companies replaced the volunteers in 1865. Until that time, Columbian Engine Company 14 was located at the corner of Vesey and Church Streets in lower Manhattan.[54] While it could have been installed outside the firehouse as a type of sign, it is more likely that, as a commemorative figure, it occupied a place of honor in a meeting room or some other interior space.

Among those heroes with a less-dangerous profession were baseball players. By the 1880s, the game was already heralded as the national pastime and images of baseball players were nearly ubiquitous throughout the United States. As shop figures, batters and pitchers were the most popular. An exception to the general rule, they were frequently used by tobacco shops even though they did not include any overt references to the products sold inside. They also served as signs for sporting-goods stores and a number of other commercial establishments.

One of the best surviving examples of a batter is shown here, a sturdy star in a period uniform with "Robb. Manu'f'r. 114 Centre St. NY." on its base (plate 114). Its fine state of preservation, including an old paint surface and original base, render it remarkable. Other, similar figures from the Robb shop exist in at least two sizes, attesting to the popularity of the type. A rarer, lifesize figure holding a ball that was found in Bridgeport, Connecticut, may represent a pitcher (plate 115). Alternatively, his left hand could have once rested on a bat, which would make him a more generalized image of a baseball player. In either case, he is particularly notable for the naturalistic style in which he was rendered, and, although the exact reference of the word "Briggs" that is painted on his chest has not been determined, his uniform is historically accurate in every detail.[55]

Heroes and celebrities came in all shapes and sizes, then, as the carvers continually created images of those personalities who made headlines and captured the public imagination. While this survey is necessarily limited in scope, it cannot end without recognition of that species of famous American that is regarded with the most ambivalence: the politician. From the number of figures of this type that have survived or are known to have existed, it seems that nearly everyone who achieved a certain level of political prominence was immortalized in wood at one time or another. Both shipcarvers and self-taught artists made them, in a range of styles that matches the diversity of individuals represented.

The most prominent, in terms of name recognition and amount of imagery, is undoubtedly the "Father of His Country," George Washington. It is scarcely necessary to mention that his likeness has been carved, cast, and painted for just about every conceivable purpose since the late eighteenth century. Paul Svin'in, a Russian diplomat who toured the United States between 1811 and 1813, observed: "It is noteworthy that every American considers it his sacred duty to have a likeness of Washington in his home, just as we have images of God's saints. . . . Washington's portrait is the finest and sometimes the sole decoration of American homes."[56]

The same can be said of public buildings, fraternal organizations, and countless businesses, large and small. One of the most distinctive wooden images of

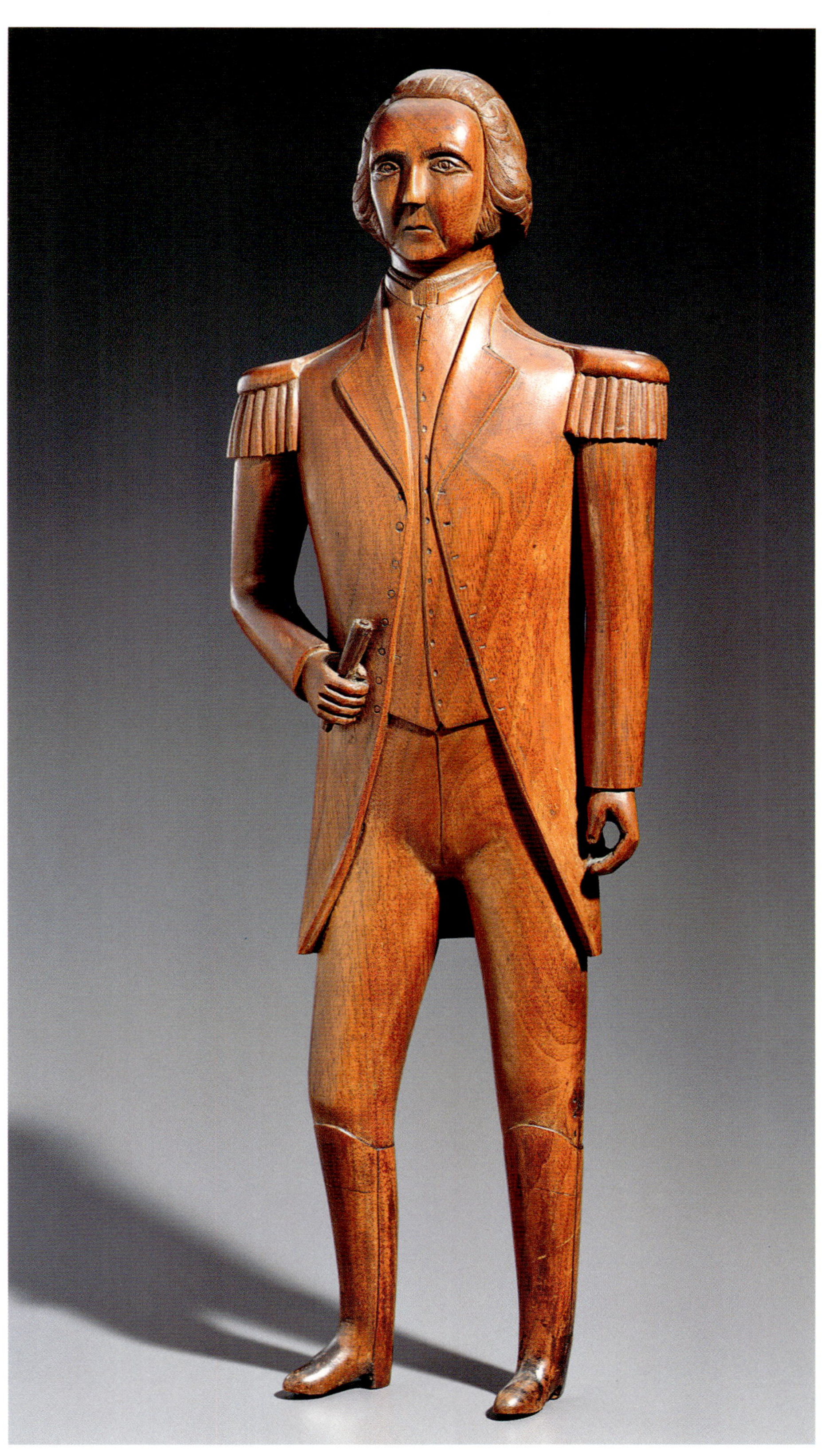

116 *George Washington*, probably Pa., mid-nineteenth century. Walnut, $24^{1}/_{2} \times 8 \times 3^{1}/_{8}$ in. (62.2 x 20.3 x 7.9 cm). American Folk Art Museum, New York. Promised gift of Ralph Esmerian (P1.2001.341)

Washington is a uniquely stylized figure thought to have been created for the Washington Masonic Lodge in Adams, Pennsylvania (plate 116).[57] The carver has captured the essence of the popular conception of George Washington with a minimum of extraneous detail. Particular attention has been paid to the head and broad shoulders emphasized by epaulets, from which the body tapers to relatively short legs terminating in the suggestion of military boots.

A monumental carving of Washington that has served as both commemorative statue and tobacconist sign provides an interesting counterpoint to this smaller figure, as well as an intriguing history that has yet to be totally unraveled (plate 117). In April 1889, the nine-foot figure was placed atop the first Washington Square Arch in New York City to commemorate the centennial of Washington's inauguration (plate 118).[58] Designed by Stanford White (1853–1906) in the fashionable Beaux-Arts style, the arch was a temporary structure made of wood and staff. The figure itself was much older, and was described in the official history of the commemoration as "a colossal wooden statue of Washington, of ancient workmanship."[59] It can be fairly well documented back to the 1840s, when it was sold at a New York City auction to a Mr. Jacques of South Norwalk, Connecticut.[60] Before that, its history is something of a mystery. For many years, it has been accompanied by a story that it was originally erected in Bowling Green or on the Battery in 1792 to replace a statue of George III that had been torn down during the Revolution. The legend was debunked in 1926 by I. N. Phelps Stokes in his authoritative work *The Iconography of Manhattan Island* but has continued to circulate to this day.[61]

117 *George Washington*, probably New York, c. 1820–40. Painted wood, 106³/₄ x 43 x 37 in. (271.1 x 109.2 x 94 cm). Historical Society of Delaware, Wilmington

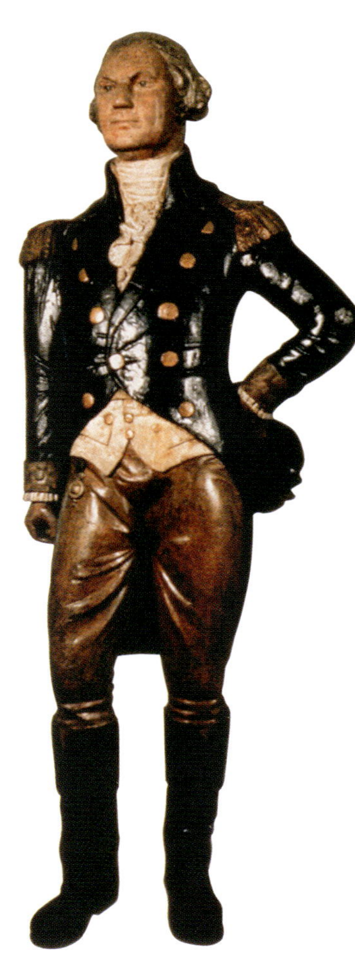

The figure was probably created sometime in the 1820s or 1830s. Stylistically, it appears to be the work of a shipcarver. This is seen particularly in the sharp folds of the jabot and the lapels and collar of the jacket, the bold strokes for hair, and the handling of the face, which, while subject to restoration over the years, still evidences the smooth planes favored by master shipcarvers.[62] Given its impressive size, it was almost certainly done as a special commission, most likely for an important civic celebration like those held during Lafayette's tour of the United States in 1824 and 1825, and the centennial of Washington's birth in 1833. Both of these events inspired commemorative works of art of all types. Passing through several hands after the 1840s auction, the piece served as a sign for a tobacconist's shop on 125th Street during the last quarter of the nineteenth century, except, of course, for its brief stint as a commemorative statue in 1889. By 1913, it was being used as a sign for a barbershop on St. Nicholas Avenue and 182nd Street. Eventually it found a home at the Historical Society of Delaware.[63]

This account has been presented at some length not only because of the importance of this venerable old statue, but also because it provides a good example of the varied histories and multiple uses and reuses of many shop figures and related carvings. They were designed to be readily adaptable, as we have seen. A purchaser could specify details and accessories that would render a particular piece appropriate to whatever purpose he or she had in mind. Whether displayed in front of stores, in gardens, theater lobbies, or on commemorative arches, they were signs of the times, reflective of contemporary trends and collective notions of a national past.

Nevertheless, the temporary marriage of the work of an early-nineteenth-century shipcarver and a commemorative arch designed in the latest style by a leading American architect may seem a bit incongruous. It is also symbolic. By the centennial of Washington's inauguration in 1889, America had embraced a new image of itself. Decades of economic development and territorial expansion after the Civil War had brought prosperity to many, and with it, visions of national greatness and international prominence finally seemed within reach. Traditional wooden figures and other images handed down from previous generations were rapidly passing into history.

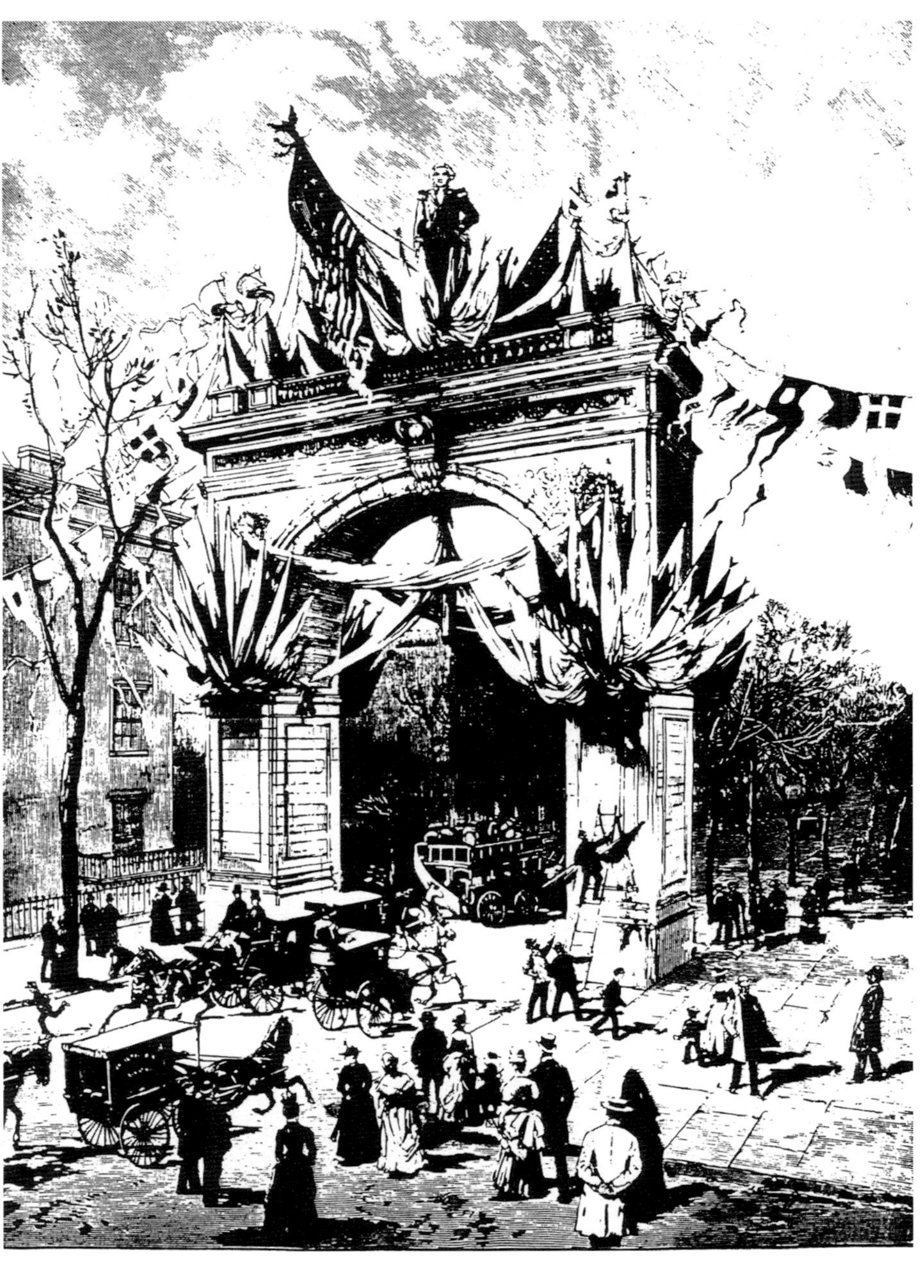

118 Charles Graham, "The Washington Arch at Fifth Avenue and Washington Square," *Harper's Weekly* 33, 4 May 1889, 343

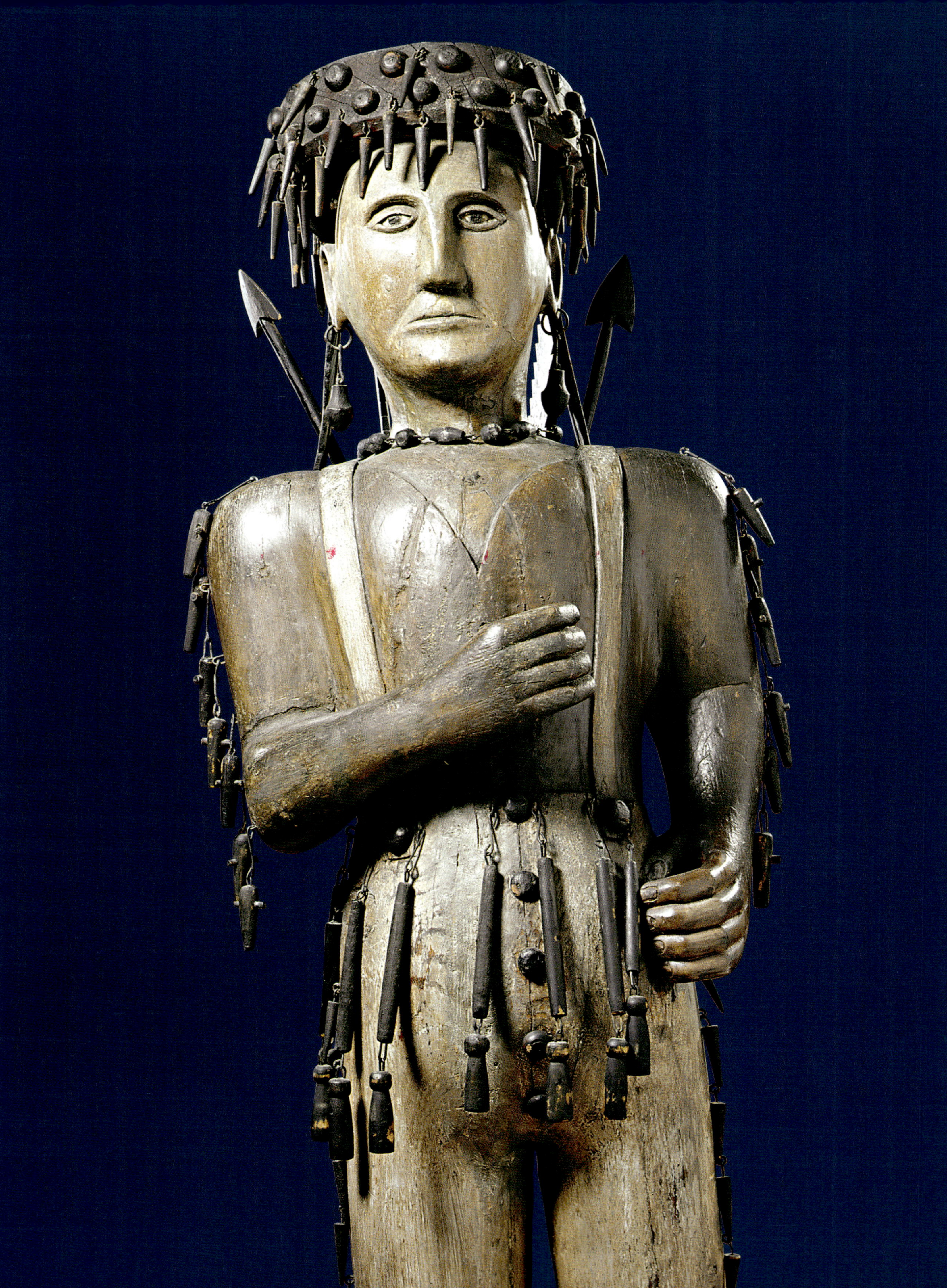

CHAPTER 5 THE END OF AN ERA

BY THE TIME THE MONUMENTAL STATUE of George Washington (plate 117) was placed on top of Stanford White's Washington Square Arch, the show-figure fad had just about run its course. As a Philadelphia journalist noted in 1892:

> Many once familiar devices for advertising have been laid on the shelf forever and have thus become obsolete. Foremost among the recently rejected methods for catching trade is the cigar store Indian, at one time the most frequent and conspicuous character of sign in this city, but which has now almost entirely disappeared and, within a few years, will be seen no more.
>
> So familiar in times past has everyone become with the cigar store Indian that we have forgotten to look for them. Thus the majority of pedestrians have failed to notice the disappearance of these figures from most of our cigar stores throughout the city. To-day not one in twenty cigar stores is so designated, while in times past every cigar store, large and small, was decorated with some character of Pompey.[1]

The article goes on to describe and illustrate several figures that could still be seen on the streets of Philadelphia. Among them were a Punch, Highlander, Lord Dundreary, Forty-Niner, and Brother Jonathan or Uncle Sam. So it seems that even as their numbers were thinning, many of the popular show-figure types remained in place as local fixtures and neighborhood landmarks. This would be the case for another twenty years or so, but, all in all, they were definitely on the decline.

The single most important reason for the disappearance of show figures from city streets was the fact that they were increasingly seen as old-fashioned, symbols of an era that was rapidly passing away. At the height of their popularity from the 1840s to about 1890, they were a vibrant and humorous form of contemporary expression that occupied an important niche in the rapidly evolving arenas of popular culture and commercial advertising. By the last decade of the nineteenth century, though, new modes of advertising and a more cosmopolitan national attitude had greatly diminished their impact. The country was changing quickly, and the brightly painted carved wooden figures did not quite fit the tenor of the times.

The year in which the article that was quoted above appeared, 1892, was also the four hundredth anniversary of Columbus's discovery of America. Celebrations in commemoration of that event were organized throughout the country. By far the largest and most impressive of these was the World's Columbian

119 Detail of plate 123

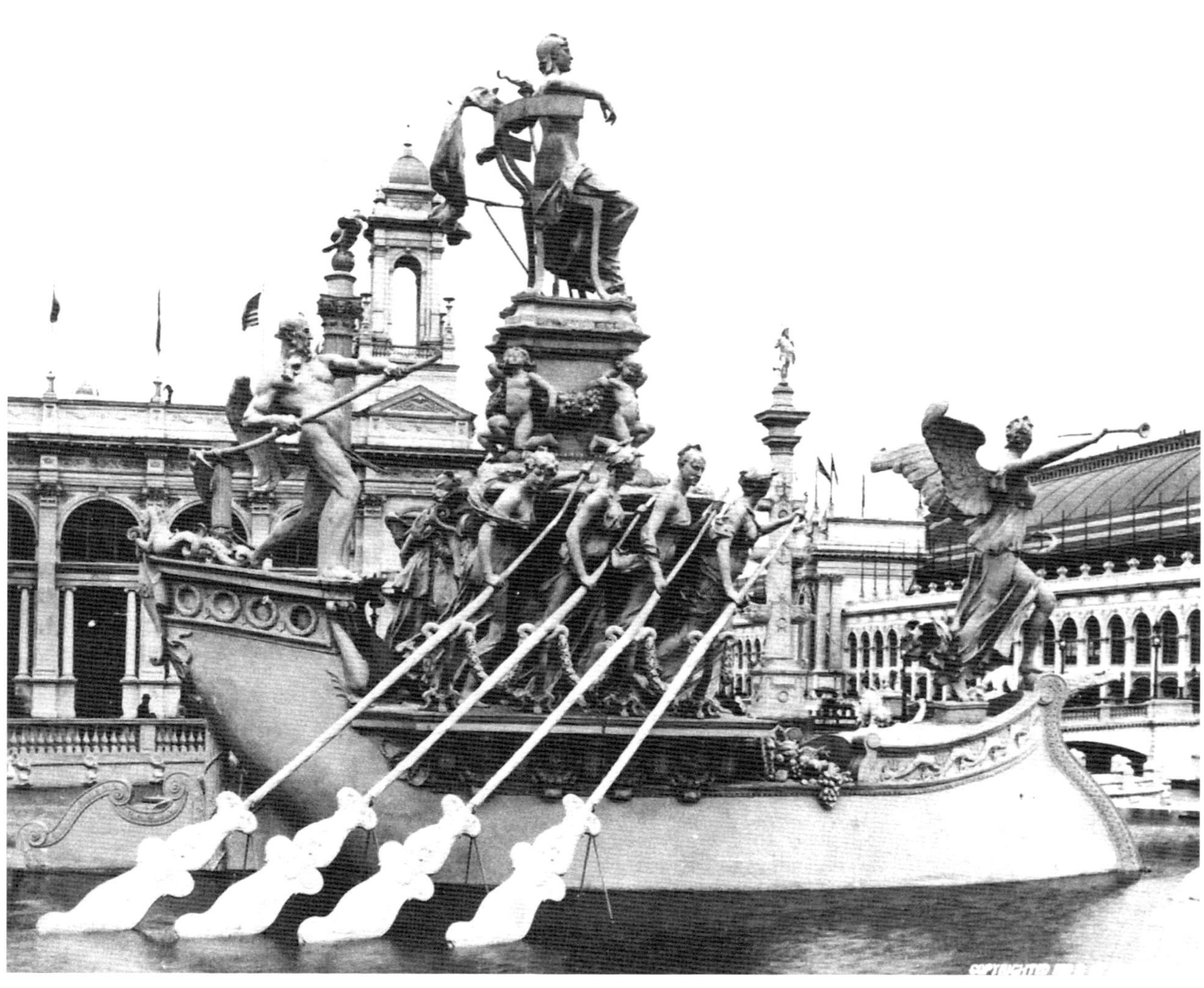

120 Frederick MacMonnies (American, 1863–1937), *Barge of State* or *Triumph of Columbia*, 1893. Staff material. Destroyed

Exposition held in Chicago from the first of May to the end of October in 1893. Set on the shores of Lake Michigan, seven miles south of downtown Chicago, the sprawling site covered over 686 acres with scores of buildings and exhibition halls, including some of the largest temporary structures ever built. During its six-month run, the fair attracted over twenty million visitors.[2]

The Exposition presented an unprecedented range of exhibits of American commercial and artistic production, as well as a large number of international pavilions. Among the fair's highlights were the Manufactures and Liberal Arts Building, Agriculture Hall, the Art Palace, and the Women's Building. Near the main entrance from a pier that jutted out into Lake Michigan was a large artificial lagoon known as the Basin that was dominated at one end by the Columbian Fountain, which featured an imposing sculptural group of a ship manned by numerous allegorical figures designed by the American sculptor Frederick MacMonnies (1863–1937) (plate 120). In contrast to this showcase of Western civilization was the Midway Plaisance, a mile-long stretch that was part–outdoor ethnological museum, part–amusement park. It featured stereotypical "native" villages from all corners of the globe, along with exotic entertainments, restaurants, and a 260-foot Ferris wheel.[3]

The largest structure in the Exposition was the Manufactures and Liberal Arts Building, with over 1.3 million square feet of floor space covering nearly thirty-one acres.[4] Among the hundreds of displays beneath its roof was, it will be recalled, a large exhibit by William Demuth and Company. In addition to several cases of elaborately carved pipes, the Demuth display featured several zinc show figures, including three Indians, a Gambrinus, and a "Moorish girl," as one article described it. It also contained four wooden figures of "Nubian boys," two of which held salvers.[5] These were not shop signs, but rather were designed for use as decorative pieces in the interior of a fashionable urban store.

One of the major goals of the fair's organizers was to demonstrate America's position as a world leader in both the arts and industries. The Columbian Exposition followed in the wake of a number of extremely popular international fairs, beginning with the famous Crystal Palace Exposition in London in 1851. Something of an exposition mania seized Europe and the United States in the second half of the nineteenth century, when nearly one hundred international fairs were attended by hundreds of millions of visitors.[6] National reputations were on the line, as each country attempted to demonstrate the strength of its contributions to Western culture and commerce. The stakes were particularly high for the United States, which was just emerging as an international player during these years.

The country had already received widespread recognition for its remarkable economic progress and its many innovative developments in technology and manufacturing. In a few short decades, it had become a world power in commerce and industry. Europeans still considered the United States hopelessly provincial in the realm of culture and the arts, however, which to many of the country's leading citizens presented a major obstacle to be overcome if America were to fulfill its destiny as the most powerful country on earth.

For this reason, the Art Palace and the fair's architecture in general were matters of great concern to its organizers. The Art Palace contained more than ten thousand works displayed in 145,000 square feet of exhibition space. Over one thousand of these were by American artists.[7] The American galleries were situated adjacent to the French in an effort to prove the superiority, or at least the equality, of American painting and sculpture. Some critics felt that the American exhibit succeeded in its intended purpose, and others did not.[8] In hindsight, however, it is clear that the Exposition was a watershed event that demonstrated that American art had come of age and could compete successfully with European art on the international stage.

As for architecture, most of the fair's major buildings were designed in the eclectic French Beaux-Arts mode, which was generally considered to be the most important contemporary style by all but some of the avant-garde. Overall, the Exposition had a pivotal impact on the future of American architecture. The first major showcase for Beaux-Arts classicism in this country, the fair established it as the quasi-official style for government buildings and the mansions of the wealthy for decades to come.

MacMonnies's Columbian Fountain exemplified the progressive and cosmopolitan attitude that America sought to project at the Exposition. Designed in France, again in the fashionable Beaux-Arts style, it was as up to date as the architecture that surrounded it. Columbia sat alert in the ship of state, with Father Time at the helm and female allegories of the Arts, Sciences, and Industries manning the oars. Fame or Victory stood at the prow, guiding the ship into a glorious future. Its rather obvious message was one of a nation come of age. One writer hailed Columbia as "a fair, youthful figure, eager and alert, not reposing upon the past, but poised in high expectations."[9]

In contrast, the wooden image of George Washington on the arch in Washington Square in 1889 was intended as a commemoration of the past, a tribute to the nation's founding and infancy. Still, it is difficult to believe that Stanford White, one of the country's leading architects, would have specified that it be used as the arch's crowning glory. He would have no doubt preferred a new work, executed in a Beaux-Arts style that would have complemented his design. In fact, a sketch of White's first study shows five figures on top of the arch, probably an allegorical group intended to symbolize aspects of America's history and development.[10] It is likely that someone else determined that the George Washington figure should be used, perhaps due to financial considerations or time constraints.

Not only was the old statue out of date, it would not have been considered high art by White and his contemporaries. According to the aesthetic criteria of the day, true sculpture was done in marble or bronze. These were the only mediums worthy of either embodying the truths that art was meant to express or immortalizing the likeness of an important personage. Wood was an artisan's medium, and shipcarving, though widely admired, was a craft in the eyes of art critics and most fine artists. It was art in the service of commerce, not higher ideals, and was not considered to be particularly edifying or morally uplifting, two of the principal characteristics of high art.[11]

Some observers took a particularly dim view of what they considered to be popular art. Lamenting the lack of artistic patronage and general appreciation of the fine arts in this country, the mid-century art critic and author Henry Tuckerman wrote in 1858, "Who, in this land of railroads and elections, stands apart rapt in solemn visions such as absorbed of old a Durer or an Angelo?"[12] He then went on to note that "The caricatures in Punch, the rude 'counterfeit presentment' of a popular statesman, the wooden filagree of an anomalous villa, the coarsely 'illustrated' paper delineating an event or a personage about which the town is occupied, bank-bill vignettes, Ethiopian minstrels, and 'the portrait of a gentleman,' form the staple art language for the masses; and in all this, there is little to kindle aspiration, to refine the judgment, or to hint the infinite possibilities of Art."[13] Even though he did not specifically mention figureheads or shop figures, he surely thought of them in the same way.

To place Tuckerman's comments in perspective, it is important to recognize the state of the arts in the United States at mid-century. In spite of a growing appreciation for painting and sculpture on the part of an increasingly affluent middle class, opportunities for American artists were still very limited. Art schools were few and far between, and those that did exist lacked resources. Some private individuals helped artists by acquiring their work or underwriting study tours of Europe, but, with the exception of sporadic portrait commissions, government patronage was nearly nonexistent. There were no public art museums, and the handful of commercial galleries that operated in major cities concentrated on European art. From the late 1830s until 1852, a number of Art Unions organized lotteries that bought works from artists and distributed them on a national scale, but these were relatively short-lived affairs. As a result, the annual exhibitions of organizations like the National Academy of Design and the Pennsylvania Academy of the Fine Arts were almost the only major venues for the display and sale of the work of American artists. Moreover, after the Civil War, many collectors and critics were not particularly interested in American art. Following the lead of their European counterparts, they considered it provincial, the same assessment that was leveled against American culture in general.

The established artistic hierarchies that dominated aesthetic thought in both Europe and America throughout the eighteenth and most of the nineteenth centuries were firmly in place.[14] The distinction between art and craft was strictly enforced, so that work like shipcarving could be appreciated for its decorative and ornamental qualities, but did not qualify as "Art." Operating from a position of cultural inferiority, intellectuals like Tuckerman were all the more sensitive to these distinctions. In response to criticism from Europe that America was marked by crass materialism and that its citizens were only concerned with the accumulation of wealth, they sought to educate the public on the importance of the fine arts in defining a national character. As a result, they were not about to cede any ground to the popular arts.

Despite the fact that he was well known in artistic circles in Philadelphia, William Rush suffered from these judgments throughout his entire career. Commenting on the figure of *Agriculture* that Rush had designed and carved for the Schuylkill Bridge in 1812, a critic wrote:

> In reviewing the works of this truly American sculptor, it is but fair to remark that he has been confined to a particular branch, namely, the figure heads of ships and other ornamental work in naval architecture, in the execution of which he has been limited, both as to time and price. . . . we will venture to say that no man in any country has ever surpassed Mr. Rush in this department of sculpture. His works have traveled with American commerce, all over the world, and are justly appreciated abroad, as well as at home; and we have no hesitation in giving it our decided opinion that, if his studies had been directed to the higher branches of art, with proper opportunities, he would have rivaled the most eminent sculptors of the present age.[15]

While he admired Rush, then, the writer clearly qualified his praise. He recognized Rush's mastery of his medium and even deemed him a sculptor. The association of his work with commerce and "naval architecture" could not be overlooked, nor could his use of wood, which, while not specifically mentioned, was obvious to anyone reading the article.

William Dunlap offered a similar assessment when he reminded his readers that while Rush had earned the reputation of "artist," his accomplishments and choice of mediums did not qualify him as a leading practitioner of the art of sculpture. In discussing Charles Willson Peale (1741–1827) and his attempt to found the Academy of Fine Arts in 1791, Dunlap noted that "The only artists named by his biographer as joining in this scheme are Ceracchi, the celebrated sculptor, and Mr. Rush, who, though by trade a carver of ships' heads, was, by talent and study, an artist."[16]

In both cases, however, the writers' comments are decidedly more positive and approving than those of Henry Tuckerman concerning the "lower" branches of art. This is no doubt partly due to Rush's prominence in Philadelphia's artistic community, an indisputable fact that presented a particular problem to contemporary critics. Then again, it is also true that this same sort of qualified admiration was frequently applied to the work of other shipcarvers, none of whom received as much notice in their lifetimes as did Rush.

In 1816, the author of an article that reviewed the state of arts in contemporary Boston echoed these sentiments in discussing Solomon Willard, the only sculptor he could identify. He wrote:

> Mr. Willard is a self-taught artist, who possesses a capacity for sculpture of no ordinary kind. He has lately been employed in carving the ornaments of two or three ships: among them the *Courier* and the *Hindu*, which have lately sailed from Boston. In viewing the freedom, the grace, and harmonious design of these ornaments, it is impossible not to regret that his talents should not be exercised on more noble and durable materials. The gentlemen who patronized him in this way, have however rendered him a service, as it develops his ability, and gives him practice, but it may be hoped that he will hereafter be occupied in higher branches of sculpture.[17]

Several years earlier, a rare diary entry made by Elizabeth De Hart Bleeker, a member of one of New York's leading families, noted that she and a group of friends visited Daniel N. Train's shop in March 1799 to "see the figure of the President belonging to the Frigate the Adams."[18] She did not offer any critical commentary in her terse passage, but the fact that she and several local worthies went to view the figurehead indicates a certain amount of contemporary appreciation for the carver's work.

Throughout the nineteenth century, many observers—particularly journalists and other writers who had less of a vested interest in the future of American art than artists and art critics—were willing to allow that carved wooden figures had definite artistic merit. At times, they were unreserved in their praise, using the words *sculptor* or *artist* without any modifiers when discussing shipcarvers and their work. More often than not, however, they qualified their judgments by calling the carvers *marine artists*, *wood sculptors*, or *sign sculptors*.[19]

One of the articles that discussed the launching of the clipper *Minehaha* in 1856 is particularly telling in this regard. While primarily concerned with Longfellow's poem and Julia Bennett Barrow's interpretation of it for the stage, the piece concluded with a description of the launch and the festivities that followed at the shipbuilder's home. The writer then mentioned that the figurehead was carved by a "Mr. Gleason," and that it was "a fine piece of work, evincing much taste, and rising to the dignity of art."[20]

These views prevailed until the end of the century. In discussing the evolution of shop-figure carving after mid-century, a journalist stated in 1890 that "The wooden Indians grew better, quite artistic in some instances." He then wrote about the carvers, "Some of them are men of decided ability and talent." In using the word *artist*, he sometimes placed it in quotation marks and sometimes not. Towards the end of the article, he attempted to create a distinction between "sculpture in wood" and "wood carving," placing the former primarily in the distant past in civilizations like that of ancient Egypt. Finally, though, he did acknowledge that, in the case of William Rush, "There was one American sculptor, at least, who worked with success in wood."[21]

The writer's discussion of ancient wooden sculpture as an art form is particularly significant. It is a rare instance in the nineteenth century in which wood was elevated to the status of an artistic medium. It is true, of course, that by citing examples from a past far removed from the present day, the author was on relatively safe ground and was not offering a radical reevaluation of figure carving. In addition, it should be noted that the article was written late in the century, at a time when members of the Arts and Crafts Movement and other avant-garde groups were extolling the virtues of handiwork and preindustrial modes of production. Still, the linkage between ancient and modern times creates a venerable artistic heritage for contemporary figure carving. A deeper aesthetic appreciation is possible within this context, even if it is not fully explored by the author.

But what of the carvers themselves? What did they think of their work and their place in the hierarchy of artistic production? On the one hand, they were clearly dedicated to their profession and approached it as artists in the twenty-first-century understanding of the term *artist* or *sculptor*. It took many long years of apprenticeship to become a master carver, and the best of them continued to hone their skills throughout their careers. One journalist noted in 1889 that "As a rule they take great pride in their work, and spend much time perfecting a feature to their mind, which they could finish in much less time if they were less artistically conscientious."[22]

The trade card of Levi L. Cushing of Boston that was previously illustrated provides some important visual evidence from earlier in the century (see plate 22). His design for a stern features up-to-date Neoclassical motifs that demonstrated that the carver was aware of the latest stylistic trends in the fine and decorative arts. At lower right, he portrayed himself as a sculptor working on a bust and wielding a mallet and chisel with a dramatic flourish. His self-identification as an artist was further reinforced by the name that he chose for the ship pictured at top. The decision to christen it the "Michael Angelo" was hardly coincidental.

As discussed, stylistic developments in shipcarving were closely related to trends in the fine arts throughout the nineteenth century. In addition, several pieces that have been previously considered illustrate their carvers' familiarity with contemporary academic styles. Among the best examples are Charles Dodge's bust of his father (plate 25) and Samuel Robb's figure of a standing Indian with bear-claw necklace that was exhibited in a metal version by William Demuth at several international expositions (plate 66). Thomas White's long-lost wooden copy of Hiram Powers's *Greek Slave* provides even more specific evidence of the carvers' interest in the fine arts. Similarly, in 1903, Samuel Robb carved a panel for a Barnum and Bailey circus wagon that featured an interpretation of John Vanderlyn's well-known mural *The Landing of Columbus*, done between 1839 and 1847 for the rotunda of the Capitol building in Washington.[23]

While they claimed a certain amount of artistic recognition for their work, though, it appears that shipcarvers generally accepted the prevailing hierarchy and the contemporary distinction between art and craft. In 1876, for example, Samuel Robb listed his occupation as "Artist in Wood" on his marriage certificate.[24] While this is certainly a statement of artistic self-identity, it is one in which Robb both proclaimed his status and qualified it at the same time. Had he believed more strongly that wood was an artistic medium on the par with marble and bronze, he would have presumably listed himself as a sculptor or an artist without feeling compelled to add a modifier. He was asserting his pride in his accomplishments, not challenging the existing system.

Another shipcarver voiced his understanding of existing aesthetic realities in an interview that appeared in *Harper's Weekly* in 1892. He began by stating sadly: "Ah, sir, the business is not what it was. Only a few American ships have figureheads now." He then continued: "One of the finest figures I ever saw is the one on the bark *Spartan*, which touches at this port frequently. It represents a Spartan warrior, bearing a shield in one hand and a sword in the other. He is in the attitude of attack, and there is a wonderful semblance of life about him. The features are finely made, and the proportions are about as perfect as they can be. It is really a piece of art-work, and would attract attention if it were anywhere else than where it is."[25]

Others were more modest in their assessments, at least in public. When asked about the nature of his work, one carver who was interviewed in 1886 answered like a true art critic. "Sculpturing?" he responded, "No, we don't call it that; just plain chopping, that's all there is to it."[26]

A cartoon entitled "In the Year Two Thousand" that appeared in *Life* magazine in 1886 presents a succinct visual summation of the general opinion of show figures and shop signs (plate 121).[27] Some of the references are obscure today, such as the mention of "Dr. Hammond's bald-headed American" in the caption. Nevertheless, the drawing obviously pokes fun at the notion of exhibiting popular art in a museum setting, while at the same time reinforcing the distinction between craft and art. Show figures belong on the street as a form of public sculpture to be enjoyed by the masses, not as objects of delectation for the connoisseur of fine art. In addition, the collections are presented as relics of a lost era, complete with labels that do not correctly identify their original purposes or histories, the implication being that they will have long since passed away by the year 2000. Fine art, on the other hand, was considered to be as eternal as the truths that it embodied.

IT IS AGAINST THIS BACKDROP that we must consider the fate of show figures. The reasons for the demise of figureheads are obvious, directly tied as they were to the shipbuilding industry. Shop figures present a more complex scenario that involves less tangible aspects of the evolving national consciousness. Victims of changing fashion and more cosmopolitan attitudes, they came to represent the past at a time when most Americans were much more interested in the future. This was particularly true of businessmen, including many of the larger urban tobacconists who were concerned with presenting a modern and sophisticated image to their upscale clientele. In 1893, a journalist noted, "One of our prominent and enterprising retailers, in speaking of this matter, said, that in his opinion the day for the Indian was passed for stores doing any proportion of fine trade; that they now marked the place for low priced goods rather than those

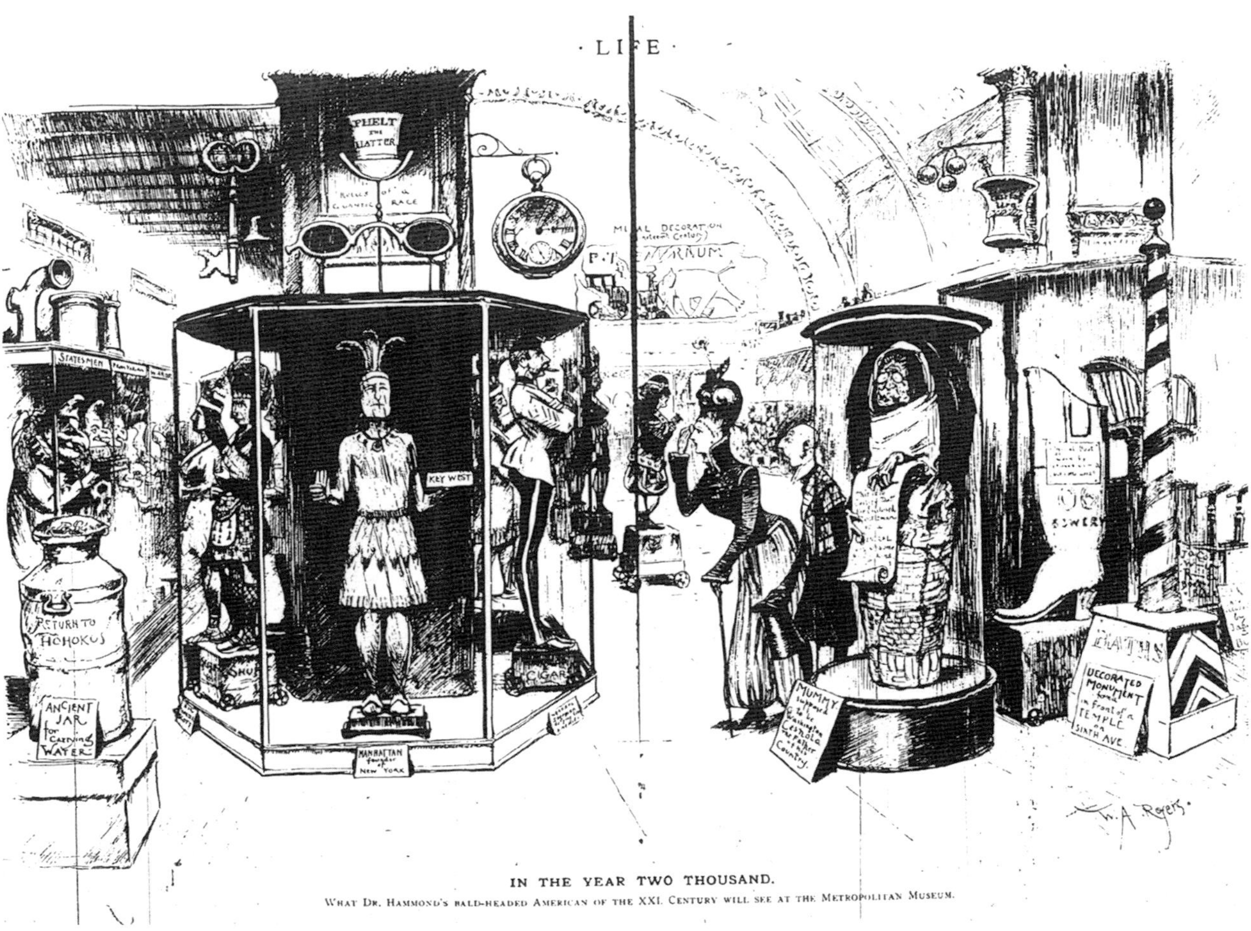

IN THE YEAR TWO THOUSAND.
What Dr. Hammond's bald-headed American of the XXI. Century will see at the Metropolitan Museum.

121 W. A. Rogers, "In the Year Two Thousand," *Life* 7 (22 Apr. 1886): 233–34

stores where an all round high class product was handled; that many of the finest Indians in the city to-day were found before stores doing a low priced trade, and that the dealer catering to a better class needed some distinctive mark."[28]

These remarks appeared in *Tobacco*, a weekly trade journal published in New York City that was a major forum for the views and opinions of tobacconists. In addition to business news and listings of current tobacco and cigar prices, the paper featured articles and editorials of interest to dealers. One long series in 1886 and 1887 concerned the history of the pipe. *Tobacco* is also the source for many of the contemporary articles on show figures and their carvers that have been quoted throughout this discussion. Most were reprinted in it after originally appearing in New York newspapers.

Besides these more historically oriented pieces, the journal also offered advice and instruction for creating the latest in fashionable interiors. Between April and June 1888, for example, it printed four articles entitled "How to Decorate a Cigar Store." Appropriately enough, the writer suggested an up-to-date masculine atmosphere, not too gaudy or elaborate, with a predominance of oak paneling and wall cabinets, shiny brass, clean glass cases, and appealing pictures on the walls. Conspicuous for its absence was any mention of show figures, either on the counter or elsewhere inside or in front of the shop. Instead, cigar lighters, which were generally figural sculptures in bronze or zinc patterned after academic work, were favored.[29]

Another article called "High Art at Conklin and Fox's" described the interior of a smoking room in a tobacco shop that was designed in accordance with the principles of the Aesthetic Movement.[30] Then, in "Art and Tobacco," the writer discussed a current trend in upscale hotels to combine a bar, cigar stand, and picture gallery that featured masculine hunting scenes and still lifes of dead game along with copies of old masters. To pique the reader's interest even more, it was noted that the galleries were frequently visited by women, but only during morning hours.[31]

If these articles provide only indirect evidence for the declining popularity of show figures among tobacconists, two editorials that appeared in 1888 stated the opinion in no uncertain terms. The first was a single paragraph without a title. It read: "The wooden Indian sign has acted well his part and has earned a well deserved rest. No first-class cigar store would be guilty of allowing one of these old tramps to loaf in front of the store. Men who use Indians generally have goods older than the squaw or buck that stands guard over them."[32] No ambiguity here; the writer clearly had no sympathy for this particular tradition, let alone a sense of nostalgia for a passing era.

The second editorial was even more blunt. It was a fairly long piece that begins with an overview of the history of cigar-store figures. The author had done some reading on the subject, because he mentioned that the first figure appeared in 1617, which was, it will be recalled, the publication date for Richard Brathwait's *The Smoaking Age, or The Life and Death of Tobacco*, the book that included the earliest known illustration of a blackamoor counter figure. The tone of the editorial quickly switched from historical speculation to racist diatribe, however, as the writer presented his views not only on show figures but also on American Indians and the Indian wars that were still fresh in the national memory. The depth and breadth of his prejudicial point of view is quite striking and revealing of the negative side of the stereotypical image of the Native American. The editorial will therefore be quoted here at some length:

> In no other country do we find the Indian, the squaw, the betting man, the "Puck," the baseball player, or the "Punch," in a series of vile caricatures that make our sidewalks hideous. The Indian was undoubtedly the father of them all, and even now is the most in demand; he served his purpose in past days, but the world is moving along, and by the survival of the fittest the live Indian is fast merging into the mass of population, or, decimated by disease and drink is dying on the reservation.
>
> It is time for the wooden Indian to move on too! There is no real use for him; the image is only a perpetual reminder of past barbarism, bloodshed, deceit, and undying hatred, that even now the strong arm of the law cannot entirely keep within bounds. We, as a nation, are tired of being perpetually reminded of the struggle we had to establish our rule through the Middle and Western States, and would fain forget its sanguinary memories. If an emblem or sign is absolutely necessary to a cigar store, why not take our national emblem, the glorious bird of freedom, which, with outspread wings, shall call to mind all that is best and highest in our national creed, instead of all that is horrible and painful in its past. Strangers make a scoff of the wooden Indian, and who can blame them; but place the bird at our doors and their lips will be closed.[33]

In this writer's mind, at least, the cigar-store Indian holds nothing but negative connotations and should be banished from sight. This intersection of art and life in the late 1880s is a vivid reminder of the bitterness and brutality that accompanied the doctrine of Manifest Destiny that most of white America accepted without question.

Some observers would have disagreed with these opinions, though, and it is easy to imagine a reply that countered his argument with the image of the Noble Savage and his pitiful vanishing race suffering at the hands of white aggressors. In "Lo, on His Last Trail," another editorial that appeared in *Tobacco* a few years later, the writer stated somewhat wistfully, "Like their prototypes in flesh and blood, the wooden Indians, who have for so long done duty as signs for tobacconists, are disappearing."[34] As previously discussed, stereotypes and misinformation abound in both of these positions. The point to be made here is that the dialogue surrounding the "Indian question" continued to affect the public reception of cigar-store figures for as long as they were a visible part of the American streetscape. The image of the American Indian ran deep in the national psyche, continually surfacing in a variety of guises. In this case, it served as a rationale for the extinction of show figures.

A second and closely related reason for the decline of the tradition was the introduction of new methods of advertising. In 1894, an article entitled "Modern Advertising" explained, "This may truly be called the era of advertising, and the firm which relies solely on old-time methods and the old stereotyped matter is neglecting its opportunities and is not going with the times."[35]

The editors of *Tobacco* recommended any number of newer techniques, particularly overhead signs illuminated by electric lights, sidewalk cases, and eye-catching window displays. As they noted in one instance, "Many dealers, having really artistic figures, are using them in the windows with good effect; and others are using on the sidewalk lettered signs on black slates, or artists' easels, the matter being constantly changed; or screens of canvas, which are lit up at night; but the Indian, as a tobacco sign, and on the frontier, is fast disappearing."[36]

By the mid-1880s, tobacco-product distributors were providing free chromolithographs to their customers. With these prints, tobacconists could create colorful window displays that featured up-to-date images in a modern format. They could also be changed on a regular basis, providing variety and a sense of novelty. An article called "Art in Tobacco Shops" that appeared in 1886 described a new type of cooperative advertising arrangement among New York dealers in which a group of paintings was loaned to one shop for a prescribed period and then circulated to another. It also noted that most advertising material in shop windows consisted of lithographs and photographs, many of which were calculated to catch the eye of potential male customers. Mention was made, for instance, of a recent crusade by the editors of the *New York Sun* against a particular lithograph of a cigarette girl that they considered indecent.[37]

One enterprising cigar manufacturer loaned full-sized, framed lithographs of the famous painting *The Angelus* by Jean-François Millet (1814–1875) to tobacconists for display in their shops. In what must be one of the earliest instances of a marketing technique that has become ubiquitous, he also advertised that he would send an unframed print to customers who submitted thirty-five cigar-box covers as proof of purchase.[38]

With the increasing emphasis on graphics in advertising, show figures were at a financial disadvantage. They were quite expensive to purchase and required constant maintenance, costs that had to be borne by the shopkeeper. Many merchants were more than happy to forego the old shop signs when manufacturers and distributors began offering free advertising. When asked the reasons for the gradual disappearance of cigar-store figures, one tobacconist responded: "In the first place a Pompey was an expensive affair, costing all the way from $25 to $200. A good figure, in fact, could not be bought for much less than $75, and this amount was necessarily a serious expenditure for a man commencing the tobacco business in a small way, and the advantages to be derived from it were in no ways proportionate. Then, too, many new devises in the way of advertising have been invented by our wholesale cigar and tobacco dealers, and, as trade was directed to them by the wholesalers, the retail men have not felt it necessary to expend any large amount of money on individual advertising."[39]

Further confirmation of this comes from another dealer who was interviewed in Baltimore in 1908. By this time, show figures were endangered throughout most of the United States, as indicated by his remarks: "Fifty years ago no tobacconist would think of opening a store without a figure. Now the men in the trade think that to put an Indian out is to waste money. When I started business in 1861, my stock cost $30, and I had a figure that cost $40. I had to have the sign, though it cost more money than the stock inside."[40]

One consequence of this investment was that the show figure came to be considered a store fixture that was sold with the shop and passed along to the next proprietor. If damaged, it could be readily repaired and given a new coat of paint. Refurbished, it was then either returned to its old spot or, if replaced by some new advertising technique, sold to someone else. The longevity of wooden figures, in combination with lessened demand and the availability of secondhand pieces, resulted in an oversupply by the end of the nineteenth century.[41]

In addition, new street and sidewalk regulations in several cities cited them as obstructions and restricted their use.[42] In other places, merchants discovered that they could augment their income by leasing their increasingly valuable sidewalk space to outdoor vendors rather than allotting it to an old-fashioned wooden figure.[43] Together these factors conspired to bring the tradition to an end. Few new show figures were made after the turn of the twentieth century.

THEN AGAIN, they were not about to give up the ghost altogether. In an article about shop-figure carving in New York that appeared in 1887, the writer mentioned: "Between two and three hundred Indians are put on the market each year. More than half of these are used in New York and the suburbs."[44] Evidently, while the opinions expressed by the editors of *Tobacco* may have been considered progressive by upscale merchants, they were far from being universally accepted. Beyond the borders of the more-fashionable business districts, show figures were still a common sight. A few years later, another observer noted: "If one would best the lion in his native lair, the rash individual must wander beyond the line of civilization marked by the Bowery, and there he will find the best instances of the aboriginal type in our city statues. Here a sense of justice blends with the love of art; and the stern, impassive Indian, bereft of all other possessions, still lives to fame as the 'stoic of the wood.'"[45]

The Philadelphia journalist who was quoted at the beginning of this chapter seconded this observation. He wrote, "These cigar figures are still to be seen only in front of small tobacco shops in old-fashioned portions of the city." Upon interviewing the proprietor of a shop that had previously produced figures, he was told, "The demand for this character of sign is now entirely from the rural districts or country towns."[46]

So it seems that show figures remained popular and prevalent in much of America at century's end. They lingered on in less-stylish urban neighborhoods and smaller towns across the country, in places where the latest opinions did not carry as much weight or were at least slower to take hold. Still, the tradition had lost its vitality and the end was in sight. One of the last articles on the subject to be published in *Tobacco* appeared in 1903. Appropriately, its author will have the final word:

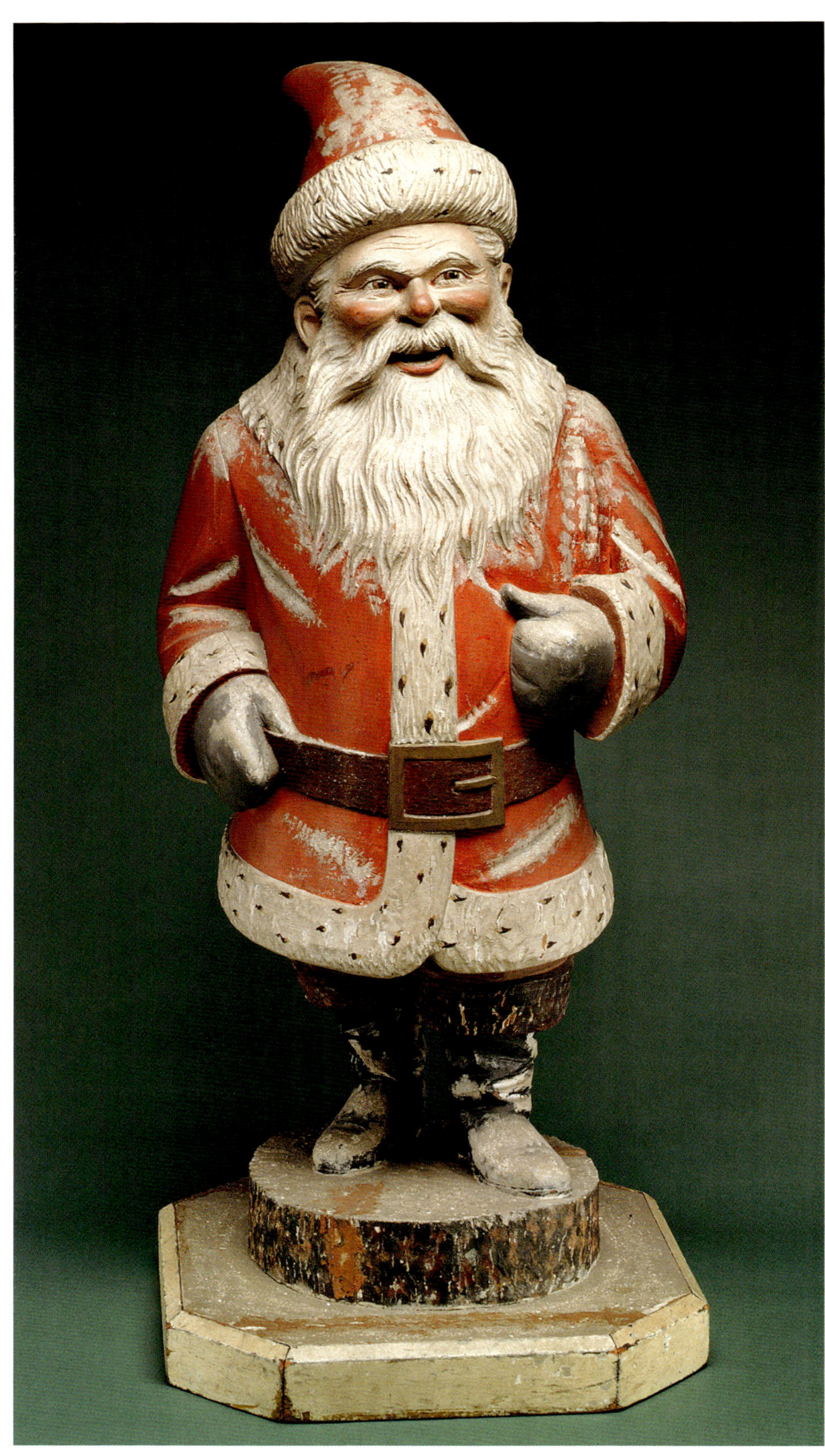

122 Samuel Anderson Robb, *Santa Claus*, New York, 1923. Painted wood, 39 x 16 x 19 in. (99 x 40.6 x 48.2 cm). American Folk Art Museum, New York. Promised gift of Ralph Esmerian (P1.2001.348)

> At frequent intervals during the past dozen years more or less elaborate stories have found their way into the secular press to the effect that the wooden Indian had had its day as a cigar store sign, and that it was only a matter of a short time when it would be seen no more.
>
> In spite of the frequence of these predictions, the wooden Indian still lingers in New York City, and there are scores and hundreds of them to be found on the streets and avenues throughout the city. Many of them are old and weather-beaten, to be sure, but others are spick and span as fresh paint can make them, and it seems likely that many a year will have come and gone before the last of them shall have disappeared.
>
> Why the wooden Indian must go, or rather why he has already gone, is not clear. It is no clearer why girls who looked so sweetly trim in little bolero jackets scarcely reaching to their waists are still more Cirean now in Monte Carlo coats that sweep the ground. "Because" is again the reason; "just because." The Indian sign is guiltless. His wooden soul remains unflecked. He is simply out of fashion.[47]

The writer could have added that the carvers, too, were headed for obsolescence by this time. Most traditional shipcarvers were out of business by 1900 or so, their art having been doomed by the advent of metal-hulled ships several decades earlier. They had, in fact, been crossing the Atlantic on a regular basis as a part of European merchant and passenger fleets since mid-century.[48] At first, American shipbuilders resisted the change, but the spectacular success of Civil War gunboats like the *Monitor* and *Merrimac* convinced even the most skeptical among them. Within a decade, the construction of wooden ships was greatly curtailed, and the urban shipyards along the East Coast that had been the carvers' mainstay were rapidly closing.

This, of course, left many shipcarvers out of work. The shop-figure fad helped for a time, but was not enough to stem the tide. The older carvers retired, and many of the younger men changed professions. Before long, no new apprentices were taken in and the old system began to break down. The case of the Brooks family is typical. After a long and productive career, Thomas V. Brooks died in 1895. His son and former apprentice, James, operated a small business called the Standard Show Figure Company in Williamsburg, Brooklyn, from 1895 until 1902, but he had no need for assistants. After closing his shop, he became a contractor and painter. He relocated several times before finally settling in Tampa, Florida, where he died in 1937.[49]

Samuel Robb closed his Centre Street workshop in 1903, not long after completing a major job creating elaborate circus wagons for Barnum and Bailey. For the next few years, he kept small shops in various locations in Manhattan, and then shared space with fellow carver Charles Brown in Brooklyn from 1908 to 1910. After that, he worked out of his home, primarily doing odd jobs and creating small-scale carvings.[50]

Robb carved his last figure in 1923, an image of *Santa Claus* that was done as a Christmas present for his daughter, Elizabeth (plate 122).[51] A lively characterization, it demonstrates that he still had the master's touch at age seventy-two. The smiling face and finely carved beard are especially engaging. He died five years later after an extended illness. The heyday of show figures was long since over by that time, and his passing can be seen as an end point for traditional figure carving.

Nevertheless, in what might be considered poetic justice for such an old tradition, show figures began to experience renewed interest as museum pieces and collector's items at the same time that they were vanishing from city streets. Beginning soon after the turn of the twentieth century, figures that had especially long histories or strong links to a particular locale were frequently donated to local historical societies and museums. Many of them were quickly relegated to storage areas or dimly lit recesses to be sure, but others assumed prominent positions in their new settings.

Collectors began to take notice of them early in the twentieth century as well, sparked by the growing antiquarian interest at the time. The first book on the topic, *Hunting Indians in a Taxi-Cab* by Kate Sanborn, appeared in 1911, not long after the last of the urban shipcarvers had given up their shops. In a breezy, anecdotal style, the author recounted some of her adventures in locating figures for her country home. She also presented the results of her research and interviews with some longtime tobacconists who had experienced the show-figure fad first-hand. The book's many photographs of figures in front of shops and on city streets are especially important as contemporary documentation.

Figureheads received even more attention than show figures around the turn of the twentieth century, as maritime historians joined antique collectors in gathering information about them and recording their reflections on the passing of the ancient tradition. As early as 1893, a naval officer wrote an article entitled "Historic Figureheads" that he commenced by noting, "It is a matter of congratulations that any of the quaint and picturesque relics of the old-time warships are preserved."[52] Instead of being destroyed or left to rot on a forlorn beach, figureheads were beginning to be recognized as important artifacts that belonged in museums and historical societies. Just as many were set up outdoors in public spaces and private gardens, which unfortunately tended to hasten their deterioration even more.[53]

By 1915 or so, figureheads and shop figures had also been "discovered" by modernist artists searching for forms of expression that they considered to be truly American. With the breakdown of academic conventions and the late-nineteenth-century experiments of Paul Gauguin (1848–1903) and others, wood was by then considered a valid artistic medium, at least by more progressive artists and critics. Wooden figures could finally be seen as sculpture, which opened up a new dimension in their appreciation among the avant-garde. Several American artists began to collect figure carvings that in turn directly inspired their work. One of the earliest instances of this occurred in 1911, when the New York artist and writer Hamilton Easter Field founded the School of Painting and Sculpture in Ogunquit, Maine. Field furnished cottages for resident artists with weathervanes, decoys, paintings, and textiles, which encouraged many of them to look closely at folk sculpture for the first time.[54]

The trend gathered momentum throughout the 1920s. Early in the decade, the sculptor Elie Nadelman (1882–1946) and his wife began collecting figureheads, shop figures, and other types of folk art. In 1926 they opened the Museum of Folk and Peasant Arts at their home in Riverdale, New York, which has the distinction of being the first folk art museum in the United States.[55] Two years earlier, in February 1924, Henry Schnackenberg had organized *Early American Art* for the Whitney Studio Club in New York, which is generally considered to be the first public exhibition of folk art. Then, in 1931, Holger Cahill curated his landmark exhibition *American Folk Sculpture* for the Newark Museum, New Jersey. Five figureheads and twelve cigar-store figures were featured, including the Andrew Jackson figurehead for the *Constitution* (plate 24), a *Trapper Indian* (plate 79), a *Turk* (plate 91), two *Girls of the Period*, and a *Captain Jinks* that had been a landmark in downtown Newark for over fifty years before being donated to the Newark Museum in 1924.[56]

That same year the influential dealer Edith Gregor Halpert established the American Folk Art Gallery in New York, the first such venture in this country. The gallery was on the second floor of her Downtown Gallery on West Thirteenth Street, which was frequented by the modernist artists whom she represented as well as by many progressive critics and collectors. At first the American Folk Art Gallery was a single room, but eventually it occupied the entire floor.[57] Her first exhibition, held in December 1931, while *American Folk Sculpture* was still at the Newark Museum, was a major success. Entitled *American Ancestors*, it attracted a wide audience and garnered critical praise.[58] The cycle of rediscovery was complete, and figure carving and other folk art genres had finally found their place in the history of American art.

It is also true, though, that wooden figures have never totally disappeared from American streets. The work of self-taught artists has continued unabated, made all the more visible in our time by the demise of many of the old craft traditions. A diverse collection of individuals, they have not been subject to the same sorts of market pressures and stylistic changes as their shipcarver counterparts. Carving on demand or for personal enjoyment, they have fashioned figures for their communities since the colonial era. Throughout the nineteenth century, they often created highly individualized pieces patterned after those made in the seaport shops. At the same time, much of the most innovative self-taught work exhibits few precedents other than the interest in the human figure that is shared by all sculptors. The possibilities are endless and the interpretations diverse. Three examples that bridge the gap between the nineteenth and twentieth centuries will be considered here.

The first two are a pair of Indian figures that first came to the attention of the art world in Boston in the 1930s (plates 123 and 124).[59] Their carver remains unidentified, as do their original purposes, although it is likely that they served as shop figures of some sort. The strength of their characterizations indicates that their maker was an experienced self-taught artist who was familiar with his medium and with the larger shop-figure tradition.[60] Highly stylized, they are par-

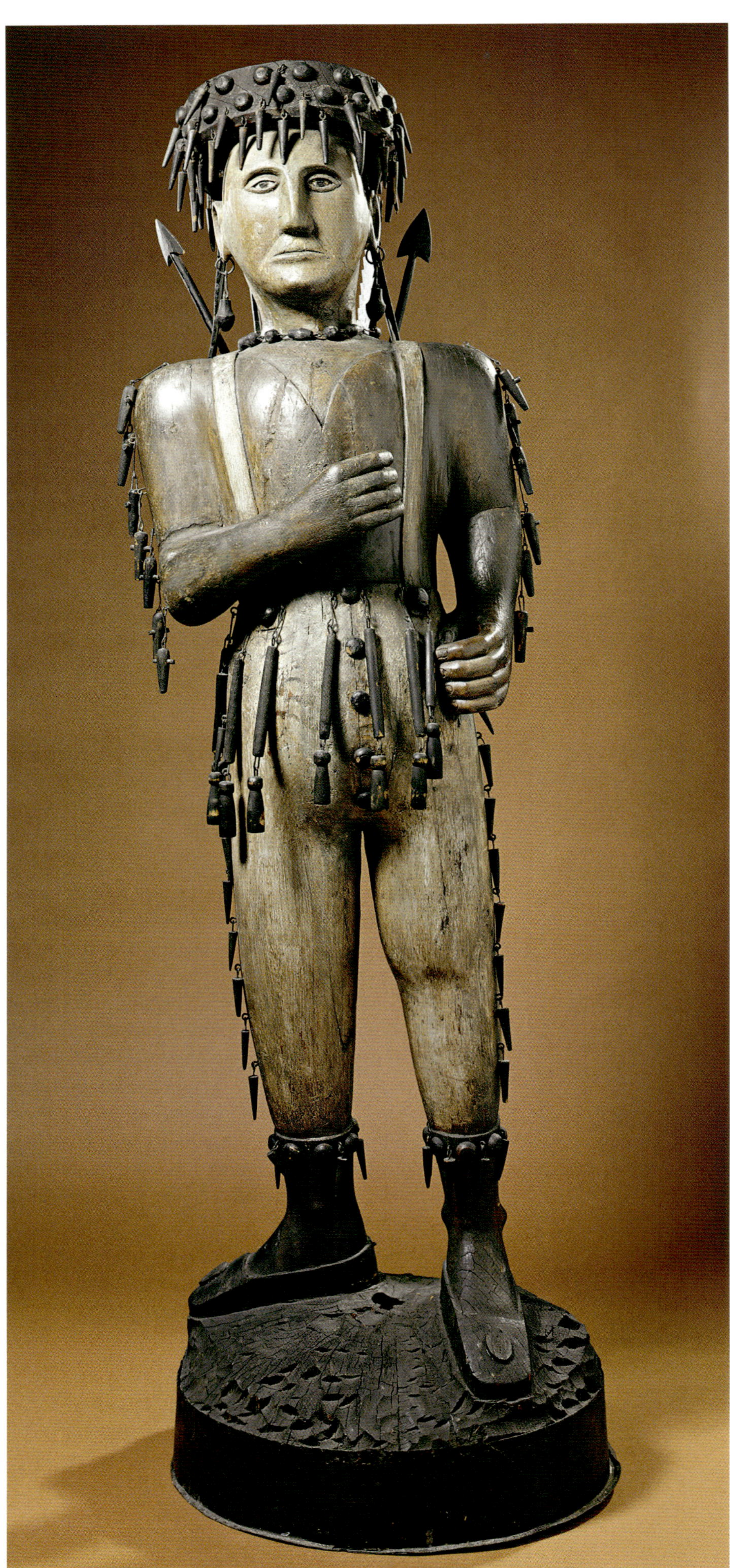

123 *Indian Trapper*, eastern United States, 1860–1910. Painted wood and metal, 60 1/4 x 29 x 19 in. (153 x 73.6 x 48.2 cm). Smithsonian American Art Museum, Washington, D.C. Gift of Herbert Waide Hemphill, Jr. and museum purchase made possible by Ralph Cross Johnson

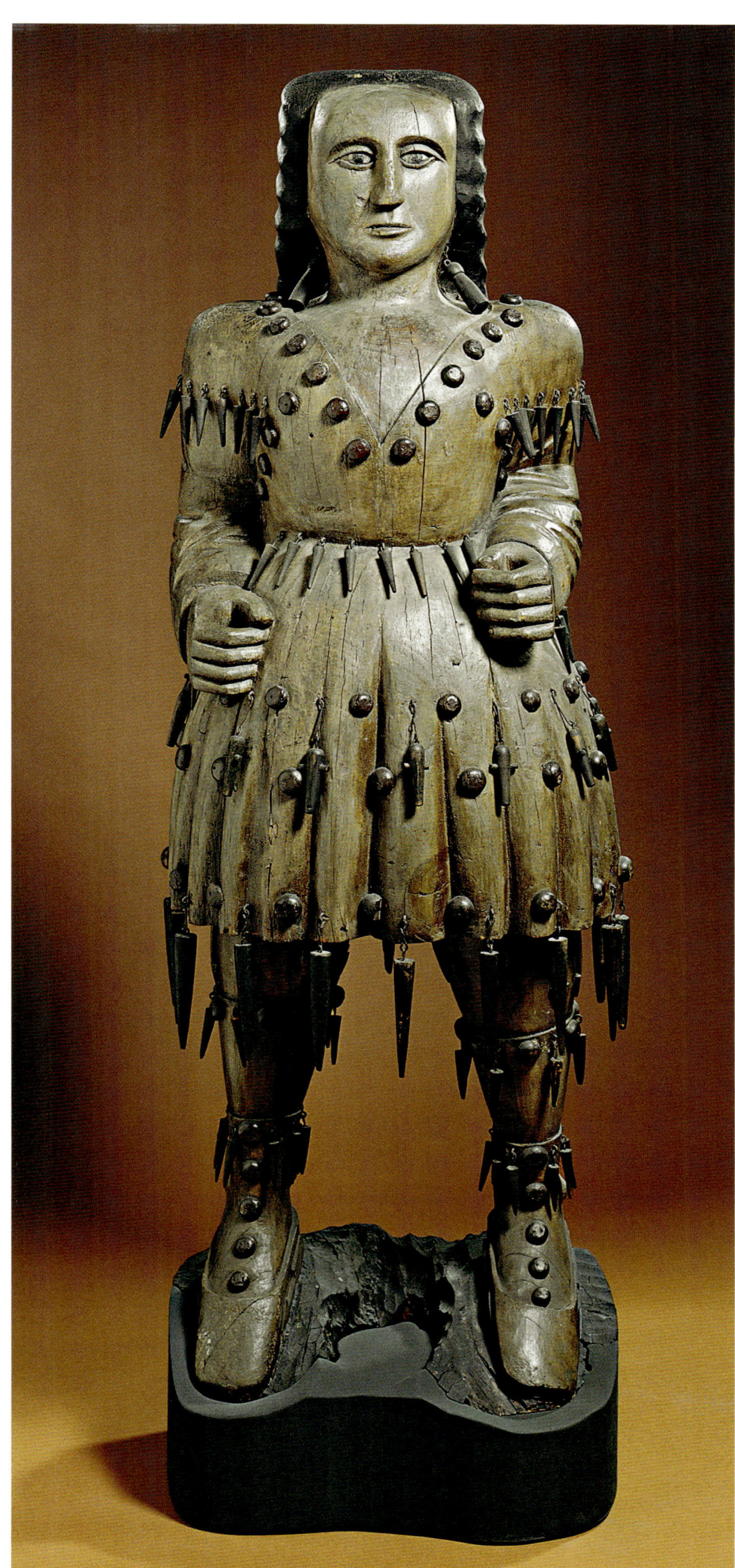

124 *Indian*, eastern United States, 1860–1910. Painted wood and metal, $48^{3}/_{4}$ x $16^{3}/_{4}$ x $16^{1}/_{4}$ in. (123.8 x 42.5 x 41.3 cm). Smithsonian American Art Museum, Washington, D.C. Gift of Herbert Waide Hemphill, Jr. and museum purchase made possible by Ralph Cross Johnson

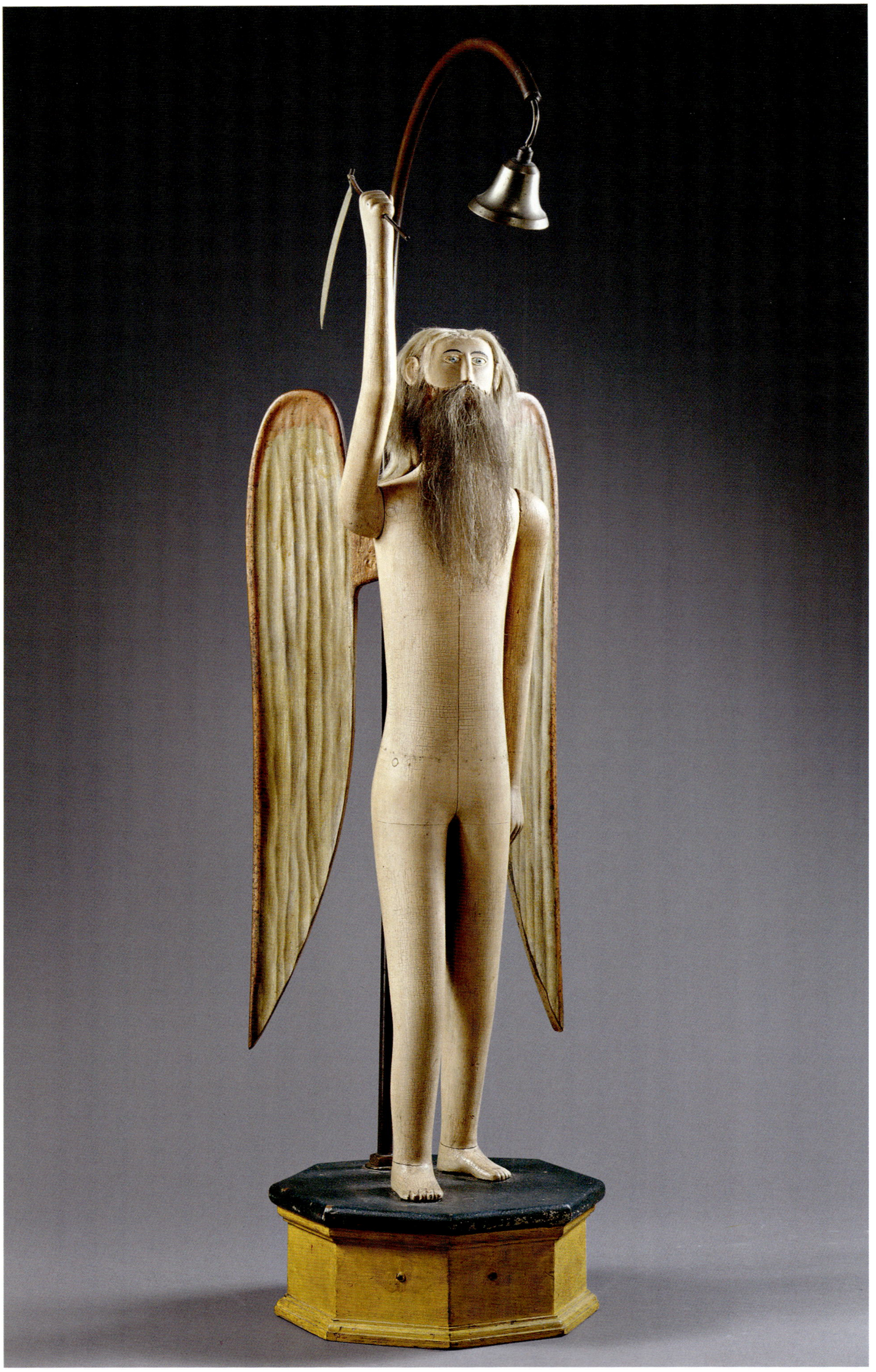

125 *Father Time*, Mohawk River Valley, N.Y., c. 1910. Painted wood, metal, and hair, 52 1/4 x 13 3/4 x 14 1/2 in. (132.7 x 34.9 x 36.8). American Folk Art Museum, New York. Gift of Mrs. John H. Heminway (1964.2.1)

ticularly remarkable for the amount of applied ornamentation on each, especially the dangling cones and bottle plugs that suggest fringed buckskin. The woman's high-topped shoes and wavy hair are typical of the types of Anglo-American features frequently applied to images of American Indians regardless of medium or point of origin.

Another outstanding piece of figure carving from the early twentieth century is *Father Time*, a counter-size piece from the Mohawk River Valley region of upstate New York that was probably created around 1910 (plate 125).[61] Although his original purpose is not certain, he is presumed to have been used in a shop, probably as a doorbell of sorts. The figure was once articulated so that the right arm moved and the sickle hit the suspended bell. He may also have originally been more modestly attired in a robe, which would seem to be appropriate for so venerable a character. As shown, he is a sleek stylization with a strong vertical thrust that accentuates the idea of an otherworldly being who marks the inevitable passage of time.

As such, he is an appropriate way to end this discussion. The art of the shipcarver gradually faded from the American scene in the early twentieth century, but figure carving remains. A number of the old show figures occupied their spots in front of shops throughout the World War II era and into the 1950s and 1960s. By then they had lost their advertising function, but they continued to serve as neighborhood landmarks that reinforced a sense of place among local residents. To others, they were objects of curiosity and nostalgia that invoked images of childhood.[62]

Many of the cultural issues that the figures embody have an even stronger hold on American society. The theme of the Noble Savage and his evil twin—the good and bad Indians, respectively—continues to haunt the national consciousness. Besides providing inspiration for countless novels, films, and plays of all types, its deeper meanings are finally becoming clearer. The pervasive nature of racial and gender stereotyping has only recently been fully understood, while their role in maintaining the status quo and the inequities in American society is still being explored.

The words *cigar-store Indian* are still current in the national vocabulary, even among those who have never seen one. Figureheads, too, conjure up romantic notions of sailing ships and an idealized American past in the minds of most people. If these mental and verbal images are much more vague today than they would have been a hundred years ago, the fact that they have survived at all testifies to the importance and longevity of the tradition. *Father Time* and the two Indian figures discussed above represent direct links between nineteenth-century figure carving and the type of self-taught work that has become popular in recent years. They and their kind have always been a part of the tradition, once vastly outnumbered by figureheads and show figures from seaport workshops. They now stand as the sole heirs, as well as a vital form of contemporary expression.

NOTES

INTRODUCTION

1 "Manufacture of Dummy Indians," *Tobacco* 2 (12 Nov. 1886): 2.

2 "Lo Takes a Spring Suit," *Tobacco* 6 (12 Apr. 1889): 1.

3 John F. Watson, *Annals of Philadelphia* (Philadelphia: E. L. Cary and A. Hart, 1830), 551.

4 Sylvia L. Lahvis, "The Skillin Workshop: The Emblematic Image in Federal Boston" (Ph.D. diss., University of Delaware, 1990), 110.

5 Marion V. Brewington, *Shipcarvers of North America* (Barre, Mass.: Barre Publishing Co., 1962), 57, 60–61.

6 Printed advertisement for William Demuth and Company, New York, c. 1871. A copy is at the National Museum of American History, Smithsonian Institution, Washington, D.C.

7 Samuel Robb identified the other four carvers as "prominent figures in the early history of the art," in Frank W. Weitenkampf, "Lo, the Wooden Indian," *New York Times*, 3 Aug. 1890, 13. Their lives were first documented in Frederick Fried, *Artists in Wood* (New York: Clarkson Potter, 1970), 177–238.

8 William Demuth and Company, *Illustrated Catalogue of Smokers' Articles and Show Figures* (New York: William Demuth and Co., 1875); Fried, *Artists in Wood*, 32–35, 60–61.

9 George B. Catlin, "Old Detroit Artists Found Trade Dull, but Market for Wooden Indians Brisk," *Detroit News*, 4 Jan. 1925, sec. 2, p. 17.

10 Weitenkampf, "Lo, the Wooden Indian," 13.

11 See Brewington's review of Pinckney's book in "Book Reviews," *American Neptune* 1 (Apr. 1941): 178–81, for a blistering assessment of the book's shortcomings. While much of his criticism is no doubt justified, he leaves the reader with the impression that the tone of the article results from other motivations.

12 Lahvis, "Skillin Workshop." Lahvis has also published two articles on the Skillins: "Icons of the American Trade: The Skillin Workshop and the Language of Spectacle," *Winterthur Portfolio* 27 (winter 1992): 213–33, and "The Skillin Workshop," *Antiques* 155 (Mar. 1999): 442–51.

13 Wayne Craven, *Sculpture in America* (Cranbury, N.J.: Cornwall Books, 1984), 26.

CHAPTER 1
Lyons, Black Boys, and Virginians: Figure Carving in England and France

1 For contemporary visual records of seventeenth-century European shipcarving, see especially the paintings of Willem van de Velde the Elder and the Younger. Two good sources are David Cordingly, *The Art of the van de Veldes* (Greenwich, U.K.: National Maritime Museum, 1982), and George S. Keyes, *Mirror of Empire: Dutch Marine Art of the Seventeenth Century* (Cambridge: Cambridge University Press, 1990).

2 Leonard George Carr Laughton, *Old Ship Figure-Heads and Sterns* (London: Holton and Truscott Smith, 1925), 77.

3 Sylvia L. Lahvis, "The Skillin Workshop: The Emblematic Image in Federal Boston" (Ph.D. diss., University of Delaware, 1990) 39–40.

4 Cesareo Fernandez-Duro, *Armada española desde la union de los reinos de Castilla y de León* (Madrid: Sucesores de Rivadeneyra, 1895), 1:324. The passage reads:

> Las capitanas se distinguian por el adorno exterior, notable en las que condujeron á Carlos V. Era el tiempo llamado del renacimiento de las artes, y á su influencia no se sustraian los bajeles; patente estaba en las figuras esulpidas en las proas, en la talla y dorado de las popas, en la forma elegante de los fanales, en las pinturas de los paveses y en el primor de los tendales, enstandartes y flámulas. El hecho de haber enviado Barbarroja al Sultán el escudo de popa de la galera de Portuondo, como joya artistica, indica la labor empleada, y todavia más se pondera la de la galera en que fué á Génova el principe D. Felipe, obra de los mejores artistas de Italia.

See also Laughton, *Old Ship Figure-Heads and Sterns*, 10.

5 Andrew Trout, *Jean-Baptiste Colbert* (Boston: G. K. Hall, 1978), 137.

6 Magli Théron, "La Décoration navale en France entre 1660 et 1830," in *Les Génies de la Mer* (Quebec and Paris: Musée du Québec et Musée national de la Marine, 2001), 44–50; Peter Norton, *Ships' Figureheads* (Barre, Mass.: Barre Publishing Co., 1976), 60; Laughton, 42.

7 Quoted in André Michel, *Histoire de l'art* (Paris: Armand Colin, 1922), vol. 6, pt. 2, p. 684.

8 Philippe Auquier, *Pierre Puget: Décorateur naval et mariniste* (Paris: D. A. Longuet, 1909), 6.

9 Ibid., 9.

10 Ibid., 5. In this regard, it is interesting to note Giorgio Vasari's well-known account of Giotto's apprenticeship to Cimabue, which holds that the young, previously untutored shepherd quickly equaled and then surpassed his master. The anecdote surely ranks as an archetype in the annals of artists' biographies. See Giorgio Vasari, *Lives of the Most Eminent Painters, Sculptors, and Architects*, trans. Gaston du C. de Vere (London: MacMillan and Co., 1912), 1:72.

11 E. Bénézit, *Dictionnaire des peintres, sculpteurs, dessinateurs, et graveurs* (Paris:

Librarie Gründ, 1976), 8:518; Norton, *Ships' Figureheads*, 60.

12 Auquier, *Pierre Puget*, 9.

13 Ibid., 15.

14 An order referring to designs for the ship *Le Brillant*, illustrated in plate 3, reads, "By command of Louis XIV, King of France, under the ministry of Jean-Baptiste Colbert, Marquis de Seignelay, from the designs of Charles Le Brun, first painter to the king, drawn and measured by Jean Bérain." Quoted in Norton, *Ships' Figureheads*, 62. See also Théron, "La Décoration navale," 46.

15 Théron, "La Décoration navale," 47–48; Norton, *Ships' Figureheads*, 18, 21. See also Michel, *Histoire de l'art*, vol. 6, pt. 2, p. 684, for an excerpt of the letter from Colbert to Puget dated 26 Dec. 1670.

16 Laughton, *Old Ship Figure-Heads and Sterns*, 14.

17 Théron, "La Décoration navale," 58; Laughton, *Old Ship Figure-Heads and Sterns*, 96; Norton, *Ships' Figureheads*, 59.

18 Norton, *Ships' Figureheads*, 52–53.

19 Ibid., 57–58; Laughton, *Old Ship Figure-Heads and Sterns*, 71.

20 Laughton, *Old Ship Figure-Heads and Sterns*, 70–71.

21 Ibid., 80–81; Norton, *Ships' Figureheads*, 72–75.

22 Norton, *Ships' Figureheads*, 10, 75–76.

23 Laughton, *Old Ship Figure-Heads and Sterns*, 25.

24 Ibid., 28; Norton, *Ships' Figureheads*, 66–67.

25 Laughton, *Old Ship Figure-Heads and Sterns*, 18–19.

26 Ibid., 28–29.

27 Ibid., 89.

28 Nina Fletcher Little, "Carved Figures by Samuel McIntire and His Contemporaries," in *Samuel McIntire: A Bicentennial Symposium*, ed. Benjamin W. Labaree (Salem, Mass.: Essex Institute, 1957), 193.

29 Norton, *Ships' Figureheads*, 85.

30 Richard Brathwait, *The Smoaking Age, or The Life and Death of Tobacco* (London: E. Griffin, 1617). "Drinking his Petoune" is an obsolete phrase that in current usage would be "smoking his tobacco." In the sixteenth and early seventeenth centuries, inhaling smoke was frequently characterized as "drinking," due to the perceived similarities in the mode of ingestion. *Petoune* is an English translation of *petun* or *petum*, which is in turn a Portuguese adaptation of a Brazilian Indian word for tobacco. See Jerome E. Brooks, *Tobacco: Its History Illustrated by the Books, Manuscripts and Engravings in the Library of George Arents, Jr.* (New York: Rosenbach Co., 1937), 1:17–19, and V. G. Kiernan, *Tobacco: A History* (London: Hutchinson Radius, 1991), 13.

31 Quoted in Brooks, *Tobacco*, 2:40.

32 "Blackamoor," "black boy," and "Virginian" are used interchangeably in the text, as they were in popular usage at the time. All three refer to two- and three-dimensional images of Africans that advertised places where tobacco was sold and consumed.

33 Ben Jonson, *Bartholomew Fair* (1614; reprint, Cambridge, Mass.: Harvard University Press, 1962), 31.

34 Cecil A. Meadows, *Trade Signs and Their Origins* (London: Routledge and Kegan Paul, 1957), 4–5.

35 Ibid., 7.

36 Ernest C. Peixotto, "Artistic Street Signs, Revival of an Old Custom as Seen in Paris," *New York Herald Sunday Magazine*, 15 Jan. 1905, 7. As the title indicates, the article is primarily concerned with signboards painted by established artists, a custom that the author claimed was experiencing a revival at the time. He mentions the famous inn sign of a white horse painted by Théodore Géricault, as well as signs known to have been created by Horace Vernet, Jean Goujon, and Antoine Watteau. He also notes that in 1826 Balzac published a small volume entitled, *Petit Dictionnaire critique et anecdotique des enseignes de Paris par un batteur de pavé*, that was essentially a catalogue of interesting street signs.

37 Meadows, *Trade Signs and Their Origins*, 7.

38 Ibid., 8.

39 Jacob Larwood and John Camden Hotten, *The History of Signboards* (London: J. C. Hotten, 1866), 26.

40 Meadows, *Trade Signs and Their Origins*, 38. See also Larwood and Hotten, *History of Signboards*, 252; and G. L. Apperson, *The Social History of Smoking* (New York: G. P. Putnam's Sons, 1916), 237.

41 In 1719, a French traveler identified as "Mission" noted, "Out of London, and particularly in villages, the signs of inns are suspended in the middle of a great wooden portal, which may be looked upon as a kind of triumphal arch to the honour of Bacchus." Quoted in Larwood and Hotten, *History of Signboards*, 26. Illustrations of some of these arches show large three-dimensional figures. See Jacob Larwood and John Camden Hotten, *English Inn Signs: Being a Revised and Modern Version of History of Signboards* (London: Chatto and Windus, 1951).

42 Brooks, *Tobacco* 1:30–31.

43 Ibid., 1:18.

44 Ibid., 1:23.

45 Jordan Goodman, *Tobacco in History: The Cultures of Dependence* (New York: Routledge, 1993), 39–40, 75–76. The ancient humoral system is believed to have been first formulated in Greece. Hippocrates is credited as the originator, with further development by Galen, whose writings were unquestioned until well after the Renaissance. In the seventeenth century, the system was based on the binary combination of four opposing qualities—hot and cold, moist and dry. The human body had four humors—blood, phlegm, black bile, and yellow bile—each of which had a specific essence. Blood, for example, was hot and moist, while phlegm was cold and moist. Healthy bodies were in humoral equilibrium. A diseased body was in disequilibrium, and it was the physician's task to restore equilibrium by drawing off excess humor through bloodletting, purging, sweating, and other practices. Being "hot and dry," tobacco was considered useful for treating imbalances relating to "moist humors." See also Brooks, *Tobacco*, 1:33.

46 Brooks, *Tobacco*, 1:32–33; Goodman, *Tobacco in History*, 79–80.

47 Brooks, *Tobacco*, 1:34.

48 Quoted in Apperson, *Social History of Smoking*, 26.

49 Quoted in Brooks, *Tobacco*, 1:404.

50 Ibid., 55–56, 401.

51 Ibid., 71, 73, 75.

52 Ibid., 78.

53 Ibid., 79–80; Goodman, *Tobacco in History*, 69.

54 Goodman, *Tobacco in History*, 59.

55 Quoted in Apperson, *Social History of Smoking*, 32, 45.

56 Goodman, *Tobacco in History*, 60.

57 Quoted ibid., 63.

58 Ibid., 67; Brooks, *Tobacco*, 1:22.

59 Apperson, *Social History of Smoking*, 57, 96–97; Brooks, *Tobacco*, 1:161; Goodman, *Tobacco in History*, 72.

60 Quoted in Goodman, *Tobacco in History*, 74.

61 In a letter to James Boswell in 1773, Johnson wrote: "Smoaking has gone out. To be sure it is a shocking thing, blowing smoak out of our mouths into other peoples mouths, eyes, and noses, and having the same thing done to us. Yet I cannot account why a thing which requires so little exertion, and yet preserves the mind from total vacuity, should have gone out." From Samuel Johnson, *The Journal of the Tour to the Hebrides* (London: Henry Baldwin, 1785), quoted in Brooks, *Tobacco*, 4:9–10. See also Brooks, *Tobacco*, 1:161, and Apperson, *Social History of Smoking*, 119.

62 Apperson, *Social History of Smoking*, 99; Brooks, *Tobacco*, 1:162.

63 Brooks, *Tobacco*, 1:167; Apperson, *Social History of Smoking*, 139.

64 Apperson, *Social History of Smoking*, 166; Brooks, *Tobacco*, 1:167.

65 Charles G. Shaw, "Black Boys and Their Playfellows," *Antiques* 25 (Mar. 1934): 101.

66 For a postmodern discussion of this, see Peter Mason, *Deconstructing America: Representations of the Other* (New York: Routledge, 1990). A structuralist perspective is provided by Bernadette Bucher, *Icon and Conquest: A Structuralist Analysis of the Illustrations of de Bry's "Great Voyages"* (Chicago: University of Chicago Press, 1981).

67 William C. Sturtevant, "First Visual Images of Native Americans," in *First Images of America*, ed. Fredi Chiappelli (Berkeley and Los Angeles: University of California Press, 1976), 1:420. The author notes that coastal Brazilian Indians were known to have worn feather belts, along with other feather adornments, but that skirts made of very large feathers such as those shown in the woodcut are not only improbable, but also would have been impractical.

68 Meadows, *Trade Signs and Their Origins*, 43.

69 Quoted in Larwood and Hotten, *History of Signboards*, 421.

70 Charles Dickens, *Little Dorrit* (1857; reprint, New York: Oxford University Press, 1953), 214.

71 Larwood and Hotten, *History of Signboards*, 426–27; Meadows, *Trade Signs and Their Origins*, 40–41.

72 Meadows, *Trade Signs and Their Origins*, 40.

73 In 1653, the British Admiralty issued a regulation forbidding smoking on all "ships at sea in the service of the commonwealth." See Brooks, *Tobacco*, 1:162. Soon thereafter, most merchant vessels adopted the same practice.

74 Quoted in Goodman, *Tobacco in History*, 63.

75 Charles Dickens, *Dealings with the Firm of Dombey and Son* (1846–48; reprint, New York: Oxford University Press, 1987), 32.

76 William Allingham, "Figure-Heads," *Nautical Magazine* 68 (Aug. 1899): 523. See also Philip C. F. Smith, "The Little Men: Carved Shop Signs of the Navigating Instrument Sellers," *American Neptune* 34 (July 1974): 197–98, 202–3.

77 Brooks, *Tobacco*, 1:37. See also Larwood and Hotten, *History of Signboards*, 431.

78 Larwood and Hotten, *History of Signboards*, 426.

79 Sidney Perley, *The History of Salem, Massachusetts* 3 (Salem, Mass.: Sidney Perley, 1928), 396–97; Marion V. Brewington, *Shipcarvers of North America* (Barre, Mass.: Barre Publishing Co., 1962), 5–6.

80 Harriet Cabot, *Handbook of the Bostonian Society* (Boston: Bostonian Society, 1979), 53; Smith, "Little Men," 199–202.

81 *Illustrated Catalogue of A. E. Brook's Collection of Antique Guns, Pistols, Etc.* (Hartford, Conn.: Hartford Press, 1899), 197. In 1882, a Colonel Perkins claimed that he had owned the figure for over seventy years and that he remembered it being attached to a signpost in front of the Backus Hotel when he was a small boy.

82 Brigham Payne, *The Story of Bacchus and Centennial Souvenir* (Hartford, Conn.: A. E. Brooks, 1876); *Illustrated Catalogue of A. E. Brook's Collection*, 189–94.

83 Charles G. Shaw, "Speaking of Wooden Indians," *Antiques* 36 (Sept. 1939): 133; Erwin O. Christensen, *Early American Wood Carving* (New York: Dover, 1972), 128. The modernist artist Charles Demuth was directly related to Christopher and John Demuth. The family home was two doors from the tobacco shop. See Betsy Fahlman, *Pennsylvania Modern: Charles Demuth in Lancaster* (Philadelphia: Philadelphia Museum of Art, 1983), 14–15.

84 Brooks, *Tobacco*, 1:138.

CHAPTER 2
The Art of the Shipcarver

1 The first warships authorized by the Continental Congress were thirteen frigates ordered in 1775 and built in 1776. Marion V. Brewington, *Shipcarvers of North America* (Barre, Mass.: Barre Publishing Co., 1962), 12.

2 Ibid., 1–2.

3 Ibid., 1.

4 Ibid., 4.

5 Quoted ibid., 2.

6 Ibid., 2, 6–8; Leonard George Carr Laughton, *Old Ship Figure-Heads and Sterns* (London: Holton and Truscott Smith, 1925), 77; Peter Norton, *Ships' Figureheads* (Barre, Mass.: Barre Publishing Co., 1976), 67, 78, 85–86.

7 Brewington, *Shipcarvers of North America*, 8.

8 Sylvia L. Lahvis, "Icons of the American Trade: The Skillin Workshop and the Language of Spectacle," *Winterthur Portfolio* 27 (winter 1992): 220.

9 Quoted in Brewington, *Shipcarvers of North America*, 8.

10 Ibid., 12–18.

11 Ibid., 2; Sylvia L. Lahvis, "The Skillin Workshop: The Emblematic Image in Federal Boston" (Ph.D. diss., University of Delaware, 1990), 36–37, 59–60.

12 Brock Jobe, "The Boston Furniture Industry, 1720–1740," in *Boston Furniture* *of the Eighteenth Century*, ed. Walter Muir Whitehill, Brock Jobe, and Jonathan Fairbanks (Boston: Colonial Society of Massachusetts, 1974), 3.

13 Mabel M. Swan, "Boston's Carvers and Joiners, Part 1. Pre-Revolutionary," *Antiques* 53 (Mar. 1948): 198–99; Mary Ellen Hayward Yehia, "Ornamental Carving," in Whitehill, Jobe, and Fairbanks, *Boston Furniture of the Eighteenth Century*, 213–15.

14 The most important Skillin sources are: Homer Eaton Keyes, "Milton, Beverly, and Salem," *Antiques* 23 (Apr. 1933): 122, 142–43; Leroy L. Thwing, "The Four Carving Skillins," *Antiques* 33 (June 1938): 326–28; Mabel M. Swan, "Simeon Skillin, Senior, The First American Sculptor," *Antiques* 46 (July 1944): 21; Swan, "Boston's Carvers and Joiners, Part 1," 198–201; Mabel M. Swan, "Boston Carvers and Joiners, Part 2. Post-Revolutionary," *Antiques* 53 (Apr. 1948): 281–85; the two previously cited works by Sylvia L. Lahvis, "Skillin Workshop: The Emblematic Image" and "Icons of the American Trade"; and her "The Skillin Workshop," *Antiques* 155 (Mar. 1999): 442–51.

15 Swan, "Simeon Skillin," 21.

16 Mabel M. Swan, "Artisan Leaders of 1788," *Antiques* 27 (Mar. 1935): 90.

17 Lahvis, "Skillin Workshop: The Emblematic Image," 69–70, 77–96.

18 Ibid., 107, 110–26. The chest is in the Garvan Collection at Yale University. The garden figures of *Pomona* and a *Shepherdess* are in the collection of the Peabody Essex Museum in Salem, Mass., and a *Shepherd* is owned by the Danvers Historical Society, Danvers, Mass.

19 Ibid., 107.

20 *Columbian Centennial*, 18 July 1793, 3.

21 Harriet Cabot, *Handbook of the Bostonian Society* (Boston: Bostonian Society, 1979), 55.

22 Giovanni da Bologna's elongated, classicized *Mercury* is a very different conception than the Skillins' figure. Given the similarities of pose, as well as the widespread reproduction of Bologna's sculpture in a variety of different media over the course of several centuries, however, it can surely be credited as the ultimate source.

23 See Lahvis, "Skillin Workshop: The Emblematic Image," 160–83, and "Icons of the American Trade," 216–24, for discussions of the relationship between shipcarving and civic pageantry in Britain and colonial America. For a more complete treatment of the pageantry tradition in England, see David M. Bergeron, *English Civic Pageantry, 1558–1642* (London: Edward Arnold, 1971), and L. J. Morrissay, "English Pageant-Wagons," *Eighteenth-Century Studies* 9 (spring 1976): 352–74.

24 John Hancock to Thomas Cushing, Connarroe Collection, Historical Society of Pennsylvania, quoted in Brewington, *Shipcarvers of North America*, 12.

25 *Pennsylvania Journal*, 23 Nov. 1791, quoted in Henri Marceau, *William Rush, 1756–1833: The First Native American Sculptor* (Philadelphia: Pennsylvania Museum of Art, 1937), 65.

26 Swan, "Artisan Leaders of 1788," 91; Linda Bantel, "William Rush, Esq.," in Linda Bantel et al., *William Rush: American Sculptor* (Philadelphia: Pennsylvania Academy of the Fine Arts, 1982), 10.

27 Francis Hopkinson, "An Account of the Grand Federal Procession in Philadelphia, July 4, 1788," *American Museum* (July 1788), 4:64, quoted in Bantel, *William Rush*, 10.

28 Pauline A. Pinckney, *American Figureheads and Their Carvers* (New York: W. W. Norton, 1940), 65–70.

29 Eugene S. Ferguson, "The Figure-Head of the United States Frigate *Constellation*," *American Neptune* 7 (Oct. 1947): 256.

30 Brewington, *Shipcarvers of North America*, 35–37; Pinckney, *American Figureheads and Their Carvers*, 70.

31 *American Daily Advertiser*, 4 Mar. 1797, quoted in Marceau, *William Rush*, 69–70. Brewington dates the article to 4 Mar. 1794, see Brewington, *Shipcarvers of North America*, 35.

32 Joshua Humphreys Accounts, 1773–95, Historical Society of Pennsylvania; Brewington, *Shipcarvers of North America*, 33.

33 John F. Watson, *Annals of Philadelphia* (Philadelphia: E. L. Cary and A. Hart, 1830), 551.

34 In the wake of the Revolution, the new government made a concerted effort to remove all royal symbols from French ships. For figureheads, allegorical subjects that embodied republican virtues were emphasized instead. Many of these were freestanding figures. The most influential design source was Pierre Ozanne, *Nouvelles décorations pour l'ornement exterior des vaisseau*, published in 1792. See Magli Théron, "La Décoration navale en France entre 1660 et 1830" in *Les Génies de la mer* (Quebec and Paris: Musée du Québec et Musée national de la Marine, 2001), 59–60.

35 *Peace* suffered fairly substantial water damage and insect infestation while serving as a garden ornament during the second half of the twentieth century, but was conserved at the Pennsylvania Academy of the Fine Arts in 1981. See Bantel, *William Rush*, 107.

36 *The American and Daily Advertiser*, 4 Sept. 1799, quoted in Lahvis, "Skillin Workshop: The Emblematic Image," 217. See also Pinckney, *American Figureheads and Their Carvers*, 69, for a slightly different transcription, presumably from another source.

37 Brewington, *Shipcarvers of North America*, 33; Bantel, *William Rush*, 13–14.

38 *Boston Gazette and Country Journal*, 30 July 1806.

39 David A. Wasson, "The Silent Pilots," *Outlook* 109 (27 Jan. 1915): 209; Swan, "Boston Carvers and Joiners, Part 2," 283; Cabot, *Handbook of Bostonian Society*, 85; Pinckney, *American Figureheads and Their Carvers*, 131.

40 Georgia W. Hamilton, *Silent Pilots: Figureheads in Mystic Seaport Museum* (Mystic, Conn.: Mystic Seaport Museum, 1984), 66–67.

41 The earliest-known identification of the figurehead as "Admiral Perry" is in the catalogue of the landmark exhibition, *American Folk Sculpture*, at the Newark Museum in 1931. See *American Folk Sculpture* (Newark, N.J.: Newark Museum Association, 1931), 15, 24, 30. Pinckney attributes it to a packet named the *Commodore Perry*, built in New York in 1822. See Pinckney, *American Figureheads and Their Carvers*, 117, 170. Another packet of the same name was built by Donald McKay in Boston in 1854, but it is a less likely candidate. A contemporary review of that ship noted that "her bow is ornamented with a bust of her namesake, in naval uniform." [Duncan McLean], "The New Packet Ship *Commodore Perry*," *Boston Daily Atlas*, 30 Sept. 1854.

42 Walter Muir Whitehill, "A Figurehead of Talma," *American Neptune* 1 (Jan. 1941), 82–83. Brewington somewhat tentatively assigned the figurehead to Isaac Fowle on stylistic grounds, but there is no evidence to support the attribution; see Brewington, *Shipcarvers of North America*, 42.

43 Carl Bridenbaugh, *The Colonial Craftsman* (Chicago: University of Chicago Press, 1950), 132–34, 136; Sean Wilentz, *Chants Democratic: New York City and the Rise of the American Working Class, 1788–1850* (New York: Oxford University Press, 1984), 28, 33–34.

44 William W. Wheildon, *Memoir of Solomon Willard, Architect and Superintendent of the Bunker Hill Monument*, (Boston: Monument Association, 1865).

45 Ibid., 29.

46 James M. Morris, *Our Maritime Heritage: Maritime Developments and Their Impact on American Life* (Washington, D.C.: University Press of America, 1979), 164.

47 John H. Morrison, *History of New York Ship Yards* (New York: William F. Sametz and Co., 1909), 40–43.

48 Ibid., 38.

49 Ibid., 57, 150.

50 Brewington, *Shipcarvers of North America*, 5; *New-York Mercury*, 21 July 1755, and *New-York Gazette and General Advertiser*, 12 Apr. 1762, quoted in Frederick Fried, *Artists in Wood: American Carvers of Cigar-Store Indians, Show Figures, and Circus Wagons* (New York: Clarkson Potter, 1970), 171.

51 *New-York Gazette and General Advertiser*, 25 May 1799, quoted in Fried, *Artists in Wood*, 172.

52 "Report of the Trustees," *Annual Report of the New-York Historical Society* (New York: New-York Historical Society, 1953), 16–18; Brewington, *Shipcarvers of North America*, 47–48; Pinckney, *American Figureheads and Their Carvers*, 92–95.

53 The original head, carved by Laban Beecher, was recently reunited with the figurehead. The Museum of the City of New York acquired it in the spring of 1998 from a private collection in France. Overall, the incident is probably the most frequently recounted story in the literature on American figureheads. See, for example, Robert G. Denig, "Historic Figureheads," *Cosmopolitan* 14 (Apr. 1893): 694–95; William Allingham, "Figure-Heads," *Nautical Magazine* 68 (Aug. 1899): 522; and Wasson "Silent Pilots," 208–9. The most complete accounts appear in Pinckney, *American Figureheads and Their Carvers*, 103–14, and Brewington, *Shipcarvers of North America*, 129–36.

54 "Report of the Trustees," 19–21.

55 G. W. Sheldon, "The Old Ship-Builders of New York," *Harper's New Monthly Magazine* 65 (July 1882): 223; Morrison, *History of New York Ship Yards*, 96–97, 118, 126.

56 Morrison, *History of New York Ship Yards*, 153–54. In "Ship-Building in New York for 1856," *U.S. Nautical Magazine and Naval Journal* 5 (Feb. 1857): 381, the editors reported that "The great depression experienced in 1855 was gradually removed during the year, and general confidence has steadily increased, although there has not been a return to the measure of activity and enterprise which has distinguished former years."

57 Morrison, *History of New York Ship Yards*, 155–58; Sheldon, "Old Ship-Builders of New York," 241.

58 Morrison, *History of New York Ship Yards*, 162; Brewington, *Shipcarvers of North America*, 77.

59 Howard Irving Chapelle, *The History of American Sailing Ships* (New York: W. W. Norton, 1935), 281–82, 84–86.

60 Brewington, *Shipcarvers of North America*, 57.

61 One of the best-known early proponents of functionalism is the American sculptor, Horatio Greenough (1800–1852), who in his book *The Travels, Observations, and Experience of a Yankee Stonecutter*, published in 1852, argued that form should follow function and be appropriate to it. Greenough also asserted that American artisans and mechanics had outstripped American artists by creating new organic forms not bound by tradition. Among other examples, he cited the racing yacht *America*, which was widely recognized at the time for its innovative design and remarkable speed. The *America* was not a clipper, of course, but it did incorporate some of the same structural principles. See Horace Bender [Horatio Greenough], *The Travels, Observations, and Experience of a Yankee Stonecutter* (1852; reprint Gainsville, Fla.: Scholar's Facsimiles, 1958). The book was essentially a collection of Greenough's essays, and newspaper and magazine articles and editorials. In "Aesthetics at Washington," Greenough wrote: "The men who have reduced locomotion to its simplest elements, in the trotting wagon and the yacht America, are nearer to Athens at this moment than they who would bend the Greek temple to every use. I contend for Greek principals, not Greek things" (p. 33). In "American Architecture," he wrote, "Could we carry into our civil architecture the responsibilities of ship-building, we should ere long have edifices as superior to the Parthenon for the purposes that we require, as the Constitution or the Pennsylvania is to the galley of the Argonauts" (p. 140). In "The Cooper Monument," he wrote: "If there be any principle of structure more plainly inculcated in the works of the Creator than all others, it is the principle of unflinching adaption of forms to functions. I believe that colors also, so far as we have discovered their chemical causes and affinities, are not less organic in relation to the forms they invest than are those themselves" (p. 162). Greenough was not the sole supporter of functionalism in his generation, of course. Among the best-known contemporary advocates was his friend Ralph Waldo Emerson. Greenough, Emerson, and others developed many of their ideas from theories of relativity and evolution that emerged from eighteenth-century empirical science and rationalist philosophy. In the realm of aesthetics, Archibald Alison's theories of relative beauty as presented in his *Essays on the Nature and Principles of Taste* (1790; reprint, Hartford, Conn.: Goodwin and Sons, 1821) were especially influential.

62 John W. Griffiths, *A Treatise on Marine and Naval Architecture* (New York: D. Appleton, 1850), 181, 185.

63 Ibid., 184.

64 Anderson's workshop was the largest in New York City in 1850. According to the Federal Census, his shop had seven employees producing figures worth $6,000, while Charles Dodge employed four, with an output valued at $3,250.

65 Octavius T. Howe and Frederick C. Matthews, *American Clipper Ships, 1833–1858* (Salem, Mass.: Marine Research Society, 1926), 1:124–25; Ralph Whitney, "Davy Crockett, Ahoy!" *Ships and the Sea* (spring 1956): 11; Brewington, *Shipcarvers of North America*, 66.

66 See, for example, "Madame Anna Thillon," *Gleason's Pictorial* 2 (28 Feb. 1852): 1. The unpublished research was conducted by Carol Olsen for the Mariners' Museum in Newport News, Va., which owns the figurehead.

67 Brewington, *Shipcarvers of North America*, 51.

68 Brewington identifies forty-one carvers active in Boston from the 1660s to the 1890s, a total that is surpassed only by New York City. See ibid., 158–59.

69 Mabel M. Swan, "Ship Carvers of Newburyport," *Antiques* 48 (Aug. 1945): 81.

70 [Duncan McLean], "The New Clipper Ship *Morning Light* of Boston," *Boston Daily Atlas*, 2 Sept. 1853.

71 The drawings are in the collection of the Peabody Essex Museum in Salem, Mass.

72 Products of Industry Schedules, U.S. Census, 1850; Jane L. Port, "Boston's Nineteenth-Century Ship Carvers," *Antiques* 158 (Nov. 2000): 758.

73 Brewington, *Shipcarvers of North America*, 62, 66–67, 143; Pinckney, *American Figureheads and Their Carvers*, 126–29; Hamilton, *Silent Pilots*, 35–37; Port, "Boston's Nineteenth-Century Ship Carvers," 758.

74 Richard C. McKay, *Some Famous Sailing Ships and Their Builder, Donald McKay* (New York: G. P. Putnam's Sons, 1928), 231; Hamilton, *Silent Pilots*, 35–36.

75 [Duncan McLean], "The New Clipper Ship *Shooting Star*, of Boston," *Boston Daily Atlas*, 6 Mar. 1851.

76 Brewington, *Shipcarvers of North America*, 67.

77 *Boston Daily Transcript*, 31 Dec. 1886, quoted in Port, "Boston's Nineteenth-Century Ship Carvers," 758–59.

78 Brewington says that Herbert was the son of Samuel W. Gleason, but this is not certain. See Brewington, *Shipcarvers of North America*, 78. See also Port, "Boston's Nineteenth-Century Ship Carvers," 759–60; and Pinckney, *American Figureheads and Their Carvers*, 136.

79 Herbert Gleason was listed as being owed $362.35 for his work for McKay on the *Glory of the Seas* in "Assignment for the Benefit of Creditors," recorded 24 Mar. 1871, book 1040, pp. 5–11, Records of Suffolk County, Mass. See Michael Jay Mjelde, *Glory of the Seas* (Middletown, Conn.: Wesleyan University Press, 1970), 24–25.

80 See p. 154, and the discussion of Hiram Powers's famous statue, *The Greek Slave*, for more on this.

81 Much has been written about the ship and her builder. See especially McKay, *Some Famous Sailing Ships and Their Builder, Donald McKay; a Descriptive Catalogue of the Marine Collection to Be Found at India House* (New York: India House, 1935; second ed., Middletown, Conn.: Wesleyan University Press, 1973), 51–52; and Mjelde, *Glory of the Seas*.

82 The sketches are in the collection of the Peabody Essex Museum in Salem, Mass. See Pinckney, *American Figureheads and Their Carvers*, plate 4, for some examples. See also Brewington, *Shipcarvers of North America*, 96, 77–78, and Port, "Boston's Nineteenth-Century Ship Carvers," 760.

83 The journals are in the collection of the Waltham Historical Society. An engraving of the weathervane appears in *Illustrated Catalogue of Copper Weather Vanes* (Waltham, Mass.: L. W. Cushing and Sons, 1883), 17. See also Myrna Kaye, "Cushing and White's Copper Weather Vanes," *Antiques* 109 (June 1976), 1225.

84 Brewington, *Shipcarvers of North America*, 42, 136; Port, "Boston's Nineteenth-Century Ship Carvers," 756. For illustrations of the figure, see Brewington, 135, and Port, 754.

85 Curatorial files, Metropolitan Museum of Art, New York; Thayer Tolles, ed. *American Sculpture in the Metropolitan Museum of Art*, vol. 1, *A Catalogue of Works by Artists Born Before 1865* (New York: Metropolitan Museum of Art, 1999), 172–74; Pinckney, *American Figureheads and Their Carvers*, 137–38.

86 See Georgia Brady Bumgardner, "Political Portraiture: Two Prints of Andrew Jackson," *American Art Journal* 18, no. 4 (1986): 84–95, and David Tatum, *John Henry Bufford: American Lithographer* (Worcester, Mass.: American Antiquarian Society, 1976).

87 Alvin R. Page, "Introduction," in *Under Sail and in Port in the Glorious '50s* (Salem, Mass.: Peabody Museum, 1950), xxix–xxx.

88 *Boston Post*, Feb. 1868, quoted in Mjelde, *Glory of the Seas*, 7–8.

89 The papers of George Greenman and Company are in the collection of the G. W. Blunt White Library at Mystic Seaport Museum.

90 The figurehead is known from an article that appeared in the *Mystic Press*, 31 Oct. 1873. An excerpt reads: "Mr. Colby is carving a likeness of himself as a centerpiece for the stern of the new schooner *John N. Colby* named after him. Even in the rough state in which we saw it is a fair likeness, though rather wooden. Messrs. Campbell & Colby are artists in the line of vessel decoration." Quoted in William N. Peterson, "Campbell and Colby: Shipcarvers at Mystic Seaport," *Log of Mystic Seaport* 27 (Oct. 1977): 69–70.

91 *Mystic Pioneer*, 31 July 1869, quoted ibid., 68–69.

92 Ibid., 68–70.

93 See Brewington, *Shipcarvers of North America*, 71–72, for an illustration of Gerrish's bust and other information about the carver.

94 Ibid., 73, 76.

95 Curatorial files, Mariners' Museum, Newport News, Va.; ibid., 88–89. For the most complete account of Bellamy's life and work, see Yvonne Brault Smith, *John Halley Bellamy: Carver of Eagles* (Hampton, N.H.: P. E. Randall, 1982). See also Victor Safford, "John Halley Bellamy: The Woodcarver of Kittery Point," *Antiques* 27 (Mar. 1935), 102–6.

96 Brewington, *Shipcarvers of North America*, 88.

97 "Fashioning Figure-Heads Once the Work of Aged Maine Man—Captain Griffith Now Dabs in Oils and Paints Portland Scenery," *Lewiston Journal*. Newspaper clipping in the Edbury Hatch scrapbook, Skidompha Public Library, Damariscotta, Maine, dated 15 July 1921, n.p.

98 William Avery Baker, *A Maritime History of Bath and the Kennebec River Region* 2 (Bath, Maine: Marine Research Society of Bath, 1973), 661–66; Brewington, *Shipcarvers of North America*, 79; Pinckney, *American Figureheads and Their Carvers*, 139–40.

99 The *Western Belle* is at the Peabody Essex Museum.

100 "Newcastle Man Carved Thousand Figureheads in His Day," article from an unidentified Portland newspaper, dated 2 May 1925, Edbury Hatch scrapbook, n.p.

101 "In the Palmy Days of the American Merchant Marine," [Bath, Maine] *Independent*, 10 Apr. 1909. Edbury Hatch scrapbook, n.p.

102 Pinckney, *American Figureheads and Their Carvers*, 138–39.

103 "In the Palmy Days."

104 Quoted in Brewington, *Shipcarvers of North America*, 83.

105 "Newcastle Man Carved Thousand Figureheads in His Day."

106 Nicholas Dean, "The Eccentric Woodcarver of Newcastle," *Down East* (Sept. 1981), 72–78.

107 H. A. Cody, "The Wood Carver of Saint John," from a publication of the New Brunswick Historical Society, c. 1955, p. 24. A copy of the article is in scrapbook 36 in the archives of the New Brunswick Museum. See also Brewington, *Shipcarvers of North America*, 95, 98.

108 Will M. Clemens, "The Man Who Carves Ships' Figure-Heads," *Harper's Weekly* 36 (5 Mar. 1892): 5.

109 Charles H. Farnum, "A Day on the Docks," *Scribner's Monthly* 18 (May 1879): 46.

110 *Western World*, Fernald and Pettigrew Papers, Peabody Essex Museum. Quoted in Brewington, *Shipcarvers of North America*, 76. The carvers also requested the dimensions of the bow in the letter. The passage is quoted here not to test the reader's knowledge of nautical terminology, but rather to demonstrate the precision with which figureheads were designed to fit the ships that they were destined to adorn. It reads:

> Your favor of the 5th inst is at hand together with the sketch of the head of the *Western World*, for which we are greatly obliged to you & which no doubt will be of some assistance to us in regard to thickness of cut water &c &c. You have sent us the rake of the stem & steve of bowsprit: if you will please let us know about the distance you want the upper-side of the lower cheek from the underside of bowsprit on the line of the stem, & the distance you want the figure to set out on the line of the bowsprit, and the distance out on the bowsprit of the inner bobstay, we shall be able to furnish a draft on a scale to set the head by: or perhaps it would be better if you would lay the model on a sheet of paper & mark the line of the stem & the shear of the wale streak, this is necessary as the butt end of the lower-cheek should start on a parallel line, & for billet heads generally starts from the same line but may be carried lower, where a greater distance is wanted for the figure.

111 Brewington believed that colored figureheads vastly outnumbered white ones. He wrote, "A few heads were undoubtedly white, but the great majority were as one carver described them 'painted to the life'; that is, in natural colors." See Brewington, *Shipcarvers of North America*, 140.

112 [McLean], "New Clipper Ship *Shooting Star*, of Boston."

113 [Duncan McLean], "The New Clipper Ship *Galatea*," *Boston Daily Atlas*, 10 Apr. 1854.

114 "In the Palmy Days."

115 Accession files, Heritage Museums and Gardens, Sandwich, Mass.

116 An illustration appears in Clarence P. Hornung, *Treasury of American Design and Antiques* (New York: Harry Abrams, 1972), 384.

117 J. Wells Henderson and Rodney P. Carlisle, *Jack Tar: A Sailor's Life, 1750–1910* (Woodbridge, U.K.: Antique Collectors' Club, 1999), 44.

118 Allingham, "Figure-Heads," 523; Accession file, Museum of the City of New York.

119 In 1878, a reporter for the *New Bedford Mercury* wrote that the figure "was created by a cunning artificer in wood named King." See *New Bedford and Old Dartmouth: A Portrait of a Region's Past* (New Bedford, Mass.: Old Dartmouth Historical Society, 1975), 58; William H. Gerdts, *"A Man of Genius": The Art of Washington Allston (1779–1843)* (Boston: Museum of Fine Arts, 1979), 13; Philip C. F. Smith, "The Little Men: Carved Shop Signs of the Navigating Instrument Sellers," *American Neptune* 34 (July 1974): 205–6.

CHAPTER 3

Wooden Indians and Noble Savages

1 "Launch of the 'Minnehaha,'" *Boston Daily Evening Transcript*, 24 Mar. 1856, 2; "Mrs. Barrow as Minehaha," *Ballou's Pictorial* 10 (17 May 1856): 305; Nina Fletcher Little, *The Abby Aldrich Rockefeller Folk Art Collection* (Williamsburg, Va.: Colonial Williamsburg Foundation, 1957), 328; Pauline A. Pinckney, *American Figureheads and Their Carvers* (New York: W. W. Norton, 1940), 127–29.

2 An item entitled "Mrs. Barrow," that appeared in *Ballou's Pictorial* 10 (12 Apr. 1856): 237, noted that the carver would use a photograph of the actress in costume as a model for the figurehead, which provides a rare piece of documentation of a shipcarver employing a technique that was more often utilized by sculptors and portrait painters. The paragraph reads in part, "Messrs. Masury, Silsbee & Case have taken an admirable full length photograph of this distinguished artiste, as she appeared in the character of 'Minehaha,' at the Boston Theatre, which is to be used for modelling the figure-head of Donald McKay's new ship, named after Longfellow's heroine."

3 For examples of the many types of objects that incorporated this imagery, and discussions of the relationships among the images of the American Indian, Goddess of Liberty, and Columbia, see esp. E. McClung Fleming, "The American Image as Indian Princess, 1765–1783," *Winterthur Portfolio* 2 (1965): 65–81, and E. McClung Fleming, "From Indian Princess to Greek Goddess: The American Image, 1783–1815," *Winterthur Portfolio* 3 (1967): 37–66; Clare Le Corbeiller, "Miss America and Her Sisters: Personifications of the Four Parts of the World," *Bulletin of the Metropolitan Museum of Art* (Apr. 1961): 209–23; and John Higham, "Indian Princess and Roman Goddess: The First Female Symbols of America," *Proceedings of the American Antiquarian Society* 100 (1990): 45–79. For broader treatments of the Indian image in American culture, see Robert Berkhofer, *The White Man's Indian* (New York: Alfred A. Knopf, 1978); Roy Harvey Pearce, *Savagism and Civilization: A Study of the Indian and American Mind* (Baltimore: Johns Hopkins University Press, 1965); and Rayna Green, "The Pocahontas Perplex: The Image of Indian Women in American Culture," *Massachusetts Review* 16 (autumn 1975):

698–716, and "The Indian in Popular American Culture," in *The Handbook of North American Indians*, ed. Witcomb Washburn (Washington, D.C.: Smithsonian Institution Press, 1988), 4:587–606.

4 See Gloria Gilda Deák, *Picturing America, 1497–1899* 1 (Princeton, N.J.: Princeton University Press, 1988), 174, for a discussion of the location and identifications of the owners of the buildings represented in the print.

5 Theodore Bolton and Irwin F. Cortelyou, *Ezra Ames of Albany: Portrait Painter* (New York: New-York Historical Society, 1955), 104.

6 John Galt, *The Life and Studies of Benjamin West, Esq.* (London: T. Cadell and W. Davies, 1817), 104–6. The veracity of Galt's account has been disputed for some time. Ann Uhry Abrams suggests that the biography was, in fact, an attempt by the elderly West to create his own apotheosis at a time when his reputation was rapidly declining. She interprets the *Apollo Belvedere* story as commentary on one of West's early paintings, *The Savage Chief (The Indian Family)* of c. 1761. See Abrams, *The Valiant Hero: Benjamin West and Grand-Style History Painting* (Washington, D.C.: Smithsonian Institution Press, 1985), 31, 75–80.

7 Both Hall's and Hicks's compositions are reversed as a result of the engraving process. In addition, West's painting did not arrive in the United States until three years after Hicks's death. See Deborah Chotner et al., *American Naïve Paintings* (Washington, D.C.: National Gallery of Art, 1992), 189.

8 Anthony W. Pendergast and W. Porter Ware, *Cigar Store Figures in American Folk Art* (Chicago: Lightner Publishing Corp., 1953), 59–61, 72.

9 While this is a fine example of figure carving, it is surely not a portrait. Black Hawk (1767–1838) was a legendary chief of the Sauks who led the resistance to white settlement of tribal lands in parts of Illinois, Wisconsin, and Missouri. A series of treaty disputes culminated in the so-called Black Hawk War in 1832, after which most of the remaining Sauk and their neighbors, the Fox, were relocated to a reservation in Iowa. Black Hawk's exploits were well known at the time, particularly in the middle states. Contemporary representations of him do not bear any resemblance to this figure.

10 See Berkhofer, *White Man's Indian*, 74–80, for a concise discussion of this transition.

11 For a consideration of the significance of the image of the American Indian in West's painting, see Vivien Green Fryd, "Rereading the Indian in Benjamin West's *Death of General Wolfe*," *American Art* 9 (spring 1995): 73–85.

12 Alexander Pope, *An Essay on Man* (1733–34; reprint, New York: Bobbs-Merrill, 1965), 9. The complete stanza is:

> Lo! the poor Indian, whose untutored mind
> Sees God in clouds, or hears him in the wind;
> His soul proud Science never taught to stray
> Far as the solar walk, or milky way;
> Yet simple Nature to his hope has giv'n,
> Behind the cloud-topped hill, an humbler heav'n;
> Some safer world in depth of woods embraced,
> Some happier island in wat'ry waste,
> Where slaves once more their native land behold,
> No fiends torment, no Christians thirst for gold!
> To Be, contents his natural desire,
> He asks no Angel's wing, no Seraph's fire;
> But thinks, admitted to that equal sky;
> His faithful dog shall bear him company.

13 See Harry Hayden Clark, ed., *Poems of Freneau* (New York: Hafner Publishing Co., 1960); and Berkhofer, *White Man's Indian*, 87–88.

14 François-René de Chateaubriand, *Atala, ou les amours de deux sauvages dans le désert* (Paris, 1801); David Wakefield, "Chateaubriand's 'Atala' as a Source of Inspiration in Nineteenth-Century Art," *Burlington Magazine* 120 (Jan. 1978): 14; Berkhofer, *White Man's Indian*, 79–80; Hugh Honour, *The New Golden Land: European Images of America from the Discoveries to the Present Time* (New York: Pantheon Books, 1975), 220–22.

15 The novel had a significant impact on popular culture as well as the fine arts. In his memoirs, Chateaubriand related that during his travels, he encountered roadside inns that were adorned with inexpensive prints of scenes from his book, and small wax figures of Atala, Chactas, and Père Aubrey that were on sale at booths in fairgrounds. See Wakefield, "Chateaubriand's 'Atala,'" 14.

16 Ibid., 19–21; Lee Johnson, *The Paintings of Eugène Delacroix: A Critical Catalogue* 2 (New York: Oxford University Press, 1981), 79; Honour, *New Golden Land*, 223.

17 "The Indians in American Art," *Crayon* 3 (Jan. 1856): 28.

18 "Indians in American Art," 28; Fryd, "Rereading the Indian," 81–82.

19 Samuel Y. Edgerton, "The Murder of Jane McCrea: The Tragedy of an American Tableau d'Histoire," *Art Bulletin* 47 (Dec. 1965): 482–83.

20 Lois Marie Fink, *American Art at the Nineteenth-Century Paris Salons* (New York: Cambridge University Press, 1990), 18–20; Wayne Craven, "The Grand Manner in Early Nineteenth-Century American Painting: Borrowings from Antiquity, the Renaissance, and the Baroque," *American Art Journal* 11 (Apr. 1979): 13–15.

21 See Edgerton, "Murder of Jane McCrea," 487–92, for a concise, if somewhat opinionated discussion of the painting's impact and representations in other media.

22 For a consideration of Longfellow, *Hiawatha*, and the construction of national memory and American history in the nineteenth century, see chapter 3, "Motifs of Morality, Myth, and Memory in Antebellum Culture," esp. pp. 82–87, in Michael Kammen, *Mystic Chords of Memory: The Transformation of Tradition in American Culture* (New York: Alfred A. Knopf, 1991).

23 Cynthia D. Nickerson, "Artistic Interpretations of Henry Wadsworth Longfellow's *The Song of Hiawatha*, 1855–1900," *American Art Journal* 16 (summer 1984): 50–53.

24 J. N. Barker, *The Indian Princess; or, La Belle Sauvage: An Operatic Melo-Drame* (Philadelphia: Palmer, 1808); Berkhofer, *White Man's Indian*, 90; Don B. Wilmeth, "Nobel or Ruthless Savage? The American Indian on Stage and in the Drama," *Journal of American Drama and Theatre* 1 (spring 1989): 42.

25 Quoted in Eugene R. Page, *Metamora and Other Plays* (Princeton, N.J.: Princeton University Press, 1941), 4.

26 Ibid., 4; Ellwood Parry, *The Image of the Indian and Black Man in American Art* (New York: George Braziller, 1974), 159; Berkhofer, *White Man's Indian*, 90; Kate Sanborn, *Hunting Indians in a Taxi-Cab* (Boston: Richard G. Badger, 1911), 28. See Richard Moody, *Edwin Forrest: First Star of the American Stage* (New York: Alfred A. Knopf, 1960), for a thorough consideration of Forrest's life and career. For an insightful discussion of Indian plays, including *Metamora*, and their role in the development of an American identity in the nineteenth century, see chapter 4, "Romantic Love, Arranged Marriage, and Indian Melancholy," in Werner Sollors, *Beyond Ethnicity: Consent and Descent in American Culture* (New York: Oxford University Press, 1986).

27 Curatorial files, Brandywine River Museum; Ann Barton Brown, "'Lo, The Wooden Indian': Prototypes for Wooden Show Figures," *Brandywine River Museum Antiques Show 1984* (Chadds Ford, Pa.: Brandywine River Museum, 1984), 6, 9.

28 Curatorial files, Historical Society of Berks County. The possible attribution to New York or Philadelphia is made by this writer, based on the high quality of the carving and the fact that Reading is not known to have had any figure-carving shops during the period.

29 "Designed by Whittling Yankees: A Studio Where Many Statues of Native Americans Are Made," *Tobacco* 1 (14 May 1886): 7.

30 New York City Directories; George C. Groce and David H. Wallace, *The New-York Historical Society's Dictionary of Artists in America, 1564–1860* (New Haven, Conn.: Yale University Press, 1957), 155; John L. Morrison, "Poor Lo Still Active," *Scribner's Magazine* 85 (Jan. 1929): 40; Marion V. Brewington, *Shipcarvers of North America* (Barre, Mass.: Barre Publishing Co., 1962), 73, 75; Frederick Fried, *Artists in Wood: American Carvers of Cigar-Store Indians, Show Figures, and Circus Wagons* (New York: Clarkson Potter, 1970), 178–80.

31 Jean Lipman, *American Folk Art in Wood, Metal and Stone* (Meriden, Conn.: Pantheon, 1948), 74.

32 Cornelius Mathews, *Big Abel and the Little Manhattan* (New York: Wiley and Putnam, 1845), 22.

33 John L. Morrison, "The Passing of the Wooden Indian," *Scribner's Monthly* 84 (Oct. 1928): 401; "Lo! The Poor Indian Finds a Happy Hunting Ground," *Reading Eagle*, 14 July 1936; Pendergast and Ware, *Cigar Store Figures in American Folk Art*, 56, 61; Curatorial files, Historical Society of Berks County.

34 Morrison, "Passing of the Wooden Indian," 394; Lawrence F. Jessup, "The Tobacconists' Tribe of Treen," *Antiques* 18 (Sept. 1930): 233; Charles G. Shaw, "Speaking of Wooden Indians," *Antiques* 36 (Sept. 1939): 133; Curatorial file, Museum of the City of New York.

35 In 1890, a journalist reported that "S. A. Robb, who has been at it for twenty-six years, is full of reminiscences concerning the history of the art." See Frank Weitenkampf, "Lo, the Wooden Indian," *New York Times*, 3 Aug. 1890, 13.

36 School Register, National Academy of Design Archives, New York; Frederick and Mary Fried Folk Arts Archives, National Museum of American History, Washington, D.C. See Fried, *Artists in Wood*, 193–238, for an extended discussion of Robb's life and work.

37 New York City Directories; Weitenkampf, "Lo, the Wooden Indian," 13; Fried, *Artists in Wood*, 195, 208.

38 The trade card is in the Frederick and Mary Fried Folk Arts Archives at the National Museum of American History. See Fried, *Artists in Wood*, 210.

39 Weitenkampf, "Lo, the Wooden Indian," 13.

40 Boston Directories; New York City Directories; Fried, *Artists in Wood*, 181–82.

41 New York City Directories; Chicago Directories; Morrison, "Poor Lo Still Active," 40; Fried, *Artists in Wood*, 182–93.

42 Fried suggested that he apprenticed with William Rush, but this remains speculative, because several members of the Millard family worked as shipcarvers in Philadelphia from the late eighteenth to the mid-nineteenth centuries, and it is not clear which of them was Rush's student. See Fried, *Artists in Wood*, 177. Henri Marceau, *William Rush, 1756–1833: The First Native American Sculptor* (Philadelphia: Pennsylvania Museum of Art, 1937), 14, and Linda Bantel, "William Rush, Esq.," in Linda Bantel et al., *William Rush: American Sculptor* (Philadelphia: Pennsylvania Academy of the Fine Arts, 1982), 10, provide information on the Millard family in Philadelphia.

43 New York City Directories; Weitenkampf, "Lo, the Wooden Indian," 13; Fried, *Artists in Wood*, 177–78.

44 Weitenkampf, "Lo, the Wooden Indian," 13.

45 New York City Directories; Fried, *Artists in Wood*, 242–43.

46 Phillips and Company's *New York Business Directory*.

47 Isaac Lewin, who had worked for Thomas Brooks for many years, took over the Chicago shop in 1895. Chicago Directories; Morrison, "Poor Lo Still Active," 40; Fried, *Artists in Wood*, 193.

48 Fried, *Artists in Wood*, 210, 214–15.

49 "Lo Takes a Spring Suit," *Tobacco* 6 (12 Apr. 1889): 1.

50 "Designed by Whittling Yankees," 7.

51 In the 1850, 1860, and 1870 schedules, the census-taker recorded several important pieces of information in a block-by-block survey organized by the old wards in New York City, in much the same way as the population census was taken. The categories included number of employees, average wages, type and value of materials used, and type and value of product, among others. Only proprietors or businesses with an annual product of over $500 are included, which no doubt eliminated a number of shipcarvers from the rolls.

52 In *Doggett's New York City Directory* for 1849–50, Cromwell is listed at 222 South Street, Anderson at 236, Dodge at 253, and Brooks at 260.

53 Weitenkampf, "Lo, the Wooden Indian," 13. James Chichester was a tobacconist who sold shop figures from his store on the Bowery. His role in the development of the show-figure business will be considered in the next chapter.

54 "Wood-Carving," *Harper's Weekly* 27 (6 Jan. 1883): 13. The "Canal Street shop" mentioned by the author was probably Samuel Robb's workshop.

55 Henry Collins Brown, *Valentine's Manual of Old New York, 1927* (New York: Valentine's Manual, 1927), 122.

56 "Designed by Whittling Yankees," 7.

57 Charles J. Dodge is listed as Deputy Tax Commissioner, and not a carver, in the New York City Directory for 1860.

58 The photo is in the Frederick and Mary Fried Folk Arts Archives at the National Museum of American History. See also Fried, *Artists in Wood,* 187.

59 *Trow's New York Directory* (1872–73); Fried, *Artists in Wood,* 182.

60 Brooks was listed at 240 South Street in the 1879 New York City Directory, but was not in the 1880 edition.

61 John Anderson was not listed in the Schedules, although he was in the 1880 New York City Directory as a "carver" at 226 South Street.

62 "Wood-Carving," 13.

63 Weitenkampf, "Lo, the Wooden Indian," 13.

64 "Lo Takes a Spring Suit," 1.

65 Ibid.

66 Brown, *Valentine's Manual of Old New York,* 122.

67 "Lo Takes a Spring Suit," 1.

68 Morrison, "Poor Lo Still Active," 40.

69 "Exhibit of Wm. Demuth & Co.," *Tobacco* 16 (2 Feb. 1894), 1, 3; Fried, *Artists in Wood,* 59–61, 212. The J. L. Mott Iron Works of New York City offered a similar figure in its 1873 and 1890 catalogues, copies of which are in the collection of the Cooper Hewitt Museum, New York, and elsewhere. It could be ordered separately or as a part of an elaborate drinking fountain for men, horses, and dogs. In *Chief Kisco and His Brothers* (Mount Kisco, N.Y.: Mount Kisco Historical Committee, 1980), Oliver A. Knapp documents the history of one such piece that has been a landmark in Mount Kisco since 1907. He also surveys over twenty other examples in cities and towns throughout the East, Midwest, and South, as well as several in museum collections. From the illustrations in his book, it is evident that not all of them were made or modeled by the same hand. Whether or not there was any relationship between Demuth and Mott or Robb and Mott has yet to be determined.

70 Lillian Sabine, "The Neighborhood Indian Passes On," *Brooklyn Eagle Magazine,* 30 Mar. 1930, 6; Curatorial file, Brooklyn Historical Society.

71 Fried, *Artists in Wood,* 176–77.

72 Harold Williams, "Eight Hundred Wooden Indians—And Then There Were Eight," *Baltimore Morning Sun,* 17 Feb. 1947, 23; Sanborn, *Hunting Indians in a Taxi-Cab,* 54.

73 Williams, "Eight Hundred Wooden Indians," 23.

74 Brewington, *Shipcarvers of North America,* 37, 62, 72, 158; Marceau, *William Rush,* 15.

75 Williams, "Eight Hundred Wooden Indians," 23.

76 Baltimore Directory (1853–54); Fried, *Artists in Wood,* 126–27.

77 Fried, *Artists in Wood,* 129–30.

78 Brewington, *Shipcarvers of North America,* 162–63.

79 Ibid., 78–79; Philip C. F. Smith, "The Little Men: Carved Shop Signs of the Navigating Instrument Sellers," *American Neptune* 34 (July 1974): 206. The figure is now in the collection of Independence Seaport Museum, Philadelphia.

80 Brewington, *Shipcarvers of North America,* 162–63; Fried, *Artists in Wood,* 122, 124; Morrison, "Passing of the Wooden Indian," 404.

81 E. Leslie Gilliams, "Cigar-Store Indians," *Philadelphia Times,* 18 Dec. 1892, 18.

82 Ibid.

83 Brewington, *Shipcarvers of North America,* 158–59.

84 Ibid., 156, 160; curatorial files, Peabody Essex Museum, Salem, Mass.; Fried, *Artists in Wood,* 156.

85 Curatorial files, Hood Museum, Dartmouth College, Hanover, N.H.

86 Mabel M. Swan, "Ship Carvers of Newburyport," *Antiques* 48 (Aug. 1945), 78–81. For illustrations of Wilson's figure of William Pitt, see Wayne Craven, *Sculpture in America* (Cranbury, N.J.: Cornwall Books, 1984), fig. 1.23, and Robert Bishop, *American Folk Sculpture* (New York: E. P. Dutton, 1974), 166, fig. 299. For more on Timothy Dexter, see John P. Marquand, *Timothy Dexter Revisited* (Boston: Little, Brown, and Company, 1960).

87 Charles Marius Barbeau, "Louis Jobin, Statuaire," *La Société Royale du Canada, Mémoires* 37, sec. 1 (1943): 17.

88 René Villeneuve, *Baroque to Neo-Classical: Sculpture in Quebec* (Ottawa: National Gallery of Canada, 1997), 35–37, 62–75.

89 Mario Béland, *Louis Jobin: Master-Sculptor* (Quebec: Musée du Québec, 1986), 11; Mario Béland, *Jean-Baptiste Côté: Caricaturiste et sculpteur* (Quebec: Musée du Québec, 1996), 26; Victoria Hayward, "Jobin—The Wood-Carver," *Canadian Magazine* 60 (Dec. 1922): 92; Charles Marius Barbeau, "Le dernier de nos grands artisans, Louis Jobin," *Royal Society of Canada, Mémoires* 27, sec. 1 (1933): 43–45.

90 Hayward, "Jobin," 93.

91 Béland, *Jean-Baptiste Côté,* 26–27, 29–30. See also Nicole Allard, "Un graveur et caricaturiste a l'aube de la Confédération," in Béland, *Jean-Baptiste Côté,* 35–65. Charles Marius Barbeau, *Côté, the Wood Carver* (Toronto: Reyerson Press, 1943), 3–4, 34, 39–40.

92 Béland, *Jean-Baptiste Côté,* 82–86; Béland, *Louis Jobin,* 41–45, 166–69.

93 Béland, *Louis Jobin,* 14–15; Barbeau, "Le dernier de nos grands artisans," 45; Hayward, "Jobin," 94.

94 Barbeau, "Le dernier de nos grands artisans," 45.

95 Ibid., 34–35, 45–46; Béland, *Louis Jobin,* 25, 45, 47, 62.

96 Béland, *Louis Jobin,* 35–36; Hayward, "Jobin," 97–98; Barbeau, "Louis Jobin," 47.

97 "Julius Melchers Suffers a Stroke: Venerable Sculptor Loses the Power of Speech," *Detroit News,* 30 May 1907; George B. Catlin, "Old Detroit Artists Found Trade Dull, but Market for Wooden Indians Brisk," *Detroit News,* 4 Jan. 1925, pt. 2, p. 17; Henriette Lewis-Hind, *Gari Melchers: Painter* (New York: William Edwin Rudge, 1928), n.p.; Pendergast and Ware, *Cigar Store Figures in American Folk Art,* 21; Fried, *Artists in Wood,* 137–38; C. Kurt Dewhurst, Betty MacDowell, and Marsha MacDowell, "The Art of Julius and Gari Melchers," *Antiques* 125 (Apr. 1984): 862.

98 "Julius Melchers Suffers a Stroke"; Catlin, "Old Detroit Artists Found Trade Dull," 17; Fried, *Artists in Wood,* 138; Dewhurst, MacDowell, and MacDowell, "Art of Julius and Gari Melchers," 862.

99 Catlin, "Old Detroit Artists Found Trade Dull," 17.

100 J. H. Junkin, "The Wooden Indian Is Passing Away," *Detroit News-Tribune*, 23 July 1899, 17.

101 Both of these attributions have been made on a stylistic basis, and by comparison with documented examples. The most notable of these is an Indian figure purchased in 1867 by the Schott Brothers Tobacco Shop in Lincoln, Illinois. It is now in a private collection in Michigan.

102 *Cleveland Plain Dealer*, 22 Mar. 1928; Curatorial files, Henry Ford Museum, Dearborn, Mich.; Lipman, *American Folk Art in Wood, Metal and Stone*, 14.

103 *American Folk Sculpture* (Newark, N.J.: Newark Museum Association, 1931), 27, 32; *Antiques* 23 (February 1933): 42; Curatorial file, Abby Aldrich Rockefeller Folk Art Museum, Williamsburg, Va.; Lipman, *American Folk Art in Wood, Metal, and Stone*, 74, 88; Pendergast and Ware, *Cigar Store Figures in American Folk Art*, 8.

104 One of the most celebrated of all cigar-store figures, this piece has attained an iconic status in the annals of American folk sculpture. Nevertheless, little is actually known about its origins, other than the oral history that accompanies it. It originally surfaced in the Elie Nadelman collection before 1940 and then passed through several dealers and collectors until it was acquired by Stephen Clark for the New York State Historical Association. Jean Lipman's attribution is the most frequently quoted source. She wrote in 1948 that it was "Said to have been made by a negro slave named Job for a tobacconist in Freehold, New Jersey in the first half of the 19th century." (Lipman, *American Folk Art in Wood, Metal and Stone*, 14). A date before mid-century is highly unlikely, though, given the treatment of the bunches of cigars and the scored fringe on the skirt.

105 John Michael Vlach, *The Afro-American Tradition in the Decorative Arts* (Cleveland: Cleveland Museum of Art, 1978), 37.

106 Almost nothing is known about the origins of this figure. The possible southern attribution is based on a statement made in an appraisal done in 1982 that seems to have been based on a vague oral history. It is, however, clearly American and dates from the second half of the nineteenth century.

CHAPTER 4
Show Figures: Caricature and Stereotypes

1 Both the figure of Father Knickerbocker and the painting of Knickerbocker Hall were donated to the New-York Historical Society in 1912 by the estate of George Shepard, the last proprietor of the stage line. It will be noted that the statue is not represented accurately in the painting. The image is reversed and appears to be larger than is actually the case. See Richard J. Koke et al., *American Landscape and Genre Paintings in the New-York Historical Society* (Boston: G. K. Hall, 1982), 3:129–30.

2 Frank W. Weitenkampf, "Lo, the Wooden Indian: The Art of Making Cigar-Shop Signs," *New York Times*, 3 Aug. 1890, 13.

3 Single-sheet advertisement, William Demuth and Company, New York, c. 1871. A copy is in the archives of the National Museum of American History, Smithsonian Institution, Washington, D.C.

4 Weitenkampf, "Lo, the Wooden Indian," 13; Frederick Fried, *Artists in Wood: American Carvers of Cigar-Store Indians, Show Figures, and Circus Wagons* (New York: Clarkson Potter, 1970), 29–30; Charles A. Flammer, "First Wooden Indians: Memories of Chichester's Cigar Store in the Bowery," *New York Times*, 4 May 1926, 26. Flammer recalled that in his youth "The Chichester mentioned as an original introducer of the wooden Indian in the '50s, was located on the east side of the Bowery, between Bayard and Canal Streets, near Charlie White's Melodeon and the Volks Garden, the Atlantic Garden being opposite, as also the old Bowery Theatre further down the block."

5 Flammer, "First Wooden Indians," 26.

6 "Death of Edward Hen," *Tobacco* 2 (6 May 1887): 3; "E. Hen's Wills," *Tobacco* 3 (13 May 1887): 3; "The Last of E. Hen's Business," *Tobacco* 3 (5 Aug. 1887): 6; John L. Morrison, "The Passing of the Wooden Indian," *Scribner's Magazine* 84 (Oct. 1928): 394–95; Fried, *Artists in Wood*, 30–32.

7 *Trow's Directory of New York City* (1855/56), 380; Morrison, "Passing of the Wooden Indian," 395; Fried, *Artists in Wood*, 30.

8 John L. Morrison, "Poor Lo Still Active," *Scribner's Magazine* 85 (Jan. 1929): 40; Fried, *Artists in Wood*, 30, 32.

9 Morrison, "Passing of the Wooden Indian," 395.

10 Morrison, "Poor Lo Still Active," 40.

11 A.W. Pendergast and W. Porter Ware, *Cigar Store Figures in American Folk Art* (Chicago: Lightner Publishing Corp., 1953), 11–13; Fried, *Artists in Wood*, 32–34, 59; "A World's Fair Exhibit," *Tobacco* 14 (7 Apr. 1893): 1; "Exhibit of Wm. Demuth & Co.," *Tobacco* 16 (2 Feb. 1894): 1, 3.

12 Fried, *Artists in Wood*, 181, 194, 196–97.

13 Ibid., 33; Morrison, "Poor Lo Still Active," 40.

14 Fried, *Artists in Wood*, 33.

15 *Illustrated Catalogue of Smokers' Articles and Show Figures* (New York: William Demuth and Co., 1875).

16 According to Fried, Demuth initially selected eight wooden figures from his line of show figures to be used as casting models by Seelig. If this was done in 1868, then it is quite certain that the figures were carved by Samuel Robb and/or some other unidentified New York shipcarver. See Fried, *Artists in Wood*, 33.

17 For an extended discussion of physiognomy and phrenology and their impact on nineteenth-century English painting, see Mary Cowling, *The Artist as Anthropologist: The Representation of Type and Character in Victorian Art* (New York: Cambridge University Press, 1989). Cowling demonstrates convincingly that most people, including artists, subscribed to these beliefs, although phrenology was not as widely accepted as physiognomy. From William Firth to William Holman Hunt and Charles Dickens to Emily Bronte, artists and writers used physiognomic distinctions in their work, confident that physical features had specific meanings that could and would be deciphered by their audience. As for the United States, the concepts of the type and typing are fundamental to Elizabeth John's analysis in her study *American Genre Painting: The Politics of Everyday Life* (New Haven, Conn.: Yale University Press, 1991). See also Charles Colbert, *A Measure of Perfection: Phrenology and the Fine Arts in America* (Chapel Hill: University of North Carolina Press, 1997); Lewis P. Curtis, *Apes and Angels: The Irishman in Victorian Caricature* (Washington, D.C.: Smithsonian Institution Press, 1971); and Judith Wechsler, *The Human Comedy: Physiognomy and Caricature in*

Nineteenth-Century Paris (London: Thames and Hudson, 1982).

18 The figure was donated to the Historical Society of Berks County in 1923. Although its exact history was not recorded at the time, accession records indicate that it was used locally. The attribution to a New York carver is made on a stylistic basis by this writer.

19 A visual record of the use of Chinese figures occurs in a watercolor entitled *Burroughs* by Jurgan Frederick Huge that is in the collection of the Bridgeport Public Library in Bridgeport, Connecticut. Done in 1876, it represents the Burroughs Building, a well-known commercial building at the time. Two Chinese figures appear in the windows of the New England Tea Store on the ground floor. See Jean Lipman, "Jurgan Frederick Huge, 1809–1878," in Jean Lipman and Tom Armstrong, eds., *American Folk Painters of Three Centuries* (New York: Whitney Museum of American Art, 1980), 115.

20 One carver's observations on the topic were noted in 1887. He is recorded as telling a journalist: "'Fidelity to nature or artistic beauty is not much looked to. That Indian,' pointing to a melancholy, flat-nosed chief, 'was done from life and we can't sell him. Buyers complain that he is too ugly. What they want is something fine-looking and attractive.'" ("The Tobacconist's Sign," *Tobacco* 2 [8 Apr. 1887]: 2.)

21 Weitenkampf, "Lo, the Wooden Indian," 13.

22 The Reverend Orville Dewey, "Mr. Powers' Statue," *Union Magazine of Literature and Art* 1 (October 1847): 236, quoted in William H. Gerdts, *American Neo-Classic Sculpture: The Marble Resurrection* (New York: Viking Press, 1973), 53. See also Richard P. Wunder, *Hiram Powers: Vermont Sculptor* (Woodstock, Vt.: Woodstock Historical Society, 1974), 25.

23 Gerdts, *American Neo-Classic Sculpture*, 52–53; Wunder, *Hiram Powers*, 25–27.

24 The earliest-known illustration of this figure was done by Elizabeth Moutal for the Massachusetts Project of the Index of American Design. The rendering shows the piece in white and identifies it as a garden figure. The word "Dove" does not appear on the base, indicating that it is a rather recent addition. See Erwin O. Christensen, *Early American Wood Carving* (Cleveland: World Publishing Co., 1952), 12, 150. The attribution to a shipcarver is made by this writer on a stylistic basis.

25 For an extended discussion, see Beverly Seaton, *The Language of Flowers: A History* (Charlottesville: University of Virginia Press, 1995).

26 Nothing is known about the history of this figure. She was found on Staten Island, and appears to have been there for some time. The attribution to a European-trained carver is made by this writer.

27 Baerer signed both sculptures. Frank Weitenkampf, "Some Signs and Others—Sign Painters and Sign Painting Artists," *New York Times*, 3 July 1892, 15.

28 "Designed by Whittling Yankees: A Studio Where Many Statues of Native Americans Are Made," *Tobacco* 1 (14 May 1886): 7; "The Puck Cigar," *Tobacco* 8 (15 Nov. 1889): 1; "Wooden Indians," *Tobacco* 26 (6 Jan. 1899): 10; Weitenkampf, "Some Signs and Others," 15. Weitenkampf was the first to note that Buberl was the sculptor who modeled the Puck offered by Demuth in his 1875 catalogue. He also states that the statue on the Puck Building in lower Manhattan was by Baerer, not Buberl, as other writers have suggested. He does not mention that there were actually two sculptures by Baerer on the building. A few versions of the zinc cigar-store Puck with "C. Buberl, sculpt." on the base have survived. For a consideration of Buberl's career, see Joyce L. McDaniel, "The Collected Works of Caspar Buberl: An Analysis of a Nineteenth-Century American Sculptor" (M.A. thesis, Wellesley College, 1976); and McDaniel, "Caspar Buberl: The Pension Building Civil War Frieze and Other Washington, D.C. Sculpture," *Records of the Columbia Historical Society* 50 (1980): 309–44.

29 "The Punch Factory under New Management," *Tobacco* 9 (31 Oct. 1890): 1; "Wooden Indians," *Tobacco* 24 (28 Jan. 1898): 3.

30 For a history of Polichinelle and other characters of the Commedia dell'Arte, see Maurice Sand, *The History of Harlequinade*, 2 vols. (New York: Benjamin Blom, 1915).

31 Frank B. Mayer relates in "Signs and Symbols," *Scribner's Monthly* 18 (Sept. 1879): 714, that "A new claimant to sign-board honors in our day, the only sovereign who in our republic asserts his prerogative of popular homage is his majesty 'King Gambrinus,' liege lord of lager-beer. His origin is mythical, and probably, like Old King Cole, of fabulous existence." A metal figure of Gambrinus or King Lager was offered as no. 49 in William Demuth's 1875 catalogue, while an illustration of a Gambrius-type figure holding cigars appeared in "Wooden Indians" (6 Jan. 1899): 10.

32 "The Girl of the Period," *Saturday Review of Politics, Literature, Science, and Art* 25 (14 Mar. 1868): 340.

33 "Modern Women," *Nation* 7 (22 Oct. 1868): 334.

34 See, for example, Winifred Sothern, "The Truth about the Bachelor Girl," *Munsey's Magazine* 25 (May 1901): 282–83.

35 One source noted that "the Girl of the Period was in great demand during the war" ("Tobacconist's Sign," 2), while another journalist, quoting Julius Melchers, wrote: "Along in the '70s the fancy figure known as the 'Girl of the Period' was quite popular. . . . The 'Girl of the Period' of which Mr. Melchers spoke was dressed in a style in vogue about 1873 with the 'Grecian bend,' high heeled shoes and a natty little cap with a squirrel perched upon the top of it." (J. H. Junkin, "The Wooden Indian Is Passing Away," *Detroit News-Tribune*, 23 July 1899, 17.)

36 *New York Clipper*, 10 July 1869, 110, quoted in Laurence Senelick, *The Age and Stage of George L. Fox, 1825–1877* (Hanover, N.H.: University Press of New England, 1988), 156. See also "Modern Women," *Nation*, 332–34.

37 The suggestion that the figure was used as a milliner's shop sign was first made by Jean Lipman in 1948. See *American Folk Art in Wood, Metal and Stone* (Meriden, Conn.: Pantheon, 1948; reprint, New York: Dover Publications, 1972), 15.

38 "Designed by Whittling Yankees," 7.

39 "Wooden Indians," (28 Jan. 1898): 3.

40 "Captain Jinks of the Horse Marines" was popular on both sides of the Atlantic. It was published by Metzler and Company in London in 1862 and by the New England Music Company in Boston and Lee and Walker in Philadelphia in 1868, among other places. In 1879, Frank Mayer noted that "'Jim Crow' and 'Captain Jinks' are almost the only instances of the hero of a song being promoted to the sign-board." (Mayer, "Signs and Symbols," 713).

41 Fried, *Artists in Wood*, 198.

42 The attribution of its use as an apothecary sign in Sellersville, Pa., is based on an oral tradition that has accompanied the figure for many years. Lipman states it as fact (see *American Folk Art in Wood, Metal and Stone*, 79), but accession records at the New York State Historical Association are not so definite.

43 As purchased and performed by John T. Raymond, the first adaptation of the novel as a play was unauthorized. Raymond then asked Twain to write a second version, which he continued to perform for several years. See "The American on the Stage," *Scribner's Monthly* 18 (July 1879): 328–30. The article illustrates a "statuette" of Raymond as Colonel Sellers, in a pose that is similar to the Cooperstown figure. The caption credits the statuette to J. S. Hartley, who was in fact well known for his stage portraits. See Rupert Hughes, "Jonathan Scott Hartley," *Munsey's Magazine* 11 (Aug. 1894): 515–20.

44 Senelick, *Age and Stage of George L. Fox*, 226.

45 "Generously Good Window Display," *Tobacco* 30 (5 Apr. 1901): 3; Curatorial files, Abby Aldrich Rockefeller Folk Art Museum, Williamsburg, Va.

46 In "Wooden Indians," (6 Jan. 1899): 10, the author noted that "when the godson of Edwin Forrest opened the cigar store still located at 744 Broadway, on the site of the Macready-Forrest riots, he had an enormous figure of the tragedian in the character of Marc Anthony outside the store."

47 A figure of George W. L. Fox that is very similar to the one at the Abby Aldrich Rockefeller Folk Art Museum illustrated ibid., 10. The author identified it as a "clown figure" and stated that "Around the environs of New York are a number of clown figures, many of them being types of famous clowns of the old-time traveling circus." See also the photograph of a Fox-type figure in Kate Sanborn, *Hunting Indians in a Taxi-Cab* (Boston: Richard G. Badger, 1911), 47.

48 For considerations of American minstrelsy, see Carl Wittke, *Tambo and Bones: A History of the American Minstrel Stage* (Durham, N.C.: Duke University Press, 1930; reprint, Westport, Conn.: Greenwood Press, 1968); Hans Nathan, *Dan Emmet and the Rise of Early Negro Minstrelsy* (Norman: University of Oklahoma Press, 1962); and Robert C. Toll, *Blacking Up: The Minstrel Show in Nineteenth-Century America* (New York: Oxford University Press, 1974).

49 For recent studies of the image of African-Americans in art and visual culture see esp. Guy C. McElroy, *Facing History: The Black Image in American Art, 1710–1940* (San Francisco: Bedford Arts, 1990); Hugh Honour, *The Image of the Black Man in Western Art*, vol. 4, *From the American Revolution to World War I* (Cambridge, Mass.: Harvard University Press, 1989); Albert Boime, *The Art of Exclusion: Representing Blacks in the Nineteenth Century* (Washington, D.C.: Smithsonian Institution Press, 1990); and Ellwood Parry, *The Image of the Indian and Black Man in American Art* (New York: George Braziller, 1974). McElroy, for example, identifies four general types of depictions of nineteenth-century blacks as "grotesque buffoons, servile menials, comic entertainers, and threatening sub-humans . . . images that denied the inherent humanity of black people by reinforcing their limited role in American society" (p. xi).

50 E. Leslie Gilliams, "Cigar-Store Indians," *Philadelphia Times*, 18 Dec. 1892, 18.

51 The story is related in Pendergast and Ware, *Cigar Store Figures in American Folk Art*, 57.

52 The editions are listed in Harry T. Peters, *Currier and Ives: Printmakers to the American People* (Garden City, N.Y.: Doran and Co., 1929; reprint, New York: Arno Press, 1976), 229–30.

53 The figure was purchased from Elie Nadelman in 1937. Its existence is documented in a lithograph of Firemen's Hall by Endicott and Company, c. 1860, a copy of which is at the New-York Historical Society. See Tom Armstrong, "The Innocent Eye: American Folk Sculpture," in Tom Armstrong et al., *200 Years of American Sculpture* (New York: Whitney Museum of American Art, 1976), 91–92.

54 Curatorial files, New York Fire Museum, New York City.

55 Curatorial files, Hood Museum of Art, Dartmouth College, Hanover, N.H.

56 Pavel P. Svin'in, *A Picturesque Voyage in North America* (St. Petersburg, Russia: 1815), 150, quoted in Avrahm Yarmolinsky, *Picturesque United States of America: Being a Memoir on Paul Svinin* (New York: William Edwin Ridge, 1930), 34.

57 Robert Bishop, *American Folk Sculpture* (New York: E. P. Dutton, 1974), 117.

58 "The Washington Triumphal Arch," *Harper's Weekly* 33 (4 May 1889): 343, 344.

59 Richard Watson Gilder, "The Washington Memorial Arch," in *The History of the Centennial Celebration of the Inauguration of George Washington as First President of the United States*, ed. Clarence Winthrop Bowen (New York: D. Appleton and Co., 1892), 409.

60 H. Dick, "This Colossal Washington a Puzzle," [New York] *World Magazine*, 20 Feb. 1921, 6.

61 I. N. Phelps Stokes, *Iconography of Manhattan Island* (New York: Robert H. Dodd, 1915–28), 5:1999.

62 The attribution is made by this writer. It should also be noted that the figure has a replaced right arm that is very poorly done and has received numerous coats of paint over the years that further obscure its original carved detail.

63 Dick, "This Colossal Washington a Puzzle," 6; "Lo on His Last Trail," *Tobacco* 10 (10 Apr. 1891): 9; Stokes, *Iconography of Manhattan Island*, 1999.

CHAPTER 5
The End of an Era

1 E. Leslie Gilliams, "Cigar-Store Indians," *Philadelphia Times*, 18 Dec. 1892, 18.

2 Robert W. Rydell, "Rediscovering the 1893 Chicago World's Columbian Exposition," in *Revisiting the White City: American Art at the World's Fair*, Carolyn Kinder Carr et al. (Washington, D.C.: Smithsonian Institution, 1993), 20.

3 See ibid., 38–44, for a discussion of the mixture of ethnological spectacle and commercialism presented by the Midway Plaisance and its contrast to the main area of the Exposition, dubbed the "White City" for the grandiose classicism and color of its principal buildings.

4 Daniel H. Burnham, *Final Official Report of the Director of Works of the World's*

Columbian Exposition (1893; reprint, New York: Garland Press, 1989), 1:94.

5 "A World's Fair Exhibit," *Tobacco* 14 (7 Apr. 1893): 1; "Exhibit of Wm. Demuth & Co.," *Tobacco* 16 (2 Feb. 1894): 1, 3; Frederick Fried, *Artists in Wood: American Carvers of Cigar-Store Indians, Show Figures, and Circus Wagons* (New York: Clarkson Potter, 1970), 61.

6 Rydell, "Columbian Exposition," 20.

7 Carolyn Kinder Carr, "Prejudice and Pride: Presenting American Art at the 1893 World's Columbian Exposition," in *Revisiting the White City*, 78.

8 Ibid., 99–106.

9 Burnham, *Final Official Report*, 4:54; Henry Van Brunt, "Architecture of the World's Columbian Exposition," *Century Magazine* 44 (May 1892): 94, quoted in Neil Harris et al., *Grand Illusions: Chicago World's Fair of 1893* (Chicago: Chicago Historical Society, 1993), 85.

10 Richard Watson Gilder, "The Washington Memorial Arch," in *The History of the Centennial Celebration of the Inauguration of George Washington as First President of the United States*, ed. Clarence Winthrop Bowen (New York: D. Appleton and Co., 1892), 409.

11 William H. Gerdts, "William Rush: Sculptural Genius or Inspired Artisan?" in *William Rush, American Sculptor*, by Linda Bantel et al. (Philadelphia: Pennsylvania Academy of the Fine Arts, 1982), 63–64.

12 Henry Tuckerman, "Art in America: Its History, Condition, and Prospects," *Cosmopolitan Art Journal* 3 (Dec. 1858): 5.

13 Ibid., 7.

14 One of the clearest expositions of this hierarchy appeared in the July 1827 issue of the *United States Review and Literary Gazette*. In a review of the second annual exhibition of the National Academy of Design, the principal types of painting, sculpture, architecture, and engraving were listed in order of importance. The categories for sculpture were:

1. Historical or Fabulous Group, in the round
2. Single statue, in the round
3. Figures in Alto-relievo
4. Figures in Basso-relievo
5. Ornamental Sculpture

While figureheads and shop figures might seem to lay claim to the final category, they were ultimately disqualified by their medium. ("The Exhibition of the National Academy of Design, 1827. The Second. New York," *United States Review and Literary Gazette* 2 [July 1827]: 243–45. See John P. Simoni, "Art Critics and Criticism in Nineteenth-Century America" [Ph.D. diss., Ohio State University, 1952], 29–31.)

15 "Review of the Annual Exhibition," *Port Folio* 8 (Aug. 1812): 145, quoted in Gerdts, "William Rush," 70.

16 William Dunlap, *A History of the Rise and Progress of the Arts and Design in the United States* (1834; reprint, New York: Dover Publications, 1969), 1:160.

17 In a footnote, the author continued: "Some may object that carving in wood, is very different from sculpture in marble. A mere ordinary carver might be unsuccessful in marble, but real talent is wasted in working upon wood. . . . Mr. Willard observed to the writer, that he could execute much better in marble, than in such a course material as wood; just, said he, as a man can write better on white paper than brown." ("For the North-American Journal," *North American Review* 2 [Jan. 1816]: 160–61. See Gerdts, "William Rush," 63.)

18 Elizabeth De Hart Bleeker Diary, 26 Mar. 1799, n.p. New York Public Library, New York.

19 To cite just two examples, the author of the *Portfolio* article quoted in this chapter uses the phrase "naval architecture" to characterize Rush's work, while later in the century, the *New York Times* article written in 1890 by Frank W. Weitenkampf (cited previously) uses both "wood sculptor" and "sign sculptor" to describe the shipcarvers who made shop figures.

20 "Mrs. Barrow as Minehaha," *Ballou's Pictorial* 10 (17 May 1856): 305.

21 Frank W. Weitenkampf, "Lo, the Wooden Indian: The Art of Making Cigar-Shop Signs," *New York Times*, 3 Aug. 1890, 13.

22 "Lo Takes a Spring Suit," *Tobacco* 6 (12 Apr. 1889): 1.

23 Weitenkampf, "Lo, the Wooden Indian," 13; Fried, *Artists in Wood*, 110.

24 Fried, *Artists in Wood*, 195.

25 Will M. Clemens, "The Man Who Carves Ships' Figure-Heads," *Harper's Weekly* 36 (5 Mar. 1892): 235.

26 "Manufacture of Dummy Indians," *Tobacco* 2 (12 Nov. 1886): 2.

27 W. A. Rogers, "In the Year Two Thousand," *Life* 7 (22 Apr. 1886): 233–34.

28 "Must the Indian Go?" *Tobacco* 14 (3 Mar. 1893): 4.

29 "How to Decorate a Cigar Store I," *Tobacco* 4 (13 Apr. 1888); "How to Decorate a Cigar Store II," *Tobacco* 4 (27 Apr. 1888); "How to Decorate a Cigar Store III," *Tobacco* 5 (11 May 1888); "How to Decorate a Cigar Store IV," *Tobacco* 5 (1 June 1888).

30 "High Art at Conklin and Fox's," *Tobacco* 1 (27 Aug. 1886): 3.

31 "Art and Tobacco," *Tobacco* 1 (30 July 1886): 2.

32 "Short Chats with Dealers," *Tobacco* 4 (24 Feb. 1888): 3.

33 "Lo—The Poor Indian," *Tobacco* 4 (8 June 1888): 4–5.

34 "Lo, on His Last Trail," *Tobacco* 10 (10 Apr. 1891): 9.

35 "Modern Advertising," *Tobacco* 17 (27 July 1894): 8.

36 "Lo, on His Last Trail," 9.

37 "Art in Tobacco Shops," *Tobacco* 1 (22 Oct. 1886): 3.

38 "The Angelus," *Tobacco* 9 (16 May 1890): 1.

39 Gilliams, "Cigar-Store Indians," 18.

40 Kate Sanborn, *Hunting Indians in a Taxi-Cab* (Boston: Richard G. Badger, 1911), 54.

41 "The Tobacconist's Sign," *Tobacco* 2 (8 Apr. 1887): 2; Gilliams, "Cigar-Store Indians," 18.

42 Robert J. Casey, "The Man Who Made Wooden Indians," in *Sidewalks of America*, ed. Benjamin A. Bodkin (New York: Bobbs-Merrill Co., 1954), 245; Sanborn, *Hunting Indians in a Taxi-Cab*, 63.

43 J. H. Junkin, "The Wooden Indian Is Passing Away," *Detroit News-Tribune*, 23 July 1899: 17.

44 "Tobacconist's Sign," 2.

45 "Lo, on His Last Trail," 9.

46 Gilliams, "Cigar-Store Indians," 18.

47 "Is the Wooden Indian Passing Away?" *Tobacco* 34 (16 Jan. 1903), 3.

48 John H. Morrison, *History of New York Ship Yards* (New York: William F. Sametz and Co., 1909), 155–56.

49 John L. Morrison, "Poor Lo Still Active," *Scribner's Magazine* 85 (Jan. 1929): 40; Fried, *Artists in Wood*, 193.

50 Fried, *Artists in Wood*, 217–23, 231, 236–7.

51 Ibid., 237. Elizabeth Robb gave this figure to Frederick Fried before she died in 1967. It is now a promised gift to the American Folk Art Museum, New York.

52 Robert G. Denig, "Historic Figureheads," *Cosmopolitan* 14 (Apr. 1893): 690. The article is a useful source of information that has been previously referenced in this discussion.

53 See, for example, Mary H. Northend, "The Garden of Figureheads," *International Studio* 75 (Sept. 1922): 505–8.

54 Hamilton Easter Field's Ogunquit School of Painting and Sculpture and its role in the rediscovery of American folk art among modernist artists and dealers, including Edith Halpert, is frequently mentioned in the literature. See especially Doreen Bolger, "Hamilton Easter Field and His Contribution to Modernism," *American Art Journal* 20, no. 2 (1988): 87–97, and Beatrix Rumford, "Uncommon Art of the Uncommon People: A Review of Trends in the Collecting and Exhibiting of American Folk Art," in *Perspectives on American Folk Art*, ed. Ian M. G. Quimby and Scott T. Swank (New York: W. W. Norton, 1980), 14–15. Bolger gives the date of the founding of the School as 1911, while Rumford states that it was in 1913. See also Elsa Rogo, ed., *Hamilton Easter Field Collection of Painting and Sculpture* (New York: College Art Association, 1930).

55 The best discussion to date of the Nadelmans' museum is Elizabeth Stillinger, "Elie and Viola Nadelmans' Unprecedented Museum of Folk Arts," *Antiques* 146 (October 1994): 516–25. Ms. Stillinger has completed a book, *The Folk Art Idea: Collecting in America, 1876–1976*, which is forthcoming.

56 *American Folk Sculpture* (Newark, N.J.: Newark Museum Association, 1931), 11, 25–38.

57 Diane Tepfer, "Edith Gregor Halpert and the Downtown Gallery Downtown, 1926–1940: A Study in American Art Patronage" (Ph.D. diss., University of Michigan, 1989), 48.

58 Edward Alden Jewel, "'American Ancestors' Show," *New York Times*, 14 Dec. 1931, 17, and "In the Realm of Art: 'Ancestors' and Other Matters," *New York Times*, 20 Dec. 1931, sec. 8, 10. *American Ancestors* was on view at the American Folk Art Gallery from December 9–31, 1931. It was not composed entirely of folk art, as evidenced by the inclusion of Raphaelle Peale's *After the Bath* or *Venus Rising From the Sea*. All in all, the exhibition was quite successful in serving Halpert's purpose of creating a link between nineteenth-century traditions and contemporary modernism. The following excerpt from "In the Realm of Art" is particularly significant because it demonstrates that many more modernist artists were aware of and interested in folk art than those relative few whose work shows a direct influence:

> The current exhibition is composed of material supplied by the Folk Art Gallery, and appears to be a great hit—especially with artists. . . . In the course of the first two days no fewer than 150 artists paid their respects to our American tradition, among them being Charles Sheeler, Stuart Davis, Niles Spencer, William and Marguerite Zorach, Alexander Brook, Glenn Coleman, Arshile Gorky, Judson Smith, Joseph Pollet, Anne Goldthwaite, Bernard Karfoil and Max Weber. As for José Clemente Orozco, his praise seems to have been the most sweeping of all. He is reported to have declared, then and there, that the entire exhibition ought to be turned into a museum.
>
> Favorites are being singled out. So far there are three: the landscape by Joseph Pickett, the "Peaceable Kingdom" by Edward Hicks and Raphaelle Peale's amazing "After the Bath," which has been likened not alone to the old masters but also to Pierre Roy. . . . When Fernand Leger saw the Pickett landscape recently he is quoted as remarking that "Pickett had nothing to learn from Picasso and Braque" and that "The Peaceable Kingdom" . . . was the greatest painting he saw in America.

59 These two figures are among the most celebrated examples of self-taught work. They were offered to Edith Halpert by A. Starnworth of the Boston Antiques Shop in 1933. For a number of years, they were in the Rudolf Haffenreffer Collection in Providence, R.I. Herbert Hemphill acquired them in 1956, and they are now in the Hemphill Collection at the Smithsonian American Art Museum, Washington, D.C. See Lynda Roscoe Hartigan, *Made with Passion: The Hemphill Folk Art Collection in the National Museum of American Art* (Washington, D.C.: Smithsonian Institution Press, 1990), 15–17, 73, 84–85.

60 Two other figures that can be attributed to the same carver on stylistic grounds are in private collections. Due to low survival rates, this is extremely rare for self-taught figures as old as these. Evidently, their talented creator was active for a number of years, and the strength of his work was recognized early on.

61 Again, little is actually known about the history and original purpose of this well-known figure. It was found in an unrecorded town in the Mohawk River Valley and donated to the American Folk Art Museum in New York in1964.

62 A typical example of this is recorded in "I Remember the Old Cigar Store Indian at Pratt and Exeter," *Baltimore Sun Magazine*, 23 Feb. 1969, 2. Its author, Mrs. Grenfall T. Kline, began the article as follows:

> When strangers in the neighborhood would ask the way to this place or that, the youngsters used to tell them to go down the street until they saw a wooden Indian, and then take a left turn or a right turn.
>
> The strangers were sometimes puzzled, but I think anybody who grew up on East Pratt street will recognize the neighborhood right away as that surrounding the corner of Pratt and Exeter streets. For the wooden Indian which stood in front of my two uncles' tobacco store was a well-known South Baltimore landmark.

APPENDIX Carvers' Biographies

Following are biographical sketches of many of the most prominent eighteenth- and nineteenth-century figure carvers in the United States and Canada, primarily those who are mentioned in the text. The list is not intended to be comprehensive. The names of numerous other shipcarvers appear in historical documents and accounts, but since for the most part, little or nothing else is known about them, they have not been included here. Many records have been lost, and much research remains to be done to identify all those who contributed to the tradition.

JACOB S. ANDERSON (1810–1857)
Born in New York, Anderson may have apprenticed with Jeremiah Dodge. He opened his first workshop around 1830 and was a partner with Charles J. Dodge from about 1843 to 1847. In 1850, Anderson's shop was the largest in New York City, with seven employees producing figures worth $6,000, according to the Federal Census. His best-known work is a figure of David Crockett carved for a ship by the same name that was built in Mystic, Connecticut, in 1853 by George Greenman and Company. Jacob died suddenly in 1857.

JOHN W. ANDERSON (1834–1904)
Son of Jacob Anderson, John entered the family workshop around 1848. His father died when he was barely beyond the apprentice stage of his career, and his mother, Jane, managed the business for a few years. In the 1860 Federal Census, she listed herself as "agent, widow of Jacob S.," head of a shop with one employee, presumably John. He was in charge of the workshop by 1870, and was a leading carver in New York through the 1890s. Among his work for ships was the figurehead of Admiral David Farragut for the clipper *The Great Admiral*, built in East Boston in 1868–69. He is also known to have carved cigar-store figures, though no examples survive that can be attributed to him with certainty.

LEMON or **LEAMAN BEADLE** (1680–1717)
Among the first native-born shipcarvers, Beadle primarily worked in Salem, Massachusetts. In 1712, he carved one of the earliest American architectural figures on record, a "handsome wooden soldier" that was placed on top of a new watch house in Salem. He was also probably responsible for several lion figureheads that were carved in Salem in the 1710s and shipped to New York City.

LABAN SMITH BEECHER (1805–1876)
Born in New Haven, Connecticut, Beecher apprenticed in Boston around 1822. By 1826 he had established his own business, and in 1834, he carved a ten-foot figurehead of Andrew Jackson for the USS *Constitution*. In 1839, he was in partnership with John W. Mason, who may have been his former apprentice. Beecher was involved in several other business ventures during his long career, including the purchase of timberland in Wisconsin, where he apparently relocated for a time. In 1870, he was listed in the Boston Directory as the president of the City Mutual Insurance Company.

JOHN HALLEY BELLAMY (1836–1914)
The son of a contractor and boatbuilder, Bellamy was born in Kittery Point, Maine, across the Piscataqua River from Portsmouth, New Hampshire. As a young man, he studied art for a time in New York and Boston and then served a brief apprenticeship with Laban Smith Beecher around 1857. Upon completing his training, he set up shop in Boston and also worked at the Charlestown Navy Yard. Returning to his birthplace, Bellamy continued to work for the government at the Portsmouth Navy Yard. In the late 1860s, he maintained a shop in Portsmouth, but for most of his life, worked out of a second-floor loft near his family home in Kittery Point. During his long career, he created numerous figureheads and other shipcarving, and a wide variety of architectural decoration, furniture and framecarving, and garden figures. He is best known for his distinctive eagle plaques, which range in size from less than twenty inches to over eight feet in length.

WILLIAM BOULTON (active c. 1860–74)
An English sculptor and woodcarver, Boulton was active in New York City. He is primarily known as one of the men for whom Louis Jobin worked during his brief sojourn in New York. Jobin later recalled that Boulton had worked in marble before coming to New York, and that he was a good teacher. Jobin noted that his shop fell into disarray because "the poor man drank like a fish."

JAMES BROOKS (1869–1937)
Son of Thomas V. Brooks, James was one of the last traditional figure carvers to practice the craft. By 1889, he was a partner with his father, listing himself as "sculptor" in the Chicago business directory. He returned to New York City around 1890 to manage the family shop there. After his father died in 1895, Brooks operated out of his home in Brooklyn under the name of the Standard Show Figure Company. He stopped carving in 1902 and began working as a house painter and contractor. He died in Tampa, Florida.

THOMAS V. BROOKS (1828–1895)
Born in New York City, Brooks apprenticed with John L. Cromwell. In 1848 he opened a shop on South Street, and the next year he entered a brief partnership with Thomas Millard, Jr. Around 1855, he began supplying figures to Edward Hen, who distributed and marketed tobacco products nationally. In the late 1850s, after Cromwell turned over much of his business to him, Brooks became the leading figure carver in New York. Brooks was instrumental in the development of the New York show-figure style. He listed two addresses in the 1860 New York business directory, one on South Street and another on Canal Street. From about 1870 to 1872, he was in partnership with Thomas J. White. In 1880 or 1881 he opened a shop in Chicago. For the next fif-

teen years, Brooks maintained workshops in both cities, though he spent most of his time in Chicago.

CHARLES BROWN (1846–1917)
Born in New York, Brown was advertising as a shipcarver in city directories by 1870. In 1872, he formed a partnership with Nicholas Collins that lasted at least six years. He later operated workshops in both the maritime district in Manhattan and across the East River in Brooklyn. In 1908, he shared space with Samuel Anderson Robb. He stopped carving around 1914.

JAMES BROWN (active c. 1883–1902)
A Philadelphia carver, Brown maintained a workshop from about 1883 to 1902. In the late 1880s he advertised in the city directory that he supplied "garden ornaments, steamboat eagles, figures, church ornaments, pompeys, and cigar Indians."

JOHN BROWN (active c. 1789–1804)
The earliest recorded shipcarver in Baltimore, Brown trained with William Rush and so helped transmit Rush's style to that city. Brown is known to have carved figureheads for the sloops of war *Maryland* and *Patapsco*.

EDWARD BUDD (active c. 1668, d. 1710)
In 1689, Budd and another Boston carver named Richard Knight presented a bill for a "Lyon" for the sloop *Speedwell*, which is the earliest-known record of an American figurehead. Testimony given in 1695 indicated that he was one of three shipcarvers working in Boston at the time.

JAMES CAMPBELL (active c. 1854–1900)
Campbell was active in Mystic, Connecticut, by 1854, and was a partner with John Colby from about 1858 to 1877, when their shop closed due to lack of business. In addition to shipcarving, the firm is known to have done architectural figures, ornate fencing, and sign gilding. Campbell apparently moved to New York City after the Mystic shop closed. He was then in San Francisco, before returning to Mystic in 1888.

JOHN COLBY (1833–1891)
Born in Winthrop, Massachusetts, Colby was in Mystic, Connecticut, in 1858, working with James Campbell. They were partners from about 1858 until 1877, when their shop closed due to lack of business. He had moved to New London by 1880, where he continued to do shipcarving, architectural work, and sign painting. He was back in Mystic in 1887, but later returned to Winthrop.

NICHOLAS COLLINS (active c. 1871–90)
Collins operated a shop on South Street in New York City's maritime district in the 1870s and had a number of partners over the years, including Charles Brown from about 1872 to 1878. He may have gone to Chicago with Thomas V. Brooks in 1880 or 1881, but was back in New York later in the decade. In 1890, he was one of five men to be mentioned in the *New York Times* as "prominent figures in the early history of the art [of shop-figure carving]."

JEAN-BAPTISTE CÔTÉ (1834–1907)
Born in Quebec City, Côté spent his entire life there. He probably apprenticed with Louis-Thomas Berlinguet, one of Quebec's leading sculptors and architects. Côté then briefly pursued architecture, but by the mid-1850s was concentrating on shipcarving. Throughout the 1860s, he also created over five hundred woodcut illustrations, which were caricatures for several satirical newspapers. With the decline of shipbuilding in Quebec after 1870, he increasingly focused on shop and garden figures, commemorative sculpture, and religious statuary and reliefs for churches and individual patrons. Among the finest surviving examples of his work is a large statue of Johannes Guttenberg, commissioned by the Society of Printers and Typographers of Quebec for a float for the Saint John the Baptist celebration in 1880.

HARVEY COUNCE (1821–after 1880)
Son of a shipbuilder, Counce spent his entire life in Thomaston, Maine, and has been credited with most of the carving done for ships built there between about 1840 and 1880. He also did a significant amount of architectural carving in the town. He was later recognized by William Southworth as one of the best-known shipcarvers of his generation in Maine.

JOHN L. CROMWELL (1805–1873)
Born and presumably trained in Boston, Cromwell had opened a workshop in New York City's maritime district by 1831. Over the course of the next thirty years, he was one of the city's leading carvers, operating shops in several different locations. He is known to have completed a number of important shipcarving commissions, including a figurehead for the ship *Samoset* built by Fernald and Pettigrew of Portsmouth, New Hampshire, in 1847. Cromwell actively diversified his business as well, and his workshop was central to the development of the New York show-figure style in the 1840s. He was also one of the first shipcarvers to create decorations for circus wagons. In 1850, his shop had five employees producing figures worth $3,000, according to census records. Later in the decade, he turned over most of his business to Thomas V. Brooks.

LEVI L. CUSHING (active c. 1830–75)
The son of a politician, Cushing is known through the advertisements that he placed in Boston city directories in the 1830s and 1840s, and a distinctive trade card, now in the collection of the American Antiquarian Society, that depicts a carver at work and the stern of a ship named the *Michael Angelo*. None of his work has been identified. Later in life, he was active in civic affairs in Cambridge, Massachusetts.

EDWARD CUTBUSH (c. 1735–1790)
A London-trained carver, Cutbush is best known as William Rush's master. Contemporary accounts indicate that he was considered the best shipcarver in Philadelphia in the 1770s.

WILLIAM DEARING (1741–c. 1838)
Born in Kittery, Maine, Dearing was active there and in Portsmouth, New Hampshire, carving for ships and architecture. In 1790, he carved a unique plaque illustrating an episode of the parable of the Good Samaritan. He also worked in Newburyport and Salisbury, Massachusetts, in 1798 and 1799, and probably at other times as well. In 1799, he did much of the secondary carving for the frigate *Congress* in Portsmouth (the figurehead was done by William Rush).

FRANCIS or **FRITZ DECKER**
(active c.1880–95)
This Austrian-born cabinetmaker is known to have created shop figures in Philadelphia in the 1880s and 1890s. His work was quite distinctive in that it was made of small blocks of wood that were glued together and carved, a technique that was fairly common among European cabinetmakers but rare in the United States.

CHARLES J. DODGE (1806–1886)
Son of Jeremiah Dodge, Charles was born

in New York City and entered the family workshop around 1820. He was a partner with his father from 1828 to 1839 and then was a partner with Jacob Anderson from about 1843 to 1847. In 1850, his workshop employed four men, with an output valued at $3,250, making it one of the largest in the city. His finest surviving work is a bust of his father, carved around 1835. He was also active in politics and civic affairs, serving as a school trustee and commissioner, an alderman, and colonel of the tenth regiment of the militia. He finally gave up carving around 1870.

JEREMIAH DODGE (1781–1860)
The son of a shipwright, he probably apprenticed in New York City with Simeon Skillin III. They were partners from about 1804 to 1811. Jeremiah then formed a partnership with Cornelius N. Sharpe from 1815 to 1828. Their best-known work is a bust of *Hercules* carved in 1820 for the USS *Ohio*. From 1828 to 1839, Jeremiah was in partnership with his son, Charles. He retired from the carving business in the early 1840s and assumed duties at the Customs House.

STEPHEN DWIGHT (active c. 1755–75)
After apprenticing with Henry Hardcastle, Dwight opened a shop in New York City in the mid-1750s. In 1762, he advertised that he "carves all sorts of ship and house work; also tables, chairs, picture and looking glass frames, and all kinds of work for cabinet-makers." He also did portraits and history painting and gave instruction in drawing.

ISAAC HOWARD FOWLE (1783–after 1854)
Fowle apprenticed in the Skillin workshop in Boston, and was directly related to the family. His father, Henry, married one of John and Simeon Skillin, Jr.'s sisters, while John Skillin himself first married Anne Fowle, and after her death, Mary Fowle (both possibly Henry's sisters). In 1806, Fowle and another former Skillin apprentice named Edmund Raymond took over the Skillin family shop. Fowle was in business by himself after 1813. Several surviving figureheads are attributed to him, but only one, *Lady with a Scarf*, done about 1820, is documented. Around 1833, his sons, John D. and William H., became his partners.

JOHN D. FOWLE (1809–1891) and
WILLIAM H. FOWLE (1813–1862)
Sons of Isaac Howard Fowle, John and William joined their father's workshop around 1833, along with another carver named Spencer Beatty. Their best-known work is a figurehead of Andrew Jackson done for the USS *Constitution* in 1846. The shop retained the name Isaac Fowle and Company until 1853, when it was changed to J. D. and W. H. Fowle. John retired in 1869, seven years after his brother's death.

WOODBURY GERRISH (active c. 1850–75)
Probably trained in Boston, Gerrish worked at the Charlestown Navy Yard for a time. He then settled in Portsmouth, New Hampshire, where he maintained a shop and continued to work for the U.S. Navy until the mid-1870s. He is best known for creating a bust of the namesake of the USS *Franklin* in 1853.

HERBERT GLEASON (active c. 1863, d. 1893)
A Boston carver, Gleason was a partner with Samuel McIntyre (1832–1920) from about 1863 to 1872. Gleason continued to operate a workshop on Commercial Street after McIntyre left and then, in 1878, entered a partnership with E. Warren Hastings, forging an association that lasted until his death in 1893. His relationship to S. W. Gleason and Sons has not been established, but it seems likely that he had family ties of some sort. Gleason is best known for his figurehead for Donald McKay's *Glory of the Seas*.

SAMUEL W. GLEASON
(b. 1800, active ending c. 1854)
Gleason was the founder of S. W. Gleason and Sons, which by the late 1840s was one of the most prominent shipcarving workshops in Boston. In 1850, the shop had five employees, including his sons Samuel W., Jr., and William B. The Gleasons worked for many leading shipbuilders in Boston and elsewhere in New England, including Fernald and Pettigrew of Portsmouth, New Hampshire. Their best-known work is a monumental eagle's head done for Donald McKay's ill-fated ship, the *Great Republic*.

SAMUEL W. GLEASON, JR.
(active c. 1847–65)
The son of Samuel W. Gleason was a partner in the family shop in Boston in the 1850s and 1860s.

WILLIAM B. GLEASON
(active c. 1847, d. 1886)
Another son of Samuel W. Gleason, William entered the family workshop in 1847 and was soon recognized as the firm's most talented carver. In 1854, he took charge of the family shop. He also did furniture carving and, in 1868, received a patent for a process for making molded wooden ornaments. By 1870, he was primarily in the furniture business, operating as William B. Gleason and Company. He later developed a method for stamping ornamental designs on wood. His obituary described him as " a leading ship carver and gilder of Boston . . . [and] inventor of the pressed ornaments commonly used on furniture."

EDWARD SOUTHER GRIFFIN (1834–1928)
Born in Portland, Maine, Griffin apprenticed with his father, John, a woodcarver and cabinetmaker. He then worked for a few years in New Haven, Connecticut, and in Boston. Returning to Portland, he opened a workshop in 1851 and concentrated on shipcarving, becoming the best-known figure carver of his generation in the city. He finally closed his shop around 1890 and spent his later years painting landscapes.

HENRY HARDCASTLE (active c. 1755)
Known through newspaper advertisements and notices, Hardcastle operated an active workshop in New York City in the mid-eighteenth century, at a time when there were few shipcarvers there. No examples of his work have been identified, but he almost certainly did architectural and furniture carving as well as ship work.

E. WARREN HASTINGS
(active c. 1854, d. 1896)
A partner in the Boston shipcarving firm of Chapman and Hastings from 1854 to 1860, Hastings operated his own workshop at various locations on Commercial Street through most of the 1860s and 1870s. In 1869, he carved a wooden model for an Angel Gabriel weathervane and a courthouse figure for Cushing and White of Waltham, Massachusetts. Hastings entered a partnership with Herbert Gleason in 1878, which lasted until 1893. A number of his designs for figureheads and sterns are in the collection of the Peabody Essex Museum in Salem, Massachusetts.

EDBURY HATCH (1849–1935)
Born in Newcastle, Maine, Hatch apprenticed with William Southworth in Newcastle for four years beginning in 1865 or 1866. Throughout the 1870s, he found occasional employment in Charles A. L. Sampson's workshop in Bath, where he helped carve

two of Sampson's most famous figureheads, the *Belle of Oregon* and the *Belle of Bath*. Due to a lack of work, Hatch gave up shipcarving in the early 1880s and took a job as a night watchman in a hotel in Boston. Returning to the family home in Newcastle twenty years later, he continued to carve ship models, picture frames, furniture, and architectural ornaments for himself and his friends and neighbors.

LOUIS JOBIN (1845–1928)
Born in St.-Raymond, Quebec, Jobin apprenticed with François-Xavier Berlinguet, one of Quebec City's leading sculptors and architects. In 1868, he went to New York City, where he worked for William Boulton. He was then employed by some German carvers, one of whom may have been Simon Strauss. Returning to Canada in 1870, Jobin settled in Montreal and opened a workshop, where he did ship and shop-figure carving, as well as religious statuary, altars, and architectural work. After five years in Montreal, he relocated to Quebec City. With the demise of shipbuilding in Quebec in the mid-1880s, he increasingly devoted himself to religious figures. In 1896, he moved to Ste-Anne-de-Beaupré, a small pilgrimage town twenty miles from Quebec on the St. Lawrence River. There he primarily fashioned saints and votive carvings until his death in 1928. Over the course of his sixty-year career, Jobin carved approximately one thousand figures. Among them was a monumental ex-voto, *Our Lady of the Saguenay*, twenty-five feet tall, which was installed at Cape Trinity on the Saguenay River in 1881.

SAMUEL KING (1749–1820)
A nautical instrument maker and a painter of portraits and miniatures in Newport, Rhode Island, King is best known as Washington Allston's first teacher, and may have given lessons to a young Gilbert Stuart. He has also been credited with carving the *Little Navigator*, which served as a shop sign for James Fales in Newport and later for his son, James, Jr., in New Bedford, Massachusetts.

ISAAC LEWIN (LEWIS)
(active c. 1871–1900)
Lewin probably accompanied Thomas V. Brooks when the latter moved from New York to Chicago around 1880. Lewin was a mainstay of Brooks's Chicago workshop in the 1880s and bought the business when Brooks died in 1895. By that time Lewin had changed his name to Lewis.

JOHN W. MASON (1814–1866)
Born in Ireland, Mason spent a few years in Canada in his infancy, but returned to his native country upon the death of his parents. As a young man, he settled in Boston, where his older brother had a printing business. He may have apprenticed with Laban Smith Beecher, for the two were partners for a brief period around 1839. By the early 1840s, Mason had a shop on Commercial Street, where for the next ten years or so he received many commissions from leading shipbuilders in Boston; Newburyport, Massachusetts; Portsmouth, New Hampshire; and other parts of New England. In 1853, a Boston journalist praised him as "our greatest marine artist." While none of his work has been identified, several accomplished drawings survive in the collection of the Peabody Essex Museum in Salem, Massachusetts. He appears to have been a poor businessman, though, which led to serious family problems and a premature end to his career in the mid-1850s.

SAMUEL MCINTIRE (1757–1811)
Born and raised in Salem, Massachusetts, McIntire is best known as the town's leading architect and architectural carver of his generation, responsible for many of its finest homes. The son of a house carpenter, he was also a furniture carver whose Neoclassical designs were much sought after. He was a shipcarver as well, but in this he apparently did not match some of his contemporaries. In 1802, the Reverend William Bentley of Salem noted in his diary: "As a Carver we place McIntire with Skillings of Boston. In some works he succeeded well. He cuts smoother than Skillings but he has not his genius. In Architecture he excells any person in our country."

JULIUS MELCHERS (1829–1909)
Born in Soest, Prussia, Melchers apprenticed with a sculptor and master woodcarver named Minstermann, who taught him to be a carver of architectural, religious, and commemorative sculpture in wood and stone. As a young man with revolutionary sympathies, Melchers was forced to flee Prussia during the Revolution of 1848. He first went to Paris, where he is said to have studied for a time with two leading sculptors, Jean Baptiste Carpeaux and Antoine Etex. In 1851, Melchers went to England and modeled decorations for the Crystal Palace. A year later, he sailed for New York City, finally settling in Detroit in 1855. He opened a workshop that for almost forty years produced a wide range of architectural sculpture, church carvings, patterns for decorative castings, maritime work, and shop figures. He also gave classes in drawing and modeling for many years and became well known in the community. One of his most important architectural projects was Detroit City Hall, for which he carved four monumental allegorical figures in 1871 and four statues of early French explorers a decade later. Among his cigar-store figures, one of the Sauk chief Keokuk is an outstanding example.

THOMAS MILLARD, JR. (1803–1870)
Born in Connecticut, Millard was the son of a shipcarver from Philadelphia. It has been suggested that he apprenticed with William Rush, but this remains speculative, because several members of the Millard family worked as shipcarvers in Philadelphia and it is not clear which of them was Rush's student. More likely, Millard apprenticed with his father. In 1827, Millard opened a shop on Cherry Street in New York City. He was a partner of Thomas V. Brooks in 1849 and 1850. In the early 1850s, he began producing shop figures for James Chichester, a tobacco-products supplier. Millard evidently played an important role in the development of the New York show-figure style in the 1840s and 1850s, although the exact nature of his contribution is unknown. In 1855, he moved to Brooklyn and worked for other carvers instead of maintaining his own shop.

ROBERT MULLARD (active c. 1708–22)
The earliest recorded shipcarver in Philadelphia, Mullard worked on the *Hope Galley* in 1708.

DAVID R. PROCTOR (active c. 1856–66)
Active in Gloucester, Massachusetts, and Belfast, Maine, from about 1856 to 1866, Proctor is best known for a distinctive cigar-store figure used by Mancell's Cigar Store in Gloucester that has been attributed to him. None of his other work has been identified.

CHARLES ROBB (1855–1904)
Brother of Samuel Anderson Robb, Charles worked in the Robb workshops on Canal and Centre Streets in New York City from about 1880 to 1903, doing some carving and painting as well as handling business affairs. He was listed on the firm's trade card for several years.

CLARENCE ROBB (1878–1956)
Son of Samuel Anderson Robb, Clarence worked in the Robb shop on Centre Street in New York City for several years in the 1890s. He also helped his father with his last major project, carving decorations for circus wagons for Barnum and Bailey at the Sebastian Wagon Company in 1902.

SAMUEL ANDERSON ROBB (1851–1928)
Son of Peter Robb, a Scottish shipwright who immigrated to the United States in the 1840s, Samuel was related to Jacob Anderson through his mother, Elizabeth. Robb was probably apprenticed to Thomas V. Brooks in 1864. He then began carving figures for William Demuth, a tobacco-products distributor. At the same time, Robb undertook some formal instruction in the fine arts. He received a certificate in perspective drawing from the Free Night School of Science and Art at the Cooper Union in 1872, and studied at the National Academy of Design, where he was enrolled in the antique class from 1867 to 1875 and the life class from 1869 to 1875. In 1876, he opened his first shop at 195 Canal Street in New York City. He continued to supply figures to Demuth, but also developed a successful business of his own, operating the largest figure-carving workshop in New York City in the 1880s and 1890s. In 1888, he moved his shop to 114 Centre Street, where he remained until 1903. After that, he operated on a smaller scale at several different locations for the next fifteen years, including sharing space with Charles Brown in Brooklyn in 1908, and finally setting up a small workroom in his home in 1910. In addition to creating countless shop and cigar-store figures, Robb's workshop was engaged in many other figure-carving projects. He was also interviewed several times by journalists. His last major undertaking was carving decorations for thirteen circus wagons for Barnum and Bailey at the Sebastian Wagon Company in 1902.

GEORGE ROBINSON, SR.
(active c. 1681, d. 1737)
Robinson was one of the earliest recorded shipcarvers in Boston. Testimony given in 1695 named him as one of three shipcarvers working there at the time. He had a large estate at his death, indicating that he was one of the most prosperous and prominent carvers of his day.

JOHN ROGERSON (1837–1925)
Born in Scotland, Rogerson traveled to Boston with his mother and brothers when he was twelve years old. His father, who was already there, died soon after their arrival, and the family relocated to St. John in New Brunswick, Canada, where his mother had relatives. John first worked with an uncle, a carver named Edward Charters, for over eight years. He then went to Boston and apprenticed with John D. Fowle for two years. Returning home, he opened a workshop in St. John and created many figureheads as well as decorative carving for ships, architecture, and furniture. One of his best-known works is a figurehead for the *Edmonton*, which was built near Quebec in 1882. He closed the shop in 1887, when a lack of work forced him to take a position at the local customs house. He continued to create portrait busts and do some architectural and furniture carving until he was in his eighties.

ARNOLD RUEF (active c. 1870–90)
Working in Tiffin, Ohio, Ruef carved a distinctive cigar-store Indian around 1880 with the help of his son, Peter. Nicknamed "Seneca John" and "The Tiffin Tecumseh," it stood in front of John Dehmer's cigar store for many years.

WILLIAM H. RUMNEY (1837–1927)
Born, raised, and presumably trained in East Boston, Rumney was a partner with Thomas J. White from 1856 to around 1866. He continued to carve until late in the century and also operated a picture and frame business for a time, along with several other unrelated pursuits, including working as an agent for a mattress company. In the 1910s, he was a carpenter for the public grounds department in Dorchester, Massachusetts. His best-known work is an over-lifesize statue of Andrew Jackson, carved around 1860 for Daniel Kelly, a prominent East Boston shipbuilder.

JOHN RUSH (1782–1853)
Son of William Rush, John apprenticed with his father and worked with him until his retirement. In 1819, William called him an "equal partner," but the actual extent of John's involvement with his father's work is unclear. John's best-known figure is *Goddess of Liberty*, done for the Berks County Courthouse in Reading, Pennsylvania, around 1840.

WILLIAM RUSH (1756–1833)
Son of a Philadelphia ship carpenter, Rush was apprenticed around 1771 to Edward Cutbush. Upon Rush's return from Revolutionary War service, he opened a shipcarving workshop that he operated for nearly fifty years. Among his major commissions was the design of figureheads for six frigates for the new United States Navy in 1795. Overall, he was the most innovative and influential American shipcarver of his day. He is credited with introducing the French style of full-length, freestanding figureheads into the American carvers' repertoire in the early 1780s, which became the standard in the nineteenth century. A figure of Peace is a well-known example. Rush also carved shop and cigar-store figures, including a Mercury for John Foble's Tobacco Store in Cambridge, Maryland, around 1830. In addition, he created many architectural figures for buildings in Philadelphia and one fountain, his famous *Allegory of the Schuylkill River* or *Water Nymph and Bittern* in 1809. Around 1810, he began modeling in clay, completing busts of many prominent citizens. He was a founding member of the Columbianum in 1795, one of the earliest art academies in the United States. He was also a founder of the Pennsylvania Academy of the Fine Arts in Philadelphia in 1805, and was active in civic affairs, serving on the Common Council and Watering Committee (waterworks) for many years.

SAMUEL SAILOR (active c. 1858–85)
A Philadelphia carver who operated several shops, Sailor is best known for a lifesize representation of a ship's officer holding a sextant that served as a sign for Riggs and Brother's nautical instrument and watch shop for nearly one hundred years.

CHARLES A. L. SAMPSON (1825–1881)
Born in Boston, Sampson was in Bath, Maine, by 1848, where he apprenticed for four years with a carver named E. B. McLain. He opened his own business around 1852 and a year later was working out of his master's former shop. After serving as a captain and then lieutenant colonel in the Civil War, he returned to Bath and was thereafter known as "Colonel Sampson." Among his best-known figureheads are the *Belle of Oregon* and the *Western Belle* of 1876, and the *Belle of Bath* of 1877. He remained a leading carver in Bath until his death in 1881.

CORNELIUS N. SHARPE
(active c. 1810, d. 1828)
A New York City shipcarver, Sharpe was a

partner of Jeremiah Dodge from about 1815 until his death in 1828. He is best known for his work on the figurehead of Hercules for the USS *Ohio*, done in 1820.

WILLIAM SHUTE (active c. 1693, d. 1743)
Shute was one of the earliest recorded Boston shipcarvers. Testimony given in 1695 indicated that he was one of three carvers working there at the time. He may have apprenticed with Edward Budd. He married Budd's daughter in 1690.

JOHN SKILLIN (1745–1800)
Son of Simeon Skillin, Sr., John apprenticed in the family workshop and remained with his father until Simeon's death in 1778. He and his brother, Simeon, Jr., then assumed control. By the early 1780s, John was the most prominent carver in Boston. He led the Boston carvers in the Federal Procession to celebrate the ratification of the Constitution in 1788 and in the entry procession of George Washington the following year. In 1796, William Rush recommended that he carve the figurehead for the USS *Constitution*, one of six frigates being built by the new U.S. Navy. He was the only carver to be so named. Along with Simeon, Jr., he worked for New England's most prominent shipbuilders, architects, and merchants, including Elias Hasket Derby and Charles Bulfinch. In all, though, only seven surviving figures can be fully documented to the Skillin workshop. John died suddenly in 1800. He was eulogized as "for many years the most eminent man in his profession."

SAMUEL SKILLIN, SR. (1742–1793)
Son of Simeon Skillin, Sr., Samuel moved to Philadelphia soon after he completed his apprenticeship in his father's shop. He worked there from the mid-1760s until about 1778, when he returned to Boston. Apparently, he was not very successful in Philadelphia, but he did operate his own carving shop in Boston.

SAMUEL SKILLIN II
(b. 1770, active ending 1816)
Samuel was the son of Richard Skillin, a blockmaker, and brother of Samuel, John, and Simeon, Jr. Born and raised in Boston, he no doubt apprenticed with his uncles. He was active as a carver and headbuilder—that is, a craftsman who specialized in mounting figureheads on ships—until at least 1816, but nothing is known of his later years.

SIMEON SKILLIN, SR. (1716–1778)
The son of a shipwright, Simeon was born in Portsmouth, New Hampshire. As a young man, he went to Boston with his father and may have apprenticed with William Shute. He established the family workshop some time after he completed his training in 1737. He was one of the most active shipcarvers in the city, though none of his work survives. In 1766, he created a bust of William Pitt for the Pillar of Liberty in Dedham, Massachusetts, which is the earliest recorded public monument done by a native-born sculptor.

SIMEON SKILLIN, JR. (1756–1806)
Son of Simeon Skillin, Sr., Simeon, Jr., served his apprenticeship in the family workshop, which he had completed by the time of his father's death in 1778. He and his brother, John, then assumed control. In addition to carving, he handled most of the business affairs for the shop. He was also involved in several real estate transactions for his family and that of his wife. From the 1780s until his death, the workshop received major commissions from the U.S. Navy, as well as from New England's most prominent shipbuilders, architects, and merchants, including Elias Hasket Derby and Charles Bulfinch. He remained a respected member of his community and died with relatively significant property holdings.

SIMEON SKILLIN III (1766–1830)
Son of Samuel Skillin, Sr., Simeon was born in Philadelphia, but returned to Boston with his father and received his training in the family workshop. He was in New York City by 1789. He was in partnership with Jeremiah Dodge from about 1804 until 1811 and then worked with two other New York carvers, James Heron and Stephen Cornell. He and his partners carved figureheads for both oceangoing vessels and those built on the Great Lakes, as far away as Detroit. In 1822, he gave up shipcarving and went into the crockery business.

WILLIAM SOUTHWORTH (1826–1909)
Born in Duxbury, Massachusetts, Southworth apprenticed with Edward Souther Griffin in Portland, Maine, and then worked in Newcastle before settling in Bath. When Charles A. L. Sampson died in 1881, Southworth bought his business and became one of the leading carvers there. Shortly before his death, he estimated that he had done carvings for more than five hundred vessels.

SIMON STRAUSS (active c. 1866, d. 1897)
Born and no doubt trained in Bavaria, Strauss had established his own carving shop in New York City by 1871, when he advertised that he was a "Carver of Figures for Segar Stores." He also did shipcarving and was one of the few German-born figure carvers who succeeded in a market dominated by Anglo-Americans. By the late 1870s, he was also manufacturing cigar boxes, which probably proved to be more profitable than figure carving. Louis Jobin may have worked for him in 1870. No figures from Strauss's carving shop have been identified.

DANIEL N. TRAIN (active c. 1799–1812)
An apprentice of William Rush, Train was in New York City by 1799, when he carved a figurehead for the frigate *President* and advertised in the *New York Gazette and Commercial Advertiser* that he had a shop on Cherry Street. He soon established himself as a leading carver in New York, along with Simeon Skillin III. Train received several important commissions in the first decade of the 1800s, including one in 1807 for a new figurehead and most of the repairs for the USS *Constitution*, which had been damaged while in service in the Mediterranean.

GEORGE WARBURTON (active c. 1729)
The earliest recorded shipcarver in New York City, Warburton was operating a workshop by 1729, at a time when most American carving was being done in the Boston area.

JOHN WELCH (1711–1789)
A leading Boston shipcarver in the mid-eighteenth century, Welch probably apprenticed with George Robinson, Jr. He married Robinson's granddaughter in 1734. In 1745, he submitted a bill in court for figures carved during the preceding nine years, which included nine lion's heads, two Neptunes, two seahorses, and four double-headed seahorses. In addition to ship work, he also did carving for architecture, furniture, and picture frames. He is best known for his *Sacred Codfish*, commissioned for the Hall of Representatives in Boston in 1736 "as a memorial of the importance of the Cod Fishery." Later in the century, he conducted a successful business importing looking glasses.

THOMAS J. WHITE (1825–1902)
Born in New York City, White probably apprenticed with John L. Cromwell. After completing his training around 1847, he apparently worked as a journeyman carver in the maritime district. Following the economic depression of 1855, he moved to Boston, where he worked with William H. Rumney. White returned to New York around 1866 and by 1870 had entered a brief partnership with Thomas V. Brooks. He then went to work for William Demuth. When Samuel Anderson Robb opened his Canal Street shop in 1876, White joined him, beginning a relationship that lasted for more than twenty years. White also worked for others during that time, including a period in the mid-1890s when he was probably employed by Charles Dare's New York Carousel Company.

SOLOMON WILLARD (1783–1861)
Arriving in Boston in 1804, Willard first worked as a carpenter. Five years later, he was carving architectural elements, and by 1813, he was working as a shipcarver. His most important surviving figurehead is a bust of George Washington for the ship *Washington*, built in Portsmouth, New Hampshire, in 1815–16. About this time, he also began creating architectural models for Charles Bulfinch and others. In 1825, he was elected architect and superintendent of the Bunker Hill Monument, a post that he held for almost twenty years. He was a founder of the Boston Mechanics' Institute and Lyceum in 1826. Later in life, he was a stone contractor and architect.

JOSEPH WILSON (1779–1857)
Born in Marblehead, Massachusetts, Wilson was in Newburyport by 1798, where he did ship and architectural carving for over fifty years. His best-known work was done for "Lord" Timothy Dexter, a self-styled aristocrat who erected on his property nearly forty painted figures of famous individuals and biblical characters mounted on fifteen-foot pedestals and ornate arches. The figures are said to have remained in place until 1815, when a hurricane toppled them and they were dispersed at auction. Wilson's figure of William Pitt survives.

JOHN PHILIP YAEGER (1823–1899)
Born in Germany, Yaeger settled in Baltimore in 1847. When he arrived, he was studying for the priesthood. Within a year, though, he was working full-time as a carver and decorator. The nature of his training is not known, but before long he was operating one of the most successful workshops in the city. In 1853, he advertised in the Baltimore Directory as a "plain, ornamental, and fancy carver" specializing in "architectural and ship work" and "moulds for castings and sculpture." He also carved altars and interiors for local churches. His most distinctive cigar-store figure is a nearly lifesize representation of a girl or woman modeled after his eighth child, Eva Isabelle.

BIBLIOGRAPHY

MANUSCRIPTS

Elizabeth De Hart Bleeker Diary. New York Public Library, New York.

Carvers Files, Elias Hasket Derby Papers, Fernald and Pettigrew Papers, and Joseph True Account Book. Peabody Essex Museum, Salem, Mass.

Connaroe Collection and Joshua Humphreys Papers. Historical Society of Pennsylvania, Philadelphia.

Dr. William Rush Denton, Jr., Scrapbook. Philadelphia Museum of Art.

Figureheads of Ships: A Compilation of Notes, Addresses, Photostats of Articles, Newspaper Clippings and Illustrations. Mariners' Museum, Newport News, Va.

The Frederick and Mary Fried Folk Arts Archives. National Museum of American History, Smithsonian Institution, Washington, D.C.

George Greenman and Company. Papers. Mystic Seaport Museum, Mystic, Conn.

Edbury Hatch Papers. Skidompha Public Library, Damariscotta, Maine.

Products of Industry Schedules, Manhattan, U.S. Census. New York State Library, Albany, N.Y.

School Register. National Academy of Design, New York.

Simeon Skillin III Receipt Books. Society for the Preservation of New England Antiquities, Boston.

DISSERTATIONS AND THESES

Béland, Mario. "Louis Jobin (1845–1928) et la marché de la sculpture au Québec." Ph.D. diss. Université Laval, Quebec, Canada, 1991.

Belisle, Jean. "La sculpture navale dans la vallée du Saint-Laurent du XVII au XIX siècle." Ph.D. diss. École Practique des Haute Etudes, Paris, 1982.

Lahvis, Sylvia L. "The Skillin Workshop: The Emblematic Image in Federal Boston." Ph.D. diss. University of Delaware, 1990.

McDaniel, Joyce L. "The Collected Works of Caspar Buberl: An Analysis of a Nineteenth-Century American Sculptor." Master's thesis. Wellesley College, 1976.

Simoni, John P. "Art Critics and Criticism in Nineteenth-Century America." Ph.D. diss. Ohio State University, 1952.

Smart, Jermayne. "The Folk Art of the Western Reserve." Ph.D. diss. Western Reserve University, 1939.

Tepfer, Diane. "Edith Gregor Halpert and the Downtown Gallery Downtown, 1926–1940: A Study in American Art Patronage." Ph.D. diss. University of Michigan, 1989.

BOOKS AND CATALOGUES

Abrams, Ann Uhry. *The Valiant Hero: Benjamin West and Grand-Style History Painting.* Washington, D.C.: Smithsonian Institution Press, 1985.

Ahrens, Hermann. *Neptuns hölzerne Engel: Schone alte Galionsfiguren.* Hamburg: H. Dulk, 1958.

Albion, Robert G. *The Rise of New York Port.* New York: Scribner's Sons, 1939.

American Folk Sculpture. Newark, N.J.: Newark Museum Association, 1931.

An American Sampler: Folk Art from the Shelburne Museum. Washington, D.C.: National Gallery of Art, 1987.

Apperson, G. L. *The Social History of Smoking.* New York: G. P. Putnam's Sons, 1916.

Armstrong, Tom, et al. *200 Years of American Sculpture.* New York: Whitney Museum of American Art, 1976.

Auquier, Philippe. *Pierre Puget: Décorateur naval et mariniste.* Paris: D. A. Longuet, 1909.

Baker, William Avery. *A Maritime History of Bath and the Kennebec River Region,* 2 vols. Bath, Maine: Marine Research Society of Bath, 1973.

Bantel, Linda, et al. *William Rush: American Sculptor.* Philadelphia: Pennsylvania Academy of the Fine Arts, 1982.

Barbeau, Charles Marius. *Côté, the Wood Carver.* Toronto: Reyerson Press, 1943.

———. *Louis Jobin, Statuaire.* Montreal: Librarie Beauchemin, 1943.

Barker, J. N. *The Indian Princess; or, La Belle Sauvage: An Operatic Melo-Drame.* Philadelphia: Palmer, 1808.

Béland, Mario. *Louis Jobin: Master-Sculptor.* Quebec: Musée du Québec, 1986.

———. *Jean-Baptise Côté: Caricaturiste et sculpteur.* Quebec: Musée du Québec, 1996.

Béland, Mario, et al. *Restauration en sculpture ancienne.* Quebec: Musée du Québec, 1994.

Bénézit, E. *Dictionnaire des peintres, sculpteurs, dessinateurs, et graveurs.* Paris: Librarie Gründ, 1976.

Bergeron, David M. *English Civic Pageantry, 1558–1642.* London: Edward Arnold, 1971.

Berkhofer, Robert. *The White Man's Indian.* New York: Alfred A. Knopf, 1978.

Bishop, Robert F. *American Folk Sculpture.* New York: E. P. Dutton, 1974.

Boime, Albert. *The Art of Exclusion: Representing Blacks in the Nineteenth Century.* Washington, D.C.: Smithsonian Institution Press, 1990.

Bolton, Theodore, and Irwin F. Cortelyou. *Ezra Ames of Albany: Portrait Painter.* New York: New-York Historical Society, 1955.

Brathwait, Richard. *The Smoaking Age, or The Life and Death of Tobacco.* London: E. Griffin, 1617.

Brewington, Marion V. *Shipcarvers of North America.* Barre, Mass.: Barre Publishing Co., 1962. Reprint, New York: Dover Publications, 1972.

Bridenbaugh, Carl. *The Colonial Craftsman.* Chicago: University of Chicago Press, 1950.

Brooks, Jerome E. *Tobacco: Its History Illustrated by the Books, Manuscripts and Engravings in the Library of George Arents, Jr.* 5 vols. New York: Rosenbach Co., 1937–52.

Brown, Henry Collins. *Valentine's Manual of Old New York, 1927.* New York: Valentine's Manual, 1927.

Bucher, Bernadette. *Icon and Conquest: A Structuralist Analysis of the Illustrations of de Bry's "Great Voyages."* Chicago: University of Chicago Press, 1981.

Burnham, Daniel H. *Final Official Report of the Director of Works of the World's Columbian Exposition.* 1893. Reprint, New York: Garland Press, 1989.

Cabot, Harriet. *Handbook of the Bostonian Society.* Boston: Bostonian Society, 1979.

Campbell, Orson. *Treatise on Carriage, Sign and Ornamental Painting.* New York: J. Bailey's, 1841.

Carr, Carolyn Kinder, et al. *Revisiting the White City: American Art at the World's Fair.* Washington, D.C.: Smithsonian Institution Press, 1993.

Casey, Robert J. "The Man Who Made Wooden Indians." In *Sidewalks of America*, ed. Benjamin A. Bodkin. New York: Bobbs-Merrill Co., 1954.

Chapelle, Howard Irving. *The History of American Sailing Ships.* New York: W. W. Norton, 1935.

Chapin, Howard M. *Early American Signboards.* Providence: Rhode Island Historical Society, 1926.

Chateaubriand, François-René de. *Atala, ou les amours de deux savages dans le désert.* Paris, 1801.

Chiappelli, Fredi, ed. *First Images of America*, 2 vols. Berkeley and Los Angeles: University of California Press, 1976.

Chotner, Deborah, et al. *American Naïve Paintings.* Washington, D.C.: National Gallery of Art, 1992.

Christensen, Erwin O. *The Index of American Design.* New York: Macmillan, 1950.

———. *Early American Wood Carving.* Cleveland: World Publishing Co., 1952. Reprint, New York: Dover Publications, 1972.

Clark, Arthur Hamilton. *The Clipper Ship Era.* New York: Putnam's Sons, 1910.

Clark, Harry Hayden, ed. *Poems of Freneau.* New York: Hafner Publishing Co., 1960.

Colbert, Charles. *A Measure of Perfection: Phrenology and the Fine Arts in America.* Chapel Hill: University of North Carolina Press, 1997.

Cordingly, David. *The Art of the van de Veldes.* Greenwich, U.K.: National Maritime Museum, 1982.

Costa, Giancarlo. *Figureheads: Carvings on Ships from Ancient Times to the Twentieth Century.* Lymington, U.K.: Nautical Publishing Co., 1981.

Cousins, Frank. *The Wood-Carver of Salem: Samuel McIntire.* Boston: Little Brown, 1916.

Cowling, Mary. *The Artist as Anthropologist: The Representation of Type and Character in Victorian Art.* New York: Cambridge University Press, 1989.

Craven, Wayne. *Sculpture in America.* Cranbury, N.J.: Cornwall Books, 1984.

Curtis, Lewis P. *Apes and Angels: The Irishman in Victorian Caricature.* Washington, D.C.: Smithsonian Institution Press, 1971.

Deák, Gloria Gilda. *Picturing America, 1497–1899.* 2 vols. Princeton, N.J.: Princeton University Press, 1988.

De Bry, Theodor. *The Great Voyages.* 13 vols. Frankfurt, 1590–1634.

A Descriptive Catalogue of the Marine Collections to Be Found at India House. New York: India House, 1935; second ed., Middletown, Conn.: Wesleyan University Press, 1973.

Dickens, Charles. *Dealings with the Firm of Dombey and Son.* 1846–48. Reprint, New York: Oxford University Press, 1987.

———. *Little Dorrit.* 1857. Reprint, New York: Oxford University Press: 1953.

Dunlap, William. *A History of the Rise and Progress of the Arts and Design in the United States.* Vol. 1. 1834. Reprint, New York: Dover Publications, 1969.

Endell, Fritz A. G. *Old Tavern Signs: An Excursion in the History of Hospitality.* Boston: Houghton Mifflin, 1916.

Fahlman, Betsy. *Pennsylvania Modern: Charles Demuth in Lancaster.* Philadelphia: Philadelphia Museum of Art, 1983.

Fernandez-Duro, Cesareo. *Armada española desde la union de los reinos de Castilla y de León.* Vol. 1. Madrid: Sucesores de Rivadeneyra, 1895.

Figureheads and Other Ship Ornaments at the Maritime Museum of Gothenberg. Gothenberg, Sweden: Gothenberg Museum, 1984.

Fink, Lois Marie. *American Art at the Nineteenth-Century Paris Salons.* New York: Cambridge University Press, 1990.

Frere-Cook, Gervis, ed. *The Decorative Arts of the Mariner.* Boston: Little, Brown, 1966.

Fried, Frederick. *Artists in Wood: American Carvers of Cigar-Store Indians, Show Figures, and Circus Wagons.* New York: Clarkson Potter, 1970.

Galionsfiguren. Hamburg: Hamburg-Altonaer Museum, 1961.

Galt, John. *The Life and Studies of Benjamin West, Esq.* London: T. Cadell and W. Davies, 1817.

Gerdts, William H. *American Neo-Classic Sculpture: The Marble Resurrection.* New York: Viking Press, 1973.

———. *"A Man of Genius": The Art of Washington Allston (1779–1843).* Boston: Museum of Fine Arts, 1979.

———. "William Rush: Sculptural Genius or Inspired Artisan?" In *William Rush: American Sculptor*, by Linda Bantel et al. Philadelphia: Pennsylvania Academy of the Fine Arts, 1982.

Gilder, Richard Watson. "The Washington Memorial Arch." In *The History of the Centennial Celebration of the Inauguration of George Washington as First President of the United States*, ed. Clarence Winthrop Bowen. New York: D. Appleton, 1892.

Goodman, Jordan. *Tobacco in History: The Cultures of Dependence.* New York: Routledge, 1993.

Green, Rayna. "The Indian in Popular American Culture." In *The Handbook of North American Indians.* Vol. 4. Ed. Witcomb Washburn. Washington, D.C.: Smithsonian Institution Press, 1988.

Griffiths, John W. *A Treatise on Marine and Naval Architecture.* New York: D. Appleton, 1850.

Groce, George C., and David H. Wallace. *The New-York Historical Society's Dictionary of Artists in America, 1564–1860.* New Haven, Conn.: Yale University Press, 1957.

Groft, Tammis. *Folk Spirit of Albany.* Albany, N.Y.: Albany Institute of History and Art, 1978.

Hamilton, Georgia W. *Silent Pilots: Figureheads in Mystic Seaport Museum.* Mystic, Conn.: Mystic Seaport Museum, 1984.

Hanson, Hans Jürgen, ed. *Art and the Seafarer.* New York: Viking Press, 1968.

———. *Galionsfiguren.* Oldensberg, Germany: Stalling Verlag, 1979.

Hanson, Hans Jürgen, and Cals Broder Hanson. *Ships' Figureheads.* West Chester, Pa.: Schiffer Publishing, 1990.

Harris, Neil, et al. *Grand Illusions: Chicago World's Fair of 1893.* Chicago: Chicago Historical Society, 1993.

Hartigan, Lynda Roscoe. *Made with Passion: The Hemphill Folk Art Collection in the National Museum of American Art.* Washington, D.C.: Smithsonian Institution Press, 1990.

Hartley, Lucy. *Physiognomy and the Meaning of Expression in Nineteenth-Century Culture.* Cambridge: Cambridge University Press, 2001.

Haswell, Charles H. *Reminiscences of an Octogenarian of the City of New York, 1816–1860.* New York: Harper and Brothers, 1897.

Hayward, Victoria. *Romantic Canada.* Toronto: MacMillan Company, 1922.

Henderson, J. Wells, and Rodney P. Carlisle. *Jack Tar: A Sailor's Life, 1750–1910.* Woodbridge, U.K.: Antique Collectors' Club, 1999.

Holmes, Oliver Wendell. *The Complete Poetical Works of Oliver Wendell Holmes.* Ed. Horace E. Scudder. Boston: Houghton Mifflin, 1923.

Honour, Hugh. *The New Golden Land: European Images of America from the Discoveries to the Present Time.* New York: Pantheon Books, 1975.

———. *The Image of the Black Man in Western Art.* Vol. 4, *From the American Revolution to World War I.* Cambridge, Mass.: Harvard University Press, 1989.

Hornung, Clarence P. *Treasury of American Design and Antiques.* New York: Harry Abrams, 1972.

Howe, Octavius T., and Frederick C. Matthews. *American Clipper Ships.* 2 vols. Salem, Mass.: Marine Research Society, 1926.

Illustrated Catalogue of A. E. Brook's Collection of Antique Guns, Pistols, Etc. Hartford, Conn.: Hartford Press, 1899.

Illustrated Catalogue of Smokers' Articles and Show Figures. New York: William Demuth and Co., 1875.

Johns, Elizabeth. *American Genre Painting: The Politics of Everyday Life.* New Haven, Conn.: Yale University Press, 1991.

Johnson, Lee. *The Paintings of Eugène Delacroix: A Critical Catalogue.* 2 vols. New York: Oxford University Press, 1981.

Johnson, Samuel. *The Journal of the Tour to the Hebrides.* London: Henry Baldwin, 1785.

Jonson, Ben. *Bartholomew Fair.* 1614. Reprint, Cambridge, Mass.: Harvard University Press, 1962.

Kammen, Michael. *Mystic Chords of Memory: The Transformation of Tradition in American Culture.* New York: Alfred A. Knopf, 1991.

Keyes, George S. *Mirror of Empire: Dutch Marine Art of the Seventeenth Century.* Cambridge: Cambridge University Press, 1990.

Kiernan, V. G. *Tobacco: A History.* London: Hutchinson Radius, 1991.

Knapp, Oliver. *Chief Kisco and His Brothers.* Mt. Kisco, N.Y.: Mt. Kisco Historical Committee, 1980.

Koke, Richard J., et al. *American Landscape and Genre Paintings in the New-York Historical Society.* Vol. 3. Boston: G. K. Hall, 1982.

Larwood, Jacob, and John Camden Hotten. *The History of Signboards.* London: J. C. Hotten, 1866.

———. *English Inn Signs: Being a Revised and Modern Version of History of Signboards.* London: Chatto and Windus, 1951.

Laughton, Leonard George Carr. *Old Ship Figure-Heads and Sterns.* London: Holton and Truscott Smith, 1925.

Les Génies de la mer. Quebec: Musée du Québec, and Paris: Musée national de la Marine, 2001.

Lewis-Hind, Henriette. *Gari Melchers: Painter.* New York: William Edwin Rudge, 1928.

Lipman, Jean. *American Folk Art in Wood, Metal and Stone.* Meriden, Conn.: Pantheon, 1948. Reprint, New York: Dover Publications, 1972.

Lipman, Jean, and Tom Armstrong, eds. *American Folk Painters of Three Centuries.* New York: Whitney Museum of American Art, 1980.

Lipman, Jean, and Alice Winchester. *The Flowering of American Folk Art.* New York: Viking Press, 1974.

Little, Nina Fletcher. *The Abby Aldrich Rockefeller Folk Art Collection.* Williamsburg, Va.: Colonial Williamsburg Foundation, 1957.

———. "Carved Figures by Samuel McIntire and His Contemporaries." In *Samuel McIntire: A Bicentennial Symposium,* ed. Benjamin W. Labaree, 179–99. Salem, Mass.: Essex Institute, 1957.

"M" Illustrated Catalogue and Price List of Statuary and Animals. New York: J. L. Mott Iron Works, 1873, 1890.

MacLaren, George. *The Woodcarvers of Nova Scotia.* [Occasional Papers #10.] Halifax, Canada: Nova Scotia Museum, 1971.

Marceau, Henri. *William Rush, 1756–1833: The First Native American Sculptor.* Philadelphia: Pennsylvania Museum of Art, 1937.

The Mariners' Museum, 1930–1950: A History and Guide. Newport News, Va.: Mariners' Museum, 1950.

Mason, Peter. *Deconstructing America: Representations of the Other.* New York: Routledge, 1990.

Mathews, Cornelius. *Big Abel and the Little Manhattan.* New York: Wiley and Putnam, 1845.

McElroy, Guy C. *Facing History: The Black Image in American Art, 1710–1940.* San Francisco: Bedford Arts, 1990.

McKay, Richard C. *Some Famous Sailing Ships and Their Builder, Donald McKay.* New York: G. P. Putnam's Sons, 1928.

———. *South Street: A Maritime History of New York.* 1934. Reprint, Riverside, Conn.: 7 Cs Press, 1969.

Meadows, Cecil A. *Trade Signs and Their Origins.* London: Routledge and Kegan Paul, 1957.

Michel, André. *Histoire de l'Art.* Vol. 6. Paris: Armand Colin, 1922.

Modern Women, and What Is Said of Them. New York: J. R. Redfield, 1868.

Moody, Richard. *Edwin Forrest: First Star of the American Stage.* New York: Alfred A. Knopf, 1960.

Morris, James M. *Our Maritime Heritage: Maritime Developments and Their Impact on American Life.* Washington, D.C.: University Press of America, 1979.

Morrison, John H. *History of New York Ship Yards.* New York: William F. Sametz and Co., 1909.

Nathan, Hans. *Dan Emmet and the Rise of Early Negro Minstrelsy.* Norman: University of Oklahoma Press, 1962.

New Bedford and Old Dartmouth: A Portrait of a Region's Past. New Bedford, Mass.: Old Dartmouth Historical Society, 1975.

New-York Historical Society. *Annual Report of the New-York Historical Society, 1953.* New York: New-York Historical Society, 1953.

Norton, Peter. *Figureheads.* Greenwich, U.K.: National Maritime Museum, 1972.

———. *State Barges.* Greenwich, U.K.: National Maritime Museum, 1972.

———. *Ships' Figureheads.* Barre, Mass.: Barre Publishing Co., 1976.

Ozanne, Pierre. *Ornaments de les proues de divers batiments.* Paris, 1799–1801.

Page, Alvin R. *Under Sail and in Port in the Glorious '50s.* Salem, Mass.: Peabody Museum, 1950.

Page, Eugene R. *Metamora and Other Plays.* Princeton, N.J.: Princeton University Press, 1941.

Panzer, Mary. *Mathew Brady and the Image of History.* Washington, D.C.: Smithsonian Institution Press, 1997.

Parry, Ellwood. *The Image of the Indian and Black Man in American Art.* New York: George Braziller, 1974.

Paulson, Hanne. *Figureheads and Ornaments on Danish Ships and in Danish Collections.* Copenhagen: Rhodos, 1977.

Payne, Brigham. *The Story of Bacchus and Centennial Souvenir.* Hartford, Conn.: A. E. Brooks, 1876.

Pearce, Roy Harvey. *Savagism and Civilization: A Study of the Indian and American Mind.* Baltimore: Johns Hopkins University Press, 1965.

Pendergast, A. W., and W. Porter Ware. *Cigar Store Figures in American Folk Art.* Chicago: Lightner Publishing Corp., 1953.

Peters, Harry T. *Currier and Ives: Printmakers to the American People.* Garden City, N.Y.: Doran and Co., 1929. Reprint, New York: Arno Press, 1976.

Pieterse, Jan Nederveen. *White on Black: Images of Africa and Blacks in Western Popular Culture.* New Haven, Conn.: Yale University Press, 1992.

Pinckney, Pauline A. *American Figureheads and Their Carvers.* New York: W. W. Norton, 1940.

Pope, Alexander. *An Essay on Man.* 1733–34. Reprint, New York: Bobbs-Merrill, 1965.

Quimby, Ian M. G., ed. *The Craftsman in Early America.* New York: W. W. Norton, 1984.

Rock, Howard B. *Artisans of the New Republic.* New York: New York University Press, 1984.

Rogo, Elsa, ed. *Hamilton Easter Field Collection of Painting and Sculpture.* New York: College Art Association, 1930.

Rumford, Beatrix. "Uncommon Art of the Uncommon People: A Review of Trends in the Collecting and Exhibiting of American Folk Art." In *Perspectives on American Folk Art.* Ed. Ian M. G. Quimby and Scott T. Swank. New York: W. W. Norton, 1980.

Sanborn, Kate. *Hunting Indians in a Taxi-Cab.* Boston: Richard G. Badger, 1911.

Sand, Maurice. *The History of Harlequinade.* 2 vols. New York: Benjamin Blom, 1915. Reprint, Manchester, N.H.: Ayer Company Publishers, 1968.

Seaton, Beverly. *The Language of Flowers: A History.* Charlottesville: University of Virginia Press, 1995.

Senelick, Laurence. *The Age and Stage of George L. Fox, 1825–1877.* Hanover, N.H.: University of New England Press, 1988.

Ship Figureheads and Other Wood Carving in the Nautical Collection of the State Street Trust Company. Boston: Rand Press, 1954.

Shoemaker, Elizabeth. *Ships' Figureheads of Old Cape Cod.* Hyannis, Mass.: Cape Cod Advancement Plan, 1936.

Smith, Yvonne Brault. *John Halley Bellamy: Carver of Eagles.* Hampton, N.H.: P. E. Randall, 1982.

Sollors, Werner. *Beyond Ethnicity: Consent and Descent in American Culture.* New York: Oxford University Press, 1986.

Stackpole, Edouard A. *Figureheads and Ship Carvings at Mystic Seaport.* Mystic, Conn.: Marine Historical Association, 1964.

Stokes, I. N. Phelps. *Iconography of Manhattan Island.* Vol. 5. New York: Robert H. Dodd, 1915–28.

Sturtevant, William C. "First Visual Images of Native Americans." In *First Images of America.* Vol.1. Ed. Fredi Chiappelli. Berkeley and Los Angeles: University of California Press, 1976.

Tatum, David. *John Henry Bufford: American Lithographer.* Worcester, Mass.: American Antiquarian Society, 1976.

Thevet, André. *Les Singularities de la France antarctique.* 1557. Reprint, Paris: Les Temps, 1982.

Toll, Robert C. *Blacking Up: The Minstrel Show in Nineteenth-Century America.* New York: Oxford University Press, 1974.

Tolles, Thayer, ed. *American Sculpture in the Metropolitan Museum of Art.* Vol. 1. *A Catalogue of Works by Artists Born Before 1865.* New York: Metropolitan Museum of Art, 1999.

Trout, Andrew. *Jean-Baptiste Colbert.* Boston: G. K. Hall, 1978.

Tuckerman, Bayard. *The Diary of Philip Hone.* New York: Dodd, Mead, and Co., 1889.

Vasari, Giorgio. *Lives of the Most Eminent Painters, Sculptors, and Architects.* Trans. Gaston du C. de Vere. London: MacMillan & Co., 1912.

Villeneuve, René. *Baroque to Neo-Classical: Sculpture in Quebec.* Ottawa: National Gallery of Canada, 1997.

Vlach, John Michael. *The Afro-American Tradition in the Decorative Arts.* Cleveland: Cleveland Museum of Art, 1978.

Watson, John F. *Annals of Philadelphia.* Philadelphia: E. L. Cary and A. Hart, 1830.

Webb, William Henry. *Plans of wooden vessels selected as types from one hundred and fifty various types and descriptions, from a fishing smack to the largest clipper ships and vessels of war, both sail and steam, built by William H. Webb, in the City of New York, from the year 1840 to the year 1869.* 2 vols. New York: William Henry Webb, 1895.

Wechsler, Judith. *The Human Comedy: Physiognomy and Caricature in Nineteenth-Century Paris.* London: Thames and Hudson, 1982.

Weitenkampf, Frank W. *Manhattan Kaleidoscope.* New York: Charles Scribner's Sons, 1947.

Welsh, Peter C. *American Folk Art from the Eleanor and Mabel Van Alstyne Collection: The Art and Spirit of a People.* Washington, D.C.: Smithsonian Institution Press, 1965.

Wheildon, William W. *Memoir of Solomon Willard, Architect and Superintendent of the Bunker Hill Monument.* Boston: Monument Association, 1865.

Whitehill, Walter Muir, Brock Jobe, and Jonathan Fairbanks, eds. *Boston Furniture of the Eighteenth Century.* Boston: Colonial Society of Massachusetts, 1974.

Wilentz, Sean. "Artisan Republican Festivals and the Rise of Class Conflict in New York City, 1788–1837." In *Working Class America, Essays on Labor, Community and American Society.* Ed. Michael H. Frisch and Daniel J. Walkowitz. Urbana: University of Illinois Press, 1983.

———. *Chants Democratic: New York City and the Rise of the American Working Class, 1788–1850.* New York: Oxford University Press, 1984.

Williams, Robert F. *An Historical Sketch of the Art of Sculpture in Wood.* 8 vols. London: Library of Fine Arts, 1835.

Wittke, Carl. *Tambo and Bones: A History of the American Minstrel Stage.* Durham, N.C.: Duke University Press, 1930. Reprint, Westport, Conn.: Greenwood Press, 1968.

Wunder, Richard P. *Hiram Powers: Vermont Sculptor.* Woodstock, Vt.: Woodstock Historical Society, 1974.

———. *Hiram Powers: Vermont Sculptor, 1805–1873.* 2 vols. Newark: University of Delaware Press, 1989–91.

Yarmolinsky, Avrahm. *Picturesque United States of America: Being a Memoir on Paul Svinin.* New York: William Edwin Ridge, 1930.

ARTICLES IN PERIODICALS AND NEWSPAPERS

Allingham, William. "Figure-Heads." *Nautical Magazine* 68 (Aug. 1899): 515–23.

American and Daily Advertiser [Boston], 4 Mar. 1794.

American and Daily Advertiser [Boston], 4 Sept. 1799.

"The American on the Stage." *Scribner's Monthly* 18 (July 1879): 322–33.

"The Angelus." *Tobacco* 9 (16 May 1890): 1.

"Apoplexy Takes Julius Melchers." *Detroit News,* 15 Jan. 1908, 7.

"Art and Tobacco." *Tobacco* 1 (30 July 1886): 2.

"Art in Tobacco Shops." *Tobacco* 1 (22 Oct. 1886): 3.

"The Art of the Shipcarver at the Peabody

Museum." *American Neptune: Pictorial Supplement 19*. Salem, Mass.: Peabody Museum, 1977.

Barbeau, Charles Marius. "Le dernier de nos grands artisans, Louis Jobin." *Royal Society of Canada, Mémoires* 27, sec. 1 (1933): 33–48.

———. "Two Centuries of Wood Carving in French Canada." *Royal Society of Canada, Transactions* 27, sec. 2 (1933): 1–4.

———. "Louis Jobin, Statuaire." *La Société Royale du Canada, Mémoires* 37, sec. 1 (1943): 17–23.

Belknap, Henry Wycoff. "Joseph True, Wood Carver of Salem and His Account Book." *Essex Institute Historical Collections* 78 (Apr. 1942): 117–57.

Bolger, Doreen. "Hamilton Easter Field and His Contribution to Modernism." *American Art Journal* 20, no. 2 (1988): 79–107.

Boston Gazette and Country Journal, 30 July 1806.

Branscombe, Henry. "Early American Wood Sculpture." *International Studio* 88 (Oct. 1927): 61–64.

Brewington, Marion V. "Book Reviews." *American Neptune* 1 (Apr. 1941): 178–81.

Brown, Ann Barton. "'Lo, The Wooden Indian': Prototypes for Wooden Show Figures." *Brandywine River Museum Antiques Show 1984* (Chadds Ford, Pa.: Brandywine River Museum, 1984): 4–9.

Brown, May Louise. "John Welch, Carver." *Antiques* 9 (Jan. 1926): 28–30.

Bumgardner, Georgia Brady. "Political Portraiture: Two Prints of Andrew Jackson." *American Art Journal* 18, no. 4 (1986): 84–95.

Catlin, George B. "Old Detroit Artists Found Trade Dull, but Market for Wooden Indians Brisk." *Detroit News*, 4 Jan. 1925, sec. 2, 17.

"Cigar Store Indian Becomes Museum Relic." *Baltimore Evening Sun*, 14 May 1926.

"Cigar Store Statuary: An Industry That Grew Out of the Decaying Trade of Ship Carving." [New York] *Sun*, 18 Aug. 1878, 3.

Clemens, Will M. "The Man Who Carves Ships' Figure-Heads." *Harper's Weekly* 36 (5 Mar. 1892): 235.

Columbian Centennial [Boston], 18 July 1793.

Craven, Wayne. "The Grand Manner in Early Nineteenth-Century American Painting: Borrowing from Antiquity, the Renaissance, and the Baroque." *American Art Journal* 11 (Apr. 1979): 5–43.

"Death of Edward Hen." *Tobacco* 2 (6 May 1887): 3.

Denig, Robert G. "Historic Figureheads." *Cosmopolitan* 14 (Apr. 1893): 689–96.

"Designed by Whittling Yankees: A Studio Where Many Statues of Native Americans Are Made." *Tobacco* 1 (14 May 1886): 7.

Dewey, Reverend Orville. "Mr. Powers' Statue." *Union Magazine of Literature and Art* 1 (Oct. 1847): 236.

Dewhurst, C. Kurt, Betty MacDowell, and Marsha MacDowell. "The Art of Julius and Gari Melchers." *Antiques* 125 (Apr. 1984): 862–73.

Dick, H. "This Colossal Washington a Puzzle." [New York] *World Magazine*, 20 Feb. 1921, 6.

Edgerton, Samuel Y. "The Murder of Jane McCrea: The Tragedy of an American Tableau d'Histoire." *Art Bulletin* 47 (Dec. 1965): 481–92.

"E. Hen's Wills." *Tobacco* 3 (13 May 1887): 3.

"Exhibit of Wm. Demuth & Co." *Tobacco* 16 (2 Feb. 1894): 1, 3.

"The Exhibition of the National Academy of Design, 1827. The Second. New York." *United States Review and Literary Gazette* 2 (July 1827): 243–45.

Fairbanks, Jonathan. "America's Measure of Mankind." *Smithsonian Studies in American Art* 2 (winter 1988): 73–87.

Farnum, Charles H. "A Day on the Docks." *Scribner's Monthly* 18 (May 1879): 32–47.

Ferguson, Eugene S. "The Figure-Head of the United States Frigate *Constellation*." *American Neptune* 7 (Oct. 1947): 255–60.

"The Figurehead and Its Story." *Scientific American* 101 (7 Aug. 1909): 92, 101–3.

Flammer, Charles A. "First Wooden Indians. Memories of Chichester's Cigar Store in the Bowery." *New York Times*, 4 May 1926, 26.

Fleming, E. McClung. "The American Image as Indian Princess." *Winterthur Portfolio* 2 (1965): 65–81.

———. "From Indian Princess to Greek Goddess: The American Image, 1783–1815." *Winterthur Portfolio* 3 (1967): 37–66.

"For the North-American Journal." *North American Review* 2 (Jan. 1816): 153–64.

Fryd, Vivien Green. "Rereading the Indian in Benjamin West's *Death of General Wolfe*." *American Art* 9 (spring 1995): 73–85.

"Generously Good Window Display." *Tobacco* 30 (5 Apr. 1901): 3.

Gilliams, E. Leslie. "Cigar-Store Indians." *Philadelphia Times*, 18 Dec. 1892, 18.

———. "A Philadelphia Sculptor." *Lippincott's Monthly Magazine* 52 (Aug. 1893): 249–53.

"The Girl of the Period." *Saturday Review of Politics, Literature, Science, and Art* 25 (14 Mar. 1868): 339–40.

Gould, G. Glen and Mrs. G. Glen Gould. "The Nadelman Ship Figureheads." *International Studio* 94 (Sept. 1929): 51–53.

Green, Rayna. "The Pocahontas Perplex: The Image of Indian Women in American Culture." *Massachusetts Review* 16 (autumn 1975): 698–716.

Greusel, John Hubert. "Art's Sake! Sculptor Julius Melchers on Sacrifices." *Detroit News-Tribune*, 22 Aug. 1897, 13.

Harris, Charles E. "Figureheads of the Constitution." *Antiques* 30 (July 1936): 10–13.

Hayward, Victoria. "Figureheads of the Old Square-Riggers." *Century Magazine* 92 (Aug. 1916): 566–73.

———. "Jobin—The Wood-Carver." *Canadian Magazine* 60 (Dec. 1922): 90–100.

"High Art at Conklin and Fox's." *Tobacco* 1 (27 Aug. 1886): 3.

Hingham, John. "Indian Princess and Roman Goddess: The First Female Symbols of America." *Proceedings of the American Antiquarian Society* 100 (1990): 45–79.

"Historical Society Gets Two Wooden Indians." *Baltimore Evening Sun*, 5 Feb. 1953.

Hopkinson, Francis. "An Account of the Grand Federal Procession in Philadelphia, July 4, 1788." *American Museum* 4 (July 1788): 64.

Hornell, James. "The Prow of the Ship: Sanctuary of the Tutelary Deity." *Man* 43 (Nov.–Dec. 1943): 121–28.

"How to Decorate a Cigar Store I." *Tobacco* 4 (13 Apr. 1888).

"How to Decorate a Cigar Store II." *Tobacco* 4 (27 Apr. 1888).

"How to Decorate a Cigar Store III." *Tobacco* 5 (11 May 1888).

"How to Decorate a Cigar Store IV." *Tobacco* 5 (1 June 1888).

Hughes, Rupert. "Jonathan Scott Hartley." *Munsey's Magazine* 11 (Aug. 1894): 515–20.

"The Indians in American Art." *Crayon* 3 (Jan. 1856): 28.

"Is the Wooden Indian Passing Away?" *Tobacco* 34 (16 Jan. 1903): 3.

Jessup, L. F. "The Tobacconists' Tribe of Treen." *Antiques* 18 (Sept. 1930): 232–35.

Jewel, Edward Alden. "'American Ancestors' Show." *New York Times*, 14 Dec. 1931, 17.

———. "In the Realm of Art: 'Ancestors' and Other Matters." *New York Times*, 20 Dec. 1931, sec. 8, p. 10.

"Julius Melchers Suffers a Stroke: Venerable Sculptor Loses Power of Speech from Paralysis." *Detroit News*, 30 May 1907.

Junkin, J. H. "The Wooden Indian Is Passing Away." *Detroit News-Tribune*, 23 July 1899, 17.

Keyes, Homer Eaton. "Milton, Beverly, and Salem." *Antiques* 23 (Apr. 1933): 122, 142–43.

Kimball, Fisk. "The Estimate of McIntire." *Antiques* 21 (Jan. 1932): 23–25.

King, Edward. "The Liverpool of America." *Scribner's Monthly* 9 (Mar. 1875): 681–95.

Kline, Mrs. Grenfall T. "I Remember the Old Cigar Store Indian at Pratt and Exeter." *Baltimore Sun Magazine*, 23 Feb. 1969, 2.

Lahvis, Sylvia L. "Icons of the American Trade: The Skillin Workshop and the Language of Spectacle." *Winterthur Portfolio* 27 (winter 1992): 213–33.

———. "The Skillin Workshop." *Antiques* 155 (Mar. 1999): 442–51.

"The Last of E. Hen's Business." *Tobacco* 3 (5 Aug. 1887): 6.

Lathrop, Constance. "A Vanishing Naval Tradition—the Figurehead." *United States Naval Institute Proceedings* 53 (Nov. 1927): 1166–77.

"Launch of the 'Minnehaha.'" *Boston Daily Evening Transcript*, 24 Mar. 1856, 2.

Le Corbeiller, Claire. "Miss America and Her Sisters: Personifications of the Four Parts of the World." *Bulletin of the Metropolitan Museum of Art* 19 (Apr. 1961): 209–23.

"Lo on His Last Trail." *Tobacco* 10 (10 Apr. 1891): 9.

"Lo Takes a Spring Suit." *Tobacco* 6 (12 Apr. 1889): 1.

"Lo—The Poor Indian." *Tobacco* 4 (8 June 1888): 4–5.

"Lo! The Poor Indian Finds a Happy Hunting Ground." *Reading [Pa.] Eagle*, 14 July 1936.

"Louis Jobin statuaire: Du Cap Trinité au Lac-Bouchette." *Saquenayensia* 28 (Apr.–June 1986): 29–69.

"Manufacture of Dummy Indians." *Tobacco* 2 (12 Nov. 1886): 2–3.

Mayer, Frank. "Signs and Symbols." *Scribner's Monthly* 18 (Sept. 1879): 704–14.

McClinton, Katherine M. "Ezra Ames, Ornamental Painter." *Antiques* 60 (Sept. 1951): 194.

"Modern Advertising." *Tobacco* 17 (27 July 1894): 8.

"Modern Women." *Nation* 7 (22 Oct. 1868): 332–34.

Morrison, John L. "The Passing of the Wooden Indian." *Scribner's Magazine* 84 (Oct. 1928): 393–405.

———. "Many Wooden Indians." *Scribner's Magazine* 84 (Dec. 1928): 98–99.

———. "Poor Lo Still Active." *Scribner's Magazine* 85 (Jan. 1929): 40–41.

Morrissey, L. J. "English Pageant-Wagons." *Eighteenth-Century Studies* 9 (spring 1976): 352–74.

"Mrs. Barrow." *Ballou's Pictorial* 10 (12 Apr. 1856): 237.

"Mrs. Barrow as Minehaha." *Ballou's Pictorial* 10 (17 May 1856): 305.

Musham, H. A. "Early Great Lakes Steamboats: The Caroline Affair, 1837–1838." *American Neptune* 7 (Oct. 1947): 298–99.

"Must the Indian Go?" *Tobacco* 14 (3 Mar. 1893): 4.

Mystic Pioneer [Conn.], 31 July 1869.

Mystic Press [Conn.], 31 Oct. 1873.

New-York Gazette and General Advertiser, 12 Apr. 1762.

New-York Gazette and General Advertiser, 25 May, 1799.

New-York Mercury, 21 July 1755.

Nickerson, Cynthia D. "Artistic Interpretations of Henry Wadsworth Longfellow's *The Song of Hiawatha*, 1855–1900." *American Art Journal* 16 (summer 1984): 49–77.

Northend, Mary H. "The Garden of Figureheads." *International Studio* 75 (Sept. 1922): 504–8.

"Old Salt on Ship's Heads." *Monthly Nautical Magazine and Quarterly Review* 2 (Aug. 1855): 396–97.

Olsen, Carol. "Stylistic Developments of Ship Figureheads of the United States East Coast." *International Journal of Nautical Archaeology and Underwater Exploration* 8 (1979): 321–32.

Peixotto, Ernest C. "Artistic Street Signs, Revival of an Old Custom as Seen in Paris." *New York Herald Sunday Magazine*, 15 Jan. 1905, 7.

Pennsylvania Journal [Philadelphia], 23 Nov. 1791.

Peterson, William N. "Campbell and Colby: Shipcarvers at Mystic Seaport." *Log of Mystic Seaport* 27 (Oct. 1977): 66–73.

"Pioneer Pipe Man Passes Away." *Tobacco* 51 (29 June 1911).

Port, Jane L. "Boston's Nineteenth-Century Ship Carvers." *Antiques* 158 (Nov. 2000): 754–61.

"The Puck Cigar." *Tobacco* 8 (15 Nov. 1889): 1.

"The Punch Factory under New Management." *Tobacco* 9 (31 Oct. 1890): 1.

Read, Helen Appleton. "Introducing the Cigar Store Indian Into Art." *Brooklyn Daily Eagle*, 17 Feb. 1924, 2B.

"Review of the Annual Exhibition." *Port Folio* 8 (Aug. 1812): 142–50.

Rogers, Clarence N. "Ships Figureheads: Selections from the Collection of The Mariners' Museum." *Shipyard Bulletin* 9 (Feb. 1946): 2–7.

Rogers, W. A. "In the Year Two Thousand." *Life* 7 (22 Apr. 1886): 233–34.

Sabine, Lillian. "The Neighborhood Indian Passes On." *Brooklyn Eagle Magazine*, 30 Mar. 1930, 6.

Safford, Victor. "John Haley Bellamy: The Woodcarver of Kittery Point." *Antiques* 27 (Mar. 1935): 102–7.

Sessions, Ralph. "The Image Business: Shop and Cigar Store Figures in America." *Folk Art* 21 (winter 1996–97): 54–60.

———."Ship Carvers and the New York City Shop Figure Style." *Antiques* 151 (Mar. 1997): 470–77.

———. "Shop and Cigar Store Figures in America." *American Art Review* 9 (Nov.–Dec. 1997): 136–41.

Severence, Frank H. "Historic Figureheads." *Buffalo Historical Society Publications* 25 (1921): 191–200.

Shaw, Charles G. "Black Boys and Their Playfellows." *Antiques* 25 (Mar. 1934): 101–3.

———. "Speaking of Wooden Indians." *Antiques* 36 (Sept. 1939): 131–33.

Sheldon, G. W. "The Old Ship-Builders of New York." *Harper's New Monthly Magazine* 65 (July 1882): 223–42.

"Ship-Building in New York for 1856." *U.S. Nautical Magazine and Naval Journal* 5 (Feb. 1857): 381.

"Short Chats with Dealers." *Tobacco* 4 (24 Feb. 1888): 3.

Smith, Philip C. F. "The Little Men: Carved Shop Signs of the Navigating Instrument Sellers." *American Neptune* 34 (July 1974): 197–210.

Sniffen, Harold S. "Figureheads and Their Subjects." *Antiques* 66 (July 1954): 37–39.

Solis-Cohen, Lita. "Tamanend the Striding

Indian Trader: 'A Fine Figure in William Rush's Best Style.'" *Maine Antiques Digest*, Nov. 1996, 28-A–30-A.

Sothern, Winifred. "The Truth about the Bachelor Girl." *Munsey's Magazine* 25 (May 1901): 282–83.

Stillinger, Elizabeth. "Elie and Viola Nadelman's Unprecedented Museum of Folk Arts." *Antiques* 146 (Oct. 1994): 516–25.

"A Stogie Display at Newark." *Tobacco* 22 (27 Nov. 1896): 3.

Swan, Mabel M. "A Revised Estimate of McIntire." *Antiques* 20 (Dec. 1931): 338–43.

———. "Artisan Leaders of 1788." *Antiques* 27 (Mar. 1935): 90–91.

———. "Simeon Skillin, Senior, the First American Sculptor." *Antiques* 46 (July 1944): 21.

———. "Ship Carvers of Newburyport." *Antiques* 48 (Aug. 1945): 78–81

———. "Boston's Carvers and Joiners, Part 1. Pre-Revolutionary." *Antiques* 53 (Mar. 1948): 198–201.

———. "Boston's Carvers and Joiners, Part 2. Post-Revolutionary." *Antiques* 53 (Apr. 1948): 281–85.

Thwing, Leroy L. "The Four Carving Skillins." *Antiques* 33 (June 1938): 326–28.

"The Tobacconist's Sign." *Tobacco* 2 (8 Apr. 1887): 2.

Tuckerman, Henry. "Art in America, Its History, Condition and Prospects." *Cosmopolitan Art Journal* 3 (Dec. 1858): 1–8.

Vaughan, H. S. "Figure-Heads and Beak-Heads of the Ships of Henry VIII." *Mariner's Mirror* 4 (Feb. 1914): 37–43.

Wakefield, David. "Chateaubriand's 'Atala' as a Source of Inspiration in Nineteenth-Century Art." *Burlington Magazine* 120 (Jan. 1978): 13–24.

Walker, Jenny Girton. "The Ship Figure-Head in America's History." *DAR Magazine* 61 (Oct. 1927): 743–56.

"Wanted, a Sign." *Tobacco* 21 (17 July 1896): 4.

Warfvinge, Svante. "Johan Törnström, Sculptor of the Swedish Admiralty." *Surveyor* 14 (Feb. 1980): 23–27.

"The Washington Triumphal Arch." *Harper's Weekly* 33 (4 May 1889): 343, 344.

Wasson, David A. "The Silent Pilots." *Outlook* 109 (27 Jan. 1915): 206–13.

Weitenkampf, Frank W. "Lo, the Wooden Indian: The Art of Making Cigar-Shop Signs." *New York Times*, 3 Aug. 1890, 13.

———. "Some Signs and Others—Sign Painters and Sign Painting Artists." *New York Times*, 3 July 1892, 15.

———. "Cigar-Store Indians." *Magazine of Art* 41 (Dec. 1948): 312–13.

Whitehill, Walter Muir. "A Figurehead of Talma." *American Neptune* 1 (Jan. 1941): 82–83.

Williams, Harold. "Eight Hundred Wooden Indians—And Then There Were Eight." *Baltimore Morning Sun*, 17 Feb. 1947, 23.

Wilmeth, Don B. "Noble or Ruthless Savage? The American Indian on Stage and in the Drama." *Journal of American Drama and Theatre* 1 (spring 1989): 39–78.

"Wood-Carving." *Harper's Weekly* 27 (6 Jan. 1883): 13.

"Wooden Indians." *Tobacco* 24 (28 Jan. 1898): 3.

"Wooden Indians." *Tobacco* 25 (13 May 1898): 9.

"Wooden Indians." *Tobacco* 26 (6 Jan. 1899): 10.

"A World's Fair Exhibit." *Tobacco* 14 (7 Apr. 1893): 1.

Zabriskie, George A. "Ships' Figureheads in and about New York." *New-York Historical Society Quarterly* 30 (Jan. 1946): 4–16.

INDEX

Page references in italics refer to illustrations.

PHOTOGRAPHY CREDITS

The photographers and the sources of visual material other than those indicated in the captions are as follows (numerals refer to plates).

PHOTO: Noel Allum (29)

PHOTO: Patrick Altman (74)

Courtesy, American Antiquarian Society, Worcester, Massachusetts (22)

Collection American Folk Art Museum, New York (7, 8, 122); photo: Gavin Ashworth, New York (114), Ali Elai, Camerarts (97), John Parnell, New York (125), © 2000 John Bigelow Taylor, New York (90, 116)

Courtesy of The Bostonian Society/Old State House (12, 18); photo: John Dean (16)

Collection of the Brandywine River Museum (54)

The Connecticut Historical Society, Hartford, Connecticut; photo: John Dean (13)

PHOTO: John Dean (57, 64, 66, 80, 93, 96, 102)

Courtesy of the Demuth Foundation, Lancaster, Pennsylvania (14)

PHOTO: Ali Elai, Camerarts (11, 58, 68, 70, 82, 87, 89, 100, 113)

From the Collections of The Henry Ford (78, 94)

Courtesy of Historical Society of Delaware, Wilmington (117)

PHOTO: David Hoffman (104)

Collection of The Hudson River Museum, Yonkers, New York; photo: Ali Elai, Camerarts (98)

© J. Welles Henderson Collection (37)

PHOTO: Rusty Kennedy (17)

PHOTO: Glenn Linsenbardt (110)

Collection of the Mercer Museum of the Bucks County Historical Society; photo: John Dean (99, 108)

Photograph © 1999 The Metropolitan Museum of Art (49); © 2004 (30)

© Musée national de la Marine, Paris (3)

Courtesy Mystic Seaport, Mystic, Connecticut (19); photo: John Dean (39)

Courtesy of The New Bedford Whaling Museum, Massachusetts (41); photo: John Dean (40)

Collection of The New-York Historical Society (25, 35, 50, 62, 77, 84, 85, 112)

Photograph Courtesy Peabody Essex Museum (26, 31); photo: John Dean (72), Mark Sexton (4, 21)

Courtesy of the Pennsylvania Academy of the Fine Arts, Philadelphia (46)

Courtesy San Francisco Maritime National Historical Park (27)

© Shelburne Museum, Shelburne, Vermont (36, 75, 92, 109)

Courtesy of Sotheby's, Inc. (44, 56)

PHOTO: John Bigelow Taylor, New York (76, 105)

PHOTO: Richard Walker (81, 101)